AF607857

Spiritual Spectacles

Religion in North America

Catherine L. Albanese and Stephen J. Stein, editors

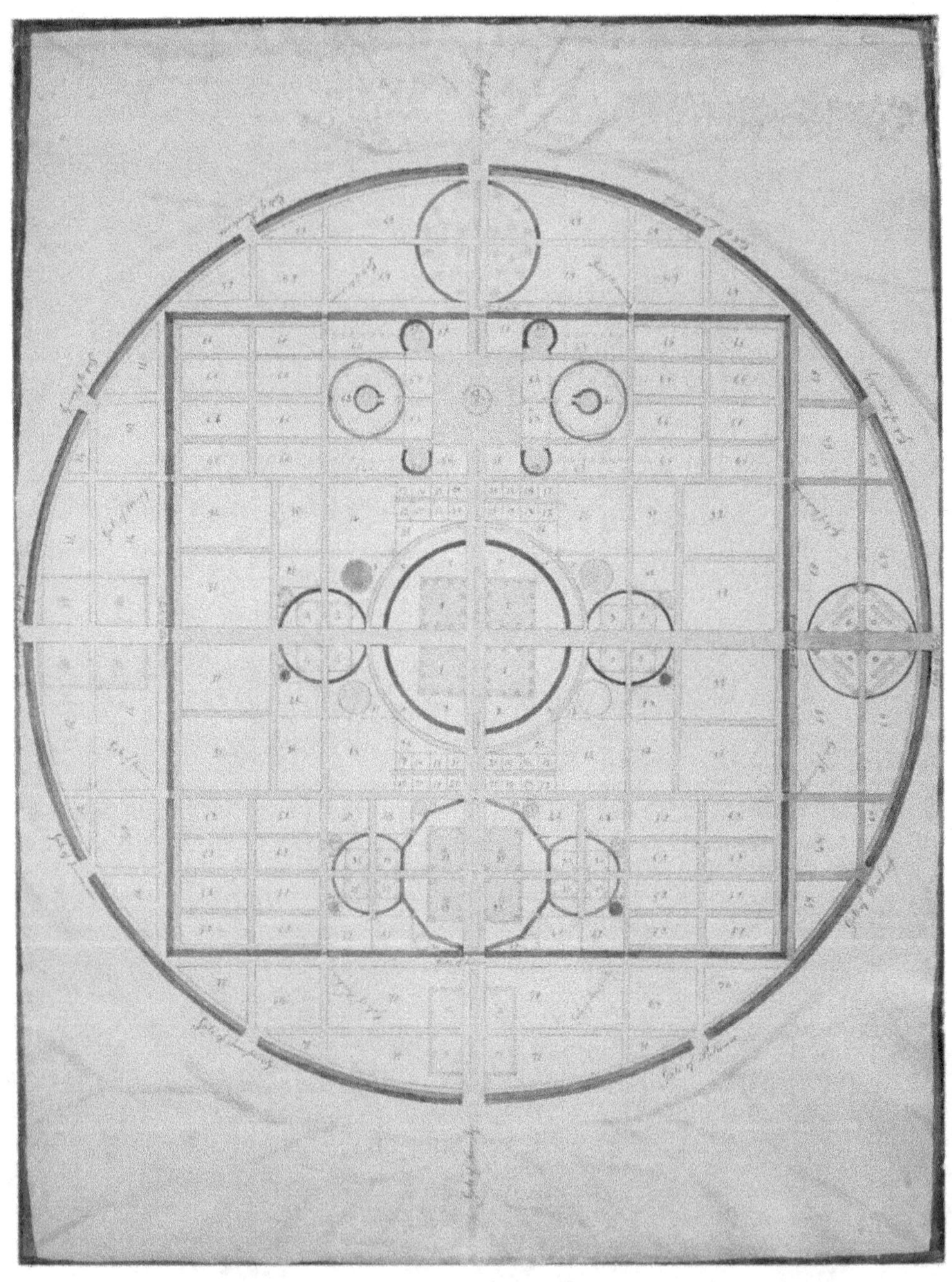

Pl. I. *The Holy City,* watercolor and ink on paper, March 1843, 31 inches by 24 3/4 inches, PMA.
Courtesy of Philadelphia Museum of Art: Gift of Mr. and Mrs. Julius Zieget

Spiritual Spectacles

VISION AND IMAGE IN MID-NINETEENTH-CENTURY SHAKERISM

Sally M. Promey

INDIANA UNIVERSITY PRESS
Bloomington and Indianapolis

Publication of this volume was aided by a grant from The Millard Meiss Publication Fund of the College Art Association of America.

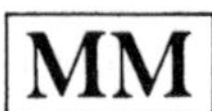

The paper used in this publication meets the minimum requirements of American National Standard for information Sciences—Permanence of Paper for Printed Library Materials, ANSI Z39.48-1984.

Library of Congress Cataloging-in-Publication Data

Promey, Sally M., date
Spiritual spectacles : vision and image in mid-nineteenth-century Shakerism / Sally M. Promey.
p. cm. — (Religion in North America)
Includes bibliographical references and index.
ISBN 0-253-34614-2 (hard)
1. Art, Shaker. 2. Christian art and symbolism—Modern period, 1500- —United States. 3. Shakers—United States—History—19th century. I. Title. II. Series.
N6510.P76 1993
704'.288'097409034—dc20 92-19337

1 2 3 4 5 97 96 95 94 93

To Roger and Anna
In memory of Velda

CONTENTS

LIST OF ILLUSTRATIONS

FOREWORD

In this volume Sally M. Promey opens our eyes to new possibilities for understanding the "gift drawings" of the Shakers, a set of artifacts almost without parallel in American religious history. "Gifts" have abounded within Shakerism, from the time of the society's origins in eighteenth-century England until the present day. Yet perhaps no period in the history of the United Society of Believers in Christ's Second Appearing has produced a greater number of concrete religious manifestations than the nineteenth-century revival era known as "Mother's Work," so named after Ann Lee (d. 1784), the principal founder of the society. Messages believed to be from the spirit world crowded in upon the Believers during the years after 1837. Thousands of such communications, most in prose or poetry, exhorted and encouraged the members of the community.

The most curious and unusual of all the spiritualistic phenomena of that era were the gift drawings that Promey examines in this volume. First "discovered" in the 1930s by Edward Deming Andrews, the pioneer in modern Shaker studies, and more recently fully catalogued by the folklorist Daniel W. Patterson, these unique examples of religious art have not yet received the focused interdisciplinary attention they deserve. This is true, even though they are now nearly omnipresent on popular culture items, including cross-stitch samplers and UNICEF Christmas cards, and also have been used frequently as illustrations in books about the Shakers. But if the analysis and interpretation of these visual texts remain surprisingly unsophisticated, Promey's work promises to alter that situation by providing us with means to see the multiple significances—religious and aesthetic—of these spiritual drawings.

Promey's study arises squarely out of the disciplinary questions and agenda of the field of religious studies. With theoretical sophistication and ease, she negotiates the world of Shaker gift drawings and advances our understanding of Shakerism and religious studies in general. She explores the contents, contexts, and symbolic pointers in the drawings that enable her to interpret the central concerns of Shaker religiosity. The drawings, according to her, evoked an experience of contact on the part of the younger generations of Believers with their first-generation founders whom they had not known firsthand. Promey demonstrates that the drawings consummately blended the conservatism of a return to "first-times" under the lawful direction of official ministries with a radically innovative use of images, long banned in the Shaker ascetic and aesthetic traditions. She thus associates these artistic expressions with a restoration impulse within the United Society, somewhat similar to the desire to return to origins widespread among other American religious movements of the time.

The careful analysis of the drawings provided by Promey in this volume features the pragmatic value of the gift images as strategies for coping with change and decline within the community. The drawings, as well as other reported spiritualistic communications, were integrally involved in the struggle between the ministry and the "instruments," or mediums, for control of communal authority. These products of ink and watercolor depicted fanciful, almost childlike emblems—hearts, balls, trees, leaves, and the like. The inscriptions they included were admittedly banal and sentimental. Yet the reception process empowered the mediums who drew and painted them.

As a student of art history and visual form, Promey in fact provides an expanded reading of the category of gift drawing that includes texts without figures. She views these texts in terms of their formal properties, including their placement on paper, their color, and their calligraphy. Perhaps the lingering effect of the Protestant religious style among the Shakers is apparent in the gift drawings, for most of them also contain words in the midst of images and may thereby reveal an unconscious suspicion of images.

Another result of Promey's investigation is new appreciation for the complexity—rather than the simplicity—of these images. The parallel structure of Shaker gift drawings and of the Believers' lifestyle, for example, is brought into focus more clearly by Promey's notice of the texture of simultaneous affirmation and denial built into the substance of both. Thus, we are shown the potential usefulness of comparing the religious aesthetic of the drawings to the famed Shaker dance. In other words, invoking images at the same time that they are banned and embracing ecstasy in the dance even as it is repudiated in the ordered life, are, in each of the oppositions, mutually supportive enterprises in establishing Shaker religiosity during the revival period. The drawings, with their attention to spatial configuration, appear as dance on paper, a "heavenly" sphere that corresponds to movements in the meetinghouse.

In sum, Sally Promey has staked out for herself a critical interpretive position over against both Edward Andrews and Daniel Patterson. Her training as an art historian allows her to offer new precision to the technical analysis of the drawings. Likewise, her knowledge of the issues involved in the comparative study of religions brings new understanding to the religious dimensions of these works, thereby freeing us from earlier sentimental readings. The net effect is greater insight into these unusual images and an improved view of the Shaker religious vision.

Catherine L. Albanese
Stephen J. Stein, Series Editors

PREFACE

At a most fundamental level mid-nineteenth-century Shakers depended in the practice of their faith upon sharp spiritual vision. A crisis of spiritual sight could produce a crisis of faith. Consequently, in the 1830s and 1840s, Shakers at New Lebanon, New York, and Hancock, Massachusetts, received gifts of "spiritual spectacles," sent to them, they believed, by the inhabitants of heaven. The spirit residents of the celestial regions intended these "vision glasses of spiritual sight" to focus the eyes of Believers more effectively and more exclusively on spiritual things.[1] At New Lebanon in 1839, the spirit of the Shaker founder gave "spiritual spectacles" to the community's ministry and elders so that they might "see clearly and not be deceived by false Spirits."[2] At Hancock on 18 September 1842, the spirit of another early leader and prophet "brought a box of spectacles for the brethren and sisters that they may see more clearly spiritual things."[3] These particular gifts of spiritual spectacles did not assume material shape or form. The eyeglasses of faith were metaphysical presents, seen by the soul's eye of the Believer.

But mid-nineteenth-century Shakers also received spiritual spectacles in a more tangible, if metaphorical, form. As early as 1839, individual members of this iconoclastic sect began producing religious drawings and paintings under the inspiration of the spirits. From the beginning, Shakers who drew and painted intended their images to enhance spiritual vision and to distribute it more widely throughout the community. The inscription on a very early drawing of a celestial leaf (1839) specified that the drawing's purpose was to allow its recipient "to see its form" (fig. 1).[4] While only some Believers were actually gifted with spiritual sight (a fact which caused considerable concern and some dissension), religious drawings and paintings, at least theoretically, allowed all present to view the things of God.[5] That is to say, these images functioned as *spiritual spectacles*. In pictures of celestial places, objects, and people, each and every beholder could see spiritual things as though possessing "corrected" spiritual eyesight. Shakers found these heavenly drawings, like numerous other presents and messages received from the heavenly sphere, to be "very useful and necessary in these eventful times."[6]

The Shaker correspondent did not exaggerate in the least when he characterized the times as "eventful." In 1837 it had been sixty-three years since the first English Shakers arrived in New York aboard the ship *Mariah*.[7] It had been fifty-three years since the death of founder Ann Lee. Other early Shaker leaders were long dead. In addition most Believers converted by Ann Lee were dead or dying. And young Shakers, lacking personal connection to the fiery zeal and commitment of their predecessors, seemed to be leaving the community in alarming numbers. Among faithful Believers a fear of losing contact with the origins of Shakerism and with the fervor that attended the early years became almost palpable. The Shaker revival of the mid-nineteenth century responded to concerns generated by this situation. Beginning in August 1837 Shaker communities underwent a period of intense spiritual commotion.[8] Shakers referred to this time as the "New Era" or "Mother's Work" (in reference to their founder "Mother Ann" Lee).[9] Historian Edward Andrews named it the "Era of Manifestations."[10]

Over the next decade and more, so Shakers believed, the spirits of Ann Lee (1736-1784) and of members of her immediate early circle traversed the boundary between heaven and earth to teach, exhort, admonish, warn, and comfort Lee's followers. When possessed by these (and other) spirits, the "instruments" of Mother Ann experienced elaborate visionary episodes, acted out extravagant spiritual pantomimes, and delivered messages and gifts direct from the mouths and hands of the spirits and the Shaker deity. Until Believers closed their services of worship to the public in 1842, seekers and other curious individuals from the surrounding towns and countryside flocked to Shaker meetings to witness these peculiar religious performances. The spectators came, depending upon their various inclinations, to be entertained, amused, shocked, or persuaded by what they saw and heard.[11] As the most tangible manifestations of the New Era, the drawings and paintings of Shaker instruments at New Lebanon and Hancock provided their recipients with both clear spiritual vision and concrete representations of a spectacular spirituality. These images were indeed spiritual *spectacles* in both senses of the word.

As they made visible heaven's extravagant promises, gift images also addressed the more ongoing pastoral, prophetic, and sacramental concerns of this ministering community. That the images participated in the full range of religious life is not surprising given the fact that Shakers understood their religious pictures to represent and to enact the relationship between heaven and earth. According to Believers, celestial beings showed the things of the spirit to chosen individuals, inspiring them to draw and to paint what they saw. Just the opposite of John Calvin who had urged artists to paint only what was visible to the natural eye, Shaker religious artists painted only the objects of spiritual sight. The images produced in this fashion were sacred presents given not to the artist, the instrument, but to some other person or group within the Shaker community.

The Shaker images and messages examined in this book fall into several subgroupings organized along a continuum from primarily text to image largely unaccompanied by word: calligraphic cards and notices; sacred sheets and rolls; texts composed as images; heart, leaf, and star cutouts; texts with emblems and/or illustrations; images with inscribed explanations; images with brief titles or captions; and images with little or no text. The instruments' drawings and paintings varied not only according to the relative proportion of picture and word, but also in scale and shape. They ranged from tiny two-inch squares to large rectangular formats of approximately nineteen inches by twenty-four inches; from the small, pastel heart-shaped cutouts to complex, multi-paged pen and ink booklets; from intricate, single color ink designs in miniature to large images painted in a stained glass palette. Despite great variety in composition, size, and shape, Shaker images employed remarkably uniform materials. The paintings and drawings were unframed and unglazed. Almost all were executed in ink or watercolor (or some combination of the two) on paper.[12] The instruments of a few gift images may have used tempera rather than watercolor.[13]

In order to emphasize, first, the community's conviction that these pictures originated in heavenly vision, in spiritual eyesight, and, second, that they were celestial presents from a divine gift-giver to an earthly recipient, I use interchangeably the terms "visionary images" and "gift images" to describe my subject. The former focuses attention on the mode of communication (visionary and visual or pictorial) as well as on one result of communication (the wider distribution of vision), the latter on the transaction represented by the material object itself. "Gift images," perhaps the more precise term if only in the sense that it distinguishes these Shaker images from visionary images produced by other groups or individuals, is a direct, though somewhat broader, adaptation of Daniel Patterson's "gift drawings."[14] I intend this modification to indicate that the gift "drawings" or visionary images considered here generally include some combination of painting, drawing, and visually organized text. Although the Shakers themselves did not use either "visionary images" or "gift images" as names for their spiritual pictures, both terms appropriately differentiate the celestial drawings and paintings from other more mundane images of Shaker life and stress the continuity between this special category of image and other manifestations of Shaker revival. Mid-nineteenth-century Believers commonly referred to a variety of visionary manifestations, images included, as spiritual "gifts."

I chose Shaker gift images as a field of research because I wanted to explore how visual images (and the idea of vision) functioned in the religious experience of a community which supposed itself to be strenuously iconoclastic. In the past, collectors and curators have obscured Shaker drawings and paintings by viewing Shaker material culture through the lens of the modernist aesthetic. Art historians have ignored or dismissed gift images as "folk art." And historians of American religion have paused only briefly to mention the visionary drawings and paintings as unconvincing aberrations of mid-nineteenth-century Shaker religiosity. In contrast, I understand gift images to embody, more tangibly than any other New Era manifestation, the central spiritual goal of Mother's Work:

Shaker visionary images restored the "visible presence" of the long-dead founder, of the early leaders who supported and expanded upon her ministry, and of the celestial world these "spirits" inhabited so that a new generation of Shakers could know and see and touch their "Mother" and her spiritual companions, and could, thereby, reclaim the experiences of the first generation of American Believers.

But, while my book illuminates key aspects of mid-nineteenth-century Shaker revival, I do not intend this work to be a comprehensive history of that revival. Very specifically, Shaker visionary images form the basis for my study; I have included or excluded material according to its relevance to an informed understanding of these drawings and paintings. In this telling, important persons, events, and places may receive only the briefest reference if they bear little relationship to the immediate context of the images. It is, perhaps, accurate to characterize the present work as a particular, localized, case study in which the specifically Shaker experience in relationship to images suggests broader methodological possibilities for the study of (1) images in religious contexts and (2) images outside the boundaries of the fine arts. In the first case, the experience of these Shakers serves to center attention on the nature of vision as a primary resource for and shaper of religious reality and, reciprocally, on religious experience as a valid context and catalyst for the formation of images. This book, then, accords a central status to visual experience. And it employs both art historical and religious historical tools in order to explore the relationship between imagery and faith in one communitarian society.[15] Not only do religious contexts and written documents require careful attention, but the specific and interdependent contributions of images clarify historical understanding as well.[16]

Moving, then, to a brief consideration of the second "case study" aspect of this book, I will demonstrate that certain (I believe nonessential) attributes of "traditional" art historical analysis have obscured our view of Shaker images. Indeed, a traditional fine arts approach to Shaker images can be limiting. Issues of individual genius, attribution, and connoisseurship reveal little here. In the past, what such an approach contributed to the study of Shaker images was an evaluative hierarchy which generally judged these paintings and drawings unworthy of consideration. The makers and recipients of these pictorial presents from heaven did not themselves understand their involvement with visionary images as a conversation with "art." In fact, the Shaker community had to create a new category for their religious drawings and paintings in order to integrate such pictures into the practice of their faith. The images, then, elicit the contextual approach characteristic of the "new American art history."[17] So, this study asks, early on, how the images came to exist in the first place and, if not as "art," how Shakers categorized what they drew and painted.

This is not to say that a traditional fine arts approach has little to offer here. In fact, if we set aside the evaluative overlay, one significant aspect of such an approach holds great promise for the study of Shaker images. What has been missing from investigations of these visionary drawings and paintings (and of other, especially American, images outside fine arts boundaries) is the kind of concentrated visual analysis usually reserved for fine arts images and objects. In this study, I intend to close the gap between careful visual scrutiny and the "non–fine arts" image. Shaker image-makers adopted a particular formal expressive language. The colors, forms, and organization of the images, as well as the iconography, shaped the meanings of Shaker paintings and determined the reception of the paintings in the community. My book attends to the visual aspects of Shaker images, examining, very carefully, the interactive relationship between form and content in the Shaker community.

My purpose is not to explore the psychology, sociology, or anthropology of Shaker individuals and groups. That is, for the most part, another task, already admirably begun by others. Neither will I consider the relationship between the mid-nineteenth-century images' spiritual value and their twentieth-century aesthetic and monetary value. As I have indicated, in this case, as in many others, issues of aesthetic quality and taste bear little relationship to understanding. There was an authenticity *for Believers* in their experience of these images. This book intends to be an expanded translating project. Its goal is to illuminate the meanings and functions of a relatively circumscribed set of visual images within a particular religious setting. I seek to contextualize and then, on the basis of context, to interpret gift images. What was going on for the creators and beholders of Shaker religious pictures? How was the religious self-understanding of the community connected with the visual? What meanings did gift images carry? How were they perceived? More specifically, why did visionary pictures emerge in a community without any previous tradition of images? And why did they appear between 1839 and 1859 and neither before nor after? The answers to these questions form the subject of this book.

Comparatively speaking, mid-nineteenth-century Shakerism represents a small moment in time and a small group of people. This is even more the case in my study, which narrows its focus to the Shaker communities at New Lebanon, New York, and Hancock, Massachusetts, where Shaker instruments produced most of the surviving gift images.[18] But the experience of these Believers illuminates more expansive concerns in significant ways. I have already suggested that an examination of Shaker images can be methodologically revealing in relationship to investigations of images in religious contexts and images outside the fine arts tradition. I will argue, further, that while the specific meanings of gift images cannot be understood without knowledge of a specific moment in *Shaker* history, the creators and beholders of these images were also firmly rooted in the broader American culture of 1830-1860. Because the mid-nineteenth-century Shaker community constantly won and lost members from and to "the world," the identities of new converts, if not their allegiances, were as much American as they were Shaker. The United Society of Believers, then, represented a particular microcosmic distillation of shared cultural concerns. For example, like many Americans, mid-nineteenth-century Shakers were millennialist and restorationist in the religious sphere and sentimentalist in the moral sphere. Among Shakers at New Lebanon and Hancock, especially, the relatively common effort among American religious groups to restore a fundamental and formative set of experiences, generally remote in space or time, took on an interesting and particularly literal form: the re-creation of a tangible "visible presence" for Ann Lee and other early Shaker leaders who constituted the core personalities in the community's construction of its own spiritual history. In addition, in a period of American history consumed by a sense of crisis in the family and concerned about the role of the home in the formation of personal character, the celibate Shakers exhibited their own peculiarly familial forms of social organization and referred to adherents in familial and generational terminology.[19] Further, as spiritualism, a decade or so later, reflected a larger cultural preoccupation with human mortality, so gift images and other celestial presents addressed similar concerns in no less dramatic fashion. Finally, and perhaps most importantly for this study, Shaker reservations about images intensified and made explicit the usually subtle and veiled but nonetheless consistent anti-iconic impulses and suspicions which characterize American aesthetic history. Within their own communal borders and on their own terms, Shakers participated in an ongoing national debate about the relationship between ethics and aesthetics, morality and beauty. Their images reveal in compelling and concrete fashion the cosmic geography and the sacred chronology developed by Shakers in relationship to this debate.

Just one decade before Edward and Faith Andrews "discovered" Shaker gift images (ca. 1930) for the world outside Shakerism, other collectors, antiquarians, and artists retrieved American "folk" art from relative obscurity. In fact, the coincidence in time of the Andrewses' discovery and of this movement to reclaim and reinterpret American folk objects was no accident.[20] In the early decades of the twentieth century, for the first time in American history, collectors desired and sought such relics of a "simpler" and less technological era.[21] The motives underlying this attraction were complex and sometimes contradictory. In most cases, the acquisition and study of folk art served to reinforce already strongly held aesthetic, nationalistic, and romantic notions about history and reality rather than to further the understanding of folk objects themselves. Casting modern abstraction as a product of American ingenuity, one prominent curator and collector expressed the popularly celebrated affinity between folk art and modern art when he claimed that folk art demonstrated "a two-hundred-year-old unbroken tradition of all that was characteristically American."[22] Another authority asserted that folk art in America represented "the very essence of abstract [read modern] design."[23] If it could be shown that American art of years past relied on the same visual principles as modern art, so this argument went, then American artists could be said to have anticipated, even "invented," modern art. Never mind the inconsistencies, historical and theoretical, of this approach. If modern art had indeed been born among American folk, then Americans might finally claim some priority in a Western art world long dominated by European perspectives.[24] Then, as one reviewer of an early folk exhibit exuberantly proclaimed, in the art world America need be "no longer a pale reflection of Europe."[25]

So an assumed affinity between the Shaker aesthetic and the modernist aesthetic engendered enthusiasm for Shaker artifacts. The collectors, antiquarians, and artists responsible for the birth of interest in Shaker material culture appreciated modern design. And they were struck by an apparent similarity between Shaker artifacts (which they saw as a particularly high-quality subset of American folk artifacts) and modern art. This group prized Shaker material culture because its clean, simple geometry looked modern and because its theologically based functional aesthetic sounded modern.[26] In fact, so impressed were these collectors by resemblances they perceived that they sought out those Shaker items which most faithfully embodied the clean lines, formal attention to function, and absence of applied decoration characteristic of their understanding of the modernist aesthetic. This early twentieth-century excitement at discovering the roots of "modern" design in the American material past has continued to shape public knowledge of Shaker artifacts.

In some significant ways, the reviews, advertisements, and installation for the Shaker exhibition at the Whitney Museum of American Art (29 May–31 August 1986) and the Corcoran Gallery of Art (27 September 1986-4 January 1987) reflected this modernist zeal. Most obviously, rather than trying to reproduce a period context for objects displayed, the designers of the striking exhibit, and of the handsome catalogue, chose to let each artifact stand alone, as though it were a piece of "sculpture."[27] This attitude, highlighting certain carefully selected features of Shaker material culture, can be traced to the modernist inclination to treat objects as things in themselves, to cut objects loose from their contexts and referents in order to prioritize formal qualities.[28] While there are instructive visual and aesthetic similarities between Shaker images and modern art and while this approach has allowed the modern beholder to see what might otherwise have been missed, the similarities between Shaker and modernist aesthetics have to do with form, not content or context. With Roger Stein, I believe that works of art are "culturally embedded systems of signification." Because "meaning is historically inscribed in works of art," interpreters depend upon historical understanding as an indispensable tool.[29] In a field (Shaker material culture) long dominated by another mode (comparison with modernist form) I recontextualize Shaker gift images and propose a unique interpretation based on this recontextualization.[30] Undeniably consideration from a variety of perspectives enriches the study of images and objects. From my point of view, however, Shaker artifacts would never have been as empty, as staged, as alone, as silent as the objects we see in modernist photographs by Charles Sheeler and many others.[31] The purpose of Shaker wall pegs, after all, was to hang things. Shaker baskets and boxes were meant to be filled. And people sat in Shaker chairs.

Appreciation of the material products of Shakerism from the perspective of the modernist aesthetic has done more than highlight objects that seem most fully to reflect the formal values of modernism. It has had the unfortunate effect of obscuring objects that appear unmodern as well. Shaker gift images generally do not fit the modernist aesthetic. Of all Shaker objects, these drawings and paintings are the least amenable to the modernist reinvention of Shaker. To eyes peering through modernist lenses, most of them seem too whimsical, too representational, too intricate and lacy, too sentimental, too obscure in meaning and motive. Consequently, many people who are well acquainted with Shaker furniture and handicraft have never heard of, much less seen, a Shaker gift image.[32]

The gift images of Hannah Cohoon constitute the exception that proves the rule. These most widely known of Shaker images include the *Tree of Life* (fig. 2) which has become the logo for a number of Shaker-associated groups and industries.[33] But Cohoon's watercolor paintings are atypical of Shaker gift images in ways particularly relevant to this discussion. While her pictures irrefutably belong in the larger category of gift images, in contrast to her image-making companions, she composed large, single images of relative geometric simplicity, using a bold palette of primary and secondary hues. Unlike most Shaker instruments, Cohoon also signed her paintings, resolving any question of attribution. These Shaker drawings most familiar to twentieth-century beholders, then, are also among the few drawings most susceptible to a modernist interpretation.[34]

This study invites the reader to lay aside modernist lenses and to try on the Shakers' own "spiritual spectacles" in order to understand (insofar as it is possible for the late twentieth-century beholder to understand) how and why Shakers saw, categorized, and interpreted gift images as they did. This invitation assumes no claim to see without historical bias. In fact, my efforts to recontextualize Shaker images grow, in part, from recognition of contextual influences on my own intellectual development. In relationship to modernist ideology, this study has proceeded during a period of postmodernist critique. While I have chosen not to adopt a thoroughly postmodernist approach, my own place in time has provided a vantage point from which it is possible to see outside of and around the modernist aesthetic and so to identify modernist assumptions in earlier studies of Shaker material culture.

ACKNOWLEDGMENTS

Many people helped to shape this book. It is my pleasure to acknowledge in print their generous assistance. To Neil Harris, Martin Marty, and Linda Seidel I extend my sincere thanks for their willingness to share both scholarly expertise and personal encouragement. Their incisive and expansive thinking and teaching stimulated, enriched, and focused my inquiry. Also at the University of Chicago, Karl J. Weintraub and other members of the Committee on History of Culture supported this project from its beginning. A William Rainey Harper Fellowship in the academic year 1986-87 allowed me to complete the initial phase of the writing in a timely fashion.

Beyond the invaluable guidance of teachers, colleagues, and friends at the University of Chicago, I am especially grateful to Stephen Stein, Catherine Albanese, and David Morgan for careful scrutiny and critical readings of the text. The advice and insights of colleagues and students in the Department of Art History and Archaeology, as well as the support of the Graduate School, at the University of Maryland at College Park, I acknowledge thankfully. Further, Jean Humez graciously made available to me, through the Indiana University Press, the manuscript of her book, *Mother's First-Born Daughters: Selected Writings by Shaker Women*. My reading of this text prompted me to return again to fruitful sources and give additional thought to significant issues.

For a generous publication subsidy, I am very much obliged to the Millard Meiss Publication Fund of the College Art Association.

Completing this study would have been impossible without the collections of many archives, libraries, and museums; the able assistance of many archivists, librarians, curators, and museum directors; and permissions kindly granted by the same to quote from and reproduce texts and images. The following people graciously made available the extensive resources of their respective facilities: Robert A. Guffin, Beverly Hamilton, Thomas F. Harrington, Robert F. W. Meader,

Beth J. Parker Miller, June Sprigg, and Lawrence J. Yerdon at Hancock Shaker Village, Pittsfield, Mass.; Jerry V. Grant, Ann Kelly, Virginia McEwen, and Viki Sand at the Emma B. King Library of the Shaker Museum, Old Chatham, N.Y.; Mary Brooks, John J. Grabowski, Kermit J. Pike, Charles A. Sherrill, and Ann Sindelar at the Western Reserve Historical Society Library, Cleveland, Ohio; Leonard L. Brooks, Paige S. Lilly, Eric Mercer (of Bates College), and David Richards at the Shaker Museum and Library of the United Society of Shakers, Sabbathday Lake, Poland Spring, Maine; Donald Anderle, Mary B. Bowling, Wayne Furman, and Anastacio Teodoro at the Rare Books and Manuscripts Division of the New York Public Library; Oscar E. Gunther, Anne Havinga, Jan Howard, Tamatha Kuenz, Jack L. Lindsey, and Beth A. Rhoads at the Philadelphia Museum of Art; Carlotta J. Owens and Charles M. Ritchie at the National Gallery of Art, Washington, D.C.; Barbara Adams, Katharine Martinez, Ian G. Quimby, and Beatrice K. Taylor at the Henry Francis du Pont Winterthur Museum Library, Winterthur, Del.; Curtis Bochanyin and Ray Gadke at the Regenstein Library, University of Chicago; Ruth T. Degenhardt and Alice Trzcinka at the Berkshire Athenaeum, Pittsfield, Mass.; Sarah A. Kinter at Shaker Village, Canterbury, N.H.; James H. Hutson and Mary Wolfskill at the Library of Congress; Richard S. Reed at Fruitlands Museums, Harvard, Mass.; Elvire Hilgert at the Library of the Lutheran School of Theology, Chicago, Ill.; and staff librarians at Garrett-Evangelical Theological Seminary Library, Evanston, Ill. I also extend my gratitude to the Shakers of Sabbathday Lake, Poland Spring, Maine, and Canterbury, N.H. I will long remember their hospitality.

Finally, words cannot adequately express the debt I owe to my husband, Roger D. Fallot—for his interest, encouragement, balance, and wisdom—and to our daughter, Anna, who, since her arrival rather early in this project, has been an added source of inspiration and (especially) vitality.

❦ *Spiritual Spectacles*

Introduction

A SENSE OF CRISIS

What in the name of reason does it mean that so many are going off nowadays???—!!! . . . O shocking tho't, what a time of apostacy![1]

In the late 1830s and early 1840s, though at their numerical peak, many Shakers characterized their situation as one of crisis. In terms of subtle but sure changes in demographics and, even more significantly, in terms of Believers' own perceptions and judgments, a grave threat confronted their community. A mid-nineteenth-century manuscript written by Isaac Newton Youngs, an official scribe for the New Lebanon ministry, substantiates Priscilla Brewer's recent claim that decline among Shakers was experienced first qualitatively (1820-1840) in a diminished level of commitment to the vision of early leaders and then quantitatively (from 1840) as growing numbers of young and middle-aged adherents left the community.[2]

> Thus the state of things became very different from that in the year 1800. Many of the rising generation, and such as had been lately gathered in, had embibed much of the spirit of the world, and would hardly restrain themselves from adopting its manners and customs; they disregarded, as matters of no importance, the wholesome laws and orders which had been established by Father Joseph and Mother Lucy, and by this means many lost their protection and fell back to the beggarly elements of the world.
>
> And tho' a good portion who were honest hearted retained their integrity, and kept on good gospel ground, yet all, both lead and people, were forced to feel the darkening influence of the cloud that hung over the whole body.
>
> These things were clearly seen and known by the faithful, they bro't much tribulation upon the Ministry and Elders, and upon the faithful first born of our heavenly Parents, who embraced the gospel in the days of Mother Ann's Ministration.[3]

Between 1800 and 1850 the adult apostasy rate in the New Lebanon Church Family rose from less than 3 percent to almost 15 percent.[4] Members between the ages of sixteen and twenty-nine were most likely to leave; by 1850 this age group accounted for 21.7 percent of the Shaker population in the East.[5] Though Shakers had experienced decline in the past, demographic shifts in the community in the late 1830s and 1840s seem to have occasioned extreme uneasiness about the future of the United Society.[6] In 1853 one zealous scribe used boldface calligraphy to emphasize his own increasing sense of anxiety.

> **Awful!** Charles M. Sears, having become reprobated in his spirit, has concluded to withdraw from our communion . . .
>
> **Disgusting!** Jane Lathan has joined Satan's crew, and chosen the pleasures of sin . . .
>
> **Shocking!** Charles Smith came with a shays, and in the course of about two hours returned and took with him Mary Ann Smith, she having agreed with him, in some way (as appears evident) to come and take her! . . .
>
> **Distressing!** John Bruce went to the Office, having made up his mind to turn his back on the way of God and to try the world.[7]

By the late 1830s at least twenty years had passed since the United Society had experienced anything like the impressive numbers of conversions which occurred during the New Light Stir in the 1780s and again in relationship to the Second Great Awakening.[8] Though prospective converts continued to come to the Shakers at mid-century, their numbers were not spectacular, and individuals remained in the Society for shorter and shorter periods of time.[9]

Rates of transition in membership even more than total numbers of members began to change noticeably during these decades. Working with membership records for the New Lebanon Second Family, Lawrence Foster has demonstrated that the 1830s marked a critical juncture in the stability of at least this one Family. Prior to this decade, the average length of stay exceeded thirty years. After once entering the United Society, individuals often remained until they died. Those who entered during the 1830s, however, stayed an average of fifteen years. The rate of turnover increased again after 1840, with the average length of stay for newly gathered individuals dropping to less than ten years. This trend continued until, by the 1860s, many left the United Society after only a few years or months among Believers.[10]

By 1840 rates of defection had been for some time greatest among younger members in or fast approaching their most productive years. A New Lebanon minister worried that "many of our young people have been dreadfully beset with doubts and unbelief concerning Revelation, a future state, rewards and punishments etc. etc."[11] Longstanding members of the United Society, fearful of the degree to which this new generation resembled "the world," referred disparagingly to some of the young as "this fashionable race of believers." These youth seemed to demonstrate insufficient commitment to the simple life required of the followers of Ann Lee.[12] A personal journal entry penned sometime between April and October 1847 constituted Isaac Youngs's "*Serious Reflection*" on the crisis of faith among the rising generation.

> What does it mean? is there none of the younger part that will abide and be good for some thing—are we indeed unable to raise any children or youth among us. *Must* they and *will* they all drop off, and prove abortive, like the rotten potatoes of late years.[13]

In part, the exodus among the young resulted from the Shaker practice, begun in the early decades of the nineteenth century, of taking in increasing numbers of orphaned and indentured children too young to make a faith commitment upon entrance.[14] By 1830 the proportion of children under fifteen in the eastern communities had reached 15.2 percent and young adults fifteen to twenty-nine years of age accounted for 26.7 percent of the eastern Shaker population.[15] As these children and young people came of age, many decided to seek their fortunes in the world rather than casting their lot with Believers.[16] Earlier in Shaker history most new converts had already reached the age of religious maturity and many had experienced extended periods as religious seekers before joining the Shakers. The majority of these earlier converts had reached sexual maturity as well. Choosing a life of celibacy, the Shaker "cross," thus presented a different set of questions to later Shakers often raised from childhood among Believers. Children and youth had entered the United Society in the early years but most of these accompanied their believing parents and (often) extended families and so were nurtured in faith and insulated from some temptations of the world by the example of committed and trusted relations.[17] The contrast with the mid-nineteenth-century situation, then, is striking. In this new historical setting, although young people continued to join for reasons of faith, many who had been raised by the Shakers decided to leave instead of signing the Shaker covenant—and many who joined left the Society in a comparatively short period of time.[18]

The Shakers' economic circumstances had changed over the years as well. In the second half of the nineteenth century, William Bainbridge maintains, Shakerism became more a refuge and less a revolution.[19] The primitive Millennial Church had offered few material comforts to its first zealous adherents. They joined, instead, for primarily religious reasons. And they gave all they had to the community. As time passed and the Millennial Church grew, it promised its members, if not luxury, at least a life free from want. Often prospective converts entered, with few material possessions of their own, to partake of the Shaker bounty. While these new Believers generally shared earlier concerns about sin and salvation, economic security and social stability attracted them as well.[20] The Shaker life, however, continued to require sufficient sacrifice that few adults joined or stayed for purely nonreligious reasons. The shift in motivation was primarily a shift in emphasis. Motives for entering the United Society remained complex.

Long before Mother's Work began, faithful Believers feared a future problem with younger generations. The deaths of the early leaders and the anticipated deaths of their first converts precipitated this anxiety. In 1813 Eldress Hannah Kendal of the Harvard and Shirley (Massachusetts) bishopric appreciated the significance of the fact that "our precious good Mother [Lucy Wright (1761-1821)] is yet alive and that there is so many pillars [i.e., committed leaders] left in Zion yet."[21] In the years after Lucy Wright's death, Shaker leaders began to express more explicitly their concern for a generation threatened by distance in time from the experience of the first Shakers.[22] In fact, as early as the 1808 *Testimony of Christ's Second Appearing,* Believers started to gather up the testimony of those who had known Ann Lee.[23] This earliest published volume to include eyewitness testimony to the charism and power of Lee's personality was intended by Shakers as a tool of conversion in their Western missions, in particular. As it neared completion, eastern Shakers at New Lebanon, Hancock, and Watervliet had already begun (almost thirty years after the death of Ann Lee) to solicit and record first-person memories of "Mother Ann and the Elders." Culminating in the 1816 *Testimonies,* this project represented a specific attempt to address the need of future Shakers ("who have never seen those blessed Ministers of Christ in the body") to know about the charismatic founder and her immediate circle.[24] By the time of the 1827 *Testimonies,* forty-five-year-old recollections of Ann Lee formed the basis of a text intended to refute negative charges, circulating in contemporary anti-Shaker literature, about the founder's character.[25]

To return my narrative to the years preceding the mid-nineteenth-century revival, Believers in the mid-thirties once again focused their attention on the rapidly dwindling numbers of Shakers converted by Ann Lee and her closest companions. As more and more of these symbolically significant and generally beloved individuals "left the scenes of time," deep feelings of sorrow, loss, and anxiety permeated the documents kept by their survivors. A letter from the parent ministry visiting at Watervliet to North Union in 1834 expressed widely shared sentiments.

> There is a number more of the first call of all believers who, in all probability, must leave this mortal shore before long: And in a few more short years there will not be an individual left who ever beheld the bodily presence of our Ever-blessed Mother! What a solemn and weighty consideration must this bring upon all who feel interested in the support and increase of the work of God.[26]

In the spring of 1840, celestial communications warned younger Believers that

> before the end of the year eighteen hundred and fifty they [Christ and Mother Ann] should . . . gather the first born home from the earth. "And then, (said they) the burden will fall on you, and you will have to keep the gospel for yourselves."[27]

Throughout the Era and extending later into the century similar lamentations abound.

> The first call of believers are fast dropping away, one after another, and . . . they will soon all be harvested out of time into eternity. And unless God works in the hearts of the children of men, to awaken them to a sense of their lost state, and of

> their need of salvation, our numbers must become small; for at the present time, true conviction of sin, and a desire to be saved from its reigning power, is rarely found . . . O Lord, how long shall this state continue?[28]

Concerned Shakers feared for the future of their Church. How, indeed, would the young remain faithful once the communities lost all physical contact with the first generation? And how would the anxiety of older Believers over this crisis be assuaged? Addressing the needs, concerns, and behavior of all ages within Shaker society, the manifestations of Mother's Work provided vivid and powerful responses to these questions.

From the time of "Mother" Ann Lee, Shakers had expressed in familial language their spiritual relationship with one another. New converts exchanged "natural [i.e., biological] relations" for "gospel relations" as they entered a community system structured around large residential "families." It is not surprising, then, that Shakers thought of the relationship between older and younger Believers in predominantly familial and, thus, generational terms,[29] and that they adapted common nineteenth-century usage to describe these relationships. "First born," "second crop," and "rising generation" differentiated what I will call the first, second, and third generations of American Shakers.[30] The Shaker terminology with regard to the generations did not originate among Believers. Adherents to the gospel of Ann Lee (in the eighteenth century and in the nineteenth century) naturally appropriated many such forms of verbal expression (e.g., "rising generation") from the broader American culture. Shakers made frequent use of New England Puritan and New Light terminology, adapting Separate Baptist usage, in particular, to their own needs.[31] The attention paid to generational categories in official Shaker documents of this period, however, suggests the special importance of generational issues for Shakers. Among Believers, the first born comprised "those converted by Mother Ann"[32] or, more broadly, "all those called by the gospel while she [Ann Lee] was on earth."[33] Adapting this Shaker use of terminology, I count as the first American generation the *converts* of Ann Lee and her English companions. "Mother's first born," including Lucy Wright and Joseph Meacham (the "second parents"), constituted this "first generation."[34] Lee (the English "first mother") then generated the sequencing rather than being encompassed within it. At the other end of the mid-nineteenth-century generational spectrum, the rising generation generally included all who entered the community or came to maturity in faith after the death of Lucy Wright in 1821, i.e., those who converted during the lengthy tenure of Ebenezer Bishop, Ruth Landon, Rufus Bishop, and Asenath Clark, the parent ministry from 1821 to 1849. The second crop occupied the intermediary position, converting after the death of Ann Lee and before the death of Lucy Wright. Although Shakers understood the generations in terms of religious maturity as well as chronological maturity, the two seem usually to have been related.

The language used to describe age divisions existed within the Shaker community long before Mother's Work began. But Shaker leaders and instruments during the New Era were particularly and intensely involved in grouping and categorizing Believers according to religious and chronological maturity. Messages and gifts from the heavens frequently divided recipients into age cohorts: the "ancients" (often but not always synonymous with "first born"), the middle-aged "second crop" or "Mother's Class," and the younger "rising generation" or "Father's Class."[35] With some variation, the rising generation included those between fourteen and thirty years of age, the middle-aged those between thirty and sixty, and the ancients those sixty and older.[36] As time passed, of course, members of the Era's rising generation (my third generation) aged. Around 1849, with the death of Ebenezer Bishop, a fourth generation began to establish itself within the community. In many cases, however, terminology was slow to change so that, in the 1850s especially, a technically middle-aged Shaker of the third generation still might be classified as a member of the rising generation.[37] Ultimately, proximity to Mother Ann and the Elders (the early Shaker "Church") established the standard for the categorization of Believers with regard to religious and chronological maturity.

While I have indicated that this period of Shaker history was by no means divorced from its broader American context, neither can it be adequately accounted for simply as part of a more general cultural awakening. Aspects of the nineteeth-century American context are highly significant and, from time to time, this book will explore vital connections. In the final analysis, however, Mother's Work is best understood as an internal revival, as a "third generation" phenomenon within the Shaker community, as an extended rite of initiation for members of this new generation of American Shakers.[38]

> For these caviling young people knew not their heavenly Parents neither personally nor in spirit. Therefore they would not believe without a work of inspired manifestations and divine communications from the Heavens, attended by such evident operations as could not be disputed by the rational senses, and which brought forth the same testimony that your heavenly Parents bore when on earth, and which had always been maintained by their first born children.[39]

Central to the mid-century rite of initiation was an effort to restore to the Shaker community the charismatic and authoritative presence of Mother Ann.

> Thus have her younger children, who never saw her face,
> While she was in the body and moving in this place,
> Receiv'd her pure instructions, monitions, and have hear'd,
> As did her elder children, their precious Mother's word.[40]

Community identity in the early years had depended upon personal commitment to a charismatic woman/prophet (many said Christ), Ann Lee. In order for the third generation to internalize the level of commitment exhibited by those who had known Ann Lee, Shakers needed a process of identity formation for this later generation that would resemble the earlier process among Lee's first born. To this end ministry and instruments collaborated with inhabitants of the celestial regions to consolidate, ritualize, and personalize a mythology and a tradition for young Believers.

In divine communications inhabitants of the celestial sphere specified the rising generation as "that class for whom these divine gifts and manifestations were generally designed."[41] Heaven and earth united to aid in "renewing and reestablishing gospel order on the original foundation among the rising generation."[42] Shakers repeatedly identified Mother Ann's work during the New Era with her ministry among the first generation of Believers.[43] In a ritual communication of October 1840, Mother Ann admonished the third generation that her life on earth "was unto them [the first born] as this day is unto you."[44] Later in the same document Ann Lee's spirit addressed the first born with assurances that

> this present work was not needed so much on your account, as on account of those who are middle aged and young, for whom it was mostly designed; that they might have an opportunity to join that planting in their own souls . . . which you gained while we [Lee and the other early leaders] were upon earth.[45]

Clearly, the Mother Ann who so personified for mid-century Shakers the "mighty gifts and power of God," had become more than the historical Ann Lee. For eighteenth-century Shakers, the Second Coming of Christ had been inaugurated collectively, in the body of the Shaker "church." Though Lee played a crucial part as prophetic visionary and charismatic focal point for the community, it was not until early in the nineteenth century that Shaker leaders identified Lee herself, and not the church, as the second appearance of Christ. In the 1808 *Testimony* Shakers first expressed in print their emerging beliefs regarding the deification of their founder.[46] A few years later, the 1816 *Testimonies* intended to "prove, to all faithful Believers, that Christ did verily make his second Appearance in *Ann Lee* . . . the first spiritual Mother of all the children of the resurrection."[47] The doctrine of Mother Ann as the "manifestation of Christ in the female" continued to receive considerable attention in the years preceding and constituting Mother's Work.[48] On Ann Lee's birthday in 1841, Shakers read aloud a little book on "Christ's Second Appearance in the female, written by inspiration, Feb'y 25th 1841." According to the record-keeper,

> It is a sublime description of the work of God in calling and preparing Mother Ann for to stand in her lot as Mother of the New Creation. As the writing is and will be preserved, sacred, I need not state particulars here. It may doubtless be seen in years to come, if necessary.[49]

The doctrinal assertion of Ann Lee as the second incarnation of the Christ spirit settled the matter of pluralism and authority for those who believed Ann Lee embodied the Shakers' particular tie to the eternal. She was the chosen one of God, upon whom rested the mantle of charism, upon whom depended the truth of the Shaker way of life, a necessary partner with Jesus in the process of salvation.[50] Although Shakers dated the onset of the Era of Manifestations to

1837, a dynamic of expectation prepared the Society during the decade and a half previous to this date. Mid-century Shakers did not anticipate the second coming of Christ: that, they believed, had already occurred in Ann Lee.[51] Expectation, therefore, had a less specific content. But Shakers generally agreed that gifts from heaven would increase, resulting in a spectacular revival of zeal, purity, and commitment. A sense of urgency grew as time passed.

As long as sporadic outbursts of spiritual enthusiasm, in the years and months prior to the New Era, did not originate among the children and youth, Believers did not interpret these outbursts as anything novel or unique. After all, from the earliest days of the faith, visionary episodes had been a fundamental part of Shaker spirituality. According to the perceptions of insiders, God inaugurated a decisively new and different work among Shakers at the moment when Mother Ann and other spirits chose members of the rising generation as instruments. The solution to the crisis of faith in the third generation had to directly involve that generation.[52] Spiritual beings delivered heavenly gifts and messages through "those who were young in years, and young in the faith of the gospel" so that these "children of Zion" would believe.[53] "I [Mother Ann] have chosen those who are very young for Instruments that they may know there is a God and futurity. Those who are older and have travelled further, do not need these gifts for their own confirmation."[54]

In fact, though, the crucial New Era issue was not a point of age. It was not simply the linear succession of Shaker generations that mattered. What counted just as much was the *rhythm* of generations within the Shaker community. At the heart of what I have described as the crisis of the third generation was a sense of remoteness from the person of Ann Lee and, significantly, from the spiritual enthusiasm experienced in her time.[55] The first two generations of Shakers had successfully accomplished the transition from a loosely ordered charismatic sect to a Millennial Church with a strict hierarchy and smoothly functioning organization.[56] Without this transition Shakerism never would have flourished as it did. By the third generation, however, American Shakers had little or no direct experience with the spiritual intensity and charismatic activity of the early years. Further, the aging eyewitnesses who could provide first-hand accounts were rapidly dying. Mother's Work addressed all ages of Believers in terms of the problems raised by chronological, physical, and behavioral separation from primitive Shakerism.

What Victor Turner discusses, more generally, as the tension between "communitas" and "structure" Stephen Stein identifies, among antebellum Shakers, as a contest between "gift" and "order."[57] Each generation of Believers incorporated elements of both gift and order, charism and institution, ecstasy and organization. But the proportionate relationship between the two changed significantly over time. In the broadest terms, the history of Shakers from their origins through the years immediately following Mother's Work can be characterized as a movement from charism (first generation) to institutionalization (second generation) to charism (third generation) to institutionalization (fourth generation).[58]

Even before she came to America, Ann Lee's charismatic experiences marked her, in the eyes of her companions, as a chosen one of God. Those who followed her to America were particularly receptive to Lee's spiritual gifts. And those who converted in America were drawn to this woman as one who could herself induce others to recognize and to manifest the power of God.[59] When Ann Lee arrived in New York in 1774, William Lee, her brother ("Father William"—d. 1784), and James Whittaker ("Father James"—1750-1787) were among those who accompanied her. Lee preceded his sister in death but Whittaker began the long process of organizing the widely scattered groups of Believers. Joseph Meacham ("Father Joseph"—1741-1796) and Lucy Wright ("Mother Lucy"—1761-1821), the early American leaders largely responsible for gathering the Shakers into communal order, succeeded Whittaker in this task.[60] As American Shakerism took shape, celibacy, confession of sin, and communal ownership of property distinguished adherents from the world around them. During Ann Lee's lifetime, however, spirit possession, rather than communal ownership of property, had constituted the third essential element of Shakerism.[61]

Beginning in early August 1837, the revival the Shakers called Mother's Work brought with it the large scale restoration of the charismatic gifts which characterized early Shaker spirit possession. On 1 January 1839 a member of the New Lebanon ministry recalled:

> There are some in the senior class of believers who have retained more or less of the gifts of visions, tongues, etc, from the first of their faith; but there has not been much of these supernatural gifts among the rising generation, except in a few instances, until about two years ago, when a girl in the childrens' Order at Watervliet [New York] had a remarkable Vision in the day time as she sat at her work, and which seemed to portend something remarkable about to take place among believers. Soon after this, the children in the back families, and also some of the youth were wonderfully wrought upon by the mighty power of God, in turning, shaking, etc. Then Visions and trances followed to a wonderful degree, until it seemed as if there could hardly be anything in the spiritual world which was withheld from their view, even from the throne of God, down to the lowest regions of despair. And whatever they saw was generally spoke of, or acted out in a manner truly astonishing to the beholders.[62]

Not two years before, fourteen-year-old Ann Mariah Goff's spiritual eyes were opened and she beheld what was invisible to those around her.[63] She saw that spirits had penetrated the borders of the earthly Zion to visit among Believers. Spirit guides conducted Goff into the celestial sphere where she toured the City of Paradise, observed celestial worship, and saw Jesus and Mother Ann. Goff described one of her journeys into the spirit world to a Shaker scribe:

> At 1/2 past 7 ocl. in the morning there came a sister spirit to me, by the name of Caroline Landon, and asked me to go with her. I went with her. We seemed to travel a great distance to the north, and we came to a city. I asked the name of the city. She said it was the city of Paradise. I asked how many buildings there were in it. She said

> there were 400. And they stood in four rows. 100 in a row. Two rows were white and two of a silver color. And the Meeting house was in the centre, and it was white, and so large that my eyes could scarcely reach from one side of the building to the other. . . .
>
> We then went to another house, and there I saw a room which my guide told me was the first place that Mother Ann came to after she left the earth. The walls of the room were white and shone very bright; and there were rows of flowers of a golden color all round the room; and between the rows of flowers Mother Ann's name was written, in large gold letters, all round the room, and at the beginning and end of her name was a large golden flower. I then started for home after an absence of seven hours and a half.[64]

Mother's Work had begun. Shakers declared a time of "universal awakening throughout the whole Society."[65] Visions and spiritual gifts increased in frequency as well as intensity. The varieties of gifts included oral and written messages and presents, ritual pantomimes, songs, dances, drawings and paintings. Shaker gift images, then, constituted a visual subcategory within a larger category of spiritual presents and messages.

A letter of 19 December 1837 from the New Lebanon ministry to the elders of the community at Sodus Bay described the events of the previous several months:

> Concerning the spiritual prosperity, we hardly know what to say or how to express ourselves. It seems almost like a new *Era*. . . .
>
> . . . the Spirit of God has been poured out of late in a wonderful manner, especially among the youth and children; and wisely calculated to eradicate infidelity, and to establish souls in the belief of divine revelation. We were glad to hear . . . of the same work going on among you . . . and that this blessed work and beautiful gifts are not the exclusive privileges of any individual person or community.[66]

Lest someone mistake the account for the experience, one Shaker correspondent assured his reader:

> we live in a day of wonders and miricles which are beyond the power of tongue or pen to describe; and should we attempt anything like a description of these marvelous gifts and manifestations from a spiritual world, we might rather dishonor the cause, and at the same time fall far short of what *we*, and perhaps *you* may daily witness in meetings, and almost everywhere on our premises.[67]

Hundreds and thousands of spirits came to inhabit the Shaker Zion. Accounts of the spirits' activities in the communities dominated journals, correspondence, and record books. Certainly, the Shakers declared, this era represented the "most marvelous outpourings of the spirit of God, in revelations and inspirations, that ever was known since the world began."[68] These words indicate that some believed they participated in a restoration not only of primitive Shakerism but of a prelapsarian condition. Others expressed their astonishment more directly in relationship to primitive Shakerism:

> It can be said in truth, that of late there has been the greatest manifestation of heavenly gifts showered down upon us that has ever been realized since the first opening of the gospel in this place. Such is the testimony of the aged brethren and Sisters who have observed the various states and travel of believers from the first opening of the gospel to the present time.[69]

News of the manifestations at Watervliet (New York) spread rapidly. While the parent ministry resided, officially, at New Lebanon, they made frequent rather long term visits to Watervliet, moving back and forth with some regularity. This established pattern of contact between the two communities promoted good communication and easy accessibility. Soon after the "gifts" began, Isaac Youngs and Barnabas Hinckley journeyed from New Lebanon to Watervliet to record visions and to learn the new forms of worship given to the Shakers by the spirits.

> Those who had these gifts were called *visionists.* And their spiritual exercises consisted greatly in their being taken in a trance, attended by some guide or spirit, with whom they had become acquainted; and going on a visit to some habitation, house, village or city in the spiritual world; seeing and conversing with those they had formerly known in the body; and also frequently forming new acquaintances with spirits; very generally attending meetings with the spirits, and uniting with them in worship. . . .
>
> Most generally in the course of their visits, they had an interview with Mother Ann . . . All these things the visionist would act out externally, insomuch that spectators could ascertain the substance of what was passing in the invisible region of the spirit.
>
> But sometimes they were entirely absent from the scenes of time, and seemed inaccessible to those in the body; but they could relate what they had experienced, after they came out of their trance. Sometimes, there were verbal messages, given by the spirits to communicate to the Elders, to individuals, or in public.[70]

Shakers from other communities, too, visited to witness the wonders; messengers and letters carried vivid descriptions to those who did not send envoys to see for themselves. The early manifestations of Mother's Work were highly diverse, energetic, almost chaotic experiences of inspiration. Some Believers spoke in unknown tongues; some saw visions; some received gift songs, dances, and rituals; spirits possessed the bodies of others, causing them to shake and jerk and twirl about.[71]

Later Shaker interpretation would depict the events of these first months as preparation for 22 April 1838.[72] On this date, Shakers claimed, the spirit of Mother Ann spoke to the Church Family at New Lebanon.[73] Although the Shaker founder had made her presence known in earlier visions and messages, this was her first official and public message in the community and family which exercised most authority (real and symbolic) among Shakers. The movement from abstract perception of Mother Ann's spiritual presence to bold personification of this religious leader was significant. Recognition of Mother Ann's direct involvement was an essential element in the internal interpretation of "Mother's Work," which Shakers also called the "Second Manifestation of Mother Ann."[74] First Mother Ann, and then other early Shaker leaders, returned from the celestial world to complete the particular work that they began during their earthly life span. Mother Ann's charismatic task was "to work conviction and plant the gospel by confession and repentance"; Mother Lucy, Father Joseph, Father William, and Father James sought to "reestablish Church order, purge out disorder and superfluities, etc."[75]

> There is no new foundation to be laid says Father, but a new increase of zeal in the middle aged and rising generation, to build rightly upon that foundation which God hath already laid; for they will shortly be left to bear the burden, and keep the way of God upon earth.[76]

Though Mother's Work did not consist of vigorous efforts to attract large numbers of new converts from outside the Shaker community, Shakers described this period as a "revival."[77] Mother's Work was indeed revival in a very particular sense: it sought to revive what its promoters believed to be a more primitive, more authentic form of Shakerism. Shakers thus shared a primitivist impulse with other American religious groups. In keeping with the usage suggested by Richard Hughes, this book understands restorationism or primitivism as the notion that " 'first times' are in some sense normative or jurisdictional for contemporary belief and practice."[78] Like other Americans, Shakers tended to equate the millennium with the primordium; they were inclined to see the latter days as a return to the first times.[79] For the United Society, as for the Puritans, Separate Baptists, Mormons, Disciples of Christ, and others, the crucial contrast was between the sanctified ancients and the profane moderns.[80] In the Shaker case, however, the ancients and the moderns were separated by only one generation. The ancients were those who had known Ann Lee and the moderns were members of the rising generation. According to official documents, Mother's Work began when the ancients intervened with Ann Lee's spirit for the sake of the youth.[81] Shakers characterized the New Era, then, as a period of tribulation and dislocation which necessitated a drastic appeal. At the same time, New Era Believers knew that they lived in a marvelous age of wonders and miracles.

For Shakers over the duration of Mother's Work, the present reiterated the past. In order to focus attention on similarities between their own time and the early years of the sect, these communitarians identified and accentuated perceived parallels between the present and the past. For example, the early followers of Ann Lee suffered persecution; mid-nineteenth-century Shakers interpreted their own situation as one of persecution by the world.[82] Believers in the early Shaker church experienced visions and spiritual "operations" both in and out of worship; so did mid-century Shakers.[83] Believers in the early Shaker church had known poverty and conditions of extreme physical hardship; during Mother's Work, those under fifty who "had never known want" underwent limited periods of intentional privation, eating only bread and water, for instance.[84]

According to New Era ministry and instruments, Believers in the early Shaker church had followed the same divine rules and orders "recovered" by the mid-nineteenth-century Shaker community.[85] Like Shakers in the early years, New Era Believers embarked on several (in the mid-century case, short-lived) missionary ventures.[86]

Even the fact of Mother Ann's particular mid-century attention to the rising generation could be construed as restorationist. For during her earthly life, some noted, Ann Lee had shown a "special interest in the young believers and her ability to win their devotion."[87] After the deaths of Ann Lee and James Whittaker, Joseph Meacham intensified this focus, hoping, Clarke Garrett argues, to create a "perfected generation of young men and women" who would later be responsible for the spread of the Shaker gospel. Though this plan for a perfected generation had to be abandoned in 1798, some among the New Era's first born or ancients had participated in this early youth order.[88] The impulse to concentrate attention on the rising generation, then, was present in early Shakerism. The relationship between apostasy and spiritual discipline was reversed, however. In the 1790s severity and rigidity of discipline in the young people's order caused resentment and apostasy. In the 1840s Shakers contended that the spirits sought to revive primitive discipline to combat apostasy among the youth.[89]

The subject of this book has little to do with the success or failure of Mother's Work. The question at hand is rather the relationship between visual imagery and the principal concerns of this period in Shaker history. Throughout my manuscript, I subject Shaker images to careful and sustained visual analysis even as I locate the images firmly in their appropriate historical and cultural contexts. In Part I, I trace the movement from vision to image within Shaker spirituality, establishing the continuity between visionary experience and visual image and expanding previous definitions of gift images in a manner consistent with Shakers' own understandings of their religious pictures. (Some readers may wish to move rather quickly through this earlier material on categories and concepts, into Parts II and III which deal more directly with particular images and their immediate contexts.) Through a symbolic ordering of space which established the close proximity of earth and heaven (Part II), and a symbolic manipulation of time which organized and conflated past, present, and future (Part III), Shaker image-makers attempted to reconnect the earthly community with heaven and its inhabitants and to restore the zeal and the personalities of earlier times. Thus, gift drawings and paintings played a critical and peculiar role in the New Era revival. Among the many gifts of encouragement, exhortation, kindness, reproof, instruction, and warning, gift images occupied at first a tentative and then a more prominent position. In the context of Shaker experience, gift images were the most strikingly experimental of the many spiritual presents received from the inhabitants of the celestial sphere. Songs, dances, spiritual pantomimes, bodily seizures, visions, spirit visitations—none of these was entirely new to mid-nineteenth-century Shakerism. But religious pictures had never before found a hospitable place among traditionally iconoclastic Believers.

Part I

VISION AND IMAGE

One

From Vision to Image

CONTINUITY IN SHAKER EXPERIENCE

The initial question which stimulated this investigation of Shaker image-making might be expressed in this fashion: in a religious community with no material precedents for visual images, in a community in which images represented emphatic discontinuity with historical practice and belief, why did adherents rather suddenly begin producing religious paintings and drawings—and how did they account for this activity? It is certainly true that Believers lacked *material* precedents for religious images. In an *immaterial* form, however, a significant precedent existed. In fact, the specifically visionary foundation of the Shaker spiritual imagination created a fertile environment for images (provided, of course, that specific reservations about decorative material forms could be addressed). Far from being a nonvisually oriented people, the Shakers of the late eighteenth and early nineteenth centuries were a people of religious vision. Describing her own experience of divine inspiration, Ann Lee herself was reputed to have said, "I look into the windows of heaven, and see what there is in the invisible world."[1] Years later, the creation and auspicious reception of images in the Shaker community depended upon Shaker understandings of religious vision and its inherent value.

An impressive sight confronted Shakers in New Lebanon's First Order when they gathered for worship on Sunday 2 June 1844. One record-keeper described the "singular circumstance" of that morning's service in this way:

> When we entered the meeting room, a table stood at the head of the meeting, covered with a white Cloth.

> The Elders informed us that as there was some time ago a promise given us by the spirits, that there would yet be something further given us as a notice from the Spiritual world, and a *heart* was given us with a promise that we should yet know what was written on them—the writing was now accomplished—and the presents were ready to be given out. The brethren and sisters then came forward, kneeling down and receiving the papers, in the form of a heart, beautifully written over with words of blessing in the name of the Father.[2]

The textual account implies that each member of the First Order received a heart. Pictorial evidence suggests that children as well as adults numbered among the recipients; of the twenty-some surviving cutouts, two were addressed to individuals twelve years of age or less.[3] So as many as 148 of these celestial valentines ornamented the board prepared for Believers on that Sunday morning in June.[4]

According to the scribe's record, the act of giving and receiving the paper hearts represented the fulfillment of a spiritual gift announced sometime earlier.[5] But this gift was not complete until Believers could *see* their hearts. The liturgical presentation of these "Hearts of Blessing"[6] thus underscored the centrality of vision (both vision of the eye and vision of the soul) in Shaker religious experience (fig. 3). When First Order Believers entered their meeting room this day they saw a white-covered table arrayed with pale blue, pink, and white paper hearts. They saw that the hearts had been inscribed on both sides with fine images and words drawn in blue ink. On closer scrutiny, they saw their own names and the names of their companions, written on these celestial presents (so they believed) through the agency of God. What Believers saw both focused and magnified the spiritual power of this ritual blessing; the visibility of the hearts was a crucial component of the ritual.

Ultimately, the crisis which precipitated the mid-nineteenth-century Shaker revival can be reconstructed as a crisis of vision. Over the years the visionary experiences of Believers had contributed significantly to Shaker religious identity. Historically and spiritually, in fact, Shakers grounded their faith in the visionary ecstasies of Ann Lee and her immediate circle. As one who knew Ann Lee testified, from childhood this "first" Shaker understood religious vision in a peculiarly literal fashion.

> I have heard Mother say she used to have visions of heavenly things, and see beautiful colors when a child—and she dreaded to have her Mother get her up in the morning for fear she would open the windows and let them out.[7]

Like their forebears, Lee's mid-nineteenth-century followers continued to interpret spiritual vision as the principal vehicle of revelation. In order to rejuvenate their faith, many Shakers at mid-century believed that they needed to recover the ability of their predecessors to see and to sense spiritual things, needed to recreate for the third generation the visual and visionary experience of the first generation. In one New Era manuscript, the spirit of James Whittaker characterized the absence of sufficient commitment on the part of some Believers as an absence of vision. In this document, Father James prayed to the "Almighty Father and my Blessed Mother" that they would "*open the eyes* of souls who are unable to stand for themselves, that they may receive conviction and turn to God and serve Him [italics added]."[8] One prominent instrument recorded this admonition, castigating wayward Believers for their lack of vision:

> For lo I say unto you, Ye have set light for darkness and darkness for light; and ye have taken the shadow for the substance and the substance for the shadow; because ye were carnally minded, and saw not the things of God aright.[9]

So, among Shakers, vision had a fundamentally moral component; righteousness involved *seeing* rightly. The ministry and the instruments of Mother's Work located the separating line between regenerate and unregenerate worlds in the distinction between authentic vision and spiritual blindness.

> All that have had a desire to receive true sight, have been made able to see. But those who have had no desire to see, but have strove against the light and power, must surely be cast without the vineyard, no more to be received into the fold of Christ.[10]

Characterizing the agency of evil in similar terms, one instrument warned Believers to kill instantly with spiritual swords any evil spirit who came at them. Otherwise, "it will fly right at you and tear your eyes out, and then you cant see."[11] If sin affected sight negatively, salvation had the opposite impact. Years earlier, according to the 1816 *Testimonies,* Ann Lee herself associated sight with redemption claiming that the redeemed could see the angels of God above them. In fact, another witness maintained, Lee had specified the present millennial age as the time foretold in the Christian scriptures when the faithful would "see clearly, face to face."[12]

The power of visionary experiences (and of derivative visual phenomena) to "convince souls," and thereby to produce commitment, commanded the attention of Shaker leaders and followers alike.[13] Members of the United Society placed a high premium on certain kinds of visibility and vision. Spiritual sight, the ability to see the things of the spirit, was a gift of God for the increase of the faith. From the years of the founders on, Believers affirmed, clear sight and faith belonged together; one led to the other.[14] For this reason, New Era instruments maintained, the two persons of the Shaker godhead chose to express their "Almighty and unalterable power, in so visable a manner."[15] During Mother's Work, then, Shakers witnessed "the things of God brought to mortal view."[16] Deity "designed" these visual manifestations "as supernatural evidences" of divine activity.[17] Official correspondents of the period noted that "ocular proof" persuaded many to believe in the messages sent by the spirits.[18]

According to the inspired ones, even biblical prophets, who now resided in the Shaker spirit world, believed that visual images could serve as a significant form of evidence. On 16 May 1839, or so claimed instrument Anna Dodgson, the prophets Isaiah and Daniel visited Believers in the Church Family at New Lebanon. In Dodgson's account, Isaiah himself painted "miniature likenesses" of the sisters and brothers, as a record of the visit, to show to his companions in the spirit world.[19] Isaiah's "spiritual" paintings provided spirits with a view of natural beings. The paintings and drawings of Shaker instruments, conversely, represented the spiritual world to the creatures of nature.

Shakers both experienced a relationship with deity and expressed personal righteousness in a visionary mode. They also based on notions of visibility fundamental distinctions with regard to the organization of the universe. They measured the distance between earth and heaven, like that between sinner and saved, in terms of vision. The things of earth were ordinarily visible; the things of heaven were ordinarily invisible. Believers referred to their ministry as the "Visible Lead" in order to differentiate them from the invisible and ultimate divine authority. In the official name they chose for themselves, Shakers indicated a connection between appearance and presence. They did not think of themselves as Believers in Christ's Second *Coming,* but as the "United Society of Believers in Christ's Second *Appearing* [italics added]." They thus expressed in visual terminology the doctrine which most publicly stated the theological dissimilarity between Shakers and other Christian sects, that is, the belief that Christ's second coming had already occurred in the person, the "appearing," of Ann Lee.

In fact, though, the most significant distinction for mid-nineteenth-century Shakers was not between visible and invisible. Rather, these Shakers were essentially concerned with *different modes of visibility,* with what was naturally visible in relationship to what was spiritually visible, with things that could be seen by the natural eye in comparison with things that could be seen only by the spiritual eye. The differentiating factor was *how* the object of the beholder's vision was seen.[20] Gift images carried this interest in spiritual vision to its logical material limit. In some important ways these drawings and paintings minimized the distance between visionary (Shakers would say "visionist") and other Believers.[21] In the pictorial products of the instruments, the things of the spirit could be seen by the natural eye. For Shakers at New Lebanon and at Hancock, then, gift images made ecstatic vision concrete and tangible. Vision was both the source and the goal of image-making among Believers. For the twentieth-century beholder, gift drawings and paintings illuminate and give form to Shaker visionary experience. These images provide points of access to an otherwise relatively inaccessible aspect of the Shaker community's religious life. There was a distinct and essential continuity between visionary experience and gift images.[22]

The ministry and instruments of Mother's Work claimed that God's gift of spiritual sight to communal members passed on to them something of God's own perceptual powers. Over and over again, instruments described and depicted the deity as an all-seeing eye (e.g., figs. 4 and 28).[23] Omnivoyance characterized and identified the godhead. Believers made much of God's ability to look into the hearts of individuals, and thus to judge their moral disposition. The heart cutouts of 1844 graphically illustrate this point. The outstanding visual characteristics of these gifts were their conventional heart shape and heart size (approximating the size of a human heart) and the fact that they were inscribed on both sides with words and images. If interpreted in the context of earlier celestial gifts with similar "visual" features, it becomes clear that the 1844 hearts allowed Shakers in New Lebanon's First Order to see themselves through God's eyes. More specifically, what they saw was the pictorial visualization of their own hearts.

According to the testimony of New Lebanon Shakers some three years before the reception of the heart cutouts, in April and again in December of 1841, Holy Mother Wisdom (the personified feminine aspect of their dual godhead) came to visit them. Prior to each visit, instruments of Mother's Work repeatedly exhorted the followers of Ann Lee to prepare their hearts by examining their lives and confessing their sins.[24] Then, when Wisdom arrived, she "went round to view us, and *to read our hearts* [italics added]."[25] Also in 1841, individuals at New Lebanon began receiving celestial "presents" of hearts understood to be visible *only* to those also gifted with spiritual eyesight. Both implicitly and explicitly the instruments identified these hearts as the hearts of the recipients themselves.[26] What is noteworthy here in relationship to the formal and material characteristics of the later heart cutouts is that the instruments described the invisible heart presents of 1841 as having writing on them. In the instrument's account, Almighty Power and Holy Wisdom had written the destinies of individuals on their hearts, according to the faithfulness of their lives. The hearts of the people were visible to the Divine Pair and, through the gift of the heart presents, also to those of their followers favored with spiritual sight.

Then, on 20 March 1842, an instrument actually produced for Elder Rufus Bishop of the parent ministry a booklet titled "A Heart of Purity." This beautifully written five-page gift text celebrated Bishop's steadfast adherence to Mother Ann's gospel and promised him rich heavenly rewards. While the "Heart of Purity" described its subject in words rather than pictures, the instrument of the booklet explicitly imagined the gift heart as a two-sided object. Indeed the text encouraged the recipient to visualize the heart and specified that a certain portion of its message was written on one side of the heart, while the rest of the message apppeared on the other side. Thus, like the heart cutouts of 1844, the "Heart of Purity" was inscribed on both front and back. And, most importantly, this heart was a "true Emblem" of Rufus Bishop's own heart.

> So now receive from me, this *Heart,*
> This precious heart of *Love,*
> For with this Heart, thou shalt appear
> With me, in Heaven above.
> This precious *Heart of Purity,*
> Is but a true Emblem
> Of thy own heart,—Yet unto me
> It is a precious Gem.[27]

In this case, though Bishop could read what was written on his heart, he could only visualize the heart's shape and ornamentation in his mind's eye. In contrast, on 2 June 1844 when First Order Shakers at New Lebanon received the heart cutouts, they actually beheld, as never before, the emblems of virtue which decorated their hearts. On this day each person present saw a sight not ordinarily visible to the human eye and, in seeing, received heavenly reassurance about the ultimate truth of their Shaker way of life. Because First Order Believers could see what God had inscribed on their hearts, they could be confident of their happy reception in heaven. They knew that they were chosen of God because celestial valentines provided tangible evidence of their own designation as valued offspring of Almighty God the Father and Holy Mother Wisdom.[28]

Like most other gift paintings and drawings, the heart cutouts of 1844 addressed their recipients in pictures and in words. For New Era Shakers who generally believed pictorial and textual phenomena to be related, the central category of visionary experience grounded both gift image and gift text: "In pictures of silver and letters of gold; Rewards for the faithful, look and behold!"[29] When Shakers "saw" their founder and other Shaker spirits, the spirits often "spoke" to them. In some cases, inscriptions on visionary pictures recorded in detail the circumstances of the vision; in others, inscriptions addressed the gift's recipient directly, in the first person, requiring that they attend with their "ears" as well as their eyes to the divine presence associated with the gift. The category of vision subsumed, in such instances, both image and text: this was not a community of images or a community of texts but a community of visions.[30] The Shaker sense of the connection between visionary picture and visionary word has complicated twentieth-century attempts to define and classify gift images.

The first essential decision in a study of this nature is, of course, what to include in the category "gift images." Definitional boundaries can be fixed in a variety of ways. Most scholars have chosen to treat only those documents consisting in large part of pictures painted or drawn. This book, in contrast, will demonstrate the usefulness of expanding the definition of Shaker gift images to include a wider range of items. The most compelling reason for this broader approach is that it is consistent with the Shakers' own understanding of their religious paintings and drawings. Although adherents explicitly categorized other types of gifts, such as songs and dances, they designated no specific, generally recognizable classification for images, understanding their pictures as a visionary and visual mode of sacred communication which fell within "the line of writing."[31] For Shakers gift images were then part of the larger category of celestial communications, inspired messages, and sacred notices which flooded the communities during Mother's Work. Thus, while care must be taken to understand the images on their own terms (that is, not to conflate pictures and texts), in some important ways, pictures and texts were parallel manifestations.[32] Instead of attending to "art" per se—a category historically suspect among adherents to the gospel of Ann Lee—this study will explore the range of *visually organized* pictures and texts which Shakers believed originated with the inhabitants of the celestial sphere. A diligent effort will be made to distinguish between texts which record charismatic experiences one step removed and those which address their recipients directly, seeking to recapitulate the visionary's experience for a broader population.

"Visual organization" is the key principle of selection in determining the definitional limits subscribed to here. "Visually organized" gifts include any materially produced message or vision, with or without pictures, placed on the page so as to indicate concern for the way the beholder perceives its formal characteristics. Most ordinary Shaker correspondence and even many celestial communications followed regional and cultural conventions for the organization of text on the page (that is, date and place in the top right-hand corner, salutation below and to the left, just above the body of the letter, closing and signature at bottom right). Some gift messages, however, self- consciously heightened the visual aspects of their presentation. They were intended to be looked at, not just read. The lines of the text, the borders around the text, and even the edges of the paper were to be understood as parts of a larger visual composition. These message-images usually employed a finer, more exacting calligraphy than the average letter or communication. They were written on colored paper or in several colors of ink. They had precisely ruled and executed borders or embellishments. They were organized in two or three columns instead of one. They were often sketched in pencil before being carefully completed in ink (figs. 6, 8, 10, 23, 24, 25).

Further complicating the relationship between text and image described here, official Shaker manuscripts number drawings and paintings among those sacred gifts classified "in the line of writing." This "line" constitutes both a descriptive category including all of the pictorial and textual manifestations under consideration and a historical continuum, a chronological development, a "lineage," proceeding from text to image. For our purposes it makes sense to consider, first, the descriptive category and its ramifications for the interpretation of images in the Shaker community. Early in 1842 a scribe noted the reception of "many articles *in the line of writing* [italics added]." According to this scribe, the "articles" in question consisted of "likenesses, pictures and representations."[33] Remarking several years later on the 1844 heart cutouts, Isaac Newton Youngs recalled "a writing, in the form of a *heart*."[34] Although these heart-shaped cutouts (fig. 3) included multiple miniature images, Youngs referred to them, on yet another occasion, simply as "papers . . . beautifully written over."[35] The apparent scarcity of explicit manuscript references to images may be accounted for, in part, by a common terminology which allowed the same words to stand for both written and painted gifts.[36] As Daniel Patterson has pointed out, Shakers most frequently designated their images in terms of a particular function, format, or symbolic mode. Believers employed nouns like "reward," "notice," "message," "gift," "token," "card," "sheet," "emblem," "sign," "figure," and "type" with far greater regularity than the descriptives "drawn" or "painted."[37] Each of these nouns could be used to name a written document, a drawn or painted document, or a document containing both text and image. On many occasions, then, the languages of image and word were interchangeable. Shakers not only classified images "in the line of writing," they "drew," "sketched," and "pictured" events in words as well.[38]

Thus, in the language of Shakers, images sometimes sounded like texts. On the other hand, text itself could function as image. Inscriptions composed of native spirit characters or of sacred script appeared to most Believers as a mysterious series of intricate designs arranged in patterns on a page.[39] Only an inspired instrument could translate these elaborate visually organized messages (figs. 6 and 17). During Mother's Work, Shakers experimented with new and visible symbols for oral communication. One instrument drew a picture of the "Prophet Daniel's Prayer when in the Lion's Den" and "The Heavenly Father's Word" (fig. 7).

The classification of gift paintings and drawings with other phenomena "in the line of writing" was consistent with the fact that Shakers believed gift images to embody *correspondence* with the inhabitants of heaven. In many cases, those who composed the drawings and paintings chose a letter format, or referred in some fashion to the format of letter writing, in order to underscore this message status (figs. 6 and 8). Occasionally an instrument retained certain elements of contemporary correspondence while discarding others. For example, the instrument of one watercolor painting rendered images and words on the kind of paper typically used for letter writing. Like most Shaker correspondents, she chose for her composition a seventeen by ten inch sheet of stationery folded once in the center to form four surfaces (recto and verso) of about eight and one-half by ten inches.[40] Other instruments created envelopes for their drawings. In 1844, a matching blue envelope accompanied Elder Ebenezer Bishop's blue-on-white heart cutout.[41] Furthermore, and perhaps most significantly, instruments frequently inscribed gift drawings and paintings on both front and back, indicating that they conceived of these images as messages or correspondence rather than potential wall hangings.

The idea of image as *message* implied the import of process and product alike. Shakers explicitly conceived of gift images as a mode of visionary communication, even communion. At celestial initiative, individual Believers received messages which, according to the instruments, were also presents from heaven's inhabitants. Shaker image was *gift* as well as message. Although both message and gift share in common a giver and a recipient, it can be argued that gift entails a permanence and a concreteness frequently not implied by message. Gift also generally indicates a more intimate level of relationship, a greater degree of mutual responsibility. The transfer of (usually) material object, of property, from one party to another creates or maintains a bond.[42] The 1844 heart cutouts, like other gifts from the heavenly sphere, indicated the special position of Believers as chosen ones of God. Such gifts thus reaffirmed Shaker understandings of an ancient partnership and created a sense of obligation to be faithful to that covenant. In the case of the heart cutouts, the communal presentation of the gifts strengthened Believers' sense of relationship and responsibility to each other as well.

The conceptual framework which gift images shared with gift texts, songs, dances, bodily spirit possession, and spiritual pantomime, for example, pointed up very real similarities between these phenomena. Grounded in Shaker ideas about the nature of celestial communication and revelation, about the role and character of spiritual imagination, each initially charismatic form exhibited a significant visual component. What was different about gift images was not visionary status itself, but the specific material form the visionary message took, the ability of that form to communicate ideas in a particular fashion, and the content of the form itself, both within the Shaker community and the wider culture. While Shakers consciously referred to gift images in ways which blurred distinctions between image and text, in some crucial respects images differed from both gift texts and textual accounts of visions.

Not only do particular images convey particular meanings (related to what and how they picture) but visual images in general, simply by assuming this visual and material form, transmit a set of cultural understandings about the expressive properties of the form.[43] Images possess a special ability both to present "things-ordinarily-seen" in new and striking ways and to demonstrate the visual characteristics of "things-ordinarily-unseen." Images grant a sort of eyewitness status to beholders who view the depicted subject as though with their own eyes. The encounter carries with it the sense not only of clarity but of facticity, of verification, that accompanies seeing something for oneself.[44] By embodying values and ideas in visual and tangible form, images make these values and ideas seem more "real," more concrete, more inevitable, especially for those who otherwise might not "see" at all.[45] In the mid-nineteenth-century Shaker community, gift images both recorded evidence of divine manifestations and placed celestial visions and gifts themselves before the eyes and in the hands of the people. In gift images the things of heaven became tangible; they could be seen and touched.

The "line of writing" was, I have claimed, both a descriptive category and a historical "lineage." In the highly visionary Shaker context, where envisioning was so central to religious activity, where adherents understood images and texts principally within the larger classification of inspired gift or message, which classification fell, in turn, within the even larger category of religious vision, it makes historical and conceptual sense to demonstrate the construction of a continuum from visionary imagination to gift image. The emergence of such a continuum, such a "lineage," indeed characterized mid-nineteenth-century Shaker spirituality. During this period, the followers of Ann Lee moved from the use of a highly visual and sensory language about the things of the spirit, to the visual organization and composition of written sources, and finally to religious images themselves. The conviction that visionary experience was a principal mode of divine revelation grounded the ideational framework which generated this continuum. Again, Believers based their confidence in visionary experience on the ecstatic visions of their founder. From this foundation, and always in relationship to it, Shakers over the years elaborated a set of mental, verbal, and graphic images which reflected both their own sectarian history and the imagery of the

Jewish and Christian scriptures. In the years immediately prior to the advent of gift images, then, the experience of visions, the use of visual language, and the visual organization of textual material were all important aspects of Shaker religious life. Furthermore, none of these earlier forms vanished when the instruments began to draw and paint. The process was cumulative; all of these expressions continued throughout the period of Mother's Work—and all but the drawings and paintings continued beyond it.

Shaker "visual language," in both oral and written forms, helped to accomplish the transition from sanctified word to suspect image. At least from the time of their first written manuscripts, Shakers exhibited a highly pictorializing imagination in describing their religious experiences.[46] As Mother's Work began, however, Shaker "visual language" usage took an interesting turn. Not only did highly visual descriptions of visionary encounters increase in number and intensity, but Believers introduced an unusual form of visionary communication. According to the instruments, celestial beings now gave gifts of spiritual *pictures,* depicting heavenly people, places, and objects. The instruments' accounts of these spiritual pictures (which never assumed material pictorial form) provided a bridge between verbal and graphic images. It is a peculiarity of this period of Shakerism that Believers wrote so frequently and explicitly about spiritual pictures and so infrequently and abstractly about actual gift images. This peculiarity notwithstanding, the spiritual pictures were, in some important ways, the experimental forebears of gift paintings. If the Shaker ministry deemed textual references to spiritual pictures useful and appropriate, then picturing itself might be useful as well. As Shaker hymnody moved from wordless songs to worded ones, Shaker iconography moved from "pictureless" images (i.e., vivid but strictly verbal descriptions of spiritual pictures) to gift paintings and drawings.[47]

A record of January 1842 noted the reception of

> Numerous spiritual presents . . . Among these are fruits of many kinds, delicious eatable things, rich drinks, cordials, wines, etc. Garments, Ornaments, articles of delight to look upon; Utensils for labor in different branches. Books in abundance to write in—and to read, etc. *Many articles in the line of writing—Likeness[es], pictures, and representations of many things and scenes in the other world and ancient things in this world etc. etc.*—Such is the nature of those peculiar manifestations from the spirit world, very abundant of late among us [italics added].[48]

While this quotation might have referred to early, and subsequently destroyed, gift images, other manuscript evidence and the fact that no drawings or paintings fitting this description survive from 1841 or 1842 suggest that the writer described the reception of numerous "spiritual" paintings and portraits that could be seen only by those with spiritual eyesight.

The Shakers' own words indicate most strikingly the character of textual references to *spiritual* picturing and representation. On 28 December 1841, the scribe recorded, Lydia Mathewson received a large ivory bandbox full of presents from her eternal, heavenly, and spiritual parents. This box and its contents were visible only to the eye of the soul. "On the inside of the cover [was] drawn the likeness of Holy Mother and Christ the Savior, also the names and likeness[es] of all the twelve patriarchs."[49] On 21 July 1842, Believers received a gift communication in the form of a booklet containing detailed descriptions of spiritual clothing to be worn for Holy Wisdom's Passover.

> For both brethren and sisters, there is a fine linnen pocket handkerchief, white as the driven snow and in the middle of them is the picture of the Holy of Holies, the Eternal Throne, and the Eternal Two in One setting upon it. In one corner is the likeness of Holy and Eternal Wisdom even myself, when descending to earth, in my chariot of brightness and elegancy, with twenty thousand Angels each side of the same; and twenty span of white horses before, which drew the chariot of glittering brightness. In another corner is the likeness of the Holy One, the great *I Am,* holding his sword of wrath in his hand, and words of terror and judgment coming from his lips. Upon the other corners are printed the names of all your Heavenly Parents, with each one's seal of love and approbation in the form of a star at the end of their names; and the name of the one that shall receive it under theirs.[50]

"A Short Word of Notice" to Jane Blanchard recounted a gift from Father William:

> A glass band box, lined with pink parchment, on the cover Holy Mother has printed your name in letters of gold, and surrounded it with a circle of Jasper stone set in gold diamonds, on the side of the Box, is Her likeness sitting on her Eternal Throne, and 4 Thousand of the Holiest Angels in heaven, obtaining Wisdom from her gracious hand. . . . Mother Ann has put in [the box] a white satin dress embroidered with pink silk, in the figure of roses, on it is a flounce of blue silk, . . . and a silver buckel; whereon is engraven the picture of the children of Isreal, . . . Father James sends a complete moddle of King Solomon's Ivory Throne. . . . He also sends a gold card, with the writing seen by Belshazzar, Mene Tekel Upharsin etc., on one side, and the picture of this memorable event on the other side. This was drawn by obadiah of old and by him presented to Sennacherib and John the Revelator received it of him and took it to the Isle of Patmos, there he pictured it again on the leaf of Alanug [?] tree . . . this was set in a gold frame by Tubil Cane, and by him presented to Father James. Father Joseph sends . . . 4 gold table spoons bearing the likeness[es] of Christ, The Ancient Kings of Judah, and Prophet Amos. Mother Lucy sends a lace cap trimed with gold and pink riben, and on one large star is the likeness of all your Heavenly Parents.[51]

Although similar references to spiritually visible pictures can be found prior to 1841 and after 1843, these descriptions multiplied rapidly beginning in 1841, peaking between 1841 and 1843. This is significant in light of the fact that very few, usually predominantly textual or calligraphic, gift images predate 1843. And, 1843 is the first year for which numerous more complex images survive. During this year also the variety among surviving drawings increases markedly. Very likely a relationship existed between increasing numbers and variety in Shaker religious images and the authority provided by the increase of heavenly prototypes mentioned in gift texts. It may even have been the case that Shakers initially classified images "in the line of writing" because the images grew out of these other "pictorial" phenomena "in the line of writing."

Further, by 1841 written records of spiritual presents assumed transitional material forms which provided a context for the later reception of gift images and contributed to their meaningful interpretation. In 1838 large numbers of adherents at New Lebanon and Hancock had first received spiritual "presents" from the celestial sphere. Instruments had described these gifts to recipients in concrete and vivid terms, but the presents themselves remained visible only to the spiritual eye. Over the months and years the spiritual presents increased in quantity and complexity. By 1840 nearly every person in the New Lebanon community had received a gift of some sort from the spirit world.[52] Individuals compiled long and detailed lists, usually in a bound format, of the presents they received. An excerpt from one such list of gifts for the First Order at New Lebanon reads:

> A cup of pure waters and a bowl of balsam for the singers from Father William and Mother Lucy.
> Two hundred Holy Angels to replace those sent to Harvard.
> A little lamb from Mother Ann.
> Help of the Lord against the mighty by Governor Clinton.[53]
> Drums given to the brethren by Father William.
> A jewel of simplicity to hang about our necks from Elder Brother John [Warner?].
> A fan of faith from Mother Ann.[54]

Significantly, in terms of this discussion, by 1841 records of spiritual presents no longer appeared only in such lengthy, generally bound, lists. Instead, individual snippets of paper communicated a single gift to an individual or group. At first these scraps appeared to have been cut with scissors by community members from the longer lists (e.g., fig. 9). By the end of 1841, however, notations of individual spiritual gifts began to appear as neatly bordered cards and notes (e.g., fig. 10). From this time on, in addition to being reminded by lists of a succession of gifts received over several years, an individual could retain and view again and again a single-sheet rectangle or square of paper representing the reception of a particular gift from the heavens. Thus, on an individual level, spiritual presents assumed a more visual, material, and portable devotional form. From visionary experience, to "visual language," thence to visually organized textual gifts: in the years that followed, cards and notices and heart and leaf cutouts represented similar, but more visually sophisticated, reproductions of spiritual presents given to individuals in the Shaker community.

Mary Hazard's book of gift songs, dated 15 June through 10 December 1839, represented a variation on this sort of transitional form. The book included highly decorative clef and repeat signs, the design for each sign different from the others. True, the primary purpose of this document was to retain the words and music of gift songs received by individuals in her community. But Mary Hazard chose to enhance the visual presentation of these songs. In her textual descriptions, Hazard reminded her readers that occasionally a song would be given in the (spiritually visible) shape of a heart, diamond, or leaf. In one instance she actually drew the exquisite leaf shape of a song received, specifying that the spirit who gave the "leaf" wanted the recipient to "see its form" (fig. 1).[55]

One additional and distinctly visionary transitional form in the movement between Shaker vision and Shaker image is more difficult to locate on the continuum outlined here. Nonetheless, the understanding and ritual enactment of prophetic signs informed the creation of gift images and enriched the interpretive context. The instruments of Mother's Work were intensely concerned with signs. For Shakers, signs were natural and spiritual phenomena, actions, or objects which pointed to divine activity in the earthly sphere.[56] According to Shakers, Almighty God the Father and Holy Mother Wisdom, Jesus Christ and Mother Ann often communicated in signs and symbols.[57] Signs had meanings. Sometimes deity told an instrument how to interpret a sign, sometimes significance was implied, sometimes an instrument plainly admitted that the meaning of a sign was unknown or had yet to be revealed. Whether the precise meaning of an individual sign was openly interpreted, implied, or left unknown, the principal import of signs was that they preceded and pointed to the end of time and the final celestial triumph. Many Shaker signs enacted in liturgical settings closely resembled Shaker images in the sense that both signs and images made use of visually striking and carefully arranged configurations of shapes and colors. The instruments of many signs wrote, drew, or placed figures on sheets of paper or cloth. Usually the instruments laid out these configurations of shapes and colors on the floor, in the clear view of worshippers. Sometimes they hung them from the four walls of the meeting room. Sometimes instruments inscribed strange characters on the sheets of paper or cloth; sometimes instruments intended the arrangement of paper and cloth shapes itself to communicate prophetic messages. Often the instruments folded the sheets of paper or cloth into significant patterns and/or sealed them with colored sealing wax.

The similarity between enacted signs and gift images indicates that the *act* of drawing or painting as well as the product of this activity could function symbolically. On certain occasions instruments made prophetic "pictures" during the course of a service of worship. For example, an astonishing display of mysterious signs marked Shaker worship and Shaker life during the early months of 1843. At this time, one Shaker scribe documented the liturgical creation of a visual equivalent for speaking in tongues.[58] Both the description and the 29 January 1843 date of the scribe's record suggest that, quite probably, these drawings had some connection with the gift images called Sacred Sheets (see fig. 17 and discussion in chapter 5).

> The female Angel, accompanying Holy Wisdom's Angel [both represented by instruments], requested 5 sheets of paper, two of white, one of dark blue, one of light

blue, and one of red—and also a box of seals, pen and ink—these were all brot into meeting.

The first signs, after we assembled, and while we were singing a song of blessing, were waving the white sheets of paper, and white cloths, around among the brethren and Sisters. After this exercise, the accompanying Angels to Holy Wisdom's [Angel] came forward into the centre of the room, with all the writing apparatus. . . .

The Instrument for the Angel, now took one of the sheets of white paper, and seemed to try very hard to tear it, by jerking it etc.—it did not tear. She then carefully folded it, and wrote upon it four lines partly in English, and partly in unknown words,—the purport of which was not to be clearly understood from the writing, but it seemed to be a word to the nations of the Earth. This was sealed up [with sealing wax]—and the red sheet taken and wrapped around the white one thus written upon—and sealed. The[n] the Angel said, Where is he who is chosen scribe in Israel? Joseph (Babe,) now came forward and seated himself at the stand, and the Angel bade him write the following word upon the red wrapper.

Hear the word of the Lord, O ye nations, and declare it in the Isles afar off. . . and say ye, he that scattereth Israel, shall gather him and keep him, as a shepherd does his flock. . . . [59] The instrument for the holy Angel, now took the dark blue paper and tried to tear it, in the same manner as the white, and behold, it was easily done and torn in many pieces; these were subsequently strewed around all over the floor and the brethren and Sisters requested to pick them up and tear them untill each one had a piece.

At this time 4 lamps were in square form placed in the center of the floor the 2 white sheets crossing each other in the center and the folded red one placed on them. . . . [While Believers sang a song given by the Holy Angel] the 4 brethren chosen as Instruments encircled the lamps holding each other by the hands and standing in a square. Two of the sister Inst were marching east and west waving their white handkerchiefs, while the other two inst stand looking verry steadily and aparently with intense interest at the lamps, papers and seals. When finished, H.A. [Hannah Agnew?] picks up the white sheet and examins the writing on the red. Various figures were now made on the sheets and the instruments all unite in the dance, carrying the white sheet and waving white handkerchiefs.[60]

The "various figures" of the last sentence might have been *drawn* figures made on the sheets of paper or they might have been *danced* figures performed on the sheets of cloth. Shakers used the word "figure" in both senses and the context here leaves the specific intent unclear. Both types of "figures" were taken as signs of God's activity, present and future, within the community and beyond. The use of the same word in reference to two different media again demonstrates the blurring of distinction between different forms of gifts and signs, the lack of sharp differentiation between word, image, and (here) symbolic body movement. As two expressive forms of spirit possession, Shaker image and Shaker dance were not unrelated. The ritual enactment of charismatic experience involved both the representation of images and the movement of bodies. The human body, like a sheet of paper, could be the medium of a spirit message; each intended to communicate a celestial content.[61] In the quote above and in other entries, many also dated January and February 1843, this scribe recorded, sometimes diagrammed, the visual and corporeal presentation of colored sheets of paper, sheets of cloth, and handkerchiefs.[62]

In relationship to prophetic signs, in particular, the language of color assumed an important role in understanding and interpreting divine messages. "Every color has its peculiar meaning, and to such as understand, all such appearances are instructive."[63] The preceding statement notwithstanding, Shaker understandings of color reveal a language of symbols with multiple recognized meanings instead of one to one correspondences. Colors, like other signs, could have shifting meanings depending on the interpreter and the nature of a specific revelation. But all Shakers believed that colors signified something beyond themselves. Among Believers, black, red, and white, especially, demonstrated symbolic possibilities. Black usually implied judgment, solemn warnings, and darkness, red the sufferings, persecution, and tribulation preparatory to salvation, and white purity, peace, hope, and blessing.[64] Gift images both *recorded* the colors and shapes of particular spiritual signs and *were,* in fact, spiritual signs made visible to the natural eyes of community members.

Even when Shakers defined images "in the line of writing," this inspired "writing" itself was already circumscribed by visionary experience. Each step in the continuum from vision to image (pictorial imagination, spiritual picturing, increasingly sophisticated visually organized textual presents) maintained, for Shakers, a conscious and deliberate connection with contemporary visionary experience and with the visionary example of Ann Lee and her early followers. Without exception, mid- nineteenth-century Shakers conceived of their religious images, too, in relationship to inspired vision. In these drawings and paintings the instruments intended either to reiterate a particular visionary experience (see Pl. IV), or to depict the visual appearance of a celestial communication (see figs. 8 and 23); both involved the ability to see spiritual objects and persons. In these drawings and paintings, the particular and concrete expressions of Shaker visual imagination, the instruments of Mother's Work represented ecstatic visions and celestial presents in a tangible and generally accessible public form.

Two

✖ *Image and Iconoclasm*

DISCONTINUITY IN SHAKER EXPERIENCE

Gift images took visionary experience as their point of departure. In this appeal to vision, the images promoted continuity with the Shaker past. But these paintings and drawings, once embodied in material form and color, also represented discontinuity in the Society's history. In fact gift images seemed to express a contradiction in New Era Shakerism. Here was a historically iconoclastic community whose religious beliefs nonetheless rested on vision and whose elaborate paintings grew out of and in relationship to visionary experience.[1] The fact that the central category of religious vision existed side by side with the prohibition of images created a persistent tension in Shaker experience. Visionaries throughout Shaker history saw spiritual things all around them, but members of the earlier Shaker community rendered in concrete form only mundane, practical images like maps and architectural diagrams. For many years Shakers believed that divinely ordained precept forbade the production and use of religious images. Accordingly, a sect which understood its history and identity in terms of visionary imagination did not picture its visions. When New Era instruments finally made a place for images in the service of charismatic restoration, the longstanding and usually unspoken tension between visionary image and religious prohibition provided a powerful interpretive framework for the instruments' pictures.

Breakers of images, after all, are not so different from lovers of images in one crucial sense. Both acknowledge art's potential to influence belief and to elicit response. Both acknowledge the efficacy of images.[2] For two decades, Shaker instruments and ministry employed a previously censored graphic mode to accomplish the goals of Mother's Work. While continuing to reject "art," mid-nineteenth-century Believers created a new category of images and tested new roles for religious drawings and paintings in their community.

Mid-century Shakers were correct in assuming at least ambivalence and often hostility toward "luxuries" like pictures, and even illustrated books, in the early years of the Society. The scarcity of material resources and "leisure" time lent credence to the argument for the absence of worldly treasures. But early Shakers opposed "finery" on ideological grounds as well, and participated in the ritual destruction of jewelry, furniture, and ornamented apparel.[3] According to New Era perceptions of the Shaker past, the founders and their immediate followers knew that true Believers should neither own nor display objects whose principal function was adornment. Instead, Shakers ought to possess only what the ministry judged spiritually useful or physically necessary. As time passed and the economic status of the Society improved, however, material goods increasingly attracted its members. By the late 1830s, although the Shaker environment was still severe by comparison to the surrounding non-Shaker culture, many feared that the United Society had become too much like the world. "An urgent call from the heavens" required the followers of Ann Lee to "retrace our steps—to come more into order and under more restraint. To sacrifice and give up many superfluous things. . . . to purge out and give up many articles, not considered as exemplary and according to good order."[4]

> Often, yea, very often of late, they [the children of the world] have been heard to say, that the time had been when the Shakers were what they professed to be; but now they are not: they have got to be about as fashionable as other people, and some of them *more* so. They are getting more and more into our manners and customs, and soon they will be no better than we are.[5]

The profusion of regulations and prohibitions generated during the mid-century years of renewal and restoration received their initial impetus from perceived transgression of the spirit of primitive Shakerism. From the beginning, Shaker converts brought with them into the Society material goods which reflected broader American cultural values and configurations. Standards for appropriate design in dress, furniture, and communal architecture had been established in relationship to the material culture of the Revolutionary and early national periods. In other words, early Shakers distinguished themselves from the world by adopting the simplest and most unadorned versions of the personal and familial furnishings with which they had entered the Society. By mid-century these "original" models would have appeared not only simple and unadorned but also antiquated in relationship to the larger culture. New converts continued to bring household furnishings with them as they entered the United Society. These newer furnishings reflected changes in taste that had occurred over several decades and, by contrast with earlier models, appeared more "worldly."[6] Of course, with aesthetic standards established in relationship to models from the material culture of the 1780s, it is not surprising that it became increasingly easy to violate these standards by 1840. It was by comparison to the early Shakers rather than to mid-century America that Believers on the eve of the New Era seemed worldly.[7] Not only had the Shakers' own economic situation improved over time, but, because of trade and changing membership patterns, contact with the world was more frequent and, often, more amicable. Shakers were aware of and interested in (though certainly somewhat ambivalent about) the rapid changes that were taking place in technology and social organization in the nation.

Legal codes issued during Mother's Work restricted images at least in part because members of the United Society owned too many images of suspect varieties.[8] Prohibition was deemed necessary because appeal was strong.

> The Deacons who have the charge of purchasing whatever supplies are needed in the Church of Christ, should be very careful indeed, says Father, and purchase that which is plain and examplary [*sic*], so far as is in their power.
>
> They should, at all times, avoid procuring that which has foolish writing or printing upon it, if it be possible; for it has not a good effect. You had better purchase that which is plain, as far as you can, even if the meterial [*sic*] is not quite so good, rather than to get that which is covered with superfluous flowers and pictures. You must remember, beloved Deacons, that a heavy responsibility rests upon you, as stewards in the house of God, and that your example will go a great way.[9]

The Holy Laws of Zion (1840), the Holy Orders of God (1840), the Holy Orders of the Church (1841), the revised Millennial Laws (1845), and other codes redefined the appropriate relationship of Believers and images by citing tradition and the authority of early Shakers.

In 1821, the first written version of the Millennial Laws had contained no explicit prohibition of images. Rather this code stated very generally that members of the United Society were "forbid making anything for believers that will have a tendency to feed the pride and vanity of a fallen nature, or making anything for the world that cannot be justified among ourselves."[10] For the most part, the writers of these "gospel statutes" could assume the absence of decoration among Believers. Behavior in 1845, on the other hand, necessitated much more specific regulation.

> No maps, Charts, and no pictures or paintings, shall ever be hung up in your dwelling-rooms, shops, or Office. And no pictures or paintings set in frames, with glass before them shall ever be among you. But modest advertisements may be put up in the Trustees Office when necessary.[11]

As these two passages begin to suggest, Shaker reservations about drawings and paintings did not rest on rejection of images per se. Rather, the historical basis for Shaker iconoclasm was the notion of "superfluity," adapted from American culture at large to fit a specifically Shaker set of circumstances. Images, Shakers generally agreed, were superfluous. Thus the charge leveled against those who coveted pictures or decorations for their walls or rooms was not that they were guilty of *worshipping* images, of confusing image with prototype. The principal argument in Shaker iconoclasm differed in this respect from the principal arguments in Byzantine and Reformation controversies about images. For Shakers, images, like other superfluities, might turn Believers' thoughts and attachments away from God. Superfluities were "stumbling blocks" that could get between the soul and the deity (were, in this respect only, other "gods"). The subject of idolatry entered this theological conversation because Shakers reconstructed idolatry as attraction to superfluities.[12]

The followers of Ann Lee defined superfluity as anything unnecessary to the lives and salvation of the faithful, anything that might distract individuals or communities from appropriate spiritual goals.

> The present testimony of our Parents strikes powerfully against all superfluities and ornamental and unnecessary articles of every description, name or nature. Against all extravagance in quality or quantity of food and raiment, utensils and conveniences.[13]

The superfluous "add[ed] nothing to . . . goodness or duribility"; it was the "merely ornamental."[14] Divine regulations required that adherents to the sect practice instead an ethic and an aesthetic of simplicity. Simplicity was the opposite of superfluity. Simplicity was "plain," "graceful," "ordered," and "uniform"; superfluity was "fancy," extravagant, potentially deceptive.[15]

A regulatory description denoting the sorts of problematic articles present among Shakers indicates the level of detail attended to by New Era rules. Part III, Section IV of the 1845 Millennial Laws lectured Believers "Concerning Superfluities not Owned":

> Fancy articles of any kind, or articles which are superfluously finished, trimmed or ornamented, are not suitable for Believers, and may not be used or purchased; among which are the following; also some other articles which are deemed improper, to be in the church, and may not be brought in, except by special liberty of the Ministry.
>
> 2. Silver pencils, silver tooth picks, gold pencils, or pens, silver spoons, silver thimbles, (but thimbles may be lined with silver,) gold or silver watches, brass knobs or handles of any size or kind, three bladed knives, knife handles with writing or picturing on them, bone or horn handled knives, except for pocket knives, bone or horn spools, superfluous whips, marbled tin ware, superfluous paper boxes of any kind, gay silk handkerchiefs, green veils, bought dark colored cotton handkerchiefs for sisters use; checked handkerchiefs made by the world, may not be bought for sisters use, except head handkerchiefs; lace for cap borders, superfluous suspenders of any kind; writing desks may not be used by common members, unless they have much public writing to do. But writing desks may be used, as far as it is thought proper by the Lead.
>
> 3. The following articles are also deemed improper: viz. Superfluously finished or flowery painted clocks, Bureaus, and Looking glasses, also superfluously painted or fancy shaped sleighs or carriages, superfluously trimmed harness, and many other articles, too numerous to mention.

4. The forementioned things are at present, utterly forbidden: but if the Ministry see fit to bring in any among the forementioned articles, which are not superfluously wrought, the order prohibiting the use of such article or articles is thereby repealed.
5. Believers may not, in any case or circumstance, manufacture for sale, any article or articles which are superfluously wrought, and which would have a tendency to feed the pride and vanity of man, or such as would not be admissible to use among themselves, on account of their superfluity.[16]

Purging out what was unnecessary was no inconsequential matter. Superfluity disrupted the universe, causing spiritual and physical disorder.[17] A scribe quoted the instrument of the first official message of Mother's Work:

> "Mother desires we would search and see if we have not gathered that which is superfluous, more than is of any kind of use to us in carrying on our respective branches in our shops; for if we gather that which is needless, it will be a clog to our souls, and engage our minds to no profit."[18]

Elsewhere spirits cautioned,

> everything wherein *fancy* is inclined to bear rule, instead of that modest, decent plainness which becomes the people of God, let it be put away. And if you are blessed with more than you need for your own comfort and support, in this order of plainness which we have mentioned, says Mother, remember the example of Christ and of us; don't spend it for that which will create little idols in the mind. Little idols, Mother says, will become great ones, if they are not purged out. But bestow upon those who are needy and destitute, and in this way you will fulfill the order of your calling.[19]

The legal codes of the New Era explicitly prohibited many kinds of images among common members and among Shaker leaders.[20]

> Almanacks shall be inspected by the Elders before being brot into the Church; and if they contain any thing of any kind, unsuitable to be in the house, it shall be cut out, before they are placed around in the rooms, and before any one has seen them; and what ye cut out of them, ye shall burn up.[21]

Believers apparently took these prohibitions seriously. A letter of 1840 recalled as a model another time "when the banisters and mouldings were torn from our dwellings, and pictures scraped from snuff boxes, tobacco boxes, etc. etc."[22] A map of New Lebanon, produced in the 1840s and attributed to Henry Blinn of the Society at Canterbury, New Hampshire, bears visible marks of this sort of censorship. Floral decorations have been scratched off of the map's handsome lettering.[23] Hervey Elkins, a sympathetic New Era apostate from the Enfield, New Hampshire community, reported:

> No image or portrait of anything upon the earth, or under the earth, is suffered in

> this holy place. Consequently clocks and such articles, purchased of the world, go through the process of having all their superficial decorations erased from their surfaces.[24]

Rules about images in the holiest places were particularly severe. Such regulations strictly proscribed certain kinds of pictures and "engraven" material objects in both the worship area or "holy sanctuary" and in the dwelling rooms of the ministry on the upper floors of the meeting house.[25] In the Holy Laws of Zion, God specified that

> my holy law does . . . strictly forbid that there should be any engravings, sculpture, pictures or images, or likenesses, either of man, beasts, birds, or any living thing, or the likeness of flowers or inanimate things either upon iron, brass, wood or stone, or any other kind of metal, be brought into my holy sanctuary, where ye assemble to offer up praises unto me, in sacred devotion.
>
> But I require everything that is attached either to the inside or the outside of such buildings, and places, should be perfect and plain, free from all unnecessary embellishments.[26]

With regard to the habitations of the ministry,

> My Holy Law does forbid, saith God, that in the dwellings of my Holy Chosen, there be any high or superfluous paintings or colors of this kind, even in their possessions, either on the ceiling, the floor or on articles of any kind whatever.[27]

In July 1840, members of the Church Family at New Lebanon removed four stoves from their meeting house because engravings on the stoves violated the Holy Laws.[28] Earlier in that year, Isaac Youngs remarked that Shakers generally "had gained a great deal by parting with . . . idols and superfluous things."[29]

As luxuries, superfluities constituted a morally dangerous category. Luxury led to corruption. In this assessment Shakers agreed with other Americans of the Revolutionary and early national periods. In the years prior to 1830 especially, Shaker anxiety about the contaminating influence of luxury reflected not a set of values distinct from the broader culture but a particularization and intensification of a widely shared American attitude.[30] For Americans at large, a republican form of government depended upon the sort of virtue fostered by simplicity and personal restraint.[31] For Shakers too, spiritual as well as political freedom could flourish only in individuals and communities liberated from material extravagance. And, because of art's association with wealth (especially foreign wealth) and aristocracy, both citizen and sectarian ranked fine art within "the dreaded category of luxury."[32]

Further, in a celibate community, especially one constituted by a relatively large number of adolescents and young adults, the relationship of material luxuries with sensual gratification was cause for alarm.[33] Luxury led to corruption and corruption to sensuality. Superfluities, in their appeal to the embodied self, might arouse the passions and jeopardize successful repression of sexual impulses upon which community spiritual life depended.[34] Among superfluities, art, in particular, made strenuous claims for physical existence, and sometimes even for physical verisimilitude. Art *was* material object and art *represented* material objects and physical beings. In the process, art placed material objects into a "permanent" and tangible idealized realm. Art was therefore doubly suspect in relationship to physical and sensual appeal.[35] Among Shakers, especially, the question of how to elicit awareness of material and visible presence without eliciting sexual awareness of the body had to be carefully navigated.

Finally, Shaker reservations about private property influenced their attitudes toward superfluities. Believers looked to the biblical account of the early church in Acts for evidence that true Christians ought to hold all things in common. On at least one occasion, a spirit communication defined idols as "things more than . . . all can enjoy."[36] So, in addition to compromising the simple life upon which spiritual and political freedom depended, in addition to stimulating concern about sensuality, superfluity threatened the aesthetic and ethical goals of uniformity and nonpartiality by promoting differentiation and self-aggrandizement based on personal property.[37]

Gift drawings and paintings could easily have been rejected as superfluities. Although gift images obeyed some Shaker proscriptions, they violated others. Instruments freely used red pigment as well as other generally prohibited "fine" colors.[38] Calligraphic intricacies, resembling lace fancywork, occupied the pens of Shaker religious artists. Symbols of heavenly mansions, golden chariots, fanciful garments, sparkling jewels, treasure chests, and ornamental fruits and flowers were wildly extravagant by Shaker standards (figs. 7, 13, 26, 28, 30). If not prohibited as images pure and simple, gift drawings might have been expelled as ornaments. Certainly the instruments' pictures resembled very closely the forbidden decorations of the world's people. Believers had to resolve this dangerous proximity in order to find a place for gift images. Throughout their history Shakers opposed images because they generally included images in the category of superfluities. If some images could be construed to be *other than* superfluities, they might find a meaningful role in Shaker life. Long before the New Era this was already true for certain mundane images like maps, architectural plans, and clothing patterns whose everyday usefulness required no further legitimation.[39] How was it that gift images, which raised a different set of issues entirely, avoided categorization as superfluities?

Gift paintings and drawings met Shaker concerns about superfluity by forcing the creation of a new category, separate from but in some obvious ways parallel to the forbidden category. In the case of these visionary images, Shakers recognized the extraordinary spiritual value of something they ordinarily would have censored. Members of the United Society had previously prohibited almost all images as a dangerous distraction and stumbling block on the narrow path to salvation. They now accepted, even encouraged, a carefully circumscribed set of visionary images as a potential means of revitalizing and thus preserving a traditional sense of community identity. Constructed in a gradual and measured fashion, the understanding of gift images that emerged in the Society during the early years of Mother's Work helped to dissipate some of the tension created by the proximity of gift images to superfluous images. Most importantly, as demonstrated in the previous chapter, Shakers identified visionary images with visionary experience. Consequently, they regarded the instruments' pictures as treasures of heaven. They thus sharply differentiated gift images from the superfluous treasures of earth which caused so much dissension and concern.[40] In numerous inspired messages of the New Era, Mother Ann admonished Believers that her gifts were "not to be treated as natural things."[41]

The spiritual hierarchy countered concerns about worldly attractions by flooding the Society with an abundance of celestial commodities. As treasures of heaven, as spiritual rather than material luxuries, gift images actually helped to compensate for tighter New Era restrictions on both behavior and worldly goods. Those in authority in heaven and on earth took objects of desire out of their material environment and placed them in a spiritual context.[42] And, through imagination and representation, instruments depicted spiritual union and spiritual treasures for all to see.

> All the presents I have sent, or caused to be sent forth unto you, must be used in the proper line of sensation, for they are all spiritual . . . They have been sent forth in this degree of nearness and semblance of material things that do exist on earth, that you may be better able to appreciate in lively colors, and thrilling sensations, the real adornings and beauties of the spiritual world.[43]

Ministry and instruments recognized and responded to the appeal of sensation by spiritualizing sensory experience.[44] The image-makers' mode of representation, in its construction of the illusion of weightlessness, underscored the conceptual distance between gift images and the forbidden treasures of earth. Even when the images suggested a sense of depth, they denied the qualities of volume and mass associated with earthly things (see, for example, fig. 22 and Pl. IV). Generally, rather than suggesting depth at all, the images instead depicted floating collections of heavenly objects (see, for example, figs. 7, 13, 26, 28, 30 and Pl. V). The celestial source changed the way Shakers experienced the otherwise superfluous form of these images. Because gift drawings came from and represented heaven and heavenly beings, Believers incorporated the drawings into their spiritual lives. As spiritual gifts, these pictures assumed a useful role in the salvation of the faithful. An amendment to one copy of the Holy Orders of 1841 demonstrates that the explicitly sacred nature of certain items exempted them from usual proscriptions. "No maps, charts, printings, writings (*sacred writs excepted*) and no paintings, shall ever be hung up in your dwelling rooms, shops nor Office [italics added]."[45]

Significantly, the visionary treasures showered upon earthly Shakers had exact spiritual counterparts.[46] Shaker instruments claimed divine prototypes for their creations; their works, graphic and literary, were "copied from the original." In the rather exceptional case of one instrument, Hannah Cohoon carefully specified in texts accompanying her images that she drew representations of representations (fig. 2 and Pl. IV). In her visions, the spirits showed her painted spiritual images which she diligently copied. Like other instruments, Cohoon believed it important for the beholder to understand that the spirits themselves established the parameters of her art. Explicit authority to paint, then, came from the spiritual world.[47] In fact, divine artists who drew and painted pictures in heaven provided role models for Shaker image-makers who drew and painted heavenly pictures on earth. New Era instruments identified the prophets Isaiah and Obadiah as well as "John the Revelator" as heavenly artists.[48] The legitimating example of celestial painters created a conceptual framework for the visionary images produced by Shaker instruments. Treasures of earth could be superfluous. Treasures of heaven could not.

Shaker founders and early leaders had often preached about heavenly treasures greatly to be desired. Never before, however, had Shakers dared to picture these heavenly treasures. Never before had Believers seen with their eyes the close formal resemblance between the things of eternity and the things of time. The subject matter and form of the instruments' images had been prohibited for many years as a threat to the purity of the sect. But a celestial content tempered and made useful this potentially radical art.[49]

In order to further insulate the new "non-superfluous" images from suspicion, instruments and record-keepers consistently collapsed gift drawings and messages into one larger category of spirit writings. The fact that gift images recapitulated visionary experiences identified these pictures as celestial (rather than earthly) treasures. The fact that Believers also understood the images "in the line of writing" further minimized correspondence with the forbidden category of superfluities and maximized their conceptual relationship with a category of objects already recognized as useful, even necessary. For those involved in the production and promotion of these most graphic manifestations of Mother's Work, perhaps the greatest value of classifying images as part of the larger phenomenon of inspired messages and writings was precisely that this method of classification allowed them to side-step the issue of whether these drawings and paintings might belong to the category "art." If the drawings were not "art," neither were the producers of the drawings "artists." The only instance in which Shakers who drew or painted called themselves "artists" involved images that were not specifically religious—like maps.[50]

For those who might have considered all images superfluous, this sort of understanding maintained that image was not really image but a subset of gift message or text. Even the media of the instruments' images supported this argument. Early drawings, especially, were executed in ink on paper. The most frequently used colors (black, blue, brown) were also those most commonly used in correspondence and record-keeping. Gradually the images began to incorporate other colors of ink (red, for example) and watercolor. By exploiting a series of associations between image and text, the instruments thus bypassed another possible set of objections to their pictures. In fact, some instruments' "drawings" were, literally, "writings." These instruments created designs of figures and signs reproducing or resembling written communication (figs. 4, 6, 7,

17, 19, 25 [border]). In a painting received by Hester Ann Adams (fig. 11) and in one produced by Joseph Wicker, for example, words formed shapes; words made pictures.[51]

In response to the conceptual challenges presented by gift drawings and paintings, then, the followers of Ann Lee reworked traditional categories of spiritual usefulness. Those in authority, both ministry and instruments, did not just decide that they would suddenly allow images. Rather, they accepted into their midst very specific kinds of images for very specific purposes. They admitted a new classification for religious images, a heavenly classification associated with textual gifts and unregulated by the category of superfluity which forbade most other kinds of images. But, as long as the ministry did not completely overturn prohibition of images, the visionary pictures permitted among Believers retained the radical charge of correspondence with forbidden forms. The fact that most extant gift images were produced at New Lebanon and Hancock, and generally in the Church Families, perhaps indicates the degree to which images remained suspect. Farther from the seat of power, instruments may have been unwilling to risk picturing their visions on paper.[52]

The new category in which Shaker instruments located their drawings and paintings did not necessarily protect all of their images. Especially in the years following Mother's Work, as the conceptual constructs which gave the images meaning weakened, there is ample evidence of the destruction of gift images. Written sources document numerous pictures that no longer exist.[53] First-hand accounts of the destruction of images, especially at Hancock, remain. For this reason, while some tentative quantitative and chronological conclusions can be offered based on the numbers and dates of extant drawings and paintings, most quantitative statements are likely to be misleading. Despite this, the fact that no gift images or similar visual documents survive from prior to 1839, that only a handful of derivatives survive from the years after 1859, and that almost all extant images were produced at Hancock or New Lebanon, suggests that it is accurate to see gift images as the relatively localized (though in some cases rather widely circulated) creations of this particular period of revival within Shakerism.

During the New Era itself, the combination of impulses in visionary pictures (tending both toward and away from superfluous objects) left the images suspended in a position of permanent ambiguity. Shaker ministry and instruments collaborated to maintain an intentional and unresolved ambivalence in relationship to gift drawings and paintings. If the members of the ministry had desired resolution on this issue, they could have revised the holy laws and orders to clarify the acceptability of gift images or they could have strengthened the existing prohibitions against images to expel the figures produced by the instruments. They did neither.

Indeed, in comparison to meticulous records detailing other sorts of spiritual gifts, the striking absence in New Era documents of specific references to gift drawings and paintings indicates the level of deliberate official ambivalence in relationship to these images. Conflicting attitudes toward images, however, represent only one extreme form of the more general and widespread ambivalence toward the charismatic manifestations of Mother's Work and toward the forces in the Society which sought to order those manifestations. It is not possible to resolve this ambivalence by labeling reactionary and progressive forces. A simple bipolar assessment of the New Era will not work. The struggle for renewal in the community took place in more subtle terms. Charismatic impulses were not necessarily innovative, nor were institutionalizing elements necessarily conservative. For Shakers, in a historical sense, charism, while potentially more disruptive because more difficult to control, actually represented a more "ancient," primitivist position, while institutionalization was relatively more modern. Further, innovation and conservation, charism and institution combined in individual persons, groups, and objects. In gift images, for example, Believers adopted a generally radical and potentially threatening form, the image, in order to restore traditional community values. A radical form claimed the attention of Shaker adherents; an often conservative content reinforced Shaker tradition in its appeal to authority and identity.[54]

As form and content cannot be separated neatly from one another,[55] neither can innovation and conservation nor charism and order in Shaker revival. Despite the necessity of discussing these elements in a linear fashion, a constant dialectic, attending Shakerism from its inception, actually pertained. The fact that the ministry felt it wise to legitimate and regulate gifts and instruments indicates that visionary phenomena and visionary persons wielded considerable, potentially disruptive power. At the same time, the ministry tolerated and even encouraged spiritual manifestations and the instruments who promoted them in order to restore and revitalize a more primitive Shaker identity.

While Ann Lee had insisted on the free operation of the spirit as a vital element of Shaker faith, it was difficult to control the spirit and those it possessed. Charismatic experience often manifested itself in bizarre and spectacular forms; it carried with it the threat of chaos and disorder. Even during the years of Ann Lee's ministry, when charism defined the very life of the Shaker community, spirit possession had simultaneously promoted disunion and apostasy. In response to the threat posed by widespread and unchecked charismatic experience, Shaker leaders in the years immediately following Lee's death had promoted restraint, regulation, and control. In other words, they moved to institutionalize a fundamentally charismatic system, to produce a "millennial church." As Clarke Garrett points out, Joseph Meacham

> transformed [James] Whittaker's intentions into an elaborate and coherent structure overseen by an equally elaborate hierarchy of elders and deacons endowed with supreme power in all matters. Henceforth everything, even the gifts of the Holy Spirit, would be subject to the hierarchy's approval.[56]

What had been disruptive in the 1780s was disruptive still in the 1840s.

But, like those who first gathered Believers into order, New Era leaders wanted to control rather than dismiss the Holy Spirit. In the persons of "official" instruments, mid-century Shakers ultimately institutionalized charismatic experience itself. Thus Shakers late in the 1830s and throughout the 1840s sought to ensure a continuing source of spiritual vitality. Thus did they recapitulate the charismatic experience of the first born in an ever-available and "safe" form.[57] The New Era Society made use of a potentially disruptive because ultimately unregulatable impulse (charism) to restore authority and identity. Ministry and instruments participated in a careful balancing act designed to recover the charismatic past in just such a way as to revive the institutions of the present.

> This is a point . . . that requires the continued exercise of great wisdom; that ye do not open the doors of communication so wide, as in a measure to let go the reigns [*sic*] of government; or shut them so close, that the body can find no access.[58]

Three

✽ *Production & Regulation of Images*

THE INSTRUMENTS AND THE MINISTRY

In many ways the tension between charism and order in mid-nineteenth-century Shaker society was embodied in the persons of the instruments. In concert with the ministry, the instruments deserve careful consideration in this book for their significant role in constructing meanings and categories for images in an iconoclastic community. Both consciously and unconsciously, instruments of Mother's Work manipulated and expanded a basic symbol system largely in place before the Era of Manifestations began. Although members of the United Society had been gifted with spiritual sight from the earliest days of their faith, during Mother's Work the role of instrument introduced a novel category of community leaders.[1] If the use of the term "instrument" was not entirely new to Believers, its mid-century form was dramatically enlarged and intensified.

Shaker instruments believed themselves "called and chosen" by the inhabitants of the celestial sphere.[2] On a given occasion, any member of the Shaker community might be inspired to speak or to perform spontaneously as an instrument of God. But the ministry blessed and anointed some of these divinely indicated individuals as "official" instruments in the Millennial Church.[3] The official instruments, especially, were set apart from the rest of the community by the sacredness of their calling and by the degree of personal sacrifice required of them. Prior to possession by the spirit, these instruments underwent periods of "mortification" or fasting and purification in preparation for their task.[4] On the one hand, the instruments represented a new center of power conceptually distinct from and sometimes in conflict with those traditionally recognized as authoritative. At least theoretically any Shaker except a member of the ministry could move into or out of this role. The addition of this office thus significantly modified the Shaker hierarchy by distributing spiritual power more widely throughout the community.[5] On the other hand, many Shaker instruments had been raised in the Society and schooled in its doctrines. These instruments were loyal to the ministry and submitted to regulation by them.

In Victor Turner's sense of the term, Shaker instruments were "liminal *personae*."[6] Not only did the instruments assume a mediate position with respect to the ministry and the membership at large, but they occupied *the* crucial threshold within the Shaker cosmos. For Believers, the presence of the instrument embodied the relationship or point of transition between heaven and earth. According to mid-century Shakers, Mother Ann intended her instruments

> to stand as mediators, mouths or instruments in our hands, to convey from the invisible to the visible, and when necessary, from the visible to the invisible.
>
> You [the instruments] have stood as the connecting link of communication between those in eternity and those in time; and the most part of you have been in this sacred position and attitude of spirit for near, or between three and four years past.[7]

Instruments exercised considerable influence within the Shaker community because of the "sacred position" they occupied. As "mediators" and "connecting links," instruments made the invisible and intangible world available to the senses of Believers.[8] They made treasures of heaven available to creatures of earth. Only through instruments did inhabitants of the celestial sphere communicate with their earthly offspring. The ministry could influence the vision of the instruments. But, almost without exception, the members of the ministry themselves did not possess the instruments' visionary capability.[9]

Instruments, Shakers believed, embodied within themselves, became symbols of, the relationship between the divine and the human. They had a particular tie to the eternal, but were also clearly lodged in the temporal. Existing as they did on the fluid edge between two worlds, they functioned as potentially dangerous and certainly powerful persons.[10] The ability of images (in general) to insist on the presence of a second, represented, world added to the liminal aura of those instruments who were also visionary image-makers. In a system which privileged union with the divine, the ones who provided visual affirmation of the possibility of spiritual union between two worlds became very important indeed. The instruments of images possessed particularly persuasive abilities to transform invisible to visible and to produce tangible and lasting evidence of contact with the spirit world.[11]

Those who saw and communicated the treasures of heaven were liminal in terms of social position and age as well as mediating role. In the months between August 1837 and April 1838, the instruments of Mother's Work, again adapting Turner's terminology, might be described as "spontaneously" or "existentially" liminal.[12] These first instruments, usually children or adolescents, often female members of the gathering orders, were, as a whole, among the least powerful members of Shaker society. In the first enthusiastic experiences they made good use of the kinds of spiritual power potentially available to them. Of Ann Mariah Goff in August 1837, the scribe commented, "it was tho't incredible by many that such a child should have such a vision."[13] The early manifestations may be seen as an attempt by young individuals in the United Society to identify with the charism of the founders, about which they had heard so much. As time passed, however, the community fashioned a "normatively" liminal category for the instruments.[14] In other words, the Shaker leadership institutionalized liminality (as they institutionalized charism) in the persons of the instruments.[15] Many of the instruments, then, became to a large extent an "official" voice in the community, generally reinforcing the position of the ministry.[16]

The institutionalization of the instrument's role reiterated the authority of women in the Shaker hierarchy and community. While many prominent instruments were men, and while men were more likely to serve as official scribes and recorders, the greatest number of instruments were women who spoke and performed in and for the community.[17] Appealing to the example of Ann Lee and pointing to the female gender of the earliest spontaneously charismatic instruments of Mother's Work, mid-century Shakers justified the personal characteristics of the instrument class.

> The peculiar exercises of this manifestation, and the speaking and writing of those sacred messages have been the most abundant among the females. And it appears reasonable that it should be so, when we consider that the second appearing of Christ was in the female, and that this is the second manifestation of Mother Ann.
>
> In the days of the primitive Church, it is evident that the female had not her equal right; her day had not come, for in that day the Son revealed the Father, and it was the Father's dispensation. But in this day, the daughter reveals the Mother; and Holy Mother Wisdom has been abundantly made known in the course of this work. It is therefore the Mother's dispensation, and the female is bro't forward in her true relation in the work of redemption.
>
> Both male and female have their equal rights in the gospel.[18]

The role of instrument, then, provided Shaker women with an increasingly public religious voice. Significantly, almost all the instruments of religious images were women. Shaker men were not without a tradition of image-making; they had been, from early years, the principal producers of maps and architectural drawings.[19] Shaker women, from 1839 to 1859, claimed their own graphic territory when they began making images of their visions.

In some important ways, watercolor was a feminine medium in the nineteenth century. Throughout the first half of the century at least, girls' academies and women's seminaries across the eastern United States taught painting in watercolor. Girls and young women entering the Shaker community may have brought with them this not unusual skill. A girls' academy which included drawing and watercolor painting in its curriculum in fact existed in the town of New

Lebanon, New York, not far from the New Lebanon Shaker community, in the early to mid–1800s.[20] The fact that women were the primary makers of religious images in the Shaker community reflected the larger cultural assumption that, apart from the fine arts which constituted a male preserve, and with regard to the medium of watercolor especially, women were more suited to this "sentimental" form of aesthetic expression. Certainly the degree of charismatic religiosity, of responsiveness to religious and emotional stimuli required of the instruments of visions (image-makers and otherwise), reflected rather precisely mid-nineteenth-century American cultural expectations about the constitution of women.[21]

Returning to the discussion of the instrument class in general, the movement from young and marginalized individuals speaking and acting spontaneously for the spirits to the creation of an instrument class is a fascinating development in mid-century Shakerism. The community had long anticipated some purifying work among the third generation. Consequently, the leadership responded to a potentially disruptive situation in which the instruments were principally young by incorporating the youth of the instruments into the official rationale for the enthusiasm; Mother Ann's gifts, they reasoned, were intended for the young. So ministry and official instruments designed the new instrument class to approximate but not exactly replicate the marginal characteristics of the first instruments even though most later instruments did not fit the profile. Though many official instruments were young adults, and though almost all were considered to be members of the rising generation, later instruments were seldom children or adolescents. Further, though young, many later instruments had significant tenure in the community. These young women and men (especially the image-makers) had been raised in Shaker schools and had demonstrated potential as future leaders in the Society. For example, among the instruments of drawings and paintings, Semantha Fairbanks entered the United Society at New Lebanon in 1813 at age nine, Eleanor Potter in 1817 at age five, Mary Wicks in 1825 at age six, Polly Reed in 1825 at age seven, and Miranda Barber in 1828 at age nine.[22] These instruments, then, though considered members of the third generation, had learned the Shaker way of life from early childhood.[23] They generally became instruments within a few years before or after the time they would sign the Shaker covenant. A significant number occupied positions (such as office deacons or trustees, schoolteachers, and caretakers of the children and elderly) which gave them more mobility than the average Shaker and greater access to books and other printed resources.

The instruments of Mother's Work who had come to the Shakers as children in the teens and twenties of the nineteenth century, by 1840 approached or had recently attained maturity in the faith. The official (or normatively liminal) instruments of Mother's Work thus continued to be *relatively* marginal and liminal in terms of age and mediating role, but the degree of their marginality and liminality changed significantly as the office of instrument came to be occupied by young women and men from the Church Families with some tenure in the community rather than by children from the gathering orders. The peculiar experiences of these instruments well prepared them to serve the interests of both institution and charism. They had been raised and socialized in the Shaker order of life; they knew, consciously and unconsciously, how to conform to the will of the ministry and the expectations of the community-at-large. On the other hand, as members of the rising generation, they also knew the sense of spiritual anxiety occasioned by remoteness from the charismatic person of Ann Lee.

The relationship between image-making instruments and their upbringing in Shaker schools provides some interesting insight into possible sources for the instruments' pictures. Extended contact between instruments and the schools usually began early in the instruments' childhood years, in some cases may even have begun before they or their families joined the Shakers since "the world's children" were often educated in these same schools.[24] At least two instruments of images became teachers, maintaining contact with Shaker schools into adulthood. Sarah Bates had come to New Lebanon in 1811 at age nineteen. By 1830 she was an influential teacher in the girls' school. Bates continued to teach during Mother's Work. Image-maker Polly Reed, widely recognized among Shakers as an excellent calligrapher, came to New Lebanon in 1825 at age seven. By 1849 she was teaching school with Sarah Bates.[25]

The association of instruments with Shaker schools influenced both the content and the form of gift images.[26] The principal object of Shaker education was "to make good Believers" of all children gathered into the United Society, "that they [might] become useful and honorable members in the house of God."[27] Teachers planned lessons consistent with Shaker life; young scholars learned appropriate Shaker behavior and beliefs as well as reading, writing, and arithmetic. In a letter about her experiences in school, fourteen-year-old pupil and future instrument Miranda Barber told Isaac Youngs (himself, on occasion, a schoolteacher) that she had learned, for example, to control anger, to use time wisely, and to honor and respect the elders. The Holy Orders of the Church specified the history of the Heavenly Parents as appropriate subject matter for young Shaker scholars.[28] As they matured, instruments raised in Shaker schools could rely on shared ethical and doctrinal knowledge in producing and organizing their paintings.

Shaker religious art also reflected the visual environment of the instruments' early childhood education. The third generation of Shakers, including most of the instruments of drawings and paintings, was the first generation with time for prolonged schooling in letters and calligraphy.[29] Literacy was essentially universal in New England by the 1840s.[30] Young Shakers acquired facility with ink and paint practicing their letters and making detailed and colorful maps to demonstrate their skill in both geography and penmanship.[31] Furthermore, Shaker teachers and their pupils had more access to pictures than the average adult Shaker. Young scholars learned to read from illustrated primers. A manuscript titled "School Instructions" counseled educators to use

> Worcesters' primer, or some other pictorial primer, containing a variety of pictures of natural things, and various kinds of animals, such as are common and well

> known to children, with the names printed under them, both in capitals and small letters. Point to the animal or thing, and let the child name it; then show them the letters which spell that name, and pronounce them, and the child will soon take the idea.[32]

This method merited attention, the author continued, because it was "plain," "simple," and "easily comprehend[ed]" and "retain[ed]."[33] New Era instruments, too, probably hoped for easy comprehension and rapid retention when they identified individual images included in their drawings and paintings with single words or short descriptive phrases written directly beneath the object depicted (e.g., figs. 7, 13, 23, 26, 28, 30). The labeled images of these instruments strongly resembled the pictures in pictorial primers, the illustrated books most familiar to the younger residents of the community.

The type boards and alphabet boards used to teach reading and writing in Shaker schools also influenced the style and iconography of gift images.[34] In 1845 Shaker educator Seth Wells wrote,

> There should be an Alphabet board hung up in a conspicuous place, in the school room, with the Alphabet in writing characters painted upon it, both in capitals and small letters, and also the pauses used in writing, and the numerical figures. By imitating these on their slates, the children will soon learn them.[35]

The letters of the alphabet boldly represented, as both subject matter and inscription, in many visionary pictures look like the clearly delineated letters Shaker students and teachers would have seen daily in their classrooms on type boards and alphabet boards (see figs. 4 and 19, for example). Finally, at the end of the term, Shaker teachers rewarded with certificates of merit pupils who showed satisfactory progress. These intricately designed and carefully executed "rewards" bear a striking visual similarity to the cards and notices received by Shakers from the celestial sphere beginning early in the 1840s. Teachers noticed and rewarded exemplary pupils as, according to the instruments, the Eternal and Heavenly Parents noticed and rewarded faithful gospel children (cf. figs. 12 and 24). Sarah Bates, the teacher who penned many rewards of merit for young Shaker scholars, was also a principal instrument of gift images.[36]

While it is interesting and informative to investigate the individual identities of Shaker instruments, Shaker images were communal creations. This art found meaning in a communal history and a communal context, and not by association with individual genius. The posture of passivity on the part of the instruments highlighted the Shaker perception that spirits rather than instruments controlled charismatic manifestations. Instruments emphasized that they remained the passive receptors of messages and visions from the spirit world. The gifts came from God through individuals open to divine influence. These gifts were treasures of heaven unadulterated by their earthly vehicles. Indeed, the title "instrument" itself intentionally underscored the notion of passive receptivity.[37] Instruments assumed an aura of liminal power because they spoke what God spoke and saw what God saw, but the initiating agent was God and not the instrument: "the instruments she [Mother Ann] has chosen are but instruments, they have no power of their own, and can communicate only what is given to them."[38]

In changing attitudes regarding publication of the instruments' identities, Shakers expressed their own uncertainties in relationship to the sort of liminal power exercised by the instruments. Regulations about written disclosures of the instruments' names changed over the course of the Era. In fact, fluctuating opinions about whether or not instruments should fix their names to copies of messages delivered through them probably left some leeway for the instrument herself to decide.[39] In some cases legal codes and regulatory messages required the inclusion of the instruments' names on celestial pictures and texts and on official records; in others they prohibited it.[40] The pictures and texts themselves reflect this disagreement; some are signed, some are not. Regulations about the instruments' names, however, were not designed to keep the identities of the instruments from the community. Instruments, official and unofficial, performed publicly. They saw heavenly people and places in public meeting. Then, sometimes only hours, sometimes weeks or months after their public visions, image-making instruments transcribed the celestial sights they had seen onto paper. Because members of the community generally witnessed the initial visionary encounter, the community knew the identities of the instruments. For the believing Shaker what really mattered with respect to the names of the instruments was the degree to which the understanding of gifts and messages came to be permanently associated with individual human talent and the degree to which any particular divine message came to be associated with a particular human personality.[41] Here again the goal was to remove the focus from the instrument and to center attention on the gift. Disagreement about the desirability of anonymity reflected once again the tension between charism and institution. From the perspective of charism, the crucial component was the spirit rather than the individual. From the perspective of institution, every detail ought to be included in the record.

For later researchers, weighting too heavily the identity of instruments can obscure the nature of gift images by centering the discussion on "individual genius" rather than on the "signifying practice" of the community.[42] Not only does focusing on attribution violate the Shaker sense of their religious pictures, but attribution can be extremely difficult to determine. What is certain is that instruments produced visionary pictures. But only a handful of image-makers can be positively identified. Most images do not include the name of the instrument. Occasionally multiple instruments collaborated on a single image or set of images.[43] In sum, my argument relative to visionary pictures depends not on the identities of individual instruments but on the general characteristics of the instruments of Mother's Work, on the reception of the images within the Shaker community, and on the roles played by the instruments' paintings and drawings. But, while many factors can make the identities of the image-makers difficult to determine with certainty and while attribution is not the prior question in terms of understanding Shaker images, the identities of the instruments are not irrelevant. Among other things, knowledge about individual instruments provides information about the status of the instrument/artist in the Shaker community and about the sorts of people most frequently chosen as instruments of Mother's Work.

Mother's Work made great demands on both instruments and ministry. Figuratively speaking, the instruments' performances, in particular, required skills not unlike tightrope walking. These women and men had to conduct themselves in ways expected enough to be believed and unusual enough to be dramatically persuasive. In discussing spirit possession among the Camisards and early Shakers as a form of sacred theatre, Clarke Garrett argues that the expectations of Believers determined both the behavior of the instruments and the content of spirit communications. Charismatic manifestations thus involved an essential cultural interaction between the instruments and the recipients of divine communications as well as between the instruments and the ministry. "If they [the instruments] did not conduct themselves in culturally expected ways, their claims to have been visited by alien or supernatural beings would not [have been] believed."[44]

But general compliance with cultural expectations did not remove the threat or guarantee the acceptability of charismatic gifts. Liminal and charismatic experiences offered much to a community dependent for its very existence upon spiritual vitality, on the demonstrated proximity of heaven and earth. Nonetheless, conflicts involving the instruments of Mother's Work and the celestial gifts they delivered also caused serious difficulties for Shakers. While most conformed to the religious assumptions generated by the New Era and many enthusiastically embraced the manifestations, some were genuinely dismayed. The majority of these skeptics left quietly, adding their numbers to the swelling ranks of Shaker apostates. The ministry expelled a few "troublemakers." One Randolph West found the Era so seriously disturbing that he committed suicide. Benjamin S. Youngs, a Shaker leader, copied this article verbatim from the *New York Journal of Commerce,* 3 July 1839:

> "*Suicide.*On Monday last [suppose June 22] an inquest was held by the coroner of this county over the body of Randolph West, who was found dead near the residence of Mr. Manning, in this vicinity. His body was found hanging by the neck to a rope, to a leaning sugar sapling, with his feet within 14 inches of the ground. From the evidence detailed to the jury it appeared that the deceased was about 72 years of age, and had resided at Union Village for 16 or 17 years, and who was amongst those of that society who could not travel with their brethren in the new Revelation which they proposed [professed] to have received. It did not clearly appear whether the deceased voluntarily left the society or was expelled, but it was testified that he had frequently stated, with tears in his eyes since he left the society, that he had labored at the village for sixteen or seventeen years and had expected to end his days there, but was now without a home among strangers, and not a relation in this country. The last conversation which he was known to hold was with one of his friends who had also been compelled to leave the Village on account of the new revelation. In this conversation the deceased inquired of the witness whether he had heard the

news from the Village, and on being told that the new work was still going on and believers still saw visions and held converse with Ann Lee, he exclaimed, 'My Lord, what will become of me!'

He then appeared dejected, and said but little more."[45] [Brackets in original.]

In addition, several prominent official instruments left New Lebanon when the ministry neglected the testimony of one of their number.[46] Shaker journals provide evidence that Believers felt very deeply the impact of this apostasy.

> We have a most shocking circumstance to record this day—namely, four young people went from the first Order to the world!!! John Allen, Derobign Bennet and his sister Letsy Ann, and Mary Wicks; this feels awful beyond description, and has caused many tears, and is such an occurrence as this family never experienced before since we began to gather together in the year 1787.[47]

Of the four apostates, three (excepting Letsy Ann Bennett) were prominent instruments, and one, Mary Wicks, was an image-maker.[48] In the west, communications delivered by a young instrument assisted in discrediting a venerable Shaker leader.[49] With the cautious support of the New Lebanon ministry, Richard McNemar (named Eleazar Wright by Lucy Wright) regained his union with the Ohio Shakers. He never returned to his former position of influence, however, and he died shortly after the ordeal. This early case demonstrated that it could be a very dangerous thing to allow any and every member of the community to speak publicly for the spirit world. The messages of such members might openly contradict or subvert the purposes of Mother's Work and the desires of the ministry. Shaker scribes recorded their communities' concern that some instruments might "lose their protection," might speak for "evil spirits" rather than good spirits. In a letter to the Union Village ministry, a New Lebanon correspondent noted,

> It seems hard for the Ministry at North Union to believe that instruments may be employed by both good and evil agents: or in other words; to believe that Mother will not protect her instruments in all cases—Well, we have no doubt but She will protect all who are obedient, but none else—Disobedient Visionists and prophets are as liable to fall and become tools in the service of the devil as any other characters: And we need not expect that, because they have been so wonderfully noticed, their free agency will be taken away, while all the rest of us are left to the freedom of our own choice.[50]

In addition to the threat posed by disobedient and disbelieving instruments and by individuals skeptical or jealous of the instruments' position and influence, gift manifestations themselves aroused disruptive feelings of envy, suspicion, embarrassment, and even boredom in some.[51] Repeatedly, the ministry cautioned against using heavenly gifts as "common things."

> And above all things ye ought never to allow yourselves to unite with any others,

> either directly or indirectly in making light of the sacred and precious givings of God; or to make a common talk of them. Ye should be exceedingly careful not to speak and feel in respect to them, as ye do in relation to common and every day concerns.
>
> "If ye do not regard this," says Mother, "ye will be guilty of a very great sin, and that which will shut my blessing from your souls . . . Souls ought continually to pray for a spirit of reverence and respect to the gifts of God.["][52]

On another occasion, referring specifically to tangible forms of gifts, "Mother expressed her displeasure with the manner in which her gifts were written and handed around as every day things like the news of the day."[53] While many accepted heavenly gifts "with humble and thankful hearts," "by some they have been used like filthy drugs; by some they have been thrown away, trampled upon, yea, and carnal pleasures picked up in their stead, and prised above them."[54] Further, those who received few gifts were likely to be jealous of those who received many.[55] Mother Ann urged her instruments not to be disheartened or dismayed "when you feel, see or hear frowns, sneers, scoffs, or rubs, from this one or that, in respect to the work of the late manifestation, in which you have been called."[56] In his farewell address, Elder Ebenezer Bishop warned against "that soul-damning spirit of unbelief, which will twist, and turn, cavil, and reason, and try, if possible, to pick some flaw in the precious gifts of God."[57] Far from stemming the tide of apostates and encouraging the revival of a more primitive Shakerism, for some the gifts of Mother's Work presented an occasion for ridicule and doubt.

But, while some abandoned both their faith and the United Society because of their discomfort with the spectacle of Shaker spirituality, many others found their Shaker identity confirmed and supported by their participation in Mother's Work. For every Richard McNemar or Randolph West, there was, for example, a John Edwin Long. Long requested that he and his family be readmitted to the United Society after the Era began, because, he claimed, he never would have left if the gifts of God had descended prior to his departure.[58] And Frederick W. Evans, a Shaker leader of the latter half of the nineteenth century, wrote in his autobiography:

> It was by spiritual manifestations . . . that I, in 1830, was converted to Shakerism. In 1837 to 1844, there was an influx from the spirit world, "confirming the faith of many disciples" who had lived among Believers for years, and extending throughout all the eighteen societies.[59]

Evidence that the ministry and the majority of the instruments recognized and attempted to respond to the threat posed by some gifts and instruments exists primarily in the elaborate apparatus for interpretation and regulation of instruments and gifts that developed early in the Era. Both the ministry and the instruments moved swiftly to legitimate and institutionalize the potentially disruptive aspects of Mother's Work. However, neither ministry nor instruments wanted to subdue gift manifestations. Rather, those authorized to lead acknowledged the power inherent in celestial gifts and inspired persons and desired to enlist that power in their campaign for a return to a more fundamental Shakerism. After two decades of anxiety about gradual spiritual decline, Shakers naturally seized upon the enthusiasm of the late 1830s as a reiteration of the spiritual gifts widely available during the ministry of Ann Lee.[60] From the beginning of Mother's Work, individual Believers recognized in spiritual manifestations possibilities for influencing behavior and belief. In this early phase, many were inclined to accept Mother's Work as true because it began among Watervliet's children.[61] The young were precisely those in desperate need of direct contact with their spiritual forebears. The community rejoiced that even the ministry could learn from the counsel of the youthful inspired ones. Initial reactions, however, were not entirely unmixed. On 8 October 1837, Rufus Bishop, a longstanding member of the parent ministry, recorded his opinion: "to be honest about the matter I think there was rather too much of the wind, fire, and earthquake to satisfy Believers who have had a long and fruitful travel."[62] But those in positions of some authority very soon became invested in promoting Mother's Work.

Members of the parent ministry visited Watervliet (their second "home") to observe the manifestations shortly after the visions and spirit visitations began.[63] In 1838 Isaac Newton Youngs recorded official New Lebanon's reaction to the first manifestations.

> Sometime in September and October [1837] we began to hear about extraordinary gifts at Watervliet of visions and trances. After a while we were favored with the hearing of the visions in writing—The work kept increasing, till Joseph H. [Joseph Hodgson] came down here, on the 30th of November. He bro't much additional information about the visions there. On the 5th of December I went up there and collected a good deal in writing: the visions increased very fast. I saw a good many of them. I came home on the 22nd. After this we heard but little for a good while, and we became anxious to hear at every opportunity.[64]

At the request of the ministry, Youngs traveled to Watervliet to interview instruments and record visions.[65] He learned the new forms of worship given by the spirits and later taught these forms at New Lebanon. Shortly after Youngs returned to New Lebanon, Giles B. Avery, of the Second Order, Church Family at New Lebanon, recorded these brief entries in the journal he kept:

> Isaac came up here [to the Second Order] this evening to read, and tell to us the Visions he attended, etc. I think he is nearly inspired to mimick for I never witnessed such scrutinizing mimickery before. Really I can say nothing but, Wonderful are thy works O Lord and in Wisdom hast thou made them all, and man by searching is not able to find them out. They are known only by revelation in very deed. . . .
>
> . . . Attended meeting at the meeting house in the afternoon to try the new manner of labouring. Beautiful! Beautiful—There were 5 new manners laboured to day. Never before did I behold such a meeting.[66]

Hancock, the community geographically closest to New Lebanon, caught the excitement early. Frequent visiting took place between members of the Church Families at New Lebanon and Hancock during the first months of the Era and in the years that followed.[67] By March 1838 Shakers at Hancock had already experienced many visions and "wonders."[68]

By the time Mother's Work itself actually reached New Lebanon on 22 April 1838, the lead had adopted an authoritative response. The record for this first official gift at New Lebanon clearly demonstrates the ministry's determination to regulate charismatic manifestations. Significantly, this initial entry in the official New Lebanon record also began to suggest the authorized interpretation of the New Era as the return of "Christ and Mother and all our first parents, together with Father Joseph and Mother Lucy [the second parents]" to restore order by assisting the rising generation.[69] By the time the ministry and their scribe wrote the introduction to the official record several years later, they had fully developed this interpretation: "In the commencement of the work these gifts did not seem to indicate any extensive, express purpose; but in the course of the work a wise design has been satisfactorily present."[70] The "wise design" of Mother Ann and the other spirits had a particular content. It depended on an interpretation of history based on an ideal time and social organization in the past and on a framework of decline from that ideal.

> It will doubtless be perceived that through the whole tenor of these inspired writings much is said by the spirits, of the degeneracy of the body of Believers, from the true spirit of the gospel, and the loss of the true order of the Church as established in the first gathering thereof.
>
> The censure of these things is almost wholly charged upon the rising generation, and those called since the Church was gathered. . . . But a little reflection will show that this degeneracy was not altogether the effect of willful neglect, but from a combination of causes in a great measure unavoidable.[71]

According to the interpretation authorized by the ministry, the "real work"[72] of the revival was the restoration of "true primitive order."

> Our blessed Parents, F. Joseph, and M. Lucy have labored incessantly to reestablish the true primitive order in which the Church was first planted. It appears that as a body, we have degenerated, or fallen back considerably in many things.[73]

In one sense, the expression "primitive order" captures in its bipolar organization the tension between charism and institution which characterized the New Era.[74] "Primitive" can be understood to signify the mid-nineteenth-century appeal for an "ancient" and charismatic Shaker foundation. By contrast, "order" can be imagined to designate the necessity of social control, organization, institution in relationship to the movement of the spirit and the response of Believers. Ministry and instruments worked to consolidate community identity, to organize communal behavior, around the ongoing spiritual presence of Mother Ann and her early circle.

Interpreting the phrase "primitive order" by examining the first and second words separately also points up a crucial distinction in chronology. Not only did New Era restorationists appeal to the primitive charismatic authority of Ann Lee, but (the official instruments especially) also spoke for the ordering authority of the early Millennial Church established by James Whittaker, Joseph Meacham, and Lucy Wright. At least to a discernible degree, Lucy Wright, "the second Shaker Mother," replaced emphasis on spiritual vision with emphasis on union, and emphasis on ecstatic experience with emphasis on good behavior. A significant part of the tension and ambiguity that permeated New Era experience resulted from reference to two different models for restoration *as though* the models were one and the same. Among Shakers for whom "true Church order" was a near synonym for "true primitive order," the two models were rapidly conflated.[75] The prototypes were historically sequential and they initially entered the revival experience in their proper chronological sequence.[76] But, after April 1838, clear distinctions between the two collapsed and instruments and ministry often appealed to the mission of Lee and the ministries of Whittaker, Meacham, and Wright as though they had occurred simultaneously.[77] In their pursuit of primitive order, mid-century restorationists adopted a twofold goal. They sought to recapitulate both the initial charismatic phase of Shakerism *and* the institutionalizing phase of Whittaker, Meacham, and Wright, to revive direct contact with Ann Lee *and* to reestablish true church order. While instruments and ministry actively promoted both models, in a very broad sense the instruments publicly performed the charism of Ann Lee and the ministry the ordering authority of Whittaker, Meacham, and Wright.

The first times of Shakerism constituted normative primitive order for mid-century Believers. But *which* first times was certainly an appropriate question. Regardless of the model being pursued, however, the person of Ann Lee, the "first Mother," established the focal point and the interpretive context for New Era spirituality.[78] Mid-century Shakers mined the charismatic experience of their past to inspire and, paradoxically, to organize and control their present. The spirit of Ann Lee—the principal figure in the restoration—played at least two significant roles. In her more historically accurate persona, she authorized the spontaneous, free movement of the spirit. Assuming a second identity more like that of the Shaker leaders who followed her, she supported the official hierarchy in their efforts. So, New Era instruments and ministry reclaimed the charismatic first times while they reasserted the validity of traditional structures of authority.[79] As charism became institutionalized, charism sanctioned institutionalization.

Although Mother's Work began among the children and the gathering orders, it spread with the support and encouragement of the ministry. Exchanges of correspondence and of well-placed and trusted visitors provided for the rapid dissemination of information. As Mother's Work progressed, New Lebanon taught other communities the gifts and rituals the "Mother Church" had received from the spirits. In addition, the ministry authorized and then encouraged the spread of especially effective and persuasive gifts received in other communities as well. For example, the 4 July 1841 entry in a record of spiritual gifts received at Harvard and Shirley included the introduction in those two communities of the Narrow Path. This ritual was already being practiced at New Lebanon.[80] Henry Blinn, a later Shaker interpreter of the Era, recalled that another ritual, the Midnight Cry, had been brought to Canterbury by Believers from New Lebanon.[81] In a postscript to a letter of 20 November 1837, the New Lebanon ministry noted,

> We were at Hancock a short time since, and understood that they were zealously engaged in the present gift, and that they were wide awake at Tyringham; and Brother Grove was expecting shortly to go to Enfield to administer the gift there; and it appears that his labors have been greatly prospered and blessed.[82]

Over time, if a community had not experienced a particular degree or kind of manifestation that that community's ministry and people or the parent ministry deemed appropriate, then the community might "feel out" the gift that they believed God intended for them.[83] Often, when the ministries of other communities called on the parent ministry, they would return home laden with spiritual gifts appointed by New Lebanon.[84]

The principal legal codes of the Era reasserted the theological legitimacy and practical necessity of the traditional Shaker hierarchy.[85] Likewise, the overt content of most gift texts and images supported leaders in the accomplishment of their duties and encouraged the conformity of all levels of the hierarchy to the will of those above them. This repeated emphasis in New Era documents points to a crisis of authority which accompanied the crisis of remoteness from Ann Lee in the mid- century Shaker community.[86] In their concern with authority, Shakers were not alone among Americans of their time; the Shaker crisis reflected difficulties related to general democratizing tendencies in the broader culture. Scholars have documented movement toward less "vertical" and more "horizontal" organization in American life as a whole during this period. Karen Halttunen, in particular, presents persuasively the significant threat of changing patterns of authority outside the Shaker community, as notions of "mastery and deference" gave way to notions of "equality" in social arrangements. Her examination of mid-century advice manuals and the despair they reveal over the collapse of traditional modes of authority (family, community, church), especially in regard to America's youth, is particularly illuminating.[87] As the rate of transition in Shaker membership increased, more potential converts accustomed to egalitarian social systems entered the Society. As Believers expanded their traffic with the larger culture, the mid-century American sense of appropriate equality in social relations had more impact on Shaker perceptions. All this occurred simultaneously with an internal crisis of authority derived from remoteness from Mother Ann and intensified, as more and more young people left the community, by a diminishing leadership pool.[88] An increasingly strong American "notion of the sovereignty of the people"[89] exacerbated a Shaker situation created largely by the passage of time. First generation Believers had followed Ann Lee because of their felt spiritual need and her direct and persuasive charismatic appeal. The second generation, because of close proximity in time, was able to build on this earlier commitment and to maintain a real sense of connection with it. Members of the third generation, however, required a compelling reason to remain in the community, to heed the advice and counsel of Shaker leaders. They were no longer content with mere hearsay about earlier and more enthusiastic times.

Although the New Era brought increased status and power to the ministry, it also greatly increased their responsibilities.

> Another important difficulty has attended this work [here the charismatic practice of "taking in the spirits"]; it has had a tendency to frustrate the operations of the visible Lead, in meetings and out. They having a desire to unite with every good gift and not to stand in the way of any genuine manifestation from the spiritual world, and yet knowing it to be their duty to properly hold the reins of government, for the general harmony and good of all, were often put to a severe test to know how to exercise true wisdom. To meet all these things, and to conduct all matters aright, for the general and individual protection of all, has caused the Visible Lead, (the Ministry and elders), no small share of labor and tribulation.[90]

Developing and carrying out an appropriate "official" reply to heaven's gifts was no small task. According to the instruments, God required much of those to whom much had been given: "I have placed no power on earth, that may judge them, therefore I do require their feet to walk in a path more strait and narrow, than any others are required to walk on earth."[91] New regulations, sanctioned, the instruments claimed, by heavenly authors, challenged members of the ministry to be the "most perfect examples of every gospel virtue."[92] Personal authority enhanced formal authority. Mid-century Shakers knew well the reputation and character of the four members of their parent ministry. Elder Ebenezer Bishop, Eldress Ruth Landon, Brother Rufus Bishop, and Sister Asenath Clark had served together since 1821 (and would continue to serve together until 1849). Lucy Wright herself had designated and blessed these leaders. If gift images and contemporary documents can be taken as indicators of community sentiment, most genuinely loved and respected all four parent ministers. With significant exceptions, the local ministries too maintained the high regard of community members. Even apostate Hervey Elkins, a longtime Shaker in New Hampshire who wrote of his experience in the Society after he left for the world, maintained that the leaders were

> our every day companions; who eat, sleep, work and worship ever with us; who by humility, by patience, by honesty, by goodness, have been promoted to be the servant of all—self-denying men, who hold themselves not aloof from us, but to whom we listen, whom we obey, because we believe that it is the order of God that we should. Tomorrow the anointing may rest on another,—on you, on us—this is the simple mystery of the ordination of leaders.[93]

Very soon after Mother's Work began, ministry and instruments exerted pressure on Shaker followers to conform to the demands of the revival and its manifestations. Prophetic messages called down God's judgment upon disbelievers.[94] At New Lebanon, members signed and sealed a "Sacred Covenant" as their testimony to the reality and divinity of the gifts.[95] By 1841 a book of inspired laws and orders for the "holy anointed of Zion" required that leading elders believe in the manifestations and their heavenly origin.[96] Eventually, this document stated, those who denied God's manifestations would be cut off from Zion.[97] Through forms of peer pressure and authoritative example, the convinced sought to persuade skeptics of the truth of spiritual manifestations.

Increasingly, the ministry monitored and molded the manifestations of Mother's Work. Increasingly, the inspired messages of both official and unofficial instruments supported the authority of the parent ministry and sought to consolidate the power of the New Lebanon leaders. On 20 May 1838, Mother Ann spoke to her children at New Lebanon: "I have come to help the Lead, but not to take the lead. God will not distroy the order of his Anointing. There will always remain a visible Lead, to lead and direct the visible body of Christ on earth."[98] The spirits made it clear that the instruments, though powerful, were subject to the ministry. "It is evident that the visionists often misunderstand their own gifts, and need their elders to guide them."[99] The official role of the instruments of Mother's Work was, after all, "to assist the anointed priesthood and the leaders of the people, by divine inspiration to keep the people in the law of Christ, and to restore whatever is fallen and decayed."[100]

The methods of control employed by the ministry in relationship to celestial gifts and messages became more and more formal and standardized as the Era progressed. At first the parent ministry issued only general precautionary remarks.

> It requires some wisdom and caution to steer the young through those gifts without some loss to themselves or dishonor to the cause. The gift of God is always good, but when fallen nature lays claim to the honor of it, there is danger of great loss.[101]

Messages from spirits and pronouncements from the parent ministry encouraged the guidance of the elders in these matters. In the early months of the Era, "protection" against abuse seemed inherent in the visions.

> In the earlier part of their visions we [the ministry] were afraid that their great gifts would lift them up above their protection; but we soon found that they were kept under such strict order, and had to visit the damned so much that they were well kept down, and it was with reluctance, generally, that they followed their guides into the spiritual world after their first visit there.[102]

In 1838 the ministry began to take measures more explicit and direct. Messages delivered through official instruments began to emphasize the ministry's responsibility and prerogative to "try the spirits" in order to determine which gift manifestations were legitimate. Shakers pointed to I John 4:1-6 as biblical precedent for "trying the spirits." The Shaker exegete held that

> The apostle John gives a plain criterion by which to try the spirits. 'Every spirit that confesseth not that Christ is come in the flesh, is not of God.' I John 4.1. This is perfectly understood in the Church of Christ in this day. Confession that Christ is come in the flesh is the same as owning Christ as a Lead, and this is paramount to acknowledging Christ in a visible Lead that dwells in mortal flesh. Hence, those who own this Lead, and submit all things to its decision, possess the spirit of God, and all communications conducted by this spirit, and owned and sanctioned by this Lead, will be genuine.
>
> Such a Lead did not exist long at a time in former ages, Hence this criterion could not be applied; hence many . . . false prophets; and hence the falling away, for the Churches had no acknowledged Lead but became divided and scattered.
>
> But the kingdom is now established, forever to stand, a Lead will always remain. Of the increase of this government there shall be no end. Isa. 9.7. And on this foundation and principle has the late work been conducted throughout.[103]

Inhabitants of the celestial sphere proclaimed that the agreement or "union" of a gift's content with the position of the ministry would stand as evidence of the authenticity of the gift.

> The Apostle said, "Believe not every Spirit, but try the spirits, whether they are of God . . . when Believers are ministered to by Spirits that unite them to their proper leads, by a simple obedience, they have proof that they are of God and their gifts may be a strength and blessing to them. But on the other hand, when their gifts serve to lift them up above their Elders, and above the gifts of God, they have reason to mistrust that they are directed by a false Spirit. The good Spirit always points souls to the established order of God . . . and we find that such as keep the most subordination to their Elders, are the most signally favored and blessed in their gifts.[104]

Over the months and years, official gift messages provided increasingly specific biblical and theological rationales for the regulation of gifts and visions.[105] By mid-1840 the spirits had erected an "Altar of Wisdom" upon which the lead could "try" all gifts. "You must try the Spirits and their gifts on that Altar of Wisdom which God has placed with the Ministry and Elders and judge them accordingly."[106]

Gift messages, initially communicated verbally, could not be inspected and "tried" by the ministry and elders without written records of those messages. From the beginning, instruments and scribes wrote down selected gift messages.[107] It was not until late in February 1841, however, that the First Order of the New Lebanon Church claimed to receive word from the spirits mandating that gift messages in each of the various Shaker communities be systematically gathered, recorded, and preserved. In addition, the instruments maintained, the spirits required that each community submit its records to the parent ministry at

New Lebanon.[108] Not only did the ministry exert control over the instruments and gifts, but both ministry and instruments used the gifts themselves as mechanisms of social control. In the case of the images, in particular, "enhanced" spiritual eyesight, "corrected" spiritual eyesight, was controlled spiritual eyesight. The instruments' images came to represent not what was produced in the spiritual imagination of each individual Believer, but rather the modulation of spiritual imagination in response to regulation by the ministry and in proximity to official interpretations of Mother's Work.

Manuscript evidence suggests that regulation was a primary purpose motivating the requirement for accurate records.[109] If Believers submitted all spirit communications to the ministry, then the ministry might enlist these gifts in service of the restoration of "church order." Shakers themselves had long recognized the institutionalizing impact of textual records. In their earlier history they had assiduously avoided writing things down for fear of stifling spiritual spontaneity. By 1808 this had begun to change but some kinds of information, legal codes included, remained essentially oral until after Lucy Wright's death in 1821. During Mother's Work, however, Shakers fearful of losing connection with their past, and therefore with a meaningful present, scrambled to write down everything. Knowledge that the parent ministry would see the sights and read the words delivered through them probably tempered the content of the instruments' messages. Furthermore, the ministry issued guidelines specifying clarity and consistency within and between gifts as major determining factors in the authenticity of those gifts.[110] Members of the ministry resolved that future generations for whom the scribes preserved gift messages would not mock celestial gifts because of glaring internal contradictions. These leaders recognized, though, that they could not effectively control each of the hundreds, even thousands, of New Era visions and gifts. In fact, the parent ministry generally trusted the judgment of the local ministries and did not insist on seeing their records immediately. Rather the New Lebanon leaders expected that visions would be collected until they filled a book; the entire book would then be forwarded to New Lebanon. "So be not troubled or in haste about copies for us; for we have no knowledge, but what next year or the year after will be soon enough for us to receive them."[111]

In all likelihood, the proclamation of the requirement to record visions presented the immediate occasion for the rather sudden increase in the number and complexity of gift drawings, paintings, and visually organized messages dating from 1841 and later. Certainly this requirement would have provided instruments with added justification to make painted images in a Society previously devoid of them. For if the goal was to produce the most accurate record possible, how better to represent precisely a thing seen than to draw or paint a picture of it. To some instruments it must have seemed that the full impact of visionary experience could be recorded and preserved only if its integrity as *visual* experience was retained. In support of this argument: like the official written records, the instruments' drawings often included appended notes asserting that the pictures were exact copies of the original visions; like the written records, drawings usually specified both a date received and a date recorded or "written"; drawings to individuals contained generally positive, reassuring content because regulations prohibited the recording of negative, judgmental gift messages to individuals. Drawings with negative content were usually prophetic and always public in nature because regulations allowed recording and retention of public messages of rebuke.[112]

In addition to understanding gift images in relationship to gift texts, then, Shakers also conceived of their visionary pictures in relationship to written records of inspired communications which used words to describe aural, literary, and visual phenomena. Gift drawings and paintings were both a visual experience and a graphic record of a visionary encounter. While visionary images shared important characteristics with other New Era gifts (e.g., word, song, dance, mime), in their theoretically literal transcription of pictorial imagination onto paper, the images were unique. As they described and recorded visionary experience, gift images also represented or recapitulated that experience in something like its "original" visual language. The images combined the immediacy and affect of sacred theatre or dance with the permanence and tangibility of the textual record.

Because images themselves belonged "in the line of writing" and because images served simultaneously as gift and record, as charismatic experience and as documentation of that experience, written inscriptions figured significantly in the visionary pictures of mid-century instruments (figs. 11, 22, 26 and Pls. II–V). While words functioned differently in different gift images, inscriptions generally added a second level of clarity to the pictorial record. Included in the compositions of Shaker paintings and important as formal elements, words also supplemented images with relevant detail. Instruments used words in the interests of precision and specificity. Words connected images with particular visionary events; words located images in relationship to particular heavenly gift-givers and earthly recipients. Texts used in conjunction with images helped to ensure the "correct" context for the image and thus the "correct" interpretation of the image on the part of the novice and/or first-time beholder.

The mandate to record highlighted the tension between gift and order in New Era spirituality. Gift images, as visions, as gifts, were charismatic experiences, visible presents direct from the heavenly sphere. Gift images, as records, as documents, introduced ritual, structure, order into charismatic experience. The drawings and paintings thus presented a challenge to the Shaker church (because the pictures approximated forbidden forms and because they suggested their own equation with free charism) while they simultaneously participated in an ordering process. Because visionary, the paintings were charismatic; because concrete, they lent themselves to regulation and control.

Part II

VISION, IMAGE, AND SPACE

Four

✸ *Ethics and Aesthetics*

IN HEAVEN'S LIKENESS

Part I of this book defines the crisis among third generation Shakers as, fundamentally, a crisis of vision. Part I further suggests that, because of the distinctively visual character of paintings and drawings, gift images offered a particularly inventive and literal response to such a crisis. Parts II and III describe and analyze the content of the instruments' images in relationship to the visual and visionary needs of mid-nineteenth-century Shakerism. What did these pictures help the third generation to see? What kinds of vision(s) did the images embody? To what ends?

For Shakers in the 1830s and 1840s, and especially for younger adherents, the person of Ann Lee and the visionary experiences of the founder and her first generation converts seemed increasingly things of a different world or a distant past, belonging to the celestial sphere or to former times. In order to restore the discipline of the first days and to reestablish contact with the charismatic source of faith, models from another world (heaven) and another time (the past) had to be made available to the third generation. In visual images Shakers tapped a resource fundamentally suited to the simultaneous representation of different places and different times.[1] Although precise spatial and temporal discrimination often adheres to the creation of images, the image-maker need not necessarily distinguish visually between this place and that place, past and present, present and future. Rather, the image-maker can (and, in the case of the Shakers, does) show the beholder things that occurred in two different places or two different times as though in a single place or single time. Intensely concerned with both space and time, these drawings and paintings brought together heaven and earth, past and present, compressing and conflating these spatial and temporal poles.[2] The images provided the logical visual and tangible limit to a similar content expressed in other gift manifestations.

By arranging and rearranging configurations of space and time, Shaker religious pictures regulated behavior and restored relationships. In terms of social cosmology, or the literal and figurative orientation of space, the instruments' representations appealed to traditional understandings of Shaker organization by illustrating parallels between heavenly order and communal order, between a celestial pattern of institution and interaction and the primitive pattern of the early Shaker world (chapter 4). At the same time, developing in a somewhat different way the mutual involvement of images and spatial concerns, the instruments' pictures asserted renewed contact with the divine by depicting the convergence of heavenly and earthly spheres and by demonstrating movement between the spheres (chapter 5). In terms of sacred chronology, or the literal and figurative manipulation of time, gift images temporally located the mid-century community in relationship to the Shaker salvation story by creating a history and a genealogy for the third generation (chapter 6). Finally, and perhaps most importantly, the images conflated third generation experience and first generation experience, present and past, by restoring the visible presence of Mother Ann to the Shaker community and suggesting an atemporal dimension in the midst of the temporal sphere (chapter 7). By composing images which represented the contraction of spaces and the concurrence of times, Shaker instruments fashioned pictures which responded directly to the deepest spiritual concerns of Mother's Work.

In March 1843, according to Believers at New Lebanon, the spirits of Adam and Eve presented to them a painted map or plan of the "Holy City" (Pl. I). The sacred metropolis, the New Jerusalem generally "perceivable only by the eye of faith," thus became visible to the natural eye.[3] A hand-scripted book, an index keyed to numbers on the map's surface, accompanied this gift image, providing clues to its contents. Moving from the border of the image toward the center, the instrument directed the eye of the beholder along rivers engendered by the river of life, through an outer circular wall enclosing the Holy City and its suburbs, across the square wall of the City proper, and subsequently the circular wall of the "Great Temple" precinct, to the square wall of the Great Temple itself. The horizontal and vertical axes of the image represented gold-paved streets with the river of life flowing in a straight channel through the center of the vertical axis. Although the divine gift-giver had assigned variant meanings to the same colors in different portions of the map, the use of color in the image, the instrument explained, generally signified morally and spiritually good, or less frequently, evil qualities (e.g., wisdom, love, comfort, charity, peace or tribulation, darkness, confusion).[4] The painting measured 31 inches by 24 and 3/4 inches. The instrument fastened it, top and bottom, to wooden dowels and designated the top of the image East and the bottom West.[5] Unlike other gift images Shakers intended this Holy City, distinguished by its status as "map," to be hung for display.[6]

As the ones essentially responsible for humanity's fall from grace, it was especially appropriate that Adam and Eve be included among the instigators of restoration.[7] What was even more appropriate, Enos, the son of Seth, accompanied his grandparents. A third generation representative of the first dispensation of God's grace addressed the third generation of the fourth and final dispensation.[8] The ministry at New Lebanon responded immediately and publicly to the appearance of Adam, Eve, and Enos and to their revelation of the Holy City. A letter from the parent ministry to the Harvard ministry, dated 22 March 1843, described the visit of the first man and woman in relationship to commitment and purification.

> Adam and Eve, and Enos the son of Seth, are now visiting among us; and they are able to tell us some things which are very interesting. They appear to consider it a great privilege to come and visit the children of Blessed Mother Ann on the Earth, who are travelling out of the fall. They speak very encouraging to us; they say if we always abide faithful, we shall be more bright and glorious than they would ever have been, even if they had never fallen.
>
> Enos tells us that there is a great distinction between those who have faithfully borne the cross, and conquered their evil natures whil [*sic*] here in time, and those who do the work in the spiritual world. He says that the former look so much mor [*sic*] bright and glorious than all others, that he can distinguish them thereby, wherever he sees them in the Heavens.[9]

According to the instrument of the Holy City painting, Adam and Eve mapped out the ordered spiritual life to which all Shaker society should aspire. The map itself visually exhorted Believers to "bear the cross" and to "conquer their evil natures while here in time." Significantly, the moral content of the map depended not only on its status as divine gift, but also on its ordered composition, on the shapes of its principal figures, and on the correspondence or likeness it suggested between earthly and heavenly spaces.

The image of the Holy City held a particular meaning for its recipients at New Lebanon. For years Shakers had adapted to their own experience and situation biblical descriptions of the New Jerusalem from the book of Revelation.[10] As time passed, the Shaker conception of the New Jerusalem had become more and more concretely associated with New Lebanon itself.[11] The index of the 1843 image identified the Shaker Zion at New Lebanon as this "Holy City on earth," the perfect likeness of the celestial city in the highest heavens.[12]

> The plan of the City of the New Jersualem, or of the living God, called the *Holy City,* is a perfect patron [i.e., pattern] of the High City of the *Holy Selan* in the Heavens.
>
> The Holy Selan is right over this Holy City on earth. There is many cities between, along thro the Heavens.
>
> The Temple of the Living God and Eternal Mother Wisdom at the holy Selan, is right over this their temple in the Holy City on earth.
>
> This Holy City is three miles square now, and as the work of God increases, this

> city will also spread every way from the center till it comes to its final and perfect size, which is now marked out by a wall; the city will then be twelve miles square and include Hancock within its beautiful walls.[13]

In addition to its more emblematic function, color in this image expanded the analogy between the Shaker Holy City and the New Jerusalem of Christian scripture. Walls identified as jasper in Revelation, the instrument colored green; the streets of gold this image-maker painted bright yellow.[14]

A set of perceived correspondences between heavenly and earthly spheres grounded the central Shaker ideal of likeness. Late in the eighteenth century, first generation Shakers had arranged their lives, they believed, to conform to a heavenly pattern. According to Clarke Garrett, early Shakers organized their communities as "stage sets," "designed to serve as perpetual reminders to believers and visitors alike that heaven had come to earth in the ordered polity of the Shakers."[15] Guided by inhabitants of the spirit world, New Era ministry and instruments intended to retrieve the underlying celestial design, to elaborate upon it, and to mold the mid-nineteenth-century community accordingly. The New Era conception of primitive *order,* then, described the organization of life which most faithfully expressed likeness to the original celestial pattern.[16]

From the Shaker point of view, order was the visual and structural dimension most essential to likeness. Order was the primary attribute of likeness to God and to the celestial sphere. Order was "heaven's first law."[17] God's habitation was "a house of order, not of confusion."[18] God created the universe in order.

> I AM, the Eternal, is a God of perfect order, Harmony marks his way; in order and harmony did he create the heavens and the earth; in order and harmony did he place all the powers therein; in subjection to his eternal and unchangeable laws of order and harmony did he form the creatures thereof, and place them in order therein, and this order he has manifested in all his works to the creatures of his creation, so far as was necessary to hold them in that order wherein they were placed, so long as they walked in obedience thereto.[19]

The unregenerate chaos of the "world's people" and their "great and wicked cities" was the antithesis of heavenly order.[20] While Shakers recognized many sources of human disobedience, at the most basic level they believed that sexual union caused and characterized the disorder of the world. For, in heaven, "they neither marry nor are given in marriage" (Luke 20:35).[21] Marriage was a mode of living suitable only for those who had not yet entered the millennial age. The celibate United Society, in contrast, represented regenerate earthly order, a terrestrial manifestation of the heavenly original. Because of the fall, humans had to strive, through discipline and regulation, to restore divinely created order to the regenerate earthly sphere.[22]

Shakers used the word "order" in several principal ways. To order things or people was to arrange them in certain regular and regulated relationships to other things or people; to order carried the implication of ranking things or people physically or symbolically. "Order" as a noun was a synonym for "law" or "rule." In addition, to "enter into order" was to faithfully commit oneself to the Shaker life; three orders of Believers represented the basic units of religious and economic commitment to Shaker society. But no matter the particular sense in which a Shaker used the word, order always had a theological referent and grounding. Order described the heavenly pattern; order on earth was that which was organized according to, which *looked like,* the godhead and the celestial sphere.

"The Youth's Guide in Zion," a gift text written during Mother's Work, taught that "order is the creation of beauty."[23] Elsewhere, Shaker theologian Calvin Green declared that

> we may discover what constitutes the beauty and glory of the heavenly world; namely its regular order, perfect symetry of arrangement, proper proportions and mutual correspondent relation, and its beautious colors of which the colors in the natural creation, and its harmonious order when unobstructed are an emenation and representation.[24]

In defining heavenly order as the source of beauty itself, Shakers consciously linked the good with the beautiful and the beautiful with the good. Order had ethical as well as aesthetic implications. The community's moral disposition corresponded to its visual and structural disposition. The orientation of space in villages, buildings, individuals, and images affected the formation of character.

The Shaker community understood that its instruments had direct knowledge of heavenly order's appearance because, accompanied by spirits, the instruments had been to heaven and had seen its ordered splendors for themselves. The spirits showed the instruments visions of the heavenly sphere and described God's habitations in detail. But the image of heavenly order could also be seen in earthly order. The divinely created likeness had been distorted but not destroyed by the fall in the Garden of Eden, Shakers argued. The disorder which resulted from third generation disobedience and apostasy, if left unchecked, would obliterate further the image of God in the earthly Shaker Zion.[25] Yet the natural world was still "figurative" of the spiritual world and, as a "figure," the natural world resembled its prototype. So knowledge of visual order on earth gave Shakers insight into the appearance and workings of the spiritual world: "It was the will of God from the foundation of the world, to bring forth natural and outward things to typify and resemble, as a shadow, the inward and spiritual work of his hands."[26] The *visibility* of order was crucial. Believers insisted that "all the works of God throughout the visible creation, are evident displays of order and harmony."[27] During Mother's Work, Shakers sounded the call for the reestablishment of a communal order that would reflect and bear witness to this "evident display." The distinction between disorder and order needed to be drawn more visibly, needed to appear more as it had in the days of the early Shaker church.[28] A new generation of Shakers needed to know what primitive order and its heavenly model looked like.

The paintings of New Era instruments showed the way. As representations of heaven, heaven's inhabitants, and heavenly attributes these images embodied heavenly order. Image-makers arranged and configured space to reflect the likeness between earthly order and celestial order. But Shaker religious pictures, like Shaker rituals, were implemental as well as expressive.[29] Precisely because the instruments patterned their images after heaven's order, their drawings and paintings served as visual exhortations to conform to order and its attending moral virtues. Visual information provided practical instruction about righteous behavior; Shaker images gave ethical norms a material contour. The instruments' drawings and paintings were concrete and visual representations of a pattern offered to Believers for emulation. As such, the images assumed a mediating quality. They made the heavenly design more accessible to members of the community. They reiterated, in forms available for meditation and edification, the values of the heavenly sphere. Individuals could *see* and *touch* the patterns deemed most appropriate for their lives.

The value of this positive and prescriptive sort of patterning in the Shaker community is underscored by the fact that gift images only rarely depicted earthly disorder. One significant exception to this rule represented the way New Era Believers experienced disorder in their communities.[30] The composition of this image forced a contrast between the unregenerate chaos of doubt and disbelief and the heavenly design offered to Shakers for emulation. In this painting, the instrument depicted birds of "Discord" and self-righteousness attacking the roots of the "Tree of true union." Simultaneously, serpents and birds representing contention, hatred, strife, and "pick flaws" threatened further destruction. Confusion radiated from an off-center ink blot. The orientation of the text with respect to the image denied the viewer a single vantage point from which to make ordered sense of the activity depicted. The text of the book in which the image appeared made it clear that the judgments of God would be visited upon the disobedient. Chaos did not represent the pattern of heaven. Chaos would never be the pattern for appropriate Shaker behavior.

The Shaker idea of likeness depended upon the notion of visual and structural similarity to the celestial pattern. The Shaker community was like heaven. During the New Era, a favored designation for the Shaker society at large and for New Lebanon in particular was "the Zion of my [i.e., God's] likeness on earth."[31] The Holy City map, then, provided a "perfect pattern" of geographical and architectural correspondence, a mediating grid of likenesses which, according to Shaker conceptualizations, spatially and morally aligned the New Jerusalem on earth with the dwelling place of the godhead in the highest heavens. The plan of the Holy City was indeed a plan of New Lebanon—but it was the spiritual New Lebanon that was mapped out for the inhabitants of the earthly city. This image made visible to the natural eye correspondences otherwise visible only to the spiritual eye. Here every beholder could see the ordered celestial grid, the template for the ideal Shaker community.

Instruments and ministry intended gift images to be imitated. In a variation on earlier traditions of image-assisted empathic meditation,[32] one official Shaker writer insisted that individuals become more and more like what they look at,

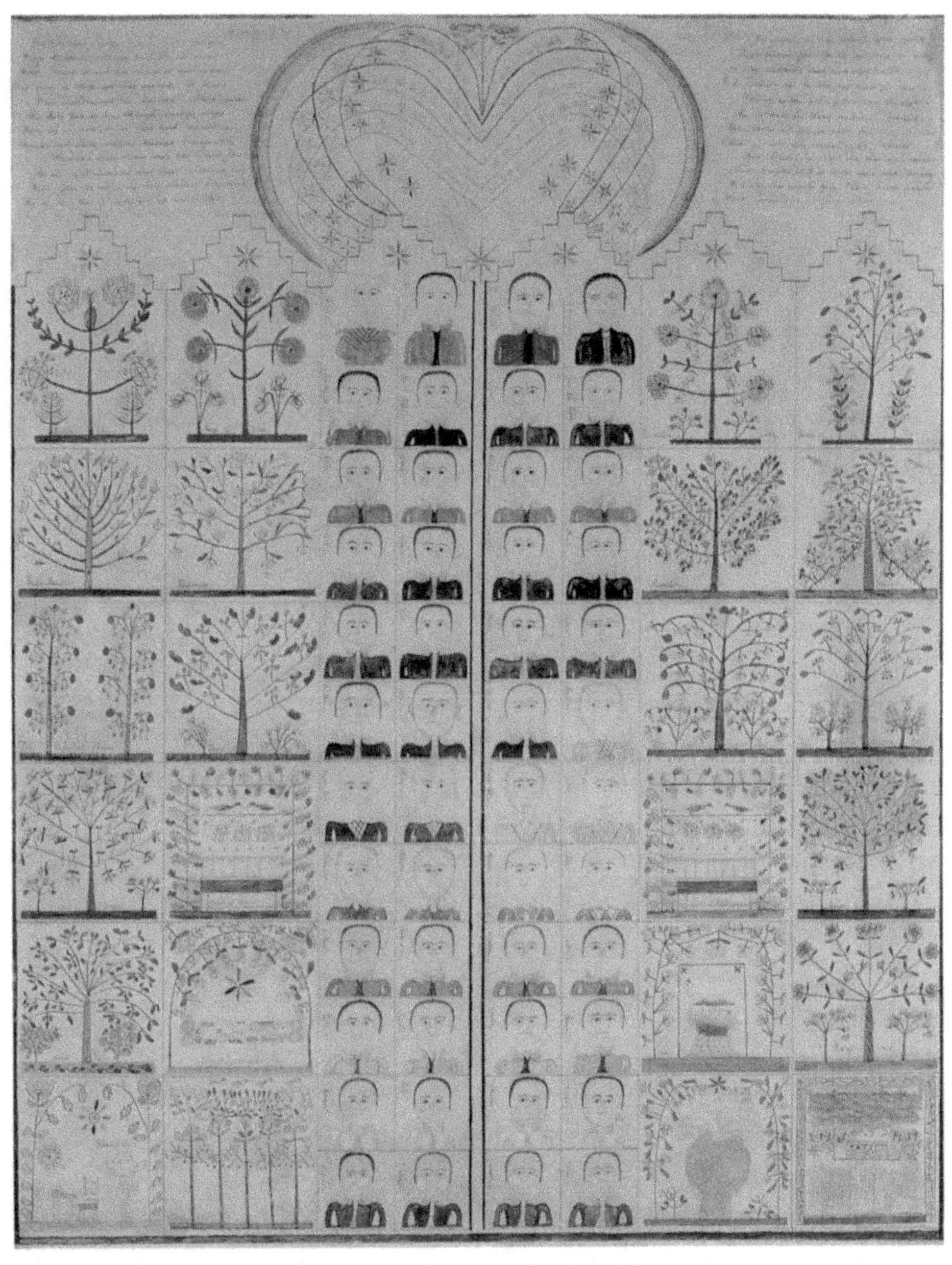

Pl. II. *An Emblem of the Heavenly Sphere,* watercolor and ink on paper, 1854, 23 3/4 inches by 18 5/8 inches, HSV.
Courtesy of Hancock Shaker Village, Pittsfield, Massachusetts

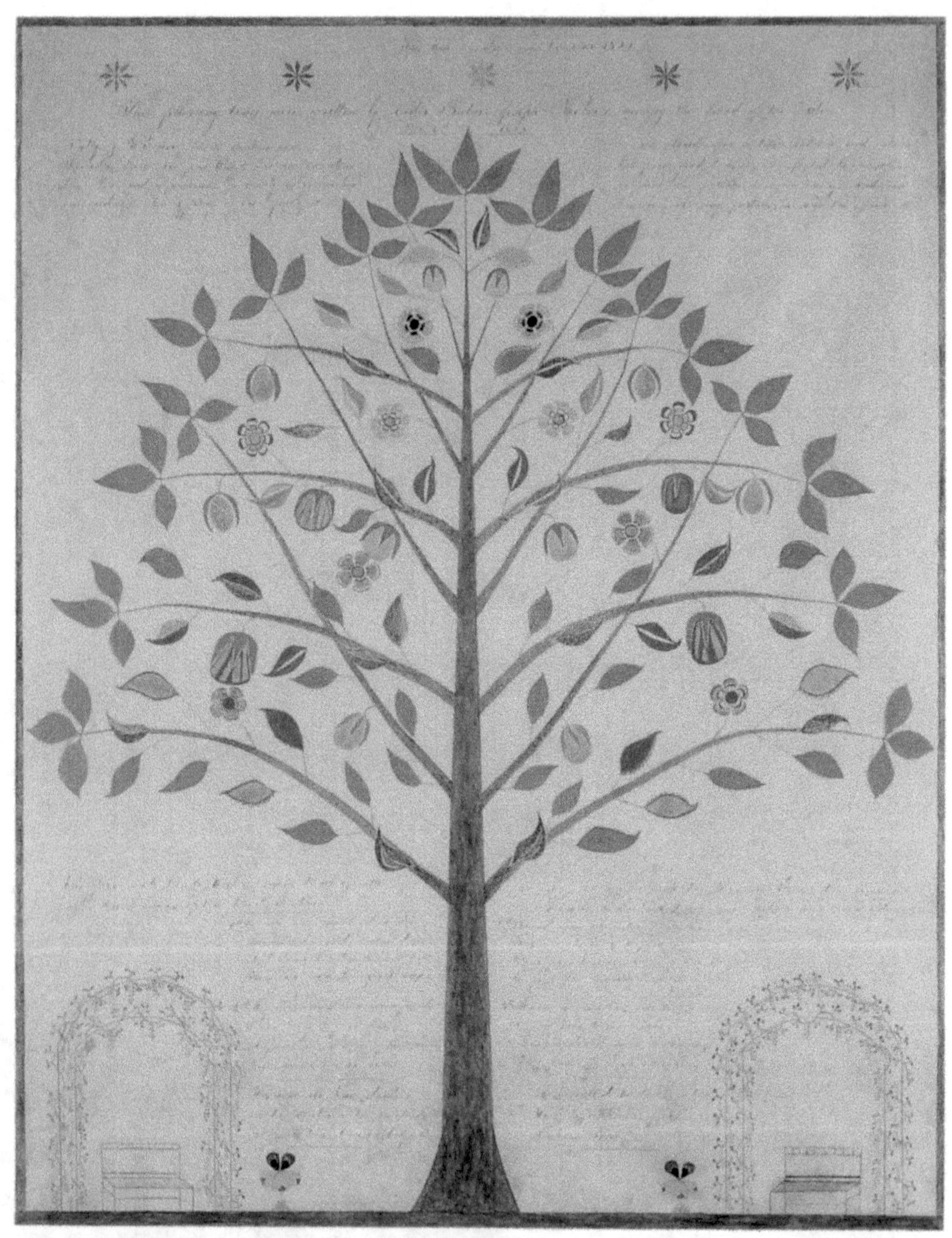

Pl. III. *The Gospel Union, fruit bearing Tree,* watercolor and ink on paper, 1855, 23 5/16 inches by 18 1/8 inches, HSV.
Courtesy of Hancock Shaker Village, Pittsfield, Massachusetts

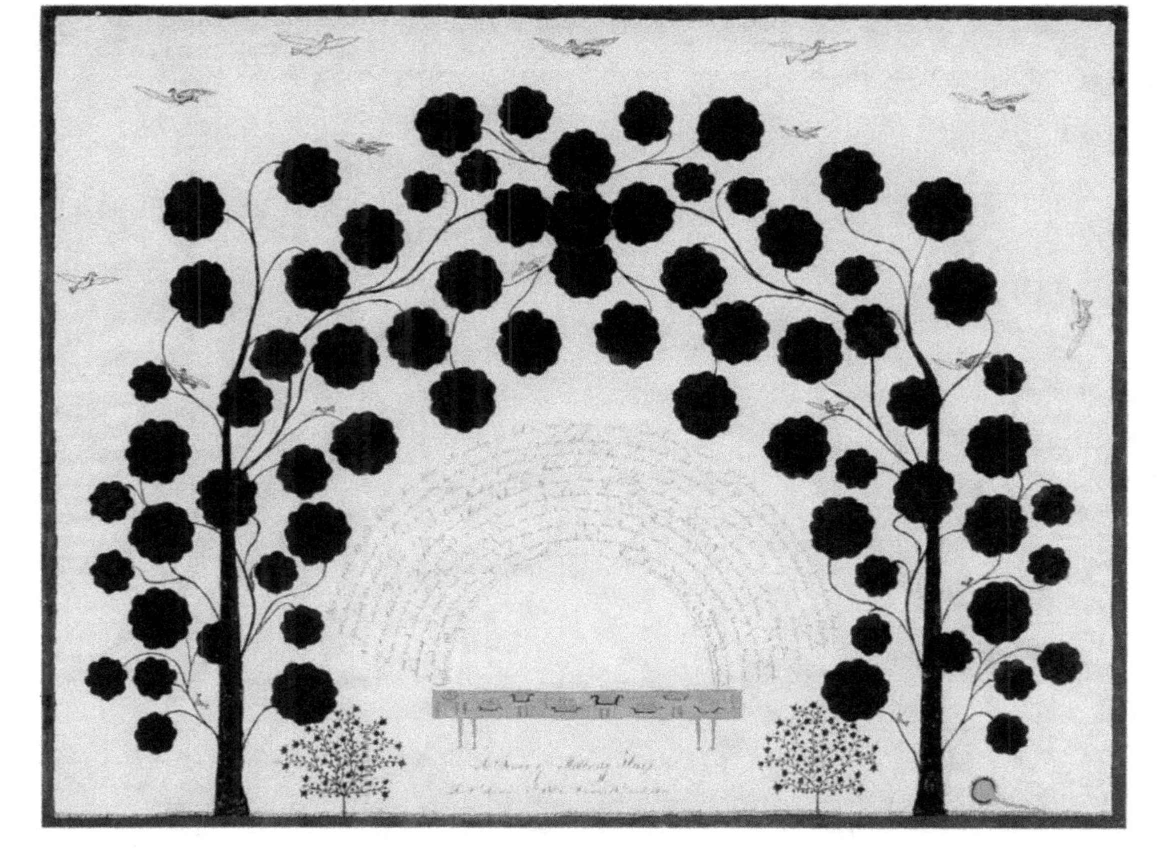

Pl. IV. Hannah Cohoon, *A Bower of Mulberry Trees,* watercolor or tempera and ink on paper, 13 September 1854, 18 1/8 inches by 23 1/16 inches, HSV.
Courtesy of Hancock Shaker Village, Pittsfield, Massachusetts

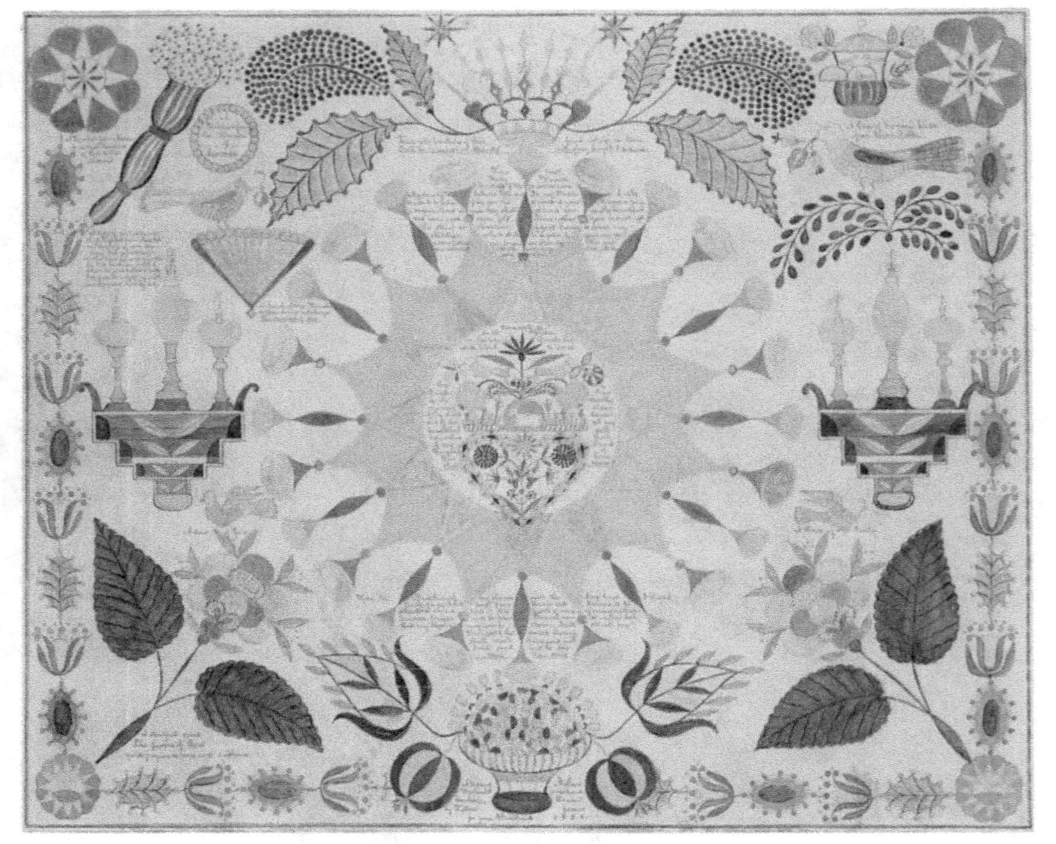

Pl. V. *A Type of Mother Hannah's Pockethandkerchief,* watercolor and ink on colored paper, 1851, 14 3/32 inches by 17 1/16 inches, HSV.
Courtesy of Hancock Shaker Village, Pittsfield, Massachusetts

more and more like the objects of their vision. "Every thing begets its likeness."[33] Further,

> it is evident to every reflecting mind that surrounding objects, have a much more lasting and powerful effect upon the young mind, than mere words or sounds.—Things out of order and things in order, are *realities* ; and they produce corresponding images or reflections in the mind.[34]

Visual lessons, Shakers believed, had a particularly powerful impact on youth and children, who so desperately needed to internalize the primitive pattern.

> Good order, and decency and cleanliness, have a powerful effect upon the minds of all people, and especially upon youth and children. For their minds are easily wrought upon, and they receive the impressions that surrounding objects are calculated to give, more readily than those whose minds are intently fixed on things more distant. Let children or youth enter a room where everything is out of order—where dirt abounds and all is *helter-skelter,* and they will at once take the impression, and show it by their unguarded language and behavior. They will have no fear of God before their eyes; because there is nothing of God or godliness visible in such a place. But let the same person enter, where all is order and neatness, and they will at once show the effect in an orderly demeanor,—a carefulness of speach and action; corresponding with the impressions, that the surrounding objects are calculated to inspire.[35]

New Era visionaries described in detail the visual and structural characteristics of heavenly order. Heaven was, for example, symmetrical, straight, and square. Mid-century Believers prized these three properties, in their visual environment and in their deportment, because, they maintained, each trait originated in the celestial design. The same adjectives that described constructed order, built or drawn, also described behavioral order.

> As God is a God of order and not of confusion; so all things that are in order, lead and direct the mind towards the fountain of order. . . . If we look at the opposite source, we shall find that the Devil is a Devil of *disorder,* confusion and uncleanness. . . . As the Devil is a crooked serpent, and has infused his serpentine nature into man; so man in nature delights or inclines to crooked ways, to disorderly ways, and to filthy ways, in all things. Man under this influence cannot bear strait lines, nor good order, nor any thing exactly square. His God must be a trinity—a trigonal, three sided Divinity; and all things around him must be out of joint, and as much as possible askew. A clean, simple strait and narrow way will not answer the purpose. . . .
>
> But the gospel is intended to bring man out of this crooked filthy nature; and when the good spirit takes its abode in man—when judgement is laid to the line and righteousness to the plummet, then the strait lines and square pillars are seen, and from the Eternal who is revealed in his order in the heavens, down to the least in the kingdom, is seen the same beautiful order; the clean, the pure and holy emenations

> from the source of all order and holiness. And this same order and cleanliness, is stamped on all things that are brought into subjection to this holy law.[36]

It was important for individuals, paths, and lines to be "straight," not only because straightness was aesthetically pleasing, but, most significantly, because straightness, as an attribute of likeness to God, was necessary to communal life and to personal salvation. If the instruments intended their images to lead the believing imagination along the morally correct path, the Holy City map of 1843 presented the beholder with a path that conformed to the symmetrical, straight, and square order of heaven. The regular geometry of this composition must have immediately impressed observers. The mid-century Shaker at New Lebanon would have known that the organization of the Holy City reflected the structure of the godhead.

As an attribute of heavenly order, visual symmetry grew from a pervasive theological symmetry.[37] Doctrinal and theological texts presented "Almighty God the Father" and "Holy Mother Wisdom" as parallel and theoretically equal aspects of deity. This divine pair constituted the "Eternal Two in One," "*two,* male and female, and from these twain proceed all goodness, purity, and holiness."[38] The Shaker idea of the feminine in the godhead originated much earlier in the sect's history. A hymn included in a collection of 1813 referred to "the Father and the Spirit" or "the Great Creator and the Holy Ghost" as parallel to "the Son and Daughter," implying that Holy Mother Wisdom evolved as a theological concept from the third person of the Christian trinity. David Benedict, an observer of the Shakers in the years prior to and including 1824, noted the peculiarity of "their notion of a Deity composed of male and female."[39] During Mother's Work, however, Holy Mother Wisdom was more emphatically personified than ever before.[40] Issues of divine gender construction engaged the Shaker community as official New Era manuscripts insisted on the equality and symmetry of the "Eternal Father" or "Almighty Power" and the "Eternal Mother Holy Wisdom."[41] "Even so it was, . . . when the earth was not, we as one did exist, the Divinity or Deity, consisting of male and female, Father and Mother."[42] The New Lebanon instruments of one series of gift drawings visually signified the parallelism of the godhead in these "Eternal Parents" by capping each composition in the series with an elevated and symmetrical representation of the "Wings of Holy Wisdom" and the "Wings of the Heavenly Father" (e.g., figs. 7 and 13).

Shakers applied their pervasive ideal of likeness even to the persons of the celestial hierarchy.[43] As Holy Mother Wisdom and Almighty God the Father were the "Eternal Two in One," so Ann Lee and Jesus (the "Heavenly Parents") were the "perfect likeness of the two in one."[44] In them, "heaven's true likeness did jointly appear."[45] The Christ spirit incorporated both "male and female principles of Deity, manifested [symmetrically] in the image and likeness of the Eternal Father and Mother."[46] From the symmetry of godhead and messiah, Shakers claimed, it followed that everything patterned after godhead and messiah in heaven and on earth ought to be symmetrical.

Gift images employed several means of suggesting this symmetry. The Holy City map, while not absolutely symmetrical, consisted largely of symmetrical arrangements of shapes. A substantial share of the image's visual impact derives from an insistent reiteration of symmetry, in the composition as a whole and in its parts. Other gift images embodied the notion of symmetry in different ways. For example, a set of visually organized gift notices received by Believers at New Lebanon on 25 January 1843 manifested theological symmetry not in terms of the shapes on the page, but through the carefully balanced organization of content in relationship to the two sides of the notices.[47] On one side of the cards, Mother Ann addressed her children. On the other side, Jesus inscribed a message. In order to emphasize the symmetrical relationship of celestial daughter and son, the instrument oriented the text on one side of the notices to read in one direction and on the other side to read in the opposite direction. Whenever one side was right side up the other side was upside down.[48] This convention isolated each of the two messages, the one from Mother Ann and the other from Jesus, and weighted equally each side of the card. Neither side gave any indication which message the divine gift-givers intended the recipient to read first. Neither side was clearly the front or the back. The gifts from Mother Ann and Jesus Christ were, in this regard, symmetrical.

Heaven's order provided a divine rationale for architectural, as well as graphic, symmetry among Shakers. In this celibate community the celestial pattern supported the practical necessity of dividing space in such a way as to create separate and equal areas for the two sexes. For example, community planners built dwellings and meeting houses with separate and symmetrical doorways and staircases for women and men. In the dwelling houses, a central hall generally divided the living quarters of male and female occupants. Men and women sat at identical but separate tables in the dining room. In Shaker meeting houses, women and men sat on opposite sides of the room. At Hancock, a "spiritual altar" located in the front of the meeting room marked a central axis dividing the two sexes during services.[49] Parallel structures in doors, windows, and interior design emphasized the symmetry and conceptual equality of men and women. Furthermore, physical movement in space (in Shaker liturgy and dance) reiterated architectural and graphic constructions of space.

If symmetry characterized the arrangement of shapes in the Holy City map, orthogonal organization of space, or "squareness," also arrested the beholder's gaze. Squareness on earth resembled the relationship of the heavenly Son and Daughter to the eternal Father and Mother. In this context of heavenly hierarchy, "square" or "four square" implied wholeness, stability, and authority. Like the celestial quaternity, the Shaker ministry was "four square" or four sided; all levels of Shaker leadership consisted of four members.[50] The meaning of the number four in relationship to earthly and heavenly hierarchies accounted not only for the square arrangement of much of the Holy City map, but also for the vigorously quadripartite presentation of its divisions and subdivisions.[51] Like symmetry, squareness in this image had practical as well as theological implications.

Translating a structural vocabulary into an expression of ethical standards, mid-century regulations called upon Believers to "square their lives by the unerring line of gospel truth,"[52] to "draw the lines squarely to the mark; squarely draw the lines and hold them there."[53] Ministry and instruments publicized an important New Era code of behavior as "that by which every soul must square their lives."[54] At a literal as well as figurative level the "squareness" of heavenly order influenced earthly geometry. Striving for resemblance to a sacred pattern, various laws and orders required Believers to construct and fence lots, fields, and gardens "in square form,"[55] to align roads, paths, fences, and buildings at right angles whenever possible, and to resist shortcuts along the diagonal.

> The haymakers, who are not otherwise employed, spend their leisure hours in beautifying the dooryard, by oblitterating the old disorderly cross paths, and making new straight and orderly paths for our feet to walk in. There is a deep interest felt in this matter which is accomplishing much good in casting out a lazy care-for-nothing sense . . .
>
> The family take much pains to make square turns at the angles of the paths, instead of cutting cross the corners.[56]

With so much emphasis on symmetry and squareness, straightness constituted a logical third visual attribute of heavenly order.[57] Adapting in a literal sense a Judeo-Christian figure for moral uprightness, ministry and instruments required that Believers sit, stand, and lie "straight." Celestial messages mandated correct posture during preparation for worship: "you are to sit in one or two straight rows, erect in your chairs, with your hands folded in your laps; no tilting back, nor sitting with your legs crossed."[58] Rather than relaxing the code in the relative privacy of sleeping quarters, the 1845 Millennial Laws stipulated that "all should retire to rest in the fear of God . . . and lie strait."[59] An excerpt from an account of an exemplary death, included in a Shaker publication "for the benefit of youth," indicated the extent to which Shakers read "straight" as "good":

> A minute or two before her breath left her body, she [Polly Lawrence] observed one of her gown sleeves was twisted. Taking her other hand, and straightening it [the gown sleeve], she said, "everything must become straight both in spiritual and temporal things."[60]

Visible order, even at the moment of death, required watchful attention.

Over and over again, instruments of gift images patterned their compositions after attributes of order suggestive of the heavenly original. Like the colleague who produced the Holy City map, the instrument of *An Emblem of the Heavenly Sphere* (Pl. II) presented the beholder with a hierarchy of spaces in vertical and horizontal registers. Clearly marked boundaries, containing and ordering each section, compartmentalized and defined these spaces. This individual framing device focused the beholder's vision on the discrete units of the painting.[61] The observer, then, had to scrutinize each separate compartment in order to reassemble and understand the whole. In this highly structured configuration, the instrument represented heavenly order as a mirror arrangement of stacked square units formed by the intersection of numerous straight lines. What was true of the organization of the Holy City map and of *Emblem* was true of the arrangement of form in *A Gift from Mother Ann to the Elders at the North Family* (fig. 14) as well. Here also the instrument imagined her drawing as a symmetrical pattern of spaces, images, parallel lines, colors, and text. These gift paintings, and others like them, thus embodied key values, values that Believers should imitate in the ordering of their personal and communal lives.

Symmetrical arrangement, squareness, and straightness were not the only visual indicators of resemblance to the heavenly sphere and thus of moral virtue. The dominant formal features of the Holy City map focused attention not on squares alone but on a series of circles encompassing squares. Here the instrument's use of the circle appealed directly to a divine prototype; heaven itself was circular. The shape of the celestial regions signified spiritual union and harmony. In 1837 Ellyette Gibbs, one of the first instruments of Mother's Work, described the beauty of heaven as "a perfect circle."[62] Like its celestial counterpart, the Shaker New Jerusalem was the "round city."[63] In the frequency of references to the heavenly *sphere,* Shakers commonly acknowledged the celestial geometry. Furthermore, while the actual landscape inhabited by American Shakers was not literally circular, Believers imagined even their earthly Zion as a circle precisely because it contained the image or likeness of the heavenly habitation.

The circular organization of the Shaker universe promoted orientation with respect to the center.[64] In fact, the idea of likeness itself was oriented with respect to the center. Closer approximation to the image and likeness of God accompanied closer proximity to the center of the earthly Zion, the Shaker society at New Lebanon.[65] "The wisdom of God in establishing a Church on earth, or center of union, for all others to gather and look to for a pattern, is plain and clear to every rational and observing mind."[66] Shakers from other communities made pilgrimages to "Zion's Centre" at New Lebanon and theoretically patterned both their behavior and their visual and symbolic environments after New Lebanon's likeness.[67] If New Lebanon as a community inspired imitation, the Church Family at New Lebanon's spiritual center was, of all earthly models, the most appropriate pattern for mid-century Believers. "Here must the laws of Zion first be revealed, here must the first increase be found; here is where all souls look for example; and here must the pattern be set."[68]

Like the Shaker universe, the map of the Holy City was oriented with respect to the center. The instrument directed the beholder's attention to this fact by beginning the sequential numbering of sections of the drawing at the center with the number one and working outward. The concentric circular organization of the image suggested the flow of traffic away from and toward the center. This compositional movement represented the extension of grace outward from the heart of the temple and the travel of souls inward toward the seat of deity. Believers accomplished the patterning of their lives and their communities after the celestial template by practicing the twelve Christian virtues inscribed within the twelve gates of the Holy City. In order to gain salvation, aspirants had to pass through these twelve ethical portals and, ultimately, approach the central holy of holies.[69]

According to the numbered key, the meeting house at the conceptual core of the earthly New Lebanon coincided with the "Temple of the Living God and Eternal Wisdom" pictured at the center of the spiritual Holy City which, in turn, corresponded with the Thrones of Almighty Power and Wisdom in the highest heavens. Divinity seated in the spiritual temple reinforced and reiterated the authority of the parent ministry who inhabited parallel terrestrial space on the second floor of the New Lebanon meeting house. The instrument provided exact measurements from celestial and terrestrial centers in order to help Believers locate the heavenly city in relationship to their own space.[70] The construction of the Holy City map as a series of apertures issuing from and converging upon the center illustrated the Era's renewed insistence upon authority. The hierarchy of the center, depicted in this case by the instrument of the Holy City map, provided celestial rationale for the exercise of power.[71] The instrument further underscored the actual correspondence between the Holy City and the earthly community by duplicating in the image such essential sacred geographical landmarks as the holy feastground.

Beginning at New Lebanon in 1842, instruments had revealed feastgrounds or holy "mountains" and had instructed that consecrated hands prepare the sites for ritual activity.[72] During the height of Mother's Work, the feast days, along with the Work of Judgment in December and early January, were among the most sacred celebrations of the Shaker liturgical year. A fundamental ritual of New Era piety, Holy Wisdom's Passover annually required significant attention and labor. Each May and September New Era Believers at New Lebanon and elsewhere marched en masse up their respective holy mountains to observe, in spiritually extravagant and spectacular fashion, the Passover of Holy Wisdom. This unusual ritual involved elaborate preparation and the reception of numerous spiritual gifts, including (according to the instruments' descriptions) brightly colored and intricately embroidered spiritual clothing intended to be worn over Shakers' own earthly dress. On the way to the feastground, the company paused at least once, at a specifically designated and sometimes named location, to rest and to receive additional spiritual gifts, before proceeding to the summit. Once they arrived at the feastground, a site Shakers believed had been divinely revealed to them, their ritual essentially created a structure for the reception and distribution of spiritual luxuries (including such articles as jewelry decorated with the images of Mother Ann and Jesus), for visitation by a variety of spirits from different times and places, and, ultimately, for the celebration of a spiritual feast with strong sacramental overtones.[73] Contemporary accounts indicate that the feast itself was strictly spiritual:

> there shall neither be food, nor drink of any kind, taken upon the holy ground, upon my feast day: but if any need other water than that which I have placed here for their souls to drink, they must go without the bounds of the holy ground to partake of it.[74]

That the feast was spiritual did not mean, however, that it might be received less than wholeheartedly. Rather,

> when ye partake of the heavenly Feast, which is now prepared for you, be not faint hearted, eat in faith, and sincerity of heart, swallow as really as if ye were partaking of natural food, do this in faith, and every one who does, they will receive a blessing that will be lasting.[75]

Much of the spring and summer of 1842 and continuing into the spring of 1843, Shakers at New Lebanon spent preparing the feastground: clearing the land, carving and erecting the Sacred Stone or Fountain Stone with "the word of the Lord," marking out the Fountain itself ("a holy Fountain of the waters of everlasting life") with cedar posts, fencing the meeting ground, and planting "a row of beautiful forest trees" just inside the fence and also along the "highway leading to this sacred ground."[76] In May of 1841, instrument Philemon Stewart testified that the *Sacred Roll and Book* had been revealed to him on the Holy Mount, the New Lebanon feastground.

Returning to the image, on the painting of the Holy City, the instrument located the feastgrounds along the vertical axis in the upper portion of the image, just inside the largest circumscribed square, at a measured distance from the central temple of the eternal Mother and Father. The center of the feastgrounds on the map, as well as the ritual focal point of the earthly site, Shakers called the Fountain of the Lord or the Fountain of the Holy Waters of Life. The painting's vertical axis represented the River of Life, flowing, according to the instrument's specifications, both east and west from the fountain. In both image and text the instrument indicated that this river formed a straight channel down the middle of a gold-paved street, lined on either side by trees of life. From the Holy Fountain, divine law and order would go out "to all the nations of the earth."[77]

With heaven made accessible to earth through a hierarchy of likeness, the distance separating the New Era community from the primitive pattern of early Shakerism seemed less significant. More accurately, since Believers understood that primitive pattern itself to have been modeled on heavenly order, the New Era community could more closely approximate primitive order by reference to the same celestial pattern. In other words, if early primitive order could be equated with heavenly order and New Era order could be equated with heavenly order, then the third generation community actually resembled the first generation community. Minimizing the distance between heaven and earth by constructing a hierarchy of parallel and analogous spaces, the concept of likeness embodied in the Holy City map reiterated and reinforced the community's relationship to heaven, the source of charismatic power and the current habitation of deceased Shaker forebears.[78] Because the concept of likeness involved ethical as well as aesthetic and theological obligations, it suggested a means for vigorously regulating behavior while it anchored a dislocated generation more securely within the Shaker universe.

The Shaker ideal of resemblance was multifaceted. Not only did shapes and their organization bind Believers to the heavenly pattern, but the skillful use of metaphorical constructions produced fruitful comparisons between heaven and earth. A more perfect likeness could be recovered through metaphor as well as through visual and compositional similarity. In a gift text of 1844, the spirit of Lucy Wright demonstrated the usefulness of metaphor in "drawing a picture" to create or reveal an instructive likeness.

> Supposing ye were called as overseers in the framing and building of an extensive edifice; say for instance like the Temple of Solomon, where the requirement was to bring all things to perfection; in order, beauty, and harmony; would it not be necessary for the master workmen and overseers to be united in their feelings, and in their goings, and all as one subject to one grand head and leading influence, in order to have the work move on prosperously and harmoniously? Truly says your Mother.
>
> But supposing one pulled one way; and another pulled another way, and some were working in direct oposition to those who were called as Master workmen, scattering their disaffected feelings among those who were merely called as individual workmen, to cause a division of feeling and sentiment among them. I say, says your Mother, look at the picture which I have drawn and reflect for a moment, and consider that ye are called as builders, and master builders in God's holy Temple, wherein naught but peace and harmony should reign.
>
> I have not spoken these things to accuse any one, but merely to draw the picture that ye might see the inconsistency of such things, and never, nay never become guilty of the like by practice.[79]

Wright's spiritual descendants, too, used metaphor to "draw a picture" in the mind of the beholder, to elicit internal visualization, to promote spiritual imagination. Image-making ultimately constituted a literal and external form of this sort of vivid "visual" description.

Many gift images incorporated specific metaphorical constructions intended to point out and to cultivate resemblances between heaven and the Shaker community or individual. These metaphorical constructions (e.g., the holy city, the heavenly mansion, the tree of life, the celestial garden, the narrow path) dominated the pictorial imagination and visual language of New Era Believers. Though some images intended to cultivate particular aspects of the threefold relationship between heaven, community, and individual, focusing perhaps most emphatically on two of the three levels (heaven and community or heaven and individual), Believers generally used these metaphorical constructions in ways that were relevant at all three levels. For example, although the Holy City image most vigorously promoted a comparison between heavenly order and the earthly community, the structure of this vision of the faithful society and its workings also suggested appropriate patterns of movement, personal appearance, and behavior for the occupants of the community. Images of celestial gardens and trees, on the other hand, often focused more deliberate attention on the individual dimension but the communal remained explicit as well. The juxtaposition of multiple levels of likeness added to the power of metaphorical constructions in the Shaker imagination.

In 1855 an instrument at Hancock produced an image of a celestial tree in a garden-like setting (Pl. III). According to the instrument, spirits called the tree the "Gospel Union, fruit bearing Tree." Like the metaphor of the holy city, the image of the heavenly tree connected three essential levels of Shaker experience. First, this tree represented the likeness of the celestial tree, that "great union tree, that spreads its branches continually before the throne of God."[80] In her painting of the gospel union tree, the instrument intended to suggest the celestial tree of life with twelve kinds of fruit described in Revelation 22:2.[81] She underscored this linkage by referring in the inscription to an assembly of the "four and 20 Elders" who sat around the throne of the most high in the biblical text. As with the holy city, a cosmic original embodied heavenly virtue and formed the basis for imitation.[82] Second, the tree also represented the earthly tree of Shaker community.[83] Mid-century Shakers in each society believed that such a tree grew in fertile spiritual soil at the center of their place of worship.[84] According to the instrument, the gospel union fruit-bearing tree flourished in the meeting room of the Church Family at Hancock.[85] This communal tree and others like it, planted among Believers by some divine being (e.g., Almighty Power, Holy Wisdom, Mother Ann) would grow as members of the United Society increased in degree of commitment and in numbers, until one day its branches would cover "the whole earth, and all Nations . . . [would gather] under its shaddow. Its fruit was for food, and its leaves were for the healing of the Nations."[86]

In the Shaker symbol system, trees, like circles, represented spiritual union and harmony. The relationship of branches to trunk and roots simultaneously modeled the appropriate subordination of the parts to the whole. So that, thirdly, the *celestial tree* growing near God's throne, as a pattern for the *communal tree* of Ann Lee's gospel on earth, also represented the *individual Believer* who, according to the text inscribed on the *Gospel Union fruit bearing Tree,* could effect changes in the appearance of the tree by his or her behavior: "it increases in beauty as ye increase in goodness." When an instrument depicted trees, fruits, flowers, and neatly fenced plots, the Shaker beholder understood this iconography in the context of a religious aesthetic urging faithful individuals as well as communities to grow as beautiful plants in the divine garden. The instruments' flowers, for example, were "emblematical" of heavenly "flowers," of faithful individuals, cultivated by God (figs. 2, 14, 22 and Pl. II). Such spectacular "blossoms" manifested the spiritual appearance of these righteous Shakers.[87] Elsewhere, some "words" sent to Jonathan Wood indicated even more clearly the relationship between individual Believers and heavenly trees.

> Lo I behold saith Wisdom, on the Holy Mount of the Most High, in the Temple of my likeness on earth, a beautiful Tree, bending down with precious fruit. This Tree was planted by the hand of God, to be an ornament in his Zion, from whence the inhabitants thereof could gather support and nourishment; and truly it is beautiful: it budeth and blossometh with innocence, and bringeth forth the fruit of purity and holiness: and the light thereof shedeth abroad as the bright rays of the Sun.

> And now I will pour upon this flourishing tree, an unbounded blessing, that the branches may spread far and wide, and gather from the four winds of the earth, people that will come and resort under its pleasant shade, that the fire of the Lord's wrath may not burn them up, in the day of his most furious judgements upon the wicked. And now my beloved child *Jere an,* who is the Tree of which I have been speaking? Is it thy self?—Verily I say it is.[88]

Although New Era regulations did not explicitly prohibit images of people, most instruments chose not to depict the human form, in a strictly literal sense at any rate. Yet, by visual and structural analogy, the *Gospel Union fruit bearing Tree,* for example, promoted the identification of the believing individual with the image depicted. While not literally representing the human figure, the verticality and bilateral symmetry of the tree implied its equation with the verticality and bilateral symmetry of the human body. Even though Shaker instruments relatively seldom painted images of actual people, then, they often *re-presented* people in their pictures. Apparently nonanthropomorphic images of trees were in fact anthropomorphic images of faithful Shaker individuals, metaphorical representations of the human figure, understood in relationship to similar communal and celestial configurations.[89]

In the collection of gift messages called Polly Collins' Book, both pictures and words richly integrate the celestial garden metaphor (see fig. 15, for example).[90] The spiritual parent who wrote one entry, "A letter from Mother Lucy to Polly Collins, March 6, 1841," described the virtuous Believer in terms of this fertile metaphor.

> O dear child, . . . if you will keep a godly fear, I will help you, and you shall be Mother's child in very deed, and bear the marks of gospel truth. And bring forth good fruit, which when fully ripe will make you shine as one of Mother's choice. . . .
>
> Child, you must be faithful to support the blessed gifts of God, they will help you thro all danger and give your spirit power to be a lovely flower in Mother's lovely garden.[91]

The instrument of Polly Collins' Book, however, neither connected particular images to particular texts nor used the short descriptive captions common in many gift images to explicate her pictures. Image and text in the book share garden subject matter but they represent two different conceptually parallel modes of rendering that visionary iconography on paper. Of the six full page paintings in Polly Collins' manuscript book, only one included any accompanying or identifying text at all. All six paintings appealed to beholders steeped in Shaker use of celestial garden imagery, to those who knew implicitly that the pictures, like the texts, admonished Believers to grow and bear fruit in God's garden.

The heavenly tree metaphor, by demonstrating relationships of likeness, thus connected the cosmic, the communal, and the individual dimensions of Shaker experience. The image exhorted individual and communal "trees" to increase in beauty and size by increasing in moral goodness, ever more closely approximating, in both appearance and behavior, the heavenly prototype. Individual Believers aspired to be the beautiful flowers and fruits growing on the celestial tree, emblems of virtue in heaven. Be fruitful, the spirits exhorted, and you will look like the living ornaments that embellish the celestial sphere. Be fruitful and you will find protection and salvation as well as beauty.[92]

In a metaphorical as well as in a compositional sense, then, a mid-century Shaker painting of a city, a garden, or a tree could represent a pattern for righteous behavior. Drawn or painted images could be patterns for Believers because visionary instruments patterned the images after the celestial original. If the images could re-present the original, however, so could Believers. Shakers based their idea of image on their own very specific sense of visual and ethical likeness to the object (or subject) represented. In a similar fashion, they claimed, the faithful life depended on visual and ethical likeness to a heavenly model, on imitation of the attributes and character of the celestial sphere and its divine inhabitants. Individuals shared with images the status of likeness. In this particular sense, then, Believers, like drawings and paintings, were images, pictures, "works of art." Individuals and paintings re-presented likenesses; individuals and paintings resembled spiritual originals. Like pictures, Shakers themselves were images, in this case, images of God, living emblems of heavenly virtues and attributes, likenesses of the eternal pair.[93]

The likeness of God that Shakers bore carried with it special responsibilities. In Shaker countenances, the world's people saw God face to face.[94] It would not do for Shakers to misrepresent God's image through their own inappropriate behavior. According to one book-length gift manuscript, the Eternal Father desired that all young Believers "be adorned" with the innocence and purity of Ann Lee and Jesus Christ,

> That ye may be their emblems unto man, that your very visage and deportment may be sufficient to convict and convert the hearts of men . . . when they behold the likeness of the Lamb of God and his image engraven upon your countenance and shining forth in all your conduct.
>
> Then will they be able to exclaim, "I have seen the Lord in his glory, in his anointed and chosen people . . . they bear no likeness of earthly and carnal things; for they are as the Angels of God in heaven. Therefore have I seen the Lord, face to face, in his people."[95]

With words such as these, deity summoned Believers themselves to manifest more fully their identity as emblems of likeness to, as images of, the heavenly sphere.

A painting of the holy city or the celestial tree bore God's image and likeness. The faithful Believer too bore God's image and likeness and was thus, like the painting, a suitable pattern for novices, for less committed Believers, and for the world's people to emulate. Shakers employed a terminology of likeness in relationship to people as well as images. "Likeness," "pattern," "emblem," "figure," "type": each could be used interchangeably; each suggested something that resembled something else in appearance or behavior, each could be used to refer to both persons and paintings. Early in the New Era, the prophet Daniel, speaking through an instrument, reminded New Lebanon Shakers that the inhabitants of heaven had called them to be "patterns of godliness, to the fallen race."[96] According to another instrument, the spirit of Father James praised New Era leader Rufus Bishop as a "true *Pattern* and *Guide*" for the third generation.[97] Later, in a heart cutout, God acknowledged Elder Ebenezer Bishop as a "saint of my likeness and an emblem of my purity." Drawings, too, fit within the category of emblems and likenesses. In fact, these terms numbered among the most common words chosen to describe drawn and painted images. The same heart cutout which addressed Ebenezer Bishop as a "likeness" and an "emblem" included miniature drawings of an anchor and a pillar, as "emblems" of Bishop's life of virtue.[98] Both Believers and images, then, were pictures: both could represent an instructive likeness.[99]

The potential usefulness of material forms of likeness (paintings as well as persons) grew as memories of early Shaker leaders and order faded. The introduction of large numbers of children into mid-century Shaker society as well as the deaths of the first born negatively influenced communal memory. In 1800, children under sixteen years of age constituted only 2.8 percent of the population of the eastern communities. In 1830, the proportion of children under fifteen had risen to 15.2 percent and those ages fifteen to twenty-nine to 26.7 percent. By 1860, children under sixteen constituted a full 26.4 percent of the Shaker population. In the New Lebanon Church Family, in particular, the proportion of children in 1855 rose as high as 30.2 percent.[100] As the numbers of children in the United Society increased and as it became clear that eventual apostasy was more likely among this youthful population, the shaping of children and youth in the Shaker way became a concern of extreme importance. By 1840 a shared mental image of appropriate likeness to the primitive pattern, and therefore to the celestial original, could no longer be assumed. The third generation of Believers required new mechanisms for internalizing the communal pattern. They needed to be shown the divine image in their communities and within themselves, needed to magnify this image by manipulating and molding their environments and their behavior, eschewing disorder and chaos, and manifesting heavenly order and harmony.

National concern about the character of youth in relationship to the social order surely reinforced the sense of urgency surrounding this issue among the Shakers.[101] In the 1830s and 40s Americans at large "came to believe that the republic's only chance for survival lay in the character of the rising generation."[102] Though the specific content of their complaints differed, Shakers and their worldly neighbors alike deplored the decline of morals among the youth. Though the specific content of their golden ages differed, Shakers and their worldly neighbors alike mourned the loss of an earlier, more virtuous era as they sought to reclaim that era by attending to the formation of character.

The equation of ethics and aesthetics permeated the broader culture as well as the Shaker community. In the popular advice manuals of the period, "appearances revealed character" and "all aspects of manner and appearance were visible outward signs of inner moral qualities."[103] The similarity between American advice manuals and Shaker codes of behavior is striking; the seemingly excessive and obsessive Shaker restrictions about body posture, etc., appear less so by comparison with similarly restrictive codes of behavior in the broader culture. According to the constellation of ideas which Karen Halttunen labels the "sentimental typology of conduct," "every aspect of social behavior should transparently display the contents of the heart."[104] Not only did dress, cleanliness, etc., indicate inner character but a common "moral language of physiognomy" asserted that an individual's face bore the imprint, visible and intelligible to anyone who understood its vocabulary, of his or her character. The righteous person cultivated physical beauty through self-improvement rather than the use of cosmetics.[105] Though the larger culture did not share the specific ideal of likeness which grounded Shaker perceptions of people and images, the person, as a moral "composition," was indeed a "work of art" in the larger culture as well as in the Shaker community. In yet another sense, Shaker perceptions distilled and focused similar understandings outside the Shaker community. Shakers believed that a person becomes more and more like what he or she looks at, more and more like the objects of his or her vision. Similarly, according to what Halttunen calls "the concept of moral influence," middle class Americans held that the disposition of a person's dress and physical carriage affected the moral disposition of those with whom he or she associated.[106] Further, the writings and architectural plans of the immensely popular mid-nineteenth-century landscape architect A. J. Downing demonstrated his firm conviction that constructed environments influenced moral behavior.

An ideology of likeness, expanded from the practice of the primitive Shaker church, informed the production and reception of images in the mid-nineteenth-century Shaker community. Among earlier Shakers the community itself was pattern, the community itself represented the coming together of heaven and earth. During Mother's Work paintings and drawings as well as constructed environments made ideal relationships and appearances concrete and tangible. Images, and the conception of images as patterns, as emblems, likenesses, and guides, played an important part in New Era spirituality. By applying the same metaphors to individuals, to groups, and to heaven, by conflating personal, communal, and cosmic representations, Shaker instruments fostered a sense of connectedness, of the unity of regenerate creation. From the products of Shaker visionary imagination, the Believer gained a sense of participation in a divinely ordered universal aesthetic. In addition to metaphorical uses of likeness, gift images, in composition, reflected patterns of order and design understood to be based on the divine image. Visual representations encouraged Shakers to shape their lives according to certain pervasive patterns of valuation. The individual as emblem of virtue, as celestial flower or tree, was also the image or icon of God and God's cosmos. The righteous individual's behavior conformed to a design ordered by its likeness to God.

Gift images, then, represented the way individuals and communities *ought* to be. These images sought to educate, to inspire, to persuade.[107] If, indeed, individuals became more and more like what they looked at and if heaven's image and heaven's order could be represented on paper and in the built and structured environment, then visual images and the visual organization of the community participated in the formation of character. Further, if the person, too, was a work of art, then character formation became a matter of aesthetics. Virtue and appearance each informed the other. The more virtuous the person, the more beautiful the image. The more virtuous the person, the closer the likeness to God's order in the heavenly sphere. Believers should aspire to be "firm pillars" in the holy city, "living branches" on the celestial tree, and beautiful emblems of heaven.[108] As firm pillars, Shakers could demonstrate unshaken faith and steadfast support of the United Society; as living branches, they could become vital parts of a divine whole; as beautiful emblems, their splendid appearances could dazzle the less committed with the glorious truth of Ann Lee's gospel.

Five

⁂ *Image as Threshold of Heaven*

PASSING THROUGH PICTURES

Paintings like the *Holy City* and the *Gospel Union fruit bearing Tree* demonstrate the celestial-terrestrial hierarchy of analogous spaces underlying New Era social and cosmic geography. But the usefulness of the instruments' images in terms of spatial configurations extended even further than this. The rising generation of Shakers needed direct contact with the heavenly world as well as assurance of likeness to it; they needed first-person experience of the sacred as well as patterns for righteous behavior. Young Believers required, in other words, not just a conviction of resemblance but a mechanism of passage. So Shakers proclaimed, in 1837, that God had opened the doors and windows of heaven. In correspondence, in journals, in record books, Shaker scribes celebrated the divine initiative.

> When this wonderful work commenced and came into full operation, it seemed astho the very doors and windows of heaven were opened. And Divine gifts, heavenly visions, and holy manifestations abounded, with prophecies and Divine revelations from our Eternal Parents, together with our heavenly Parents in the New Creation. These were sent down in copious showers of solemn warnings, searching, reproof, kind instructions and heavenly blessings, with the visitations of holy Angels and justified spirits, together with a numerous variety of angelic songs, in such a wonderful manner, that it seemed as though Zion on Earth and Zion above, had become truly joined together.[1]

As images could represent the order and organization of the universe, they could also embody this more active spatial content. Hannah Cohoon's *Bower of Mulberry Trees* (Pl. IV) recorded the Hancock instrument's vision of the convergence of heaven and the earthly community. Cohoon's inclusion of the common Shaker long table rendered the depicted sacred landscape familiar to Believers and proposed that living Believers as well as spirits could inhabit this space. Shakers would have recognized the feast table as a visual allusion to the holy meals they shared biennially at the feastgrounds. Some records of these meetings at Hancock, in particular, describe a scene that, if not identical to the one Cohoon painted, was certainly much like it, accounting even for the doves circling overhead, the use of the "long table," and the sorts of spiritual food spread upon the table.[2] Shakers would have known this spiritual space and could have literally placed themselves in the natural space, in the actual constructed environment, that was figurative of it.

The image presented in this painting at first looks flat and static, apparently removed from the space of the beholder by the border. On closer examination, however, these are not the features which most convincingly characterize the contextual import of the image. Cohoon's painting looks flat and static because it disregards modulation of color, the play of light and shade on and around objects, as a way of representing volume. Instead, other means of suggesting three-dimensionality emerge. On its own terms, Cohoon's image is neither flat (in a strictly two-dimensional sense) nor static. On its own terms, this image is, in fact, about movement in space. Compositional elements ensure the clear communication of this content.

Securing in the process a sense of three-dimensional space, of travel or passage through space, Cohoon constructed her image as a series of at least four suggested planes (represented by the bower itself, the two small trees, the Shaker table, and the bow of text) parallel to the picture plane and receding into a distance signified by such visual cues. The picture's spatial organization relied, in part, upon perceptions that size diminishes with distance, that objects located higher up on the picture plane are farther away, and that distant objects are seen less clearly than objects nearby. Demonstrating, at the very least, an intuitive grasp of the first and second of these perceptual principles, Cohoon pushed the large bower forward and down, flush with the lower edge, just one small step beyond the viewer's space.[3] Her smaller feast table and bow of text she then located, according to scale and placement, in positions above the border and well behind the bower's foremost foliage. The progressively smaller arcs of bower and text receded from the picture plane, leading the eye back into the image as into a sacred vault or canopy. The outside border of Cohoon's *Bower of Mulberry Trees,* in fact, functioned as a window or aperture through which to look or pass. The bower itself, positioned visually just "behind" the border, reinforced this framing device and contributed to the expectation of movement into the image and back toward the table and its bow of text. The instrument's image anticipated transport; her visionary bower created for the beholder a psychic bridge between heaven and earth, a waymark at the interface between two worlds.

The spatial relationship of the text to the bower, the reiterative shape of the text (a "second" bower), and the delicate line of the calligraphy assured the viewer's visual passage through this living arch. According to the third perceptual principle suggested at the beginning of the preceding paragraph, more distant objects lack the clarity of definition enjoyed by foreground objects. The text in Cohoon's image embodied this third means of creating the illusion of space. Even before the calligraphy faded, its smaller size and less dense presentation required a closer viewing than did the bower. The beholder had to look more carefully at the text in order to read it, perhaps squinting as though to see something very distant. The text, then, functioned as an invitation to the third dimension by suggesting that the words occupied space inside or behind the bolder, more clearly defined bower.

Attentive use of the properties of color as well as the size and arrangement of shapes brought the bower out toward the edge of the composition and thrust the bowed text into more distant space under and behind the bower, acccentuating deity's invitation to move beneath the mulberry trees and into sacred space. The dark green and brown of the leaves and the tree trunks tied the bower to the similarly dark blue border in the foreground. The relative lightness of the yellow table differentiated celestial furniture from foreground elements, pushing the sacred feast into its own space farther back under the bower. Cohoon's composition invited Believers to step through the border and the bower until their progress was impeded by the Shaker table and they joined the feast in the spirit world.

Over and over again, the multiple aspects of Cohoon's painting reiterated themes of passage, movement, encounter between worlds. In terms of subject matter, interpretation depended upon the beholder's knowledge that Shakers used bowers as union motifs. Expanding on this customary understanding, the instrument placed the major visual emphasis in her painting at the point of contact between the two trees. The image then conducts the beholder's eye over its painted surface, back and forth across a central assembly of three horizontally arranged leaves and up and down through an almost identical assembly of three vertically arranged leaves. Directly above the resulting cruciform configuration, a heavenly dove optically weighted the vertical axis. The central constellation of five leaves, incidentally the only leaves in the picture actually contiguous with each other, then represented the union of horizontal and vertical, of heaven and earth. At the same time, this constellation alluded to the Shaker cross, a symbol of the sacrifices required of celibate Believers and of the cosmic victory that would ultimately be theirs.[4]

Communicating a principal content of terrestrial-celestial traffic, Cohoon's mulberry bower presented two simultaneous perspectives to the eye of the beholder: the front (or mortal) view and the aerial (or God's eye) view.[5] Thus the spectator concurrently enjoyed both natural and spiritual vision. The two small trees bearing the "fruit of Paradise," the large tree trunks, the table legs, and the text the beholder saw as from an earthly vantage point. The table top, the small yellow spring at the lower right, and perhaps the central leaf configuration, the beholder looked down on from above. Moreover, the spiritual doves that circled overhead, capable of looking down at the bower as well as out at the viewer, emphasized and validated this "God's eye" view. God had opened heaven's windows and invited those who could see to acknowledge their presence in celestial space. Interestingly, even the precise dimensions of the principal image in Cohoon's composition intensified the prospect of human passage. The instrument scaled the bower to the size of the average human head. While not the size of the full human figure, the bower nonetheless suggested consideration of human proportion thus identifying the intended users of the passageway. Further, the head-sized bower, a marker of sacred space, also indicated the sacrality of individuals who would pass under it. The bower was crown, perhaps halo, as well as border.

Finally, in the text that accompanied the mulberry bower, Cohoon narrated the visionary story of the image and its reception.[6] Here she described the activity of two esteemed and deceased Shaker elders as they entered the bower and feasted at the table. But, despite the text's insistence on the presence of these two elders and many other Shaker brethren as well, the instrument depicted no human figures.[7] Rather, the painting, like many other gift images, operated as a stage set, encouraging its spectators to people it themselves.[8] The beholder then became an actor on a sacred stage, in the divine story told by Hannah Cohoon's vision. The image provided the setting, the locale, in relationship to which the beholder might imagine, perform, contemplate appropriate action.[9] The absence of figures resulted in the inclusion of the spectator in represented heavenly space.[10]

So the *Bower of Mulberry Trees* created an encounter with and an invitation into another world. Through this triumphal canopy Believers might pass and in this living arch they might experience divine presence.[11] But passage required something of the beholder. Among New Era Believers, a bower signified willing submission to God's purposes. In order to form a bower, trees had to be bent but not broken. In order to enter the heavenly sphere, New Era Believers, the rising generation included, had to respond freely and faithfully to God and to God's representatives on earth: the Shaker ministry. The form of the bower, however, signified not only appropriate individual posture. For, as Cohoon indicated, again in the text, the bower stood "four square on the ground." This allusive comparison of the bower to the Shaker ministry and to the celestial quaternity, also commonly described as "four square," would not have escaped the contemporary beholder. The ministry and its celestial counterpart then constituted the sacred canopy, sheltering and defining the arena of holy activity. It is, in fact, likely that Cohoon intended her text to suggest that her bower was composed of four mulberry trees, though she actually depicted only the two foremost. The cruciform leaf configuration at the apex of the arbor, in its composition as four leaves meeting at a fifth central leaf, hints at this possible interpretation, and the painting's bowed inscription not only describes the bower as "four square," but also refers to the small yellow "spring" in the right foreground as "just beyond the square" formed by the mulberry bower. Perhaps it was sufficient simply to allude to the other two mulberry trees, since, from the mortal viewer's perspective, the forward two would have been more clearly visible anyway.[12]

Cohoon made explicit the correct response of Shakers to God and to the ministry by including in her painting's inscription a reference to II Samuel 5:25 and I Chronicles 14:14-15. Both biblical texts tell how a rustling in some mulberry trees informed David when to attack the Philistines. The divinely assured success of David's attack led to the spread of his fame throughout the nations. If New Era Believers were attentive to God's activity among them, the visionary picture suggested, if they would be faithful like David, then they too could defeat the enemies that beset them. Ultimately, the Shakers' spiritual progeny, like David's, would spread over the entire earth and the Millennial Church would emerge victorious. This divine promise the image repeated visually by alluding, in the shape of the bower and, even more explicitly, in the shape and organization of the text, to the rainbow which figures so prominently in another biblical story of covenant.[13]

Cohoon's image of the mulberry bower facilitated visual passage between earth and heaven. It thus represented most explicitly a theme (at least) implicit in all gift images: the concern of Believers with the borders between heaven and earth and between Shakers and the rest of the earth's population. If ordered spaces were significant, so were the thresholds that linked these spaces. Perhaps an earlier way of life might be retrieved, many reasoned, if heaven came nearer to Believers and the world moved farther away. Perhaps the rising generation would persevere if the spirits connected them with the heavenly sphere and separated them from the world. Gift images made visible these most significant boundaries in the Shaker universe and encouraged movement in one direction while arresting it in the other. Inclusion in sacred space assumed separation from the world.

When God opened the windows of heaven, Shakers began closing their meetings to the public. No longer did they permit non-Shakers to attend worship.[14] The Watervliet Shakers first received the divine message which inspired the closing of the gates.[15] According to this communication, God ordered the gates closed from the day before the Savior's birthday until the day after Mother Ann's birthday. While the gates at Watervliet initially remained shut from 24 December 1841 until 2 March 1842, other communities followed somewhat different calendars. Generally, New Lebanon Believers prohibited the public from attending meetings from 1842 until 1845.[16] Shakers at New Lebanon set up crosses in front of their meeting house and office to warn the unregenerate not to trespass on consecrated ground. The simultaneous dissolution and fortification of boundaries expressed in regulations such as the one regarding the closing of the gates may be seen as a primary goal of the era of Mother's Work. Shakers intended, thereby, to become less worldly and more otherworldly. The official correspondence of the New Lebanon ministry noted explicitly that the "closing of the gates" in 1842 had the dual purpose of keeping the world out and keeping Believers in.[17]

Shaker leaders, instruments, and longstanding members blamed increasing rates of apostasy on what they called "blending with the spirit of the world."[18] In 1845 Isaac Newton Youngs repeated a common refrain when he bemoaned the fact that

> peoples [*sic*] attention is greatly turned to earthly gain, improvements in arts, etc. Railroads, Telegraphs, —etc. etc. There is so much going now days in the world, that is inviting, and we have so much connection and dealing with the world, that it has a great effect upon Believers. It is all calculated to draw out of Zion, rather than to add to. It therefore produces a state of *trial,* rather than encouragement.[19]

Shakers continued to do business with "the world," continued their involvement in charitable acts toward those outside the community, continued to pray for the salvation of all people, but codes like the Holy Laws of Zion repeatedly admonished the faithful, "Think not that ye can keep the laws of Zion while blending with the forms and fashions of the children of the unclean!"[20] Shakers ought to be separate from the world as their "first Parents and Elders" had been separate.[21] The Shaker God, after all, was a God of "searching and separating power."[22]

During Mother's Work, instruments described the duties and roles of leaders in the United Society in terms consistent with the themes of boundaries and separation. The "office deacons" functioned as buffers between the church and the world. These deacons, also called trustees, lived in the office. Conceptually if not always actually, Believers situated this building in closest proximity to the margin between the community and the world. Shakers conducted all commerce with the world in and through the trustees' office. Like the parlor, which functioned within the American cult of domesticity as a literal and figurative transitional zone between the public street and the privacy of the home's inner sanctum, the trustee's office at least theoretically and symbolically restricted access to the communal habitat while it provided Shakers with a face to the world.[23] Shaker legal codes of the mid-nineteenth century restricted the amount of time trustees could spend in the world on Society business. And, when two or more male trustees rode out together, divine regulations required them to "eat at one tavern, and sleep in one bed; and when ye walk in the street, ye shall keep so close together, that there would not be room for a dog to run between you."[24]

In addition, Believers organized communal spaces in such a way as to minimize contact between outsiders and the "holiest" Shakers, the Church Family. The members of the ministry removed themselves even further from worldly contamination. They lived alone above the meeting house and ate and worked in separate areas provided for in community designs. According to Shakers, God appointed the ministry and elders "Watchmen on the Walls of Zion," calling these men and women to guard the spiritual gates to the New Jerusalem and to regulate access to (and from) the United Society.[25] Several rather schematic gift images, most apparently by the same hand, included depictions of the "Watchmen" on the "Walls of Zion." One instrument, in particular, constructed an entire, very large image around the central idea of "picturing" the walls for the beholder to see. Here, the instrument claimed, the walls were "composed" of the holy orders of God.[26] As the natural world was a figure of the spiritual world, natural boundaries were figures of spiritual boundaries. So Shakers marked the borders to their communities with care. Visitors commented that the excellence of Shaker roads, the beauty of their lawns and fences, and the extraordinary cleanliness of the whole made obvious the crossing between world and Society.[27] This fastidious concern for communal appearances had characterized Shakers during the earlier years of communal organization as well as during their mid-nineteenth-century revival. Garrett demonstrates that

> [Joseph] Meacham realized that the contrast between the severe simplicity of the Shaker communities and the haphazard arrangement of most villages in the New England back country would make a strong impression on visitors. When he visited Harvard in 1791 in order to prepare the believers for their gathering into gospel order, he told them that their fields and gardens should all be planted in straight rows because "this will be preaching to the world[,] for they admire the beautiful outward order of the people of God."[28]

As with the composition of communities, meticulous designation of boundaries characterized Shaker attitudes toward the composition of images. A painting is, in fact, quite literally a boundary, a limit, a wall at the edge of one's vision. The image-maker can create or suggest an illusion which dissipates the image's impact as limit but the act of image-making begins with this physical reality. The Shaker instruments who produced gift drawings and paintings gave almost all their designs strongly marked borders. Compositional devices, drawn or painted elements passing over or through these borders, for example, demonstrated that some boundaries could be crossed (fig. 30). Frequently gift images had several represented borders one inside another. In some cases, instruments composed an entire picture as a series of apertures and borders, inviting the viewer to enter, visual layer by visual layer, into the composition (figs. 13, 22, 28).

Shaker usage of a motif they called the "golden chain" substantiates the notion that members read as boundary phenomena the necklaces, chains, and wreaths encircling many gift images. Shortly before her death in 1821, Mother Lucy Wright introduced the golden chain as a figure of community cohesion. She intended the chain to signify both the union of Believers with each other and with heaven, and the separation of Believers from the world.

> To my sense Believers are held together in union by a *golden Chain*. This chain is composed of the gifts and orders of God and every order is a link in the chain; and if you break any of these orders, you break this chain and are exposed to be led astray, But while you are careful to keep the gifts and orders of God, you are surrounded with this golden chain, and are secure from evil. You are on safe ground, and nothing can injure you unless by disobedience you break a link in this chain, and so expose yourselves to the enemy without, for the enemy cannot come within to injure any one.[29]

Immediately following Lucy Wright's death, Shakers circulated the golden chain address among themselves.[30] Then, just prior to the New Era, the address resurfaced and the image again assumed popularity as a boundary motif. In 1838, the spirit of Father James Whittaker explained that the spiritual gift of golden chains exemplified "that feeling of oneness, which binds us together."[31] A contemporary scribe interpreted the golden chain as an emblem of the orders of God which surrounded the Shaker Zion like a protective wall.

> Remember that the orders, rules, and regulations of the gospel are given for the strength and protection of Believers . . . They are like a golden chain encircling us around to protect us from evil; every order forms a link in this chain and if one link is broke, the chain is parted and we are exposed to evil. They are also like a wall of fire surrounding the camp of saints to defend them from the enemy of souls.[32]

In 1845 Shaker editors included a copy of Mother Lucy's golden chain address in their revision of the Millennial Laws.[33] When they encountered chains and derivative forms as images in drawings, then, Shakers reacted in a manner consistent with their knowledge of the body of material on chains as walls and borders, as tokens of union with other Believers and with heaven, and as symbols of separation from the world (figs. 25, 28, 30).

If God was a divine artist who drew a separating line between the precious and the vile, Shaker religious pictures underscored this demarcation by emphasizing the unique status of Believers as recipients of heavenly gifts.[34] The spirits did not send any gift images to the world's people. And Shakers chose not to share the visionary paintings and drawings with outsiders. Time and again, official correspondence expressed the ministry's unwillingness to let the world know any details about gift messages and visions.[35] Even if one of these images had circulated outside of the community, the peculiarly Shaker subject matter and content of these drawings and paintings would have baffled a nonbeliever. An insider's knowledge of Shaker history, myth, and iconography was necessary to the interpretation of gift images.

> The mighty manifestations of God to his chosen people, are truly wonderful, very wonderful; far beyond any thing ever before revealed on earth. It has often seemed as though the Heavens and earth had come together, and that we were in reality surrounded by heavenly hosts; yet these heavenly and divine manifestations, with which we have so often been favored, are not understood by the world of mankind; nor can they understand them except by revelation from God, or faith in the testimony of his appointed agents.[36]

Shaker images, like Shakers themselves, did not belong among the unregenerate. The pictures, in fact, were not of this world. Through these images, Believers maintained, heaven spoke to Shakers with a divine intimacy and immediacy not offered to the unbelieving.

Although Shakers did not formally define the word "boundary," they were quite clear about how they *experienced* boundaries. The Shaker conception of boundaries provided a way of marking the limits of categories and of regulating movement between them. Boundaries were borders or points of transition between ordered spaces and orders of spaces. On a cosmic level, boundaries marked the interface between worlds. Thus, Shakers distinguished the chaos and confusion of the world's people from their own regenerate sphere and highlighted the necessary transition from the faithful regenerate earth to the heavenly sphere. Shaker boundaries were barriers that could be crossed. But this passage required some change in state or condition on the part of the marginally committed Believer or some new initiative on the part of God.

In *Rites of Passage,* Arnold van Gennep discusses the potency of transitions from one state or place to another as a process of three stages: a preliminal stage of separation or dislocation; a liminal stage, fraught with power and danger, during which the subject is actually in transition, "betwixt and between" a point of departure and a destination; and a postliminal stage of incorporation and reassimilation.[37] In the course of his discussion, van Gennep examines the role of doors and thresholds (Shakers would add windows, bowers, arbors, gates) as symbolic constructions marking movement from one place and state to another.

> Precisely: the door is the boundary between foreign and domestic worlds in the case of an ordinary dwelling, between sacred and profane worlds in the case of a temple. Therefore to cross the threshold is to unite oneself with a new world. . . . rites carried out on the threshold itself are transition rites.[38]

In *The Ritual Process,* Victor Turner takes up van Gennep's argument, expanding on the notion of danger and power inherent in liminal experiences, places, and structures.[39] Turner's discussion has particular relevance in regard to the understanding of gift manifestations throughout Mother's Work. During this period, the products of the instruments, in image and word, demonstrated the significance (and danger) of doors, windows, and gates as potential points of transport. Numerous restrictions sent from the heavenly sphere governed the trespass and status of such apertures.[40] Shaker visionary paintings, like the *Bower of Mulberry Trees,* functioned figuratively as windows and doors of visual passage into heaven. These images provided Believers with invitations to cross the threshold between heaven and earth and with bridges to accomplish such passage. What an official scribe said of his account of heavenly manifestations could be said even more accurately of gift images: "Here you will see thro' the opened windows of heaven, into the immortal regions . . . cast a glance into the celestial mansions, and view the movements of the heavenly orders."[41] If the windows of heaven were indeed open, gift images became the frames through which Believers could look in order to see the celestial sphere. Visionary drawings and paintings *were,* in fact, windows on the heavens. In beholding these images, Shakers could see the glories of heaven while yet in time.[42] As mediating objects, as links between earth and heaven, gift images, like the instruments who produced them, assumed liminal status.[43]

All gift images, regardless of subject matter, exemplified visually the new and more intimate relationship Shakers desired between the celestial sphere and the regenerate earthly community. These documents had themselves passed from heaven to earth, from spiritual vision to material form, through the mediation of an instrument. If the objects and spirits represented in drawings could move freely from one realm to the other, then so might living human beings. The message status of the visionary paintings and drawings underscored their conception as boundary phenomena. In the nineteenth century, more than in the twentieth, handwritten correspondence played an essential role in communication between different people and different places. Messages, in other words, formed bridges between individuals and between worlds. Messages acknowledged and signified the existence of a relationship.[44] While, on the one hand, messages recalled physical distance to mind (why send a letter to one who is standing close by?), on the other hand, both messages and gifts assumed emotional proximity and possessed the ability to dissolve distances, to make an absent one present.[45] Because Shakers understood gift images as forms of correspondence rather than art, Believers experienced these drawings and paintings as active and dynamic communications between the inhabitants of eternity and the inhabitants of time.[46] The easily portable size and material of gift images and their status as message gave the recipient a sense of intimacy, of direct relationship, with the content and source of these images. From within this particular thoughtworld, heavenly persons and objects moved in regenerate earthly space and could be seen, approached, and embraced. At least once during Mother's Work, Shaker spirits chose to emphasize the potentially reciprocal nature of tangible correspondence between the two worlds. In 1847 adherents at New Lebanon received "a communication from all our Heavenly Parents, concerning sending gifts and presents to those of our companions in the spiritual world." According to the instrument of this message, the Heavenly Parents directed that the community's instruments be supplied with materials such as paper, ink, and pens in order to convey the appropriate gifts and presents to the intended recipients in the spirit world.[47]

Over the course of Mother's Work, different instruments chose to highlight different aspects of the Shaker concern with borders. While one image might emphasize the need for ordered separation from the chaotic world, another might proclaim the celestial infusion of Shaker space. Many drawings and paintings combined these two emphases in some fashion. The formal characteristics of Cohoon's mulberry bower invited the beholder to enter sacred space; the Narrow Path drawings (fig. 16), by materializing the Shaker spiritual travel motif, schematically and sequentially demonstrated how earthly Shakers might progress into the heavenly sphere. The Narrow Path, as an emblem of a Shaker boundary ritual and the theology that produced it, thus offered Believers an alternative visual route for transcending the boundary between heaven and earth and for separating themselves from the world.

A number of gift images include depictions of the Narrow Path, but eight surviving drawings seek to replicate the actual shape, scale, and design of the Narrow Path itself. A single caption on one of these eight strips of paper identifies the subject as a path. Other representations of the Narrow Path (all by different hands) lend support to this identification.[48] In each case, the instruments intended the paths to be emblems of the Narrow Path walked by individuals as they journeyed from earth to heaven. The group of eight very similar drawings includes seven rectangular strips measuring thirteen inches by four inches in brown or faded black ink on white paper and one strip measuring twelve and three-quarters inches by four inches with the figures in blue ink and the text in brown or faded black ink on white paper. The original status of the eight pieces with respect to each other remains speculative. All eight may have been glued together to form one long roll, or the piece composed with blue ink may have been the terminal piece of a second Narrow Path series. (This blue piece is the only one of the eight in which the path comes to an end—but it also repeats most of the figures from one of the brown pieces.) The surviving pieces may represent several series, for which multiple segments are missing, or each piece may have been given to a different individual as a representation of his or her own Narrow Path. Given the evidence which remains, any of these alternatives can be plausibly argued and none can be ruled out. The more likely scenario, however, has the pieces connected in some manner; traces of adhesive remain on each end of most of the Narrow Path strips.[49] Daniel Patterson dates the Narrow Path strip drawings, which he sees as parts of one long roll, to about 1843. He bases this date on the dates of two drawings by the same hand: a cut-and-fold booklet of 2 May 1843 and a prophetic book formed of concentric circles of 21 June 1843.[50] The year 1843 is indeed a likely approximate date because of the popularity, in the early to mid–1840s, of a ritual observance called the Narrow Path.[51]

The role played by the eight Narrow Path strips, in visualizing and ritualizing the Shaker motif of spiritual travel, can best be understood through an exploration of the narrative subject matter of the drawings and the content that subject matter was known to possess in the Shaker community. In the broader culture, the physical mobility of nineteenth-century Americans found expression in the popular genre of travel books. Shakers, who kept detailed journals of their travels between communities and in the world, recorded their journey visions and their progress in spiritual travel as well. Among the Shakers, the idea of spiritual travel was not new to the era of Mother's Work. As outlined by Mother Lucy in 1815, six years before her death, spiritual travel described the state and condition of the Believer's life both in time and in eternity.

> I expect to travel as long as I live in this world and I do not expect to stop traveling then; I do not expect to ever die; I expect my body will die; and I shall leave this earthly tabernacle to be returned to the earth like all the others. [B]ut my spirit is not agoing to die; my spirit will live always. Souls are not agoing to stop traveling if they are faithfull, But they will travel and travel till they come to the heavens of heavens; and then not stop; for there is no end to the work of God.[52]

At the moment of death a person's soul appeared in the spirit world "according to [that person's] travel in the gospel." The soul then completed what remained of the journey to secure its "entire releasement from the effects of a fallen nature."[53] Once fully "released," the soul continued to travel nearer and nearer to God.[54] Spiritual travel was both eternal and progressive. "We know that '*the way of God is strait as straitness . . . and unless believers come to it they will loose their souls.*' But this cannot be gained all at once, but by a progressive travel."[55] The New Era, then, was progressive as well as restorationist. While Shakers lived, in terms of communal history, with a rhythmic alternation between charism and institution, their personal spiritual travel, their own "private" histories, these Believers understood as ideally progressive, moving straight forward in one direction, bringing them closer and closer to their spiritual goal and their heavenly destination.

Although the idea of spiritual travel had a long Shaker history, the motif enjoyed increased popularity during Mother's Work. In this particular historical setting, the ritual observance of the Narrow Path and its pictorial expression embodied the convention of spiritual travel.[56] Instruments communicated the intention of spirits that these gifts, like other manifestations, would "hasten the spiritual travel" of Believers, would move them along in the Narrow Path.[57] Shaker leaders and instruments adopted the figure of the Narrow Path to describe the way individuals ought to accomplish the transition from earth to heaven and to signify the appropriate relationship between Shakers and the world. On 1 November 1840, adherents to the gospel of Ann Lee first received the Narrow Path ritual as a gift from the heavens. An official journalist of the New Lebanon Church Family recorded the occasion as a sort of participatory spiritual theater.

> Fr Wm had brot for each of us a strait and narrow path to walk. it was strait as straitness, no turning to the right nor left. And he desired we would each of us devote 10 minutes every day to walk in this path. Daniel [Boler] and Betsey [Bates] showed us how we were to walk placing one foot just before the other—walk in solemn meditation, and in the fear of God—this doing daily, until our heavenly parents should meet with us, which would be in their own time.[58]

One mid-nineteenth-century manuscript indicates the conviction that celestial beings presented with emblems of repentance, tribulation, and divine support Shakers who diligently observed the Narrow Path ritual.[59] Perhaps the Narrow Path drawings constituted such emblems. In form, the "straight" and "narrow" paths of Shaker spiritual travel resembled paths in the earthly Zion. On a literal level, members of the United Society moved throughout their communities on paths that were straight and narrow. On a figurative level, they traveled between the Shaker Zion and its celestial prototype on the Narrow Path. Divine laws admitted no shortcuts, either on earth or in heaven.

So spiritual travel was a figure for Shaker life as a whole, a description of what happened during many visions, the content of a particular communal ritual, and an expression of the progressive nature of divine revelation and activity. Numerous references to the Narrow Path demonstrate the pervasiveness of the metaphor as a figure of Shaker life; these notations also fill out the rich interpretive context that surrounded the rather schematic Narrow Path drawings.[60] During their lives, Shakers traveled a straight path "adorned" (like the eight Narrow Path segments) with "heavy scenes of tribulation."[61] The instrument of the drawings represented these "heavy scenes" in the emblems of serpents, spears, traitors, axes, whips, etc. The emblems reminded Believers that the faithful life required much of them. Not only did God command them to bear a daily cross of celibacy, sacrifice, and humility, but the world, so they thought, expressed its opposition to God's way by persecuting the faithful and by attempting to lure them away from the Millennial Church. In the context of the difficult challenges presented to them in the course of their spiritual travels, Shakers frequently used interchangeably the words "travel" and "travail." Spiritual travel involved a process of bringing forth a new creation, of giving birth to a new self. This task required dedication and effort.[62]

The Narrow Path ritual and drawings reminded Shakers of their belief that choosing the straight and difficult way of God separated them from the world.[63] God called them to walk in the Narrow Path leading to heaven. The world, Shakers maintained, strayed in "Hell's broad way"[64] leading to the "Valley of Deth."[65] The forms and fashions of the world had to be left behind; there was no room for them in Shaker life.[66] Spirits guiding Believers on the Narrow Path instructed the children of Mother Ann to deny all vehicles of worldliness as stumbling blocks on the road to salvation. If the Narrow Path separated Believers from the ways of the world, it also bridged the gap between earthly Shakers and heaven. It led the faithful adherent to Mother's living fountain in the celestial sphere.[67] By walking this path, Believers found union with and encouragement from their Heavenly Parents who had traveled the narrow course before them.[68] In this path, good spirits kept the faithful safe, though snares were all around.[69]

According to Shakers, every individual had to prepare during his or her life a path to walk in eternal life. Visually, each person's path was an emblem or memorial of the life that person had lived and the degree of spiritual perfection attained. A wayward individual might have a very crooked path full of stumbling blocks to travel in the celestial sphere, or even no path at all. On the other hand, those faithful to Ann Lee's gospel had beautiful paths lined with flowers and watched over by heavenly angels. The path that guided first born Eliab Harlow to the heavenly sphere "was straight and smooth, and appeared to be set with bright shining diamonds, and it was without spot or blemish: it was a path of perfect beauty."[70] An instrument described and depicted Rufus Bishop's narrow path as a splendid celestial carpet marking the threshold of his mansion in eternity.[71] Any person's Narrow Path, by the way it looked in the collective visual imagination, then, revealed that person's status before God.[72] The Narrow Path strip drawings translated into material form a ritual or sacred pantomime already conceived of by Shakers in visual terms. Narrow Path drawings and emblems demonstrated to the recipient the actual visual appearance of his or her own path. "I have set my Messenger, even your beloved Father William, to give you a way you all could see, a strait and narrow path, wherein your feet must walk."[73]

Several visionary manuscripts in particular described the Narrow Path in ways suggestive of the eight strip drawings.[74] Although none of these literary references to Narrow Paths (with regard to rolling the paths for storage, to their widths, to their segmentation, or to descriptions of their spiritual ornamentation) can be said with certainty to correspond with actual drawings, the images and words reflect parallel and related objects and experiences in a single visual universe. For example, a number of instruments and scribes referred to the paths as being given "rolled up."[75]

> Father Wm . . . spake more or less—and also said he was round last night and viewed all the paths that had been given us; and he found them in good order, well paved, bright and shining . . . and said he, What do you think I did with them? Why I took them all and rolled them up, and laid them here on the bench, and if you will ask the beloved Ministry for them, you may have them, and they will be yours forever.—So we went and asked if we might have our path and they said yea, so we took them and put them on our heads—then F. Wm said he wanted we should walk them a little at this time—so we took them from our heads and unrolled them on the floor, and walked on them—a while, and then rolled them up again and put them on our heads.[76]

In a communication of 1848, the spirit of Elder Sister Olive Fairbanks brought rolled paths representative of the Narrow Paths of each person present.[77] Such "rolled" paths might have been easily translated to strips of paper, "well paved" with images.

Early in 1842, New Lebanon Shakers received a lengthy gift message brought by the spirit of Mother Ann Lee. The instrument titled the message "Holy Wisdom's Path . . . discribed on a Ball of pink coloured *Tape*."[78] This detailed account of Wisdom's Path not only explained in writing what the path looked like, it also invited Shakers to clearly visualize the gift and to place themselves within it, at least in their mind's eye. Wisdom's Path was a model in relationship to which individuals might judge their own paths. In Holy Mother Wisdom's Path, Almighty God the Father would pass to view his people. The instrument of the message told how the rolled ball of pink tape was unwound so that she could see it. It was six inches wide and 600 yards long. It was numbered every 100 yards to form six sections. Diamonds, stars, flowers, and heavenly fruits decorated the path Wisdom herself had paved. This path ran throughout Zion on earth and led directly to the kingdom of heaven and the mansion of eternal happiness. Though snares and swords and beasts and monsters might be laid in the way, God would lead the faithful to safety. Holy Mother Wisdom walked this path and drew her footprints upon it in gold for those with vision to see and to follow.[79] The six-inch width of Wisdom's Path in this message and the four-to-six-inch width of a path walked by William Deming in a vision of January 1843 both suggest the possibility that the instruments' verbal descriptions bore some relationship to the use of four-to-six-inch strips of paper to represent the Narrow Path.[80] The eight surviving strip drawings are approximately four inches wide.

Detailed visions of the spiritual adventures encountered by individuals as they walked their paths give insight into the symbols and emblems which surround the central part of the path in the strip drawings. In 1842, "A Sensation or View of the narrow path to Heaven" guided the visionist past threats of destruction and tribulation toward the celestial sphere. Here a path of four inches in width was guarded by angels with swords of mercy, truth, forbearance, charity, patience, meekness, tribulation, sufferings, repentance, comfort, etc. Large serpents, a lake of fire, and a forest filled with wild beasts lay in wait just outside the path for those who deviated from the straight and narrow way.[81] A Miranda Barber vision of 1855 combined similar symbols with an expanded description of the most heavenward sections of the path. In this narrative, after passing bravely through deep tribulation, the visionist and her spirit guide entered a brightly illuminated and beautifully ornamented part of the Narrow Path. Here, at the end of her spiritual journey, the instrument could see into the celestial sphere itself. She returned to earth to tell her communal companions what lay in store for the faithful as they passed from earth to heaven on the Narrow Path.[82] If Shakers intended the eight strip drawings to be placed end to end in one or more series, the progressive and sequential movement of the images simulated the Narrow Path visions. The segments of the drawings, with their whips, spears, and serpents, surely represented the earthly end of the path, the beginning of the journey. The representations of flowers, fruit trees, angels, and walls of Zion signified the passage of the faithful into salvation and the heavenly sphere. If these eight strips reproduced, instead, the paths of eight different individuals, the strips reflected the various "degrees of travel" or spiritual conditions of the individual recipients.

Like the Mulberry Bower and the Narrow Path, the drawings known as Sacred Sheets reflected the New Era's consciousness of boundaries. In this case, however, the drawings presented neither invitations to enter sacred space nor schematic tokens of the course of traffic between earth and heaven. Rather, by reiterating a familiar border symbol in a novel and mysterious context, Sacred Sheets manifested notions of both separation and passage. New Lebanon beholders of Sacred Sheets would have recognized immediately the figure of the diagonal cross employed in many of these mysterious designs (fig. 17). In 1842, one year before the first Sacred Sheets appeared, Believers at New Lebanon had erected precisely this sign, the diagonal cross, as a symbolic boundary marker (fig. 18). Some months earlier, these Shakers had closed their worship services to the public and had posted "Advertisements" and "Proclamations" to advise the world to that effect. In an official journal a scribe noted that

> sometime in April there were signs made by divine requirement, in the form of a cross, and words of the Savior painted thereon. These were to be placed up in plain

> view, one in front of the Meeting house and one in front of the office: and were first put up on the first of May, this year. *Words and form as follows.* [Here the scribe inserted a sketch of the two crosses, giving their dimensions and recording these inscriptions.] Enter not within these gates, for this is my Holy Sanctuary saith the Lord. But pass ye by, and disturb not the peace of the quiet, upon my Holy Sabbath [Meeting House]. This is a place of trade and public business. therefore we open it not on the Sabbath. So let none contrive evil against my people saith the Lord, lest with my hand I bring evil upon them [Office].[83]

A separate "Confidential" journal entry was somewhat more specific.

> There had been two wooden crosses prepared, and painted white with writing upon them. These were, by Order of the Savior, each to be placed on a post, one just within the pickets, fronting the Meeting House facing the road, the other, just within the Fence fronting the Office, facing the road; they were to be prepared, by the Elders of the Second Order, and put up on the first day of May: the day of our first Sacred, and holy Feast on the Mount; and these crosses were to go up every Sabbath thro' the present season. All this was, for many weeks done according to direction.[84]

New Era Believers encountered other celestial signposts too. Divine models of varied descriptions served as prototypes for signs Shakers envisioned around them.[85] According to the instruments, celestial beings posted spiritual signs, sometimes sufficient in themselves to mark the borders around and within Zion as a "sign and a warning to the children of this world,"[86] sometimes to guide Believers in the placement and content of their own religious billboards. Often the spiritually sighted ones described elaborate celestial scenes painted by inhabitants of heaven on signs unseen by those who possessed only ordinary vision. Although instruments mentioned spiritual signs of many descriptions in contemporary manuscripts, the diagonally oriented cross appears to be the only such boundary marker actually executed in wood. The sign of the diagonal cross both warned the world away *and* characterized celibate Believers, in opposition to the world, as a people who bore the cross of sacrifice and salvation. One Shaker maintained, "I am thankful for that cross that draws a strait line, and marks a separation between us and the world. I love the cross of Christ, which brings salvation to the world."[87]

Individuals, like territory, could be set apart, marked for salvation, by the sign of the cross. In one ritual, Shakers received the love of their long-deceased spiritual forebears William Lee and James Whittaker in the shape of a cross.

> They send it to you in this manner or form, that ye may know you have gained their love by bearing the cross. Place the cross on your foreheads that ye may be known when ye enter eternity as faithful crossbearers.[88]

The "Closing Roll" of 1841 described a "large GOLDEN CROSS" given to each Shaker instrument. An angel placed these crosses

> upon each and every one of your breasts . . . and from the ends of this cross, is extended a shining band of silver over your shoulders and back under your arms, to the cross again; and on the cross is written "GOOD AND FAITHFUL CHILDREN, AND FAITHFUL INSTRUMENTS IN THE HANDS OF YOUR MOTHER AND HEAVENLY PARENTS."[89]

Only a diagonal cross could have been worn in this fashion. Furthermore a gift image received by Mary Hazard depicted a diagonal cross for her to wear.[90] When Believers encountered the diagonal cross symbol in the intricately detailed and enigmatic Sacred Sheets, then, they recognized the significance of the figure as both a warning against the trespass of sacred space and as an emblem of spiritual distance from the world.

The instruments of Sacred Sheets constructed many shapes which were subtly analogous to other familiar forms in the Shaker sacred environment: the prophetic and cosmographical symbols of sun and moon, and forms resembling the holy feastgrounds and the fountain stone, for example. The instruments made no attempt to imitate exactly the heavenly orbs and earthly spaces that they pictured. Neither did these visionaries specify an exact or absolute correspondence between a drawn form and any single referent. Rather, the shapes on the sheets suggested, implied, connoted, powerful forms from a recognizable vocabulary of sacred landscape. The shapes were intelligible but not explicit. They conveyed both familiarity and strangeness. In fact, the designs on the sheets were intentionally cryptic; they relied on a sense of celestial mystery for their impact. In a sense these paintings were like cosmological treasure maps, locating celestial valuables within Shaker territory.

Shakers received the surviving dated Sacred Sheets during the first quarter of 1843. In a journal account for March 1843, a scribe observed,

> about this time and a few weeks past, there has been a remarkable manifestation from the spirits, in writing certain mysterious sheets, containing many hierogliphics, and generally more or less english, and abundance of mysterious writing in unknown characters. These sheets were written and given to individuals, with their names on them.
>
> They are said to contain much that will be revealed. I cannot present a specimen of them here, but doubtless they can be seen, if desired.[91]

The enigmatic signs and symbols on these "mysterious sheets" captured the scribe's imagination. The designs on the sheets were formed of characters which appeared to be letters and words but which the scribe could not decipher. He was confident, however, that their content would at some point be made plain. The ambiguity of this sacred script was decidedly useful. The script admitted of multiple "intentional" meanings, depending upon the instrument's translation. No one could challenge these meanings because only heaven and the instruments understood their significance. When translations were forthcoming, they could address a specific situation which might not yet have arisen when the community first saw the image itself. Thus the messages exercised a certain prophetic power in the community. An instrument with spiritual sight might also "read" these gifts in such a way as to meet the particular needs of an individual recipient—and the message might change as the needs changed.

Instruments composed the images on Sacred Sheets from seemingly impenetrable calligraphic characters representing a visual equivalent for the charismatic experience of speaking in tongues.[92] According to William J. Samarin, this form of spiritual writing might be called "glossographia."[93] Sacred Sheets were not the only manifestations of the Era containing such sacred script. Other types of gift messages, some predominantly text, some predominantly image, included this "mysterious writing."[94] Some Shaker glossographia resembled no known language; some bore similarities to Hebrew or Arabic; some used a variation on the English alphabet, with letters combined in incomprehensible patterns; and some used ordinary English letter combinations to form readily understandable words but so disguised the letters with flourishes and a "broken" style that only close examination made recognition possible.[95]

The boundary significance of the script on the Sacred Sheets lay in the Shakers' acknowledgment of this script as the native tongue of the celestial sphere.[96] Heaven spoke directly to the Shaker community. Only through the special relationship of believing instruments to the heavenly sphere could these cryptic symbols be understood and communicated with authority. In a booklet of 1843, given at Watervliet, an instrument demonstrated his ability to translate the language of heaven. The title page and the first six pages of celestial script, the instrument repeated verbatim in the remaining English pages of the text.[97] Within Shaker society alone was such a translation possible. The celestial sphere would speak comprehensibly, in its own tongue, only to this chosen people. By virtue of the characters the instruments used to build their images and the inclusion of suggestively familiar yet somehow inexplicit forms, Sacred Sheets drew Believers closer to the divine mystery and separated them from a world which did not understand.

In a range of religious pictures, instruments demonstrated some of the visual and conceptual possibilities for dissolving and reinforcing boundaries. Each image showed Shakers how to live within or move across the significant borders they encountered in their lives. The Mulberry Bower used the elements of its formal composition to create sacred and celestial space into which the spectator could imagine his or her own movement. The Narrow Path, in its reliance on shared understandings of spiritual travel and shared ritual experiences, materialized a form that community members recognized as emblematic of their own boundary rituals and boundary theology. Sacred Sheets reiterated meaningful visual forms in a mysterious and heavenly script.

If Mother's Work sought to restore order in the third generation Shaker community, a second, perhaps even more important goal, was to reestablish contact with celestial sources of faith. Though an institutionalizing impulse rapidly shaped and channeled the New Era, the desire for personal charismatic experience remained a powerful motivator. Boundary-challenging mechanisms in gift images facilitated contact by mediating passage between earth and heaven. Gift images visualized not only the organization of the universe, but also movement within the universe. Images made heaven available as a model for behavior and as a locale in which to experience the divine. The conviction of an ordered universe provided a sanctifying ethic, a primitive pattern, according to which the mid-nineteenth-century community might more perfectly resemble the heavenly sphere. But the celestial original which determined this pattern was itself accessible to regenerate Believers on earth who, having put on spiritual spectacles, peered through heaven's windows and traveled through heaven's doors.

Part III

VISION, IMAGE, AND TIME

Six

[Re]collecting History

A VISIBLE GENEALOGY OF "GOSPEL RELATIONS"

Remoteness from the person of Mother Ann Lee constituted the principal threat to the third generation of Shakers, or so many mid-century Shakers in positions of influence seemed to believe. Because this sense of remoteness was temporal as well as spatial, concerning the gap between past and present as well as the distance between heaven and earth, ministry and instruments embraced a solution that involved time as it did space. The celestial gifts of Mother's Work connected their New Era recipients and the communities gathered around them with a former age as well as a faraway place.

But it was the sense of time itself and not just the past that was important. Shakers were not so interested in the "good old days" that they neglected the novelty of the *New* Era. Neither were they so involved with a prophesied future that they repudiated the present. Rather, they sought to reclaim from times gone by identity-instilling and initiating experiences (in terms of both charism and institution) in order to live effectively in the millennial age inaugurated by Ann Lee. Like other American religious groups (Puritans, Mormons, Pentecostals), Shakers were both restorationist and millennialist, primitivist and progressive. In the case of the Shakers, restorationism served essentially millennialist goals. Restorationism involved an orientation toward the present with respect to the past; millennialism involved an orientation toward the present with respect to the future. The combination of restorationism and millennialism might have produced a consistent tendency on the part of

Believers to straddle the present, to use the past to catapult themselves into the future. But one important circumstance prevented this situation: for Shakers the millennium was now. The final dispensation had already begun. The thousand-year reign of the Christ spirit before the Last Judgment took place in their own time. Instead of a full-scale retreat into the past, New Era Shakers staged expeditions of recollection. They intended to resolve a contemporary predicament by bringing the past forward in time to create a new and more persuasive present. They aimed to renew commitment to the millennial vision of Ann Lee by reconstructing past history in the present tense, and they wanted to order and interpret the present in light of future glory.

Richard T. Hughes and C. Leonard Allen have suggested that restorationism in American religion is generally ahistorical.[1] Their argument is compelling. But as Hughes himself implies in a later essay, it is the particular use of history and tradition by restorationists, not necessarily historicity or ahistoricity, which is most illuminating.[2] For historicity is always a relative quantity. All records of the past involve construction and reconstruction, involve the interdependence of history and memory, the differential valuation and subjectively informed remembering of various historical periods.[3] The historian never captures the actual lived past.

To some degree, Shaker "ahistoricity" was muted by the comparative accessibility of the principal past Shakers chose to recall. American Puritans appealed to a distant biblical and early Christian primordium. Enlightenment thinkers appealed to the primordium of Eden, of nature.[4] For mid-nineteenth-century followers of Ann Lee, the most significant "primordial" past was the relatively recent past, the period of "primitive" Shakerism. Because of this, the past that Shakers reconstructed involved lived historical memory as well as sacred memory, profane time as well as sacred time.[5] Granted, Shakers identified their own primordium in relationship to primitive Christianity and even to a prelapsarian era. But the fourth and final dispensation inaugurated by Ann Lee was, according to Lee's followers, the most perfect revelation of God's will and grace and the principal pattern for Believers.

Conflations and disjunctions, as well as selections and abbreviations, characterized Shaker historical consciousness. For example, mid-nineteenth-century adherents to the sect, in a sort of condensation of history, collected both historical persons and inhabitants of the atemporal celestial sphere to populate their present. They introduced a cyclical notion of time by representing the ideal present as a retrieval of past experiences and behaviors and as a figure of a future celestial state. But Shakers also marked time in a linear fashion. Incorporating a dual notion of linear time, they combined a belief in a decisive temporal break, a future and final Last Judgment separating good and evil, with a sure sense of progressive and universal salvation. Shaker dispensationalism, too, displayed both linear and cyclical faces. Four sequential ages or dispensations proceeded one after the other. But the movement from beginning to end of one dispensation resembled the movement from beginning to end of each of the other three, suggesting a cyclical arrangement of events within the linear sequence.

Actually, the most revealing question is not whether Shakers can be more adequately described as historical or ahistorical. As Sam Hill has pointed out (and as I think Hughes and Allen would agree), "restorationism in all its forms has something to do with views of history."[6] Mid-nineteenth-century Shaker instruments and ministry had an acute sense of historical person and historical event and of the potential use of the past to shape religious selfhood and communal identity. The most revealing question here is, rather, how did these Shakers receive and use their past? How did they appropriate and articulate the dimension of time? Before addressing specifically the mid-nineteenth-century Shaker (re)configuration of the past(s), it is helpful to examine some broader temporally related conceptions within the Shaker community.

A prophetic sense of God's activity placed Shaker historical time within the context of sacred time. Assisted by their prophets, Believers gained the means to interpret both past and current events within the framework of salvation history.[7] The instruments of Mother's Work, producers of both gift images and gift texts, were, so Shakers believed, latter-day prophets.[8] According to these instruments, a verb in the heavenly tongue, "sevene," described the action that instrument-prophets performed on the part of the community. To sevene meant to reveal, to uncover, and, sometimes, to interpret, a divine perspective.[9] Shaker prophets, then, conveyed a sacred story. Shaker preachers proclaimed this story; Shaker scribes recorded and elaborated upon it. The story connected a remembered and cherished past with the less certain present and connected the less certain present with the divinely ordained future. The connections the prophets drew revealed the fabric of meaning and movement from which Believers fashioned their history.

Many images, including a significant number of those already discussed, Shakers interpreted prophetically. Some gift drawings and paintings gave explicitly prophetic voice to Shaker history. They anchored the Shaker past and present to an ultimate divine purpose and sequence of events. Their strange signs and complicated constructions provided visual and material evidence of the work of God in the Shakers' midst. During worship on 1 May 1843 Believers at New Lebanon received an apocalyptic book of boldly drawn and very colorfully painted geometric signs and symbols (e.g., fig. 4).[10] This book appears to be by the same hand that drew the cut-and-fold booklets, the Narrow Path segments, and at least two other pictorial prophetic documents. The instrument conceived the "geometric" book (like the cut-and-fold booklets discussed in the following pages) as a complex material form. Many pages folded; some pages opened up, some down, some out to one side or the other.[11] And, although the intended principal vantage point of the beholder remained consistent and unmistakable, the instrument oriented words and letters on a single sheet to face several directions. In other words, while the vantage point was conceptually clear, it was experientially less certain; the beholder had either to move physically around the large pages of the book or to turn the book itself around in order to read all of the text and to comprehend all of the images.[12] Even after exerting themselves in this fashion, even after carefully examining this primarily pictorial document, beholders would not be able to fathom the precise meanings of the instrument's depictions. The mysterious letters, numbers, and figures of the prophetic book remained fully comprehensible, the instrument claimed, only to God.

Most of the images in this book concerned prophetic vision. Spiritual sight was, after all, synonymous with prophetic ability. Shaker prophetic ministry depended on the ability to see and make known the things of the spirit.[13] When the instrument wrote in English, she favored words like "watch" and "see." In one painting, she depicted a giant eye-like image (fig. 4). In all likelihood, the instrument intended this sign to suggest the discerning eye of God in the act of seeing, perhaps even reading the hearts of Believers as the day of judgment approached. In another drawing the instrument floated the caption "the eyes" across the page. The instrument's words about sight received considerable emphasis because they were among the few words and signs that beholders in general could translate or interpret. What could be "seen" in the images and signs of the times, the instrument noted, announced the imminent judgment of God and prophesied ultimate salvation for the faithful. The strategic use of red and black paint, signifying sacrifice and commitment, tribulation and judgment, highlighted prophetic intentions.[14] But "stranger and mightier things shall ye yet behold in this your sacred place of worship than was ever known in the days of my Ancient Prophets," promised the deity.[15]

The images and text of the four surviving components of cut-and-fold or puzzle booklets were characteristic of pictorial prophetic signs (fig. 19). Instruments cut and folded these little booklets from two sheets of paper, usually with the addition of a separate cover piece. After registering the appropriate images and words on each numbered segment of a cut and folded sheet, an instrument fitted the two sheets together like a puzzle. For example, "Words by Signs to the Watchmen" and "To the Instrument Writers" folded into each other to form one gift message with pages 1, 2, 5, 6, 9, 10, 15, 16, 19, and 20 in one segment and pages 3, 4, 7, 8, 11, 12, 13, 14, 17, and 18 in the other.[16]

The individual pictures and words of these booklets recorded signs. The small size, the stark contrast of black ink and white paper, and the elaborate, sharp-edged ink images contributed to the booklets' striking visual impact. In addition, instruments interpreted the intricate and ingenious nested form of the booklets as a sign of God's activity in their community, as evidence that the hand of God was in this work. "The Word of the Savior by Signs" of 2 May 1843 also came to the faithful in the

> form of a little book which I made with mine own hand and by this may you understand that God will turn and overturn, that he will divide and subdivide, and that which was once closely joined together will be part asunder, even, as this little book is. Yet, let this remain a sign, that God is ever able to confound the wisdom of the wise, and bring to naught that which mortals may in their inventions join together. . . . Watch ye the signs which your eyes behold, and ye may understand a little of what is known in Heaven. . . . Let this [booklet] be kept even as it is now, that all

> may see that God is mighty, and he doeth that which is marvelous in the eyes of man. So, my word is, let it remain untill the end. Amen.[17]

In order to prepare the cut-and-fold booklets, the instrument had to "turn and overturn," "divide and subdivide" the paper. Thus, the instrument maintained, the very motions required to create the booklets reiterated the artistry of God among the Shakers and in the world. In response to God's activity, Believers ought to stand as closely united to one another as did the two pieces of each cut-and-fold booklet. Furthermore, the union of each segment and its companion piece symbolized the appropriate relationship of body and soul.[18] One instrument declared that signs and figures from the spiritual world "were made as plain and clear to me, as any natural things that I can see and apprehend with my natural senses, so that I knew of a certainty, that they were divine truths."[19] The task of the Shaker prophet/instrument was to make visible and tangible to others these gifts and judgments of God.[20] Drawings and paintings were ideally suited to this goal.

The content of prophetic images typified the content of the Shaker prophetic narrative in general. Shaker gift paintings participated in New Era prophetic ministry by embellishing and reiterating the story of a special people with a divine mission living in God's time. Shaker prophecy was both eschatological and apocalyptic. Shaker instruments promoted a particular understanding of the end times, the ultimate and divine goal of history, *and* they appropriated a complex system of symbols, set over against the dominant cultural system, in order to express their concept of the oncoming eschaton.[21] A sense of living in a final era after the Second Coming of the Christ and before the imminent judgments of God characterized Shaker prophecy. Believers divided sacred history into four ages of time or four dispensations of the "providence and grace of God."[22] From the Fall of Adam and Eve to the bondage of the children of Israel in Egypt constituted the first or Abrahamic dispensation. The second or Mosaic dispensation began with the Exodus and ended with the mission of John the Baptist. The period from the First Appearance of Christ (Jesus) until the Second Appearance of Christ (Ann Lee) constituted the third dispensation. And the fourth dispensation or "great and last display of God's grace to a lost world" began with the Second Coming of Christ in Mother Ann. During this millennial period inaugurated by Ann Lee, the gospel would be preached to all the nations, followed by the final Judgment and the end of time.[23] Such eschatological and apocalyptic thinking intensified the sense of urgency many felt about the spiritual conditions of wayward companions.

Shakers used the word prophecy in both its "forthtelling" and "foretelling" senses.[24] Shaker instruments told forth the will of God for their own day *and* they foretold the future in which, they believed, God's will and purpose would be accomplished. According to their prophets, Shakers lived in divinely punctuated time; they participated in a sacred narrative. Though the middle of the story was uncertain and fraught with tribulation, the end of the story was known: Almighty Power and Holy Wisdom would vindicate their chosen ones.[25] The losses which precipitated the New Era revival would not be the final word. Not only would the gospel of Ann Lee survive and flourish, but Lee's followers had a unique and essential role to play in accomplishing God's ultimate plan of progressive and universal salvation.

> I called and chose you out from among many, and made you my own. and ye shall work with me, and I will work with you saith Wisdom; and the weak shall become strong and the strong stronger until God's work is perfected.
>
> Behold the time has come for my people to be known in the earth, and the fame of those whom I have chosen to serve me, and do my will shall spread from pole to pole. And the children of this world shall know where the Lord reigneth and where his Temple is builded. . . . [Prepare yourselves for] ye shall be the glory of the earth and a light to all nations.[26]

Shaker prophecy, like its biblical model, was constantly dialectical. Shaker prophets balanced their words of judgment with words of hope, their words of castigation and warning with words of edification and comfort. They exhorted and converted the doubtful and wavering and they supported and encouraged the faithful. They broke down and they built up. They demolished one world and called forth another.[27] The Shaker liturgical year, as it developed during the New Era, expressed this dialectic. The annual Work of Judgment, or Yearly Sacrifice, was observed in December through early January. This was a period of serious soul-searching, confession, and repentance. Every evil thought was to be exposed, infidelity and unbelief purged. Documents of the period used harsh language to describe the difficult work Believers undertook in expelling all sin from themselves. Although Shakers introduced the Work of Judgment prior to Mother's Work, they expanded and intensified such ritual observances of cleansing and purification during this time. On the other hand, the spring and fall feasts on the sacred mountains, instituted during Mother's Work, were happy occasions for the celebration of membership among God's chosen and for the reception of spiritual gifts. Image and text as well as ritual periodization embodied this fundamental movement of Shaker prophecy. One series of prophetic paintings juxtaposed pictures of "terrible winds in the earth and fire and hail, and dreadful earthquakes" with representations of "Peace on Earth and good will to Mankind."[28]

A dual sense of the Shaker future accompanied the prophetic dialectic between immediate judgment and sustaining hope. History moved toward imminent cataclysmic events which would rapidly culminate in the final separation of good and evil. And history contained the persistent, progressive revelation of God's will working incessantly for the salvation of the entire world. When it came to setting dates, Ann Lee had counseled her followers to conduct themselves simultaneously as though they would die tomorrow and as though they would live a thousand years.[29] Shakers maintained a sense of both immediate crisis and distant triumph; they moved in God's time, they believed, and only God knew *precisely* how and when history would unfold. Shaker prophets consistently avoided specifying a date for the Last Judgment. Particularly during the frenzied search for signs of prophecy and fulfillment that accompanied Mother's Work, ministry and official instruments diligently rebuked those who dared to suggest an exact time for this cataclysmic event. This is not to say that Shaker prophets never designated exact days or, more often, years. But, in such cases, the ministry and others urged caution. These times should be taken seriously but not literally. The fulfillment of such specific prophecies might occur "spiritually" or the predictions might accord to "some other calculation than ours."[30] The Shaker expectation of imminent divine intervention, then, offered an interpretive framework which allowed for constant revision.[31]

New Era images explicitly incorporated the determination of Shaker prophets to retain a sense of divine mystery about sacred chronology. One series of prophetic drawings featured prominent pictures of clock faces (e.g., figs. 7 and 13). These timepieces functioned as both memento mori for individual recipients and as announcements of imminent judgment for the community. The instruments always depicted the hands of the clocks pointing to a particular hour; judgment would occur in time. But the clock images on different drawings rarely indicated the same hour. The instruments who drew the clocks deliberately used this device, this disagreement between images, to avoid predicting the exact hour of judgment. Both individual and communal destiny remained entirely in God's hands. The pictorial context of the clock faces in the prophetic series underscored the instruments' eschatological intentions. Image-makers flanked their timepieces with representations of the darkened sun and bloodied moon of biblical eschatology. The inscription above the clock in one drawing paraphrased the scriptural source: "I will show wonders in the Heavens and in the Earth. Blood and fire, and pillars of smoke. The Sun shall be darkened and the Moon turned to blood, in mine own time, saith the Lord."[32] Shakers believed that their God required constant vigilance. "Watch and pray, for ye know not the hour of my coming."[33] In addition, the instrument of another series of prophetic paintings (see, for example, fig. 20) quite deliberately jumbled the chronological sequence of her images. Lest the beholder misunderstand her purpose, the instrument added a note (dictated to her, she claimed, by the prophet Isaiah) to the page of text preceding the fourteen paintings in her book.

> These signs I shall show after the order that Wisdom hath commanded, and this is thus to be that no one may know the order, the times and seasons of the Lord's work. This I know not, for this they reserve in their own power and wisdom, that mortal man may not judge them. Therefore the signs will not be regular as things will come to pass, but scattered.[34]

Although the particulars remained hidden, God shared with Shaker prophets a general blueprint for the course of events during the fourth and final dispensation. Many of the predictions made by Ann Lee and her immediate followers had already come to pass, bolstering the confidence of Believers in subsequent revelations. For instance, Lee's small and struggling band had indeed increased rather suddenly during her own lifetime. This growth had continued until Shakers midway through the fourth decade of the nineteenth century could judge themselves successful in numbers and material holdings but increasingly unsuccessful in spiritual fervor and commitment. The instruments of Mother's Work insisted that this came as no surprise to them. Ann Lee herself had prophesied a great decline, the "purging of Zion," which would try the faith of the chosen before God's final triumph.[35] The increasing rate of apostasy, these prophets suggested, could be explained by Ann Lee's earlier prophecy.[36] This argument was strengthened by the perceived fulfillment of a second "ancient" prophecy, that times of tribulation would accompany and succeed the deaths of Mother Ann's first born.[37]

Almost with the same breath which foretold decline and tribulation, however, Shaker prophets heralded an increase of spectacular proportions.

> The time will come, that many will flock to this Zion, to hear the word of the Lord . . . begging for something to save their souls. . . . This generation shall not pass away, untill there are hundreds, yea, thousands called to partake with you in this lowly way.[38]

When the hundreds and thousands did not appear, Shaker prophets searched for a way to understand the apparent discrepancy in God's word to them and to their ancestors in faith. They concluded that God had not intended them to convert the living. Rather, God desired that they assist in the salvation of millions of unconverted dead from previous generations around the world.

> When our First Parents were on Earth they testified that souls would yet flock to Zion in such great multitudes that our streets would be so filled that one might walk on their heads for miles. All this is fulfilling in this our own day. But we never knew, till lately, that they would be the Spirits of those who had lived in all ages of the world, from the beginning unto the present time; but so it is; they seem to be coming, some of all nations.[39]

Only after the unconverted inhabitants of the spiritual world had been saved would the gathering of earth's inhabitants begin.[40]

Eighteen forty-three was a year of particularly vigorous prophetic activity. In 1843, Shaker instruments created many of their most explicitly prophetic images.[41] An astonishing display of mysterious and prophetic signs marked the early months of the year. A symbolic vocabulary of color and shape had been developing and found expression in worship. Earlier Shaker prophecies designated 1843 as the year of the "third opening of the gospel." The gospel had been "opened" first by Mother Ann herself in the founding years of American Shakerism. The second opening had been "in the west," in Ohio, Kentucky, and Indiana. The third opening brought to fruition all prior efforts in the "opening of the gospel to the world."[42] It did not go unnoticed that the third opening of the Shaker gospel coincided with the year of expectation singled out in Millerite prophecies.[43] Fulfilling Shaker prophecies of converts from the world, many former Millerites joined Shaker communities after the "Great Disappointment."[44]

At New Lebanon, much of 1843 was taken up with the massive effort required to prepare official instrument Philemon Stewart's visionary manuscript, the *Sacred Roll and Book,* for publication. Shakers sent the public version of the lengthy text to the leaders of governments all over the world. The experiences surrounding the preparation of this prophetic book formed one backdrop against which New Lebanon Shakers experienced all other manifestations of a prophetic genre in the year 1843.[45] At Watervliet, 1843 witnessed the reception of a second book-length manuscript in the prophetic genre: *Holy Wisdom's Book,* delivered through instrument Paulina Bates.[46]

Shaker prophecy from the earliest years had maintained not only that the world would flock to Zion, but also that manifestations like those of Mother's Work would break forth among the world's people after Ann Lee's own had received her gifts and been prepared for judgment.[47] In 1849, then, when Shakers began to read in the public papers of spiritualist phenomena in neighboring towns and villages, they felt certain that this prophecy had been fulfilled and that Mother's Work had indeed begun among the children of the world.[48]

> Our attention was much attracted to this interesting subject, by many reports from abroad, and also various ones of our society witnessed many facts while out among the world, of mysterious knocking or rapping, communications by questions and answers; also moving of material things, evidently done by some invisible, intelligent agency.
>
> It would appear that the prophecies among us a few years past, were verily coming to pass, that the gifts of Inspiration and manifestations from the spiritual world would shortly break forth in the world. . . .
>
> This year seems as the commencement of a New Era in religious matters in the world.[49]

The advent of the New Era in the world in the late 1840s and early 1850s signaled an anticipated decline, but not cessation, in gifts among Shakers. If anything, the onset of American spiritualism probably extended the attraction of Shaker New Era manifestations beyond what would likely have been an earlier and perhaps more conclusive resolution.[50] According to the mid-century followers of Ann Lee, having first concentrated their efforts on rooting out sin from among Shakers, celestial beings now busied themselves with saving the rest of the world. But, before non-Shakers could be saved, Almighty Power and Holy Wisdom would offer every opportunity to their chosen people. To communal members, then, it appeared that deity revealed its will most clearly within the United Society. And deity recruited the assistance of Believers in order to accomplish the salvation of the nations.

Shakers expressed great interest in the American spiritualist movement. During the second half of the nineteenth century, Shakers formed a variety of opinions about the usefulness to the United Society of these spiritualistic phenomena. "What the extent or end of these things will be, time must determine, but they are surely very interesting and useful to the spiritually minded," commented one intrigued Shaker leader, Giles B. Avery.[51] In making sense of spiritualism, Shakers suggested a hierarchy of spiritual experiences with their own visions at the pinnacle. "The Rappings are one degree above the mere moving of tables, chairs, etc. And the magnetic sleep is the third degree, the trance next, then the visions, such as is common amongst us."[52] Later in the century Shaker Henry Blinn conceived of the manifestations of Mother's Work and the manifestations of spiritualism in the world as different expressions of the same spiritual phenomenon.[53]

Because Shakers understood God to inspire the creation of gift images, some scholars have compared the Shaker religious pictures with the "automatic" drawings and texts of nineteenth-century American spiritualism. In the case of gift images, however, the instrument always "saw" the visions she drew; the figures did not just flow through her. In addition, the act of recording gift images in ink and paint was removed from the initial visionary experience by hours, days, weeks, and even months or years. The gift image, then, was a re-presentation and interpretation of the visionary experience. The act of drawing did not constitute the event itself. Furthermore, as spontaneous products of spontaneous occurrences, automatic drawings were almost always completed in a single inspired sitting. The instruments of gift images, on the other hand, left patterns, drafts, preliminary pencil markings, and sketches which indicate the unhurried precision, skill and care with which Shaker visionaries depicted heavenly persons, places, and objects.[54]

The Shaker prophetic narrative articulated time, its beginning and end, its dispensational structure, from an overarching divine perspective. But the particular events of history had yet to be integrated with this outline. Mid-nineteenth-century Shakers enhanced and expanded an already well established prophetic story. They also created a "new" historical narrative designed to maximize correspondence between their own (American, biblical, and Shaker) story and their God's story. Before the rising generation could encounter Mother Ann as had their predecessors, before these younger Shakers could feel personally connected to their founder, they needed to know more about this charismatic leader and her companions. Much earlier, Shakers had begun to address the concern for a communal history. During Mother's Work Believers revived this concern, pursuing the documentation (and creation) of a historical record with renewed vigor. Ministers and instruments, in concert with the heavenly sphere (so they believed), elaborated a coherent religious history designed to attract and retain those who were young in years and those who were young in the faith. It can almost be said that, during the years of Mother's Work, the ministry and the instruments *collected* a history by combining what was remembered or recorded of their own tradition with popular selections from American history and biblical history. Of course, Shakers understood the resulting narrative to be both a lived story (shaped from the experience and reported experience of their own predecessors) and a revealed story (the divine "truth" about American and biblical history communicated to them through their prophets).

For those who entered the United Society after the first two generations, this "new" history connected familiar figures and events from American and biblical pasts with the unfamiliar cast of Shaker history. Shakers counted religious images among the educational tools available to them in disseminating new historical information. The visual products of the instruments embodied and embroidered the Shaker religious story for all to see.

An important past, recorded in a rather small number of publications, seemed to be slipping rapidly away from nineteenth-century Shakers. With the loss of this past, a sense of present identity and commitment appeared to be waning also.[55] Ann Lee herself had been virtually illiterate. She left no writings of her own. The contemporary record of her life and ministry is almost nonexistent. More than two decades after Lee's death, her followers began to write about their founder, publishing, first, the 1808 *Testimony of Christ's Second Appearing* as part of their campaign to win converts in the West. In 1812, when Lee had been dead for twenty-eight years, some leading members of the United Society expressed an interest in gathering stories and oral testimonies about Ann Lee "while many were yet living who were personally acquainted with her."[56] In 1816 Lee's followers printed around twenty copies of the manuscript that resulted from their labors. Though they sometimes referred to the text as the "Secret Book of the Elders," because the average member knew its content only through hearing the elders read aloud from the book, Shakers formally titled this early collection *Testimonies of the Life, Character, Revelations and Doctrines of Our Ever Blessed Mother Ann Lee, and the Elders with Her.* In 1827 a second book with a similar title contained testimonies of those personally converted by Ann Lee (the New Era's "first born"). As time passed and mid-century neared, interest in preserving and elaborating the words of Ann Lee and accounts of her ministry intensified and proliferated once again. In 1856, Isaac Newton Youngs lamented,

> For many years there was but little attention paid to the keeping of Journals, and what was written was generally very imperfect, in giving satisfactory information; so that it is to be regretted that there were many important events and matters, of which there are now no traces to be found on record.[57]

By the time Mother's Work came to a close, this inadequacy of record-keeping had been addressed. Printed texts, spirit communications, resources for worship and for religious education, correspondence, manuscript books, and paintings and drawings circulated detailed information about Ann Lee and other early Shakers. These materials encouraged adherents to know not only what their Heavenly and Spiritual Parents said, but also what they looked like, where they came from, and what happened to them as they sought to live according to their faith.[58] Through the instruments, Believers maintained, Mother Ann's spirit companions residing in the heavenly sphere as well as living witnesses to her ministry contributed to the stories of the founder treasured by her followers. Shakers regarded as scripture the words of Ann Lee as remembered and recorded by some members of the Society. The 1845 manuscript, "Sayings of Mother Ann Lee," edited by Roxalana Grosvenor, highlighted, in particular, the charismatic spirituality of the Shaker founder.[59] By reclaiming and revering the places, times, objects, and people of the first generation, members of the United Society sought a surer sense of continuity with a sacred past.

Spiritual sites within Zion's borders gained significance as the shrines of a sacred history. Many New Era travel journals read like accounts of eager and often self-conscious pilgrims making their way to Shaker holy places.[60] In 1843, Shaker Giles Avery wrote about his travels in the eastern societies. A diary entry described Avery's visit to the community at Harvard.

> Here we are shown the very rooms where our ever blessed Parents served the Lord both with hands and hearts, the same stairs which have so often borne their supple knees, and, also, drink at Mother's Well, not of spiritual water only but at the self same proverbial well where so many of our gospel parents have quenched their thirst when dripping with sweat on a cold winters night from laboring in the work of God . . . Yea, here is the same old well porch and cirb [curb]—and, I don't know but the same bucket, I here drew water from Mother's well with my own hand, a privilege long to be remembered. O Mother, Mother art thou near, While I thy mansion do revere, And dost thou hear my infant cry, O Mother do not pass me by? Truly my child, I hear thy voice; And in this mansion now rejoice, Where once I suffered grief and pain, That Zion's children here might reign.[61]

Not only did New Era Shakers surround the historical sites within their borders with an increasing aura of sanctity, they also erected new monuments and acquired additional properties in places they considered historically significant. In 1845 Shakers purchased the Eleazar Grant house, "where once transpired the scene of a riotous Mob and biter persecution in which Mother Ann was the principal object of abuse."[62] After completing the business transaction, Believers held a service of dedication at the house. During the proceedings, according to the instrument, the spirit of Mother Ann appeared, blessing this act of recollection.

> The account of the scene of the Mob, as recorded in Mother's Sayings was read. Mother soon made herself known, thro' an Inst and spake much of her love to us, her children, and her special delight that we had thus turned out to notice this place, and to commemorate the scene of her sufferings on earth.[63]

Some years later the Shaker community at Harvard planned to erect a marble slab, near their borders, "on the spot whereon Beloved Father James was so cruelly whipt by his persecutors . . . so that we can hold meetings there."[64]

In addition to holy places, the instruments recommended an expanded calendar of sacred holidays to reach the hearts and minds of the rising generation. Ann Lee's birthday assumed a status parallel to the Christmas birthday of Jesus

Christ.[65] New Era Believers frequently celebrated the birthdays of other prominent Shaker ancestors as well.[66] And August 6 took on sacred significance as the day Mother Ann and her English followers landed in New York.[67] New articulations of time marked years as well as days in relationship to the life of Mother Ann. Shakers devised a chronology based on the births of *both* Jesus *and* Ann Lee to date testimonies appended to the "Holy Laws of Zion." According to this new system, the testimonies originated in 1841, "in the year of our blessed Lord and Savior," and in the year 105, "from the birth of our ever blessed Mother Ann Lee."[68] The United Society continued this practice in dating similar contemporary documents.

Material fragments of sacred history, too, figured significantly. During Ann Lee's lifetime some converts considered it a privilege just to touch the garments of their charismatic leader.[69] Years later, in the 1840s and 1850s, Believers expressed a similar attitude when they accumulated and treasured relics representing a personal connection with Ann Lee's bodily presence.[70] Contemplating these fragments of history moved the thoughts and devotion of the faithful to persons now beyond history. A poem interpreted a scrap of Mother Ann's skirt as it was passed down over the years.

Unborn generations
Who come to Mother's fold,
May feel some satisfaction
This relic to behold;
To know that Mother saw it,
And held it in her hand;
To know it cross'd the Ocean
With her, from Britain's Land;
Will please her faithful children,
And bring her spirit near,
The Mother of all Zion,
Who lived and suffered here.[71]

Other Shaker relics included the bones of Mother Ann and Father William. In 1835, Believers exhumed the remains of these revered predecessors so that they could be buried in the cemetery of the Shaker society at Watervliet where Mother Ann and Father William first planted their gospel.

[11 May 1835] Elder Ebenezer and I [Rufus Bishop] went with most of the elders of this society and some others, to the North farm and took up the bones of Mother Ann, Father William, and William Bigsby [a first born Believer]. We found them in a better state of preperation than was expected, notwithstanding they had lain in the sand more than half a century. Even the bones of the fingers and toes were in pretty good shape. We took them up and filled the graves and returned home before noon. The Brethren prepared a small and decent coffin for each. During which preparation the society had free access to view the bones of these venerable messengers of peace and salvation who first brought life and immortality to light in this our day, and

> who waded through sore afflictions, privations, and cruel persecutions, both in England and America for the good of lost souls.
>
> Some marks of their sufferings were yet visible—On the left side of Mother's scull could be seen a fracture said to be made when she was drgged [*sic*] down stairs feet foremost by her persecutors, when at Petersham.
>
> Also a fracture of an inch and half was plainly seen above Father William's left temple, which according to his own account when living with us, was made by one of his persecutors who gave him a severe blow with a fire poker while in England.
>
> [12 May 1835] About half past One Oclock, P.M. these remains were decently entered in our Grave-yard, near the Centre. So Mother Ann's bones lay the next north of Mother Lucy's, and Father William's at Mother's left—all in one row.[72]

But not all Shaker relics were actual historical objects. Shakers not only preserved relics, they created them.[73] Foremost among "new" relics, gift images met all necessary criteria for establishing a sense of personal connection with the owners of items represented: they were visible, they were tangible, and they were passed to Ann Lee's followers on earth directly from the hands of deceased ancestors resident in the spirit world. Gift pictures (and texts too) sometimes took the form of intimate personal articles belonging to the Heavenly and Spiritual Parents. No one had saved Mother Hannah's pocket handkerchief, but Father James pictured it for Jane Blanchard in a painting dated 1851 (Pl. V). Here was a reasonable equivalent for one not fortunate enough to have inherited a piece of Mother Ann's dress or apron. Such a representation made the memory of the Heavenly and Spiritual Parents concrete and transferable from generation to generation. A handkerchief might seem a strange choice for a relic but many Christians in the past would not have thought so. The renowned Veronica's Veil was, after all, the kerchief with which this saint was said to have wiped Christ's brow on the road to Calvary.[74] Ample evidence survives to indicate important religious as well as personal uses of pocket handkerchiefs among Shakers. These articles of dress figured in Shaker prayer at mealtimes,[75] in burying the dead,[76] in drying tears of sorrow,[77] and in exchanges of material and spiritual gifts.[78] Shakers employed pocket handkerchiefs in enacting prophetic signs[79] and as wrappers or containers for sacred items.[80] Semantha Fairbanks, an important instrument of messages and drawings (eventually a member of the parent ministry) was also a handkerchief-maker.[81]

A Type of Mother Hannah's Pockethandkerchief was reliquary as well as relic. Within this holy container, the instrument pictured other treasures of a sacred history: "A Necklace from the Woman of Samaria," "A Fan of Mother Hannah's, to blow away buffetings," "A Trumpet from Moses," and so on. Similarly, many other gift images functioned as reliquaries of Shaker history and tradition (e.g., figs. 7 and 13 and Pl. II). The smaller pictures which fill the inner spaces of numerous drawings and paintings (sometimes resembling individual motifs on samplers or quilt blocks) often represented a selection of choice presents bestowed upon the recipient of the image by inhabitants of the spirit world. The reliquary analogy was borne out in design and composition as well as subject matter. The borders painted around the edges of these religious pictures gave the viewer a clear sense of interior and exterior which visually paralleled the experience of a precious box or vessel filled with spiritual treasures.

Shakers would likely judge useful the analysis of their visionary images as reliquaries of sacred history and heavenly gifts. In fact, New Era Believers recorded the reception of spiritual "treasure boxes" visible only to the instruments, containers of sacred objects for distribution among members of the community. On 22 November 1841, Isaac Newton Youngs mentioned a "Box of Holy Sacred and Heavenly treasures, given by Mother Ann at Watervliet, for all her faithful and true hearted children at the Holy Mount of God [New Lebanon]."[82] A number of images too Shakers conceived as (and labeled) treasure boxes. One amply illustrated gift booklet the instrument titled a "Beautiful Box of Gifts and Emblems of the Presents Given to Calvin Green as a Token of Eternal Blessings from all the Eternal and Heavenly Parents."[83] The gifts from inside the box, the instrument painted on the pages of the booklet: a "Crown of Fortitude" from Mother Ann, a "Trumpet of Declaration" from Father Joseph, a "Sap Vine of Love" from Mother Lucy, for example. Another gift image, a small, meticulously composed sheet given to Molly Smith in 1854, the instrument described as "A Little Box of presents" from Eldress Ruth Landon (d. 1850).[84] On one side of this decorated message, Ruth Landon addressed Molly Smith, praising her faithfulness, assuring her of a "glorious reward," and describing the contents of her "Little Box." The box, according to the text, held gifts from Mother Ann, Father William, Father James, Father Joseph, and Mother Lucy as well as from Eldress Ruth Landon, with whom Smith had been well acquainted. Included among the spiritual treasures bestowed upon Smith was "a *pair of Spectacles,* to see your pretty treasures with," and "a nice *Pockethandkerchief,* with a *Blue Border.*" The reverse side of the image then constituted a facsimile of the pocket handkerchief, the blue border of the image duplicating the border of the handkerchief, the central text recording the "Verses written on the Handkerchief." The instrument ornamented the handkerchief at the corners with painted pink "Rose[s] of love from the rest of your former Ministry and one from Sister Susanna, with a little dove on it." In such novel and relatively durable pictures, Shakers retained for posterity objects of great personal and historical value.

In other gift paintings too, instruments made Shaker history visible. One large picture, *The Tree of Light or Blazing Tree* (1845), depicted a visionary image critical in the religious self-understanding of the United Society.[85] Such a blazing tree, seen by James Whittaker in a "vision of America," convinced Ann Lee and her small group of English followers that "the Church of Christ . . . [would] yet be established in this [American] land."[86] The burning tree image also connected the Shaker story to the story of God's people in an earlier dispensation; the followers of Ann Lee knew very well that God spoke to Moses through a burning bush.[87] In this and many other gift images, instruments sketched signs and symbols from Shaker history. The Albany prison in which the sect's founder was incarcerated, the ship on which she crossed the Atlantic, and her "crucifixion" all figured prominently in the instruments' paintings (figs. 7, 20, and 28).

The wide circulation of an official sacred history allowed mid-nineteenth-century Shakers to share a set of memories with their ancestors in faith. Knowledge of holy places, dates, and objects now connected the third generation with Mother Ann and those converted by her. In fact, the first born themselves, as representatives of the living link between Ann Lee and later generations, played a role in the history the mid-century Society promoted.

> Living among you are many worthy and beloved souls, who have taught you of my sufferings, and ardent labors and persecutions, while planting the gospel among them and their toiling companions, who have done their work on earth and gone home to the mansions of eternal rest.[88]

Beginning in the years preceding Mother's Work, Shaker journalists and scribes provided a detailed chronicle of the diseases and deaths of the first born. Members of the Society kept one another informed of the passing of individuals from the original English band as well as the demise of each person converted during Mother Ann's life time.[89] The first born not only taught Shaker history, they were a crucial part of that history. As repositories of the collective historical memory the first born, in a sense, themselves became sacred relics.[90] Their personal connection with Ann Lee granted them a sort of analogous status with material objects Ann Lee had possessed or touched. The first born, like both actual and represented relics, gained influence and value because they had been in direct contact with a celestial gift-giver. According to Shaker chroniclers of Mother's Work, the first born pillars of the Millennial Church spent their days on earth building a solid foundation for later followers of Ann Lee.[91] Instruments assured Shaker congregations that the first born were, in fact, responsible for the "refreshing showers" of the Era of Manifestations. The prayers of the first born caused God to open heaven's windows. The faith of the first born kept the judgments of God at bay so that more recent converts might turn from sin and be saved.[92] In a communication of 27 April 1839, Ann Lee's spirit spoke these words:

> I . . . appeared on earth, the second time . . . among my children for the consolation of my first born, that they might see and know that my gospel was firmly planted in the rising generation, that they might leave this world in peace.[93]

Spiritual gifts and messages awarded to the first born encouraged recognition of their years of service and commitment to the Shaker cause.[94] When the elders distributed gift notices on 25 January 1843, some surviving first born members (and other "ancient" Shakers) merited, in addition, special cards representing choice presents from the heavenly sphere. According to one of these visually organized messages (fig. 10), carefully bordered and calligraphed on delicate pastel colored papers, celestial beings clothed Molly Smith in beautiful garments clearly visible to those gifted with spiritual sight. In the religious imagination of the believing community, these and similar gifts symbolically marked the first born as worthy models for emulation. (Coincidentally, at just about the same time that the last of the first born were "passing from the scenes of time," Shaker instruments stopped producing gift images.[95] For a variety of reasons, any intentional or causal correlation here must remain purely speculative. To the degree, however, that the images facilitated communal grief about and, ultimately, acceptance of the loss of "direct" contact with the early years, the synchronic pattern is revealing.)

As the chronological and experiential gap between the Shaker community and the first Shakers widened, ministry and instruments encouraged heightened respect and veneration in regard to Shaker founders and those converted by them. But *Shaker* history alone was insufficient if the appeal was to be truly effective among the young and recently converted. For this was a history foreign to those with little or no previous exposure to Shakerism. When knowledge of the Shaker founders was no longer familiar to the majority of those who entered the United Society, dedicated adherents constructed a history which *was* familiar. Instruments of Mother's Work turned the giants of a popular and widely disseminated American and biblical history into the heroes of communal history.[96] In image and in text these instruments construed Shakerism as the centerpiece of this new and more generally familiar historical narrative. One very large gift painting (Pl. II) ranked a miniature portrait of the widely known Christopher Columbus in the top register, adjacent to Mother Ann and her less widely known companions, Father James and Father William. Clearly identified in the caption to the left of the image, Columbus was made to occupy a position of high esteem in the compositional hierarchy represented here. George Washington, William Penn, Lafayette, Napoleon, and great numbers of Native Americans also figured prominently in the new condensed version of Shaker mythology.[97] If the rising generation experienced Mother Ann as a relatively unknown quantity, they certainly knew and revered Washington and Columbus. As "Brother Washington" noted in an early manifestation, "you have all heard, or read of me."[98]

Shakers did not vote or take up arms, and they were often at odds with their state legislatures. But, they insisted, theirs was the *true* American heritage. In fact, Shakers promoted Ann Lee and her followers, arriving in America in 1774, as inaugurators of the American struggle for freedom. In the Shakers, so the argument went, spiritual freedom made its initial appearance in this land. In a few short years, political freedom (which, Shakers reasoned, depended upon the spiritual variety) would also belong to Americans.[99] According to Shaker historians, however, God had been at work in America long before the eighteenth century. Divine providence directed that "the wilderness of America" be "the field for the manifestation of Christ in the female."[100] Shaker instruments recreated Christopher Columbus as a John the Baptist figure, "preparing a way in the wilderness" for Ann Lee, the second appearance of Christ.[101]

> I [Mother Ann] have proved the bearer [Christopher Columbus] of this my word unto you; for ever since he first found me and confessed his sins, he has walked in obedience to the gospel; and also some others who you have heard of, who were

> noticed of God, to form the Constitution of the United States. Many of them, who have left the body, have proved to be faithful children to obey the gospel.[102]

So Mother Ann had personally converted Columbus in the celestial sphere. He testified to his gospel faith: "Now when ye think of me, if ye will but consider me as a little one among you, and a small child of my Mother, it is all I desire."[103] In a detailed communication of 25 August 1840, Mother Ann recounted her own version of Columbus's voyage to America.[104] At each point of crisis in the preparations for the journey and in the crossing itself, Almighty God the Father and Holy Mother Wisdom urged Columbus on, until he came to the land upon which the Divine Pair would build their Shaker Zion.

Similarly, Believers reconstructed George Washington as "an instrument in the hands of God [sent] to prepare the way for his peculiar people." According to this Shaker conformation, God worked through George Washington "to bring about the independent freedom of this American land."[105] Washington, a man "whose name [was] very dear to every true American,"[106] thus "paved the way" for the "blessed gospel" of Mother Ann.[107] During the years of Mother's Work, Washington visited his Shaker brothers and sisters even more frequently than did Columbus.[108] A letter from New Lebanon to Groveland in April 1840 recorded one of these visits.

> On the 25th ult. [of March] George Washington attended meeting with the Second Order at Watervliet, he said I have come to unite with you in the beautiful worship of God, and I want to drink with you of the spirit of thanksgiving to God for . . . Mother's pure gospel; for it is what my soul loves. He said he saw Mother [in a vision] once when he was on earth, and he thought then she was the most beautiful woman he ever saw.[109]

The writer of this letter included what purported to be Washington's own description of his visionary encounter with Mother Ann. In the course of their meeting, the correspondent maintained, Mother Ann recognized Washington, the "Hero of the Earth, and Father of the free."[110] The nation's Revolutionary hero and revered first president, then, became a reliable eyewitness to the work of the Shaker founder. When Shakers peopled their heavenly sphere with heroic Americans, they sought to create a relevant and convincing history for present and future generations. Christopher Columbus and George Washington represent just two members of an impressive contingent of patriots, inventors, political and religious leaders adopted by mid-nineteenth-century Shakers.[111]

Native Americans as well as renowned individuals of European descent figured in the Shaker historical reconstruction. Believing exegetes of Ann Lee's gospel identified the natives of the North American continent with the ten tribes of Israel in Jewish and Christian scriptures.[112] Like many biblical peoples, American Indians, then, were part of the *figurative* Israel which laid the foundation for God's *literal* Israel, realized in the followers of Mother's gospel.[113] Centuries before Shakers ever set foot on the continent, adherents claimed, native prophets had foretold the foundation of the Millennial Church in the New World.[114] The energy and imagination required to speak for Indian spirits attracted many young instruments, in particular, to this task.[115] In November 1842 one of these instruments delivered an especially intriguing message. At the request of William Penn, George Washington, Thomas Jefferson, and their compatriots in the spirit world, the instruments asserted, Mother Ann had agreed to redress the grievances of Native Americans against the colonists and citizens of the United States by inviting native spirits to share the blessings of her gospel.[116] The spirits of William Penn and company pled their cause convincingly: "For when we review our past lives, there is nothing but what we can feel is freely forgiven, but our repeated cruel acts to the poor Natives who inhabited the woods of America."[117] In the remaining paragraphs of this communication the instrument recorded Mother Ann's request that her followers on earth participate in the conversion of native spirits. In this way, the spirit of the Shaker founder suggested, living Shakers might assist in compensating American Indians for past European transgressions, simultaneously multiplying the number of Shakers in the celestial sphere in an effort to balance losses on earth.

Despite the fact that native spirit messages employed a unique historical mythology, they generally expressed the same themes found in other gift messages. In their most striking visual form, communications from Indian spirits arrived encoded in elaborate native notation (fig. 6). As one Believer remarked,

> Some of the Native spirits write beautiful letters in their own language, which is beyond our art to imitate. When they translate their Letters (as they generally do into broken english), one page will fill three, or a little more. These Instruments for the Natives will as readily read these leters [*sic*] as we could print, altho we might as well read a piece of Chintz, as to read these letters, before they are translated.[118]

To the average Shaker, the ornamented surfaces of most native spirit correspondence looked more like coded fields of ink lace than like written language. In some cases both the original notation and the "translation" survive. In others, the only record is the "broken english" penned by the translator. Occasionally an instrument illustrated gift messages delivered in a "Native American tongue" or its translation with small recognizable images. In 1845 booklets to members of the parent ministry "brought by a native spirit" included sketches of objects and persons drawn from Shaker perceptions of Native American life.[119] Because the ordinary Shaker could not decipher "a piece of Chintz" or a field of lace, native spirit texts functioned as exotic spiritual designs, as visible pieces of Shaker history, similar in some respects to the mysterious Sacred Sheets.[120]

Not only American history, but also biblical history served in the creation of the Shaker historical narrative. Shakers reconstructed and adapted biblical history as enthusiastically as they incorporated the American past, and with the same fundamental goal: to create a cohesive, persuasive, and moving narrative for the rising generation and for those who would follow after them. From the beginning, the followers of Ann Lee had identified themselves as the true Christian Church. Judeo-Christian scriptures, then, were Shaker scriptures. During the New Era, however, Shakers more elaborately and explicitly integrated biblical characters, places, and events into their own religious story. While adherents to the gospel of Mother Ann appropriated as their own the Christian bible, they understood this sacred book as an incomplete, even imperfect, record of God's activity, useful only when correctly interpreted in the context of the *living* word of God which addressed Believers in Christ's Second Appearing.[121] Once the millennium had been inaugurated by the celestial Daughter, Ann Lee, older scriptures assumed for Shakers a figurative status.[122] The Shaker American Zion was, they claimed, the *literal* Israel. America was the true site of Creation,[123] "Cain slew Abel in the hollow near the Holy Mount,"[124] and Noah built his ark on Shaker territory.[125] New Era Shakers raised an altar on their feastground in memory of the biblical spirits who peopled their lands.[126] Their own landscape, they believed, contained the holy sites of Jewish and Christian scriptures.[127] Like the Mormons, then, Shakers "sacralized the nation's landscape."[128] Rather than living in the sacred past, that past became a present spiritual reality in the retrieved persons, places, and events of Shaker history. According to Believers, biblical figures, like all truly great Americans, enthusiastically joined the Shaker cause by accepting Mother's gospel in the heavenly sphere. Adam and Eve, Moses and Miriam, Abraham and Sarah, Isaiah, Daniel, Jeremiah, Esther, Judith, Mary, Deborah, Nicodemus, Peter, and many, many others gave testimony in words and pictures to the fulfillment in Mother Ann of God's will for the universe.

For at least some mid-nineteenth-century Shakers, the inclusion in their spiritual pantheon of widely acclaimed and admired figures from American and biblical history made Shaker history more compelling, in part because more familiarly heroic. The history Believers created validated their own experience. Such eminent persons could not be wrong. If the greatest heroes of both religious and secular history claimed Ann Lee as their spiritual Mother, then Shakers possessed God's highest revealed truth. In addition, the new historical narrative gave Believers a sense of participation in a venture of critical importance; this understanding of the past assigned them a crucial role in the course of the nation and the course of the universe. And finally, the new history provided a coherent umbrella for other significant aspects of Shaker and prospective Shaker lives; Shaker history framed national, religious, and familial loyalties.

The creation of a convincing communal history was crucial in a society rapidly losing the young who could not recall Mother Ann. The new historical concretion invited both young and old to celebrate the glorious past of the sect. But persuasive memories of the charismatic founder and the early years of zeal truly belonged only to those who had lived in those days. Somehow the rising generation needed to make the communal memory and the communal history its own. The sectarian, American, and biblical aspects of the new Shaker historical narrative came together to form a spiritual genealogy for the United Society. This genealogy occupied an intermediary position between recollecting history and recreating experience, between knowledge of the past and encounter in the present. Ann Lee was, after all, not only the historical founder of Shakerism, she was also the spiritual Mother of her New Era children. Ultimately, the history that Shakers recalled was a *family* history. The ties designed to hold Shakers together were *family* ties. Ministry and instruments collaborated with their Heavenly and Spiritual Parents in the celestial sphere to help Mother's children in the rising generation experience their full inclusion in the Shaker family.

The Shaker ideal mandated that "gospel relations" (the true familial ties between spiritual relatives) supplant "natural relations" (ties of blood between biological relatives). In the eighteenth century, Ann Lee and James Whittaker had adopted a familial model for understanding spiritual relationships. Joseph Meacham expanded this metaphor significantly. Under Meacham and Lucy Wright, the Shaker community became a spiritual family of gospel brothers and sisters with the early ministry for parents.[129] Mid-nineteenth-century initiates to Shakerism joined a family which counted among its members the heroes of American, biblical, and Shaker history. Acknowledging the full integration of Washington, Lafayette, Governor Clinton, Columbus, and tribes of Native Americans into Shaker society, Believers welcomed these individuals as "dear Gospel Relation[s]."[130] Ministry and instruments encouraged young members of the Shaker family to walk in the footsteps of their gospel parents, to follow their spiritual forebears in the Narrow Path, to be like the generations of Shaker ancestors that had gone before.[131]

The concern of Shakers for the children and youth among them reflected a much broader antebellum American sense of crisis in the institution of the family. While issues of adolescent individuation and psychosexual development undoubtedly intensified the situation in the communal and celibate Shaker context, Americans in general worried about the moral correctness, obedience, and familial attachments of their children. In *Religion and Sexuality,* Lawrence Foster argues that several factors, including increased economic differentiation, geographic mobility, and individualism, produced a significant sense of dislocation and dis-ease and ultimately focused attention on the family home as both the locus of the problem and the most likely site for a solution.[132] On many fronts, in terms of domestic architecture (Andrew Jackson Downing) and the concurrent cult of domesticity as well as in religion (Horace Bushnell), Americans launched a crusade to shape and reshape their offspring in morally acceptable ways. If (as Bushnell claimed) god-fearing parents and a Christian home might produce salvation in the young, if (as Downing claimed) the family was the only social institution capable of restraining materialism, individualism, and competition, then the domestic environment, the happy home, became both a surrogate for the church and a pillar of American democracy. Antebellum Shakers, adapting the domestic ideal of their American contemporaries, frequently construed the crisis among their youth as a crisis of family and familial associations. Instructions given to Shakers who cared for the youth and children urged a sense of "parental obligations" toward those placed in their custody.[133] The communal home, like the Shaker heaven, constituted a refuge in relationship to the world—heaven was, after all, the ultimate cosmic "home."[134] Again, even the conceptual organization of the Shaker community with its trustees' office was similar to the organization of the antebellum home with its parlor. Parlor and office funtioned as transitional zones, protecting the inner sanctum of the home from the world outside.[135]

As part of the larger narrative of familial history reshaping the New Era community, gift images displayed a *visible* family line. Drawings and paintings enhanced the individual's sense of inclusion in a cohesive family unit which extended beyond the terrestrial sphere into a spiritual world inhabited by great women and men who were "dear gospel relations." The instrument who included Columbus in *An Emblem of the Heavenly Sphere* (Pl. II) represented the celestial regions as a genealogical garden. As Christian iconography's Jesse Tree established the lineage of Jesus, this *Emblem* depicted Shaker lineage. The arrangement of the central part of the composition around a trunk-like form from which blossom "regions of delight" suggests a resemblance between Shaker forebears and a living family tree bearing heavenly fruit.[136]

The consistent organization of the painting into ranks and sets of four reinforced orthodox Shaker genealogical history. Here again four dispensations, inaugurated by Abraham, Moses, Jesus, and Ann Lee, comprised Shaker familial descent as four human "pillars" comprised the contemporary Shaker ministry. Although this quartered or "four square" composition maintained a dispensational content in a painting representing celestial lineage, the instrument made no attempt to depict an exact correspondence between columns of people and particular dispensations of time. Rather, by selecting and grouping together miniature portraits representing individuals from all four dispensations, the instrument underscored the notion that each of the biblical and historical figures included in her painting had embraced Ann Lee's gospel in the spiritual world. All thus enjoyed membership in the mid-nineteenth-century Shaker family by virtue of their posthumous conversions. So each portrait represented a "contemporary" gospel sister or brother as well as an ancestor in the faith.[137] The likenesses of four of the immediate forerunners of American faith (Mother Ann, Father James, Father William, and Columbus) across the top register suggested that the stout trunk of the family tree would continue growing—would in fact, soon include Shakers still on earth at the time of the *Emblem*'s production. The text of the painting reiterated this visual promise:

> An emblem of the happy land above!
> Where Angels join the choral song in love,
> Is here portraid, that you may faintly see,
> But half can not be told, nor shone, to thee.
> Rejoice, go on, you'l yet obtain the sight,
> An entrance in those regions of delight.
> Your praise will mingle with the happy throng,
> And to their holy circle you'l belong.[138]

The rising generation, images like *Emblem* insisted, enjoyed a familial connection with Mother Ann, her first born, and their spiritual forebears. Tangible images of this sort signified both longevity and continuity in Shaker lineage. As genealogical chart, as family tree, *Emblem* represented the notion of the family as a repository or archive of historical meaning and as a site of its manufacture.[139]

In *Emblem* the instrument adapted to her own purposes a broader visual tradition for representing lineage in the form of a tree. The instruments of other gift images as well freely adapted forms from popular familial depictions. These instruments did not so much copy forms from the culture outside the United Society. Rather, they established a sufficient visual resemblance to suggest in the mind of the beholder the possible sources of their images and the familial significance of those sources. At Hancock, Massachusetts, in 1854, instrument Hannah Cohoon modeled her striking *Tree of Life* (fig. 2) on an image she may have remembered from a quilt applique.[140] But this image very closely approximated an eighteenth and nineteenth-century form of decorative family record popular in New England and especially in Massachusetts.[141] The familial content of this resemblance has been suggested recently, perhaps unwittingly, in the cover image of a 1979 publication by George R. Stewart titled *American Given Names* which conflates Cohoon's image and the New England record of familial generation.[142] On the cover of Stewart's book appears a very slightly modified version of the Shaker image with popular American given names superimposed over the fruits of Cohoon's tree of life, producing a synthesis which suggests naming traditions within American families.

Shakers adapted at least one additional popular art form which, in its original context, communicated a distinctly familial and generational content. Three surviving gift drawings (see, for example, fig. 21) are strikingly similar in design to the ceramic commemorative plates popular among American folk groups of English and Continental descent contemporary in time and place with Shaker instruments.[143] Once again, the transcription was not exact. In this case, Shakers changed the medium of the original objects from clay to paper and they implied a possible alternative status for these family plates as "balls of love."[144] Nonetheless, it was not at all uncommon for a gift image to be associated with more than one heavenly gift or source. The image could be both plate and ball of love. And, significantly, the text of one of the three drawings (dated 1847 to Grove Blanchard from Holy Mother Wisdom) specifically identified the image as a "plate": "For surely I your Mother true, have sent this plate to comfort you." Other internal evidence supports the interpretation of these drawings as commemorative plates. Unlike many other gift images, Shaker "plates," like the ceramic family plates, had images on only one side. Also, Shakers recorded the reception of spiritual gift plates on numerous occasions. Believers described some of these plates as bearing writing and images.[145] In one message, Hannah Blake and Giles Avery (both instruments rising in Shaker ranks) received "little white plates" "covered all over" with Mother Ann's love and blessing. The words accompanying these plates addressed the youth and middle aged, in particular, as "Ye who must soon bear the burden in the house of God."[146] Gift plates were vessels to hold heavenly food, sustenance for New Era Believers.[147] Even in the unlikely event that the instruments did not consciously intend all three works to represent family plates, the visual similarities, especially of the two drawings not textually identified as plates, are remarkable. Furthermore, like the family plates which honored ancestors and commemorated important family occasions (marriages, for example), these circular compositions identified promising young Shaker leaders as the spiritual offspring of beloved Shaker parents.

Daniel Boler received one of these drawings (fig. 21) from Mother Ann on the same day (2 November 1845) that Eliza Ann Taylor received a second from Father Joseph. These two Shaker "plates" represented a living and intimate connection between young leaders of the rising generation and the founders and first generation leaders of the Millennial Church. The outer ring of the drawings established earthly lineage. On Eliza Ann Taylor's plate, the encircling text read,

> **Father Joseph** was born February 22nd 1742. Deceased August 16th 1796, being 54 years 5 months and 24 days of age. **Mother Lucy** was born February 5th 1761. Deceased February 7th 1821, being 61 years and 2 days of age.

Daniel Boler's plate recorded similar information about Mother Ann:

> **Mother Ann** was born February 29th, seventeen hundred and thirty six. Landed in America August sixth, seventeen hundred seventy four. Deceased September eighth, seventeen hundred 84, being 48 years 6 months and eight days of age.

The inner circle of the plates emphasized the continuing presence of these gift-giving Shaker ancestors. The ministries of Mother Ann, Father Joseph, and Mother Lucy visibly embraced and nurtured the lives and work of their daughter and son in the rising generation. When Taylor and Boler received their plates, they held the junior positions in the eldership of the Church Family at New Lebanon. While they were not yet members of the parent ministry, their companions in faith knew that they were among those to whom the mantle of leadership would pass.

The instrument of Taylor's plate depicted two pillars representing the kind of stable leadership upon which the future of the sect would depend. In words inscribed next to the pillar crowned with a harp, Father Joseph appealed to this third generation daughter to "stand as a permanent pillar in the house of your Mother when her first born are called home," urging her to identify with her Shaker forebears, the original "first born" pillars of the Millennial Church, by assuming their role as strong columns supporting the Shaker terrestrial home. The calligraphers who drew these plates gave visual expression to the places of Eliza Ann Taylor and Daniel Boler in the Shaker ancestral line. By promoting this visible genealogy of gospel relations, both instruments and ministry hoped to strengthen the familial link between the rising generation and the earliest converts of Ann Lee.

Instruments worked and reworked the communal, biblical, and American pasts to create a collective historical memory that would shape the Shaker present and future.[148] To a large extent, after all, the New Era predicament involved the recollection of past experiences. Identity-informing memory constituted, in fact, a critical distinction between first born and rising generations. Far more important than biological age cohort, the content of memory figured in the Shaker comprehension of generation. The first generation of American Shakers shared a set of memories which did not belong to later generations of Believers.[149] Somehow these memories had to be made accessible, had to be restored, to the mid-nineteenth-century Shaker community. The New Era re-collection of history aimed to accomplish this goal. The entire cast of figures from the Shaker historical narrative arrived to help the rising generation "remember." Gift images and other sacred communications helped to fix, define, and organize appropriate memories. Images, especially, established a material relationship to an ideal past.[150] They not only rationalized memory but made it concrete. Of all celestial gifts, the instruments' pictures most tangibly manifested the visionary performances which preserved the memory of early Shakerism.

But memory alone was insufficient; for memory, in large part, signified loss. Memory functioned as "a substitute, surrogate, or consolation for something that [was] missing."[151] Not only did members of the mid-nineteenth-century Shaker community need to recollect historical memory, they also needed to reconnect memory with the experiences that produced it. Shared experience, as the context for shared memory, was the critical factor. Appropriate memories could be produced, to a degree, by teaching the story, the historical narrative. But memory could be more persuasively instilled by repeating the original experiences. Only in conjunction with personal experience could familiarity with the past revitalize communal memory and stimulate conviction.

Seven

Restoring Relationship

IMAGE AS "VISIBLE PRESENCE"

The missing "something," the experience which had so permanently grounded the early Shaker community, involved, of course, the person of Ann Lee, her charism and authority, and her ability to facilitate the expression of charismatic gifts and to "work conviction" in others.[1] Even the first young visionists at Watervliet defined the immediate problem of the third generation in terms of loss of contact with Ann Lee. Most of these initial instruments, in the course of their spiritual visitations, found themselves being "interviewed" by this most significant "Mother."[2] On 16 August 1837, one of the instruments "was asked what she saw; she answered, 'The first I knew Mother Ann came to me, and she asked me if I knew her, I said nay; she said "Did you ever hear of Mother Ann?["] I said yea; she said, ["]My name is Mother Ann." ' "[3] The first official gift message delivered at New Lebanon envisioned Mother's Work as the revelation of the Shaker founder to those who had never seen her, as the "second appearance" of the early leader, manifested "with power and evidence, not to be mistaken or evaded."[4]

> For these caviling young people knew not their heavenly Parents neither personally nor in spirit. Therefore they would not believe without a work of inspired manifestations and divine communications from the Heavens, attended by such evident operations as could not be disputed by the rational senses, and which brought forth the same testimony that your heavenly Parents bore when on earth, and which had always been maintained by their first born children.[5]

Curiously, it was the *visual* component of Mother Ann's absence that seemed most to disturb mid-nineteenth-century Shakers. Surviving documents establish beyond a doubt the centrality to Believers of their founder's *visible* presence.[6] The rhetoric of vision, of visibility, these Shakers found most compelling, most reassuring. "Seeing" Ann Lee was a pivotal event in Shaker experience even during Lee's lifetime. The 1816 and 1827 *Testimonies* contain multiple accounts of the relationship between seeing Lee and conversion or confirmation of faith. "When Anna Northrup first saw Mother, she received faith in the second appearance of Christ, in Mother, confessed her sins and received the power of the Holy Ghost."[7] Esther Bracket received from Lee the "gift of vision," "so that she [Bracket] could see Mother and converse with her, at any time, when she labored for it, as well as though they had been present together in the body."[8] In one of the latest recorded (1857) testimonies of a first born Believer, Thankful Goodrich (who converted with her parents at age ten) described her childhood experiences of Ann Lee. The initial words of Goodrich's testimony stress the importance of the visual encounter.

> I will now relate some of the blessed privilledges I enjoyed, at an early age, of beholding the faces, and hearing the words of our Heavenly Parents; which have ever remained fresh on my mind. They looked more lovely to me than any objects my eyes ever beheld; their soft voices, and the beauty of their lovely countenances filled my little soul with reverence and Godly fear.[9]

For Believers, a crucial part of the experience of Lee's death was the loss of their ability to "see" her. The founder was no longer visibly available to her followers. In the first edition of the *Testimony*, Benjamin Youngs described Ann Lee's passing as the disappearance of her "visible presence" "from the view of the world."[10] In reference to the earlier death of William Lee, Youngs wrote,

> The decease of Elder William served as a particular means of preparing the minds of believers for a still heavier trial, in being deprived of the visible presence and protection of Mother, the thought of which seemed almost insupportable to many; however, having finished the work which was given her to do, she was taken out of their sight.[11]

Distinguishing the rising generation from the first born on the basis of visual contact with Ann Lee, scribes and instruments addressed these spiritually younger Shakers as "you who never saw." From the Shaker perspective, this visual omission in past experience characterized a whole generation of adherents to the gospel of Ann Lee.[12]

As early as 1815, in order to minimize difficulties created by the loss of visual contact with Mother Ann, Lucy Wright offered an alternative means of sensing connections.

> The young that never saw Mother and the Elders, may sometimes feel to mourn because they have not seen them, it is not in seeing Mother, that joins us *to* Mother.

> If you are obedient to the present gift of God [as revealed to the ministry and communicated through them], you will be as really joined as I am, according to your measure.[13]

Wright's solution addressed a need for charismatic contact with an institutionalizing response. Union with the ministry and the community, she suggested, might replace vision, orderly behavior might replace ecstatic experience.

> You will have feelings that you will want to know if you are in union with Mother, but you need not labor for gifts to dream dreams or see visions, if you keep your union together as good brethren and sisters there will be nothing to separate you from Mother. You ought to go forth in union in all that you do with a calm and peaceable spirit—and Mother's spirit will be with you and God will bless you.[14]

For some this response was insufficient; for some union was no substitute for vision. The passing years only exacerbated the problem. By 1837 the young not only had no memory of the visible presence of Mother Ann, but most had never seen *any* of the early leaders—and the communities were fast losing the first born who alone could provide them with eyewitness accounts of the early people and events. A scribe for the Second Family at New Lebanon sounded a note of despair that Shakers would soon "be left without one who ever saw the face of the first Elders, or founders of the *holy Church*!"[15] At Watervliet, on 25 February 1844, another scribe's list of "The Names and Births, of the Brethren and Sisters, now liveing in the first part of the Church that have ever seen Mother Ann" was distressingly brief.[16] An official scribe at New Lebanon captured the dilemma precisely when he paraphrased Proverbs 29:18 to stress the passage of time rather than change of locale: "*When* there is no vision the people perish [italics added]."[17] At a time in Shaker history when Ann Lee and the first Elders could not be seen, how could her third generation followers experience contact with their founder?

According to the accounts of the instruments, those who now populated the heavenly sphere tailored a response to fit the problem: the gifts and messages of the New Era would provide the rising generation with the opportunity to see and hear Mother Ann for themselves. Through their young instruments, Mother Ann and other deceased Shaker leaders established a direct and immediate relationship with the new generation. The inhabitants of eternity and the inhabitants of time spoke "spirit to spirit, and face to face . . . as two friends would converse together."[18]

> It is a time of great encouragement for youth and children; as they do not now have to live on hearsay reports about the mighty gifts and power of God and about Mother and the Elders, who they formerly thought had been dead more than fifty years, for they have been made partakers of that blessed power, and by frequent visions and trances have become well acquainted with our blessed Parents and Elders in their glorified state and converse with them very often, and receive messages from them to communicate to the Brethren and Sisters.[19]

As Brother William Leonard testified, the Era was designed "to give us a more perfect presentation of our Eternal Parents than was ever made before to spirits in flesh and blood."[20] Some claimed that the visionists themselves, when possessed, actually bore a "remarkable resemblance," in "voice, gestures and manners of expression," to the "peculiar traits" of the spirits for whom they communicated. "This then must be a strong evidence that the invisible spirit did inspire the Instruments, inasmuch as they were unborn in the days of our Parents and knew nothing personally of their peculiarities."[21] A member of the New Lebanon ministry summarized the impact of the new and intimate relationship between past and present, between time and eternity.

> It feels to us like a peculiar notice and blessing, especially to all our junior brethren and Sisters, that they can now daily see or hear from our Ever-blessed Mother, and all our beloved Parents in the gospel, and can form an acquaintance and feel as near a relation to them as those who knew them when they were clothed with human flesh. Therefore, if there are any now among us who have doubts concerning revelation, or a future state, they must bear it themselves, for they must be wilfully blind.[22]

In visionary episodes third generation instruments experienced the "visible presence" of a spiritual mother they had never seen. On the basis of this experience, the third generation like the first could speak authoritatively of their aquaintance with Ann Lee.[23] Joseph Wicker, an instrument of gift messages and drawings, "spoke of his love and confidence in Mother altho' he never saw her face in the body; yet he felt much acquainted with her, he had seen her lovely form and could testify of her."[24]

But not every member of the rising generation enjoyed spiritual vision. Those without this gift depended on their spiritually sighted companions for knowledge of Mother Ann's presence among them. They depended on the vision of others, that is, until the spirits commissioned instruments to prepare drawings and paintings of celestial objects, people, and places. As members of the older generations passed away, gift images replaced these first born as visible reminders of Mother Ann's presence and ministry. In fact, the sudden appearance of images in a previously anti-iconic community can be attributed directly to the need not just for Mother Ann's presence but for her *visible* presence, for visual contact with the sect's founder. The rising generation re-presented their spiritual mother in their own time by creating for her a meaningful "image." When they needed vision, Shakers produced a religious art; when they needed eyewitnesses, they provided alternative objects of vision.[25] For the mid-nineteenth-century Shaker community, then, gift images were experiments in visible presence. Granted, the majority of the drawings and paintings did not depict the physical features of Ann Lee. The connection between picture and prototype did not depend on literal resemblance to Lee's bodily appearance. Nonetheless, these images signified and materialized the first Mother's presence by offering visible proof of parental affection and concern.[26]

For example, in 1853 the Hancock ministry received an exquisitely drawn and brilliantly colored *Floral Wreath* (fig. 22). In this composition, image and text together formed a successive layering of concentric circles leading the beholder's eye inward toward the central flower. The instrument underscored this gravitation toward the center by numbering the text's verses in ordered sequence, circle by circle, from the outermost ring moving inward. She called the viewer's attention to this intended ordering by locating the verse numbers along a vertical axis visually punctuated at the top and bottom of the wreath by two prominent red strawberries. The text urged the ministry to identify in their struggles with the persecuted Ann Lee. According to the text, Mother Ann had in fact placed her love in the center of the wreath to comfort Hancock's leaders through months and years of trial. This heavenly Mother's love the instrument represented in the single open blossom at the hub of the composition. The recipients of this gift, following the insistent centripetal movement of image and text, located themselves visually at this floral center, surrounded by a celestial garland, in space perfumed by Mother Ann's love. Surely Mother Ann and, indeed, the entire heavenly sphere (reproduced in the sacred circular shape of the wreath) embraced the ministry in all their tasks. Likewise, in a visionary painting addressed to Hester Ann Adams, the instrument identified the image itself with the love of Ann Lee: "receive this sheet, it is her [Mother Ann's] love" (fig. 11).[27]

The subject matter and form of the instruments' pictures demonstrated visual connections with the Shaker founder at multiple levels. While most of the images did not depict the physical form of Ann Lee, they did provide beholders with what Shaker William Leonard might have agreed was a "more perfect presentation" of the spiritual forebear "than was ever made before."[28] In fact, by not representing the physical body of Ann Lee, gift images suggested that her actual presence was more all-encompassing, more permanently available than her mortal body. Shakers based their understanding of visible presence on a particular construction of aesthetics, ethics, cosmology, and history in relationship to Ann Lee and to the heavenly sphere (cf. chapters 4, 5, and 6). What the instruments drew and painted, then, were the most fundamental characteristics of the Shaker primitive way exemplified in the "appearance" of Mother Ann: structural order, spiritual extravagance, moral virtue, heavenly enclosure and embrace, "familial" regeneration and bonding. So, paradoxically, gift images restored Mother Ann's essential visible presence generally without picturing her. This is visible presence in a very particular but also very broad sense: gift images re-presented Mother Ann in tangible and visible form by depicting some of her most powerful, compelling, and reassuring characteristics. Precisely because the images did not reduce her presence to a picturing of her physical form, they were able to draw upon an immense range of traits (behavioral, relational, structural) associated with her and to bring these traits into direct relationship with the beholder. Material evidence of a Mother's love could be handled and treasured far beyond the actual years of her visitation. By recording images and words on paper, Shaker instruments ensured that not only the third generation but others who followed after them might see.[29]

In gift images the instruments represented in a new time both the charismatic experience of vision exemplified in Ann Lee and the visible presence of the Shaker Mother herself. While the instruments identified many heavenly gift-givers (e.g., Mother Lucy, Father James, Father Joseph, Almighty God the Father, Holy Mother Wisdom, Jesus, and even George Washington, Christopher Columbus, and numerous named and unnamed native spirits), Ann Lee remained the pivotal figure in relationship to whom Lee's Shaker offspring interpreted all others. Images recalling the "second Mother" Lucy referred the beholder to the "first Mother" Ann. Mother Ann's visible presence then subsumed and included the visible presence of other Shaker leaders, conflating historical personae to carefully maintain the balance between charism and institution. Usually explicitly, at the very least implicitly, the instruments suggested that Lee had a hand in every gift of her Second Manifestation. This was, after all, *Mother's* Work. Even the deity was more clearly revealed through the person of Ann Lee. The Eternal Parents, the Heavenly Parents, the Spiritual Parents, the spirits of more recently deceased Shakers—all were arrayed around Lee and all gifted Shakers with visions, images, operations, messages which evoked Lee's presence.

In terms of its place within the framework of this book as a whole, this chapter considers gift images as a visible and tangible mechanism for expressing the concurrence of times, the retrieval of models from other times and outside time, the suggestion of an atemporal dimension in the midst of Shaker temporality. In terms of its own organization, however, it demonstrates exactly what this contraction, this simultaneity, offered mid-nineteenth-century Believers. In addition to re-presenting the "appearance" of Mother Ann in a variety of characteristics, Shaker images promoted three principal modes of restoring her visible presence. Shaker images revealed the caring, sacralizing, decorating (and decorated) presences of the Shaker Mother. This chapter will examine sequentially these three modes of expression, beginning with the caring or pastoral presence.

Mother's Work and Mother's presence operated at both communal and personal levels. The mid-nineteenth-century Shaker revival issued principally from a restorationist agenda. The alleviation of a particular *communal* affliction constituted its motivating source. But Believers also experienced intensely *personal* needs; the gifts of the spirit addressed these personal afflictions (physical, emotional, spiritual) as well as the communal concerns. The generally religious character of the United Society as a whole has not been disputed, but scholars have seldom considered Shakerism from the perspective of its particular ministries. Shakers defined themselves, individually and collectively, in terms of Christian history and tradition. They adapted traditional Christian symbols to their own circumstances, investing these symbols with new fourth dispensational meanings. As material resources of prophetic, pastoral, and sacramental ministries, sacred pictures and celestial communications addressed the religious needs of the mid-century Shaker community. At New Lebanon and Hancock, at least, leaders and followers alike integrated gift images into their understanding and practice of ministry. Celestial images and texts became particularly powerful visual and material resources in a ministry of pastoral care.[30] "Likenesses," both spiritually and naturally visible, became media of comfort.[31] In times of illness, death, and mourning, as simple encouragement in life's trials, as notices of personal forgiveness and salvation, as signs of protection from on high, gift paintings and visually organized notices healed, consoled, and reassured their recipients. Among mid-century Shakers, the ministry of pastoral care was, in fact, a ministry of *presence*. Gift images and related messages participated in this ministry in two ways. First, the subject matter of these pictures and words from the spirit world provided explicit, thoughtful, and convincing responses to specific troubles. Second, in form, the gifts were material tokens, visible "proof," of the compassion of a celestial mother/minister, of the reality of the celestial sphere, and, in many cases, of the continued existence of deceased spiritual relatives.

Among Shakers, as among the somewhat later spiritualists, a most pressing pastoral concern was the desire for assurance of personal as well as communal immortality.[32] Mother Ann's presence, of course, signified her immortality which guaranteed the Believer's immortality and the immortality of the Believer's loved ones. The vision that inaugurated Mother's Work not only "introduced" the third generation to Ann Lee, it also commented directly on the nature and reality of an otherworldly afterlife. In this vision, Ann Mariah Goff claimed that she entered the spirit world conducted by Beulah Downs, a sister from Goff's Shaker family who had died about eight months before. When asked why God now gave this gift of vision, Goff repeated Downs' reply, "We mean your people shall know what there is in another world."[33] Soon after this, Shaker instruments began to recount instances of the spirits of the dead visiting, often attending their own funerals, comforting those who mourned with assurances that life continued.

> At Watervliet they have had two deaths, one of them was a small boy, say three years old, at the South Family, of scarlet fever. After the little spirit had left its clay tenement, one of the visionists being present saw it, and likewise some other Spirits which the little thing seemed to eye pretty closely, and as they were strangers to him, he crawled up into the lap of a Sister who had nursed him in his sickness.[34]

In a description of recent deaths in the community at New Lebanon, a member of the New Lebanon ministry wrote:

> five others have gone to the spirit land, from which, it was formerly said, that no traveller returned. However, in these wonderful days they generally and frequently return in spirit, and minister comfort and consolation to their surviving friends.[35]

In 1839 Rufus Bishop described the impact of spirit visitations on attitudes toward death.

> Lucy Clark and Hannah Fairbanks, in the First Order here, cannot continue in their clay tenements much longer, as they are gradually failing, as to their bodily strength. But neither they nor we have anything to mourn about for the veil between us and the spiritual world has become so transparent, in these days, that our good friends

> seem much more active after laying aside the clay tabernacle than they did when they were bound and fettered by it.[36]

Spirits not only conducted tours of the celestial sphere and made visits to their earthly brothers and sisters, they also sent material emblems of comfort and consolation to reassure the sick and dying, to provide anxious and mourning survivors with hope and encouragement, and to offer words of grace and thanksgiving to the caretakers who nursed dying Shakers through their final days.[37] For example, at Hancock, in 1847, Molly Smith received an illustrated letter "written" in 1845 by Israel Hammond, who had died on 9 August 1841 at New Lebanon.[38] Hammond had been severely injured in a fall on 14 July 1831 and had been an invalid for ten years prior to his death.[39] Smith was one sister responsible for Hammond's care during the decade of his disability. In the 1847 gift letter, the spirit of Israel Hammond thanked Smith for her attentions and sought to relieve her of any guilt she might have felt regarding her inability to restore Hammond's health or preserve his life.

> Much Respected Sister,
>
> I have obtained permission of my blessed Mother [Ann], to manifest my thankfulness to you, for your neverending kindness to me, while in my afflicted situation; I know that you strove to do all that you could for my comfort and spared no pains for my relief.
>
> I have many times conversed with Mother about it, and told her I was afraid I had not done my duty in returning my thanks, as I was neither able nor capable of doing it while in the body; and that I should be glad if Mother would give me liberty to notice you now with a little present.
>
> Mother answered me and said; Israel, this is your duty; and you shall have my union in it. Take this little Box, and fill it with my love, blessing and thanks for the same; tell her that these trying scenes have not passed unnoticed by her parents in Heaven, and every act of kindness to the suffering and afflicted is recorded in Gold letters, and will remain there all eternity.[40]

A circular motif in colored inks painted on the reverse side of the letter pictured the key to and the round cover of a box of spiritual treasures sent to Molly Smith from Mother Ann as a reward for Smith's steadfast care of Hammond (fig. 8).

> Good Sister as you can only see the Cover to your little Box, I must tell you what is in it. It is filled with the Seeds of Thankfulness, with Blessed Mother's Love packed in tight on the top. It is also locked up, as you will see the key hangs upon the lock with a Silk Ribbon in it. Also in the Cover you will see a Seal of the Love of your Heavenly Parents; and the Birds of Paradise gathering the fruits of heaven to feed you with, and blessing the Trumpet of peace and good will to the children of Mother.[41]

When Holy Mother Wisdom's instrument urged recipients to keep such gifts in their dwelling rooms and to "labour to derive comfort, strength and support therefrom," she commented on the intended relationship of individual and image.[42] The nature of the interaction between Shaker beholder and visionary picture was more individual than communal, more private than public, not in the sense of isolation from the communal context but in the sense that the interaction itself elicited an intimate conversation between the spirit(s) involved in the production of the image and the beholder/recipient. Certainly the images had significant public and communal aspects: Believers often received images during communal meetings for worship; images participated in the ritual life of the sect; visionary experience in the sect (the basis for the creation of images) was a public performance; images drew upon the collective symbol system for subject matter, form, and content, privileging a particular shared visual code; image-makers influenced one another within communities and across community borders; an instrument in one community might produce an image for a resident of another community.[43] Ultimately, however, gift images in the Shaker community functioned as vehicles for interiorization and reflection; ultimately the images had more to do with personal devotion than with group experience. In content and in the circumstances of initial reception, images served the communal purposes of Mother's Work. But these complex visual messages addressed individuals or small groups and required attentiveness and concentration in order to achieve maximum effectiveness.[44] In most cases, the sheer abundance of separate compositional elements combined with precise and meticulous representation to create an image which demanded careful and close scrutiny. Some have argued that the individual or private aspect of gift images in a communal sect detracted from the images' power and usefulness.[45] On the contrary, precisely this aspect contributed significantly to the images' impact. In the Shaker context, gift images compensated for the general restriction of the private sphere. Particularly during the period of Mother's Work when new and renewed regulations, authorized in pursuit of true "primitive order," put additional constraints on individuals, gift images responded to legitimate personal needs.[46] The private, devotional impulse in gift images differentiated the pictures and visually organized personal messages from other manifestations of Mother's Work (song, dance, physical operations) which were more completely public in nature.[47] While public messages to communities or to sizable groups within communities were officially recorded and kept by the ministry, individuals retained personal gifts and messages in their own dwelling rooms, immediately available, to be contemplated, "perused, and preserved with great care."[48] In a multitude of ways, then, gift images directly communicated the caring presence of Mother Ann in personal struggles as well as in communal concerns. These images expressed and embodied Mother Ann as a source of nurture, sustenance, reassurance, comfort. In the images the strength of the founder, the strength of other early Shaker leaders, became accessible, could be drawn upon repeatedly, could be internalized as a fount of personal fortitude.

Historically, David Freedberg notes, certain forms of meditation depended upon "real images for the production of mental ones." "Image-assisted meditation" aimed to produce empathic associations or to facilitate the recovery of "that which [was] absent, whether historical or spiritual."[49] According to this contemplative method, the mind ascended from material image to mental image to spiritual image.[50] Image aided both concentration and ascent by directing attention to spiritual beings, objects, places. In the case of mid-nineteenth-century Shakers, who created religious images in direct response to and as representations of their relationship to specific spiritual presence(s) and subsequently contemplated the images to recall presence(s), image-assisted *invocation* more precisely describes the operative mechanism. Here among the followers of Ann Lee, the invocatory relationship of visibility and presence was explicitly sacramental. Tapping this second mode of pictorially restoring visible presence, Shaker religious images brought the sacred reality of Mother Ann and the celestial sphere into direct, intimate, and ongoing contact with the earthly realm.

Assisted by visual images, Believers invoked a *sacralizing* presence. Historian of religion Gerardus van der Leeuw understood sacrament as "nothing more than image, than 'sign,' through which that which is represented is made present."[51] Visibility and presence: representation is also re-presentation. It is the assertion of a presence. E. H. Gombrich calls attention to the "natural tendency to endow an image with presence."[52] Freedberg calls this the "epiphanic nature of representation," the ability of the image to declare and make present that which is absent, to function as a sort of reincarnation.[53] What is more, the created presence requests a reciprocal presence—the presence of the beholder, the active engagement of the senses.[54] A painting or a drawing is always half of a "physical" proposition. Beholder and image address one another. The beholder is one partner in an interaction called forth by the image.

While, technically speaking, the United Society was a nonsacramental church, *sacralizing experiences* punctuated its spiritual life. In the broadest sense, anything and everything could be sacrament to those whose lives were constantly interrupted by the mighty gifts of God. Shakers rejected the traditional sacraments of the Protestant Christian churches because they believed that these "third dispensation" rituals were spiritually archaic. The Lord's Supper and Baptism, Shakers maintained, belonged to the period of Christ's absence between the First and Second Comings. "Eating the Lord's Supper . . . proves the absence of Christ; 'For as often as ye eat this bread and drink this cup, ye do show forth the Lord's death till he come,' not afterwards."[55] In Ann Lee, Christ had already made a second appearance. A new dispensation, the fourth dispensation, required new sacramental objects and rituals. All celestial communications were sacralizing phenomena: instituted, according to Believers, by Mother Ann, they served to remind and reassure Shakers of divine presence. Spirits and community leaders strictly enjoined the sect's adherents to respect the character of heavenly gifts, to "keep them sacred and choice."[56]

Gift images, in particular, operated as visible signs of invisible presence. They called into being a spiritual community which explicitly included the heavenly gift giver(s) and earthly recipient(s) in present and visible relationship with one another. Shakers would have recognized Mother Ann in their images not because of a sense of identity between founder and image, but because image created a locus of presence, a site for the experience of contact, because image demonstrated accessibility between different times and different places. Instructions about the use of gift images and visually organized messages adopted or paraphrased the words of institution used by Jesus at the Last Supper.[57] The inhabitants of heaven counseled their earthly offspring to contemplate celestial pictures and words "in remembrance" of the Heavenly and Eternal Parents (fig. 23).[58] Celestial beings thus compared the reception of cards, notices, and emblems by Shaker individuals to the reception of the bread and cup of the sacrament by Christians of the previous dispensation.

Beholding a gift image, though a relatively "private" experience, was hardly a solitary one. When Shakers received gift images "in remembrance of Mother Ann" and those who bore witness to her, they experienced her presence with them. Sacramental remembering was active remembering; memory made present. The inscription on one gift image announced Mother Ann's intention for the gift in relationship to its recipient: "'twill bind thy soul and mine together" (fig. 25). Interestingly, at just the time that Americans in general were discovering and celebrating the ability of the new photographic image to "replicate experience," Shakers introduced gift images to accomplish deceptively similar ends.[59] While gift images functioned in certain respects like the photographic image (i.e., they both "reduc[ed] [a] world to proportions that could be taken in at a glance, [and] [held] it still long enough to let [the beholder] look closely"[60]), Shaker images obviously differed from photographs in their celestial subject matter and content as well as in their charismatic origin and its relationship to the personal charism of the Shaker founder and thus in sacramental association. Shaker image did not suggest visual surrogacy but provided a locus for presence. In the Shaker case, image became a moment of divine encounter.

In August 1842, in concert with the ministry, instruments presented a series of cards of "Love and Notice from Holy Mother Wisdom" in preparation for her early September feast day on the holy "mountain" at New Lebanon (fig. 24). Isaac Newton Youngs recorded the reception of a "special notice from Holy Mother—a *Card,* well written, containing blessings, praise and promises, very choice and in beautiful language."[61] Each card from Holy Mother Wisdom was "given" on 10 July 1842 and "copied" by the instrument from its spiritual original between 1 and 20 August 1842. At least sixteen of these cards survive in various archives. While none included drawn or painted images, all were visually compelling and physically tangible manifestations of the spiritual world. The instruments composed Wisdom's notices in blue ink on a delicately colored pink paper. Borders and underlining accentuated the visual appearance of the papers. On 21 August,

> The whole Church, or all who were over 20 years of age, Met at half past 8 a.m., in the Holy Sanctuary, to receive a beautiful card, as the last present, from our Holy and Eternal Mother; These cards have all been coppied on to a small piece, of peach blow coloured paper: These were given to each individual by the hands of the Ministry.[62]

A matching pink and blue booklet, tiny but handsome, accompanied the cards, advising recipients about proper use of these and similar presents in relationship to sacramental memory. Holy Wisdom desired those gifted in this way to

> make a wise use of the same, and not handle them as common things. But when they read them, read them in remembrance of their Holy Mother, and all their heavenly Parents, and treat them as *a blessing of great worth.*[63]

Furthermore, the instruments claimed, Holy Mother Wisdom instructed her children to keep these tokens of remembrance and to read them each year before ascending the Holy Mount to celebrate the feast day of Wisdom's Passover.[64] For Shakers, these and other sacramental images and texts recalled to mind the divine correspondent and traced a visible outline for an invisible presence. When Shakers rejoiced in receiving "abiding substances" and "durable Gifts" from the heavens, they did not necessarily mean that all of these gifts actually posessed material form.[65] Precisely because of their tangibility, however, gift images were particularly suited to representing permanent and "durable" spiritual "substances." Gift images allowed Believers to see, to touch, and to retain the spiritual objects and presences represented in the images. Gift images made the vision of one person, one place, and one moment available to other persons, in different places, over time.

Symbolically manipulating time (in the subject matter, form, and content of their images), New Era instruments restored to Mother Ann a literally visible presence. What the first times and eternity had in common, after all, was the (visible) presence of Ann Lee. Ordering, condensing, conflating the temporal as well as the spatial dimension of experience, the instruments simultaneously retrieved the Shaker founder from the past and recalled her visible presence from an eternity beyond time, from a larger, atemporal sphere which encompassed finite existence. The instruments' images appealed to their recipients, then, as sacred mementos of past persons and experiences *and* as visible and material proof of the continued existence of such persons and experiences in an atemporal celestial sphere, intimately related to their own temporal terrestrial world.

Many images demonstrate this sacralizing capacity. However, one painting is especially suited by its own form and its accompanying text to explicate the ways in which the temporal community and its inhabitants might experience intimate contact with the inhabitants of eternity. The large watercolor called *A Type of Mother Hannah's Pockethandkerchief* (1851) (Pl. V) gave third generation Jane Blanchard (1812-1884) of New Lebanon the opportunity to experience the continuing visible presence of a sizable group of deceased Shaker leaders involved in the production of the image.[66] According to the instrument of the painting and its accompanying gift booklet, the handkerchief itself belonged to the founding eldress of the Harvard and Shirley (Massachusetts) communities, Mother Hannah Kendal (d. 1816), a missionary companion of Ann Lee. The three who originally served in the Harvard ministry with Kendal, Father Eleazar Rand (1763-

1808), Elder John Warner (1758-1834), and Eldress Rachel Keep (d. 1823), enclosed their love and a gift for the current (1851) Harvard ministry.[67] Mother Lucy Wright and Eldress Ruth Landon (d. 1850) attended to the details of the gift. Father James Whittaker "actually" painted the picture on the handkerchief. And, "better than all," "blessed Mother Ann" perfected the entire project with her love.[68]

Much of what Blanchard knew about the production of her image, she would have learned not from the image, but from the narrative booklet probably delivered with the painting or a short time before it.[69] *Mother Hannah's Pockethandkerchief* was, in this respect, a somewhat unusual Shaker image: at least in terms of the surviving evidence, no other gift painting seems to have been accompanied by anything like this relatively lengthy and extremely detailed textual narrative.[70] In the booklet, the instrument claimed that the spirit of first born Eunice Wyeth (1756-1830) dictated the story surrounding the creation of Blanchard's image.[71] The words, apparently written by the same hand that penned the calligraphy on the image, framed the picture in relationship to a series of specific visionary encounters experienced by Wyeth (who, by 1851, when the instrument painted the image, had been dead for twenty-one years). The narrative jumps here and there, recounting out of linear sequence different episodes in Wyeth's story, moving back and forth between 1815 and 1850 as well as between time and eternity, describing the living and the dead often without distinguishing between the two. Early in the account, in the voice of Wyeth's spirit, the instrument revealed the sacramental intention of image and text: "O that I could make her [Jane Blanchard] *remember* that time and . . . *realize* the blessedness of the kind care of a true Mother [Ann Lee]" (italics added.)[72]

In the case of *Mother Hannah's Pockethandkerchief*, graphic and textual accounts of three separate but related visionary episodes reportedly experienced by Eunice Wyeth in 1815 and 1850 complemented and supplemented each other. Text and image contained related and consistent but by no means identical information. The text, while its careful narrative form clarified the specific visionary context of the image, created in the reader a marked sense of disjunction resulting from the author's movements of the narrative back and forth between different points in time.[73] To a large degree, the point of both narrative and image was that such chronological distinctions were ultimately irrelevant, that the third generation of American Shakers enjoyed the same relationship to Ann Lee and other early leaders as did the first generation. In order to ensure this interpretation, the instrument placed the whole enterprise within a conceptual fabric of spiritual gift-giving and ornamentation which assumed Lee's active participation. But the image, much more persuasively, much less ponderously, than the gift booklet, actually embodied the seamless conflation of times. Image more vigorously represented the "free communion" of first and third generation; text more clearly distinguished between the times the image conflated. Unlike the narrative booklet which ordered and prioritized its presentation sequentially (if only in the sense that one word, phrase, or sentence appeared *after* another, that the end could not be "seen" at the beginning[74]), the image established priority in a different fashion, by inviting the beholder, after the initial engagement of the whole, to make a closer examination of some visually "privileged" parts of the painted surface. While images, like texts, may address their audience in a linear and sequential mode, unlike texts, they do not necessarily prescribe a single "beginning," "middle," and "end." An image-maker may indeed privilege certain parts of an image in relationship to their claim on the beholder's attention. But choices about where to begin the task of looking and understanding remain to the viewer.[75]

In the instrument's pictorial representation of the sacred pocket handkerchief, relics of Shaker and biblical pasts mingled with "new" treasures of heaven in contemporary presentation. For *Mother Hannah's Pockethandkerchief* included pictures which the instrument claimed were created on at least two different occasions probably separated by many years. In her textual narrative the instrument distinguished between the two sets of depictions, describing the one as figure (the star) and the other as ground (the decorated handkerchief); in the painting, she substantially diminished this differentiation, tying the central star, in terms of organization and color, to the emblems in its orbit. The star, designating Blanchard as a witness to Mother Ann's love and blessings, became a celestial ornament *like* the surrounding wreath of spiritual gifts earlier bestowed upon Mother Hannah Kendal, as celestial ornaments for her linen handkerchief.[76]

Repeatedly, the instrument relayed Eunice Wyeth's delight in the open communion that existed between Ann Lee's spiritual children in eternity (where all Shakers who had "left the bonds of time" could see their founder) and in time (where visions and visionary images provided evidence of her presence). When, through the instrument, Wyeth described how, in a charismatic episode in 1815 at the Church Family in the Harvard community, she "could feel that relation to Christ and my blessed Mother thro their children, that was worth sacraficing [*sic*] and suffering all things for," she wanted Blanchard to "feel her relation" as well. The link between Eunice Wyeth ("who received the gospel immediately from Mother and the Elders")[77] and Jane Blanchard was not accidental. One dramatically parallel life experience made sense of the connection. Peculiar circumstances had prevented both third generation Blanchard and first born Wyeth from spending their adult lives where each felt most at home, within the borders of the Shaker community at Harvard.

First responsibility for the care of a crippled daughter and then the fears of Shaker leaders about the instability of husband Joseph Wyeth's faith prohibited Eunice Wyeth from permanent residence in a Shaker community for several decades after her conversion. In the 1850 gift booklet, Wyeth's spirit referred to this difficult period, describing her outside residence as her "cottage of sufferings."[78] Finally, five years before her death, she and Joseph were "gathered at the Square House, where she finished her work and left this world in union and beloved by all."[79] Jane Blanchard (1812-1884), like many other third generation Shakers, entered the United Society as a young girl and was raised from early childhood by the Harvard Shakers. Her tenure there overlapped with Wyeth's Harvard association by at least fourteen years (1815-1829). Blanchard undoubtedly knew Eunice Wyeth, who worked and worshipped with the Harvard Shakers despite her "outfamily" status. As Blanchard approached adulthood, the parent ministry decided that she belonged in the First Order at New Lebanon. Accordingly, she changed her place of residence in the summer of 1829. While the reasons for this move are not entirely clear, the evidence suggests that Blanchard's "natural" mother, Emma, an apostate who left the Shakers late in 1823 along with one Benjamin Winchester, Jr., was attempting to convince Jane to join her in the world.[80] Those in authority deemed New Lebanon a safer haven than Harvard for this promising but contested young soul.[81] Blanchard accepted and complied with the ministry's decision but, for years thereafter, she missed her spiritual family (which included many of her biological relatives) at Harvard and longed for her original Shaker home.[82] Blanchard's difficulties increased during the period of apostasy preceding and accompanying Mother's Work when friends and companions left the United Society for the world.[83]

According to the narrative booklet attending *Mother Hannah's Pockethandkerchief*, the painting represented an image seen on Jane Blanchard's face at Harvard in 1815 by visionary Eunice Wyeth. "A very bright Star on [Blanchard's] forehead, which mostly covered [her] infant face" designated the three-year-old as a witness for Wyeth's testimony to the truth of Ann Lee's gospel.[84] When the child requested a picture of her star so that she could keep it forever, the instrument continued, Wyeth assured Blanchard that she would have the picture but she would need to wait until after Wyeth "got to heaven."[85] Shortly thereafter, a second vision transported Wyeth in space (from Harvard to New Lebanon) and time (from 1815 to the period of Mother's Work) where she observed Blanchard, the child now grown to adulthood, her face still decorated with the same star. In 1850, when (according to the instrument) Wyeth's vision came to fulfillment, her spirit remarked on the perfect resemblance between her 1815 vision of the New Era "Mother Church" and the sights seen during her posthumous visit there in the company of the recently deceased Eldress Ruth Landon, the "blessed Parents," and attending spirits.[86] As in her earlier vision, Wyeth indeed saw the mature Jane Blanchard with a star on her forehead. In response to this sight, Wyeth concluded, "God has knowledge of all and will in his own will and wisdom, become all things to all generations."[87] Soon, Blanchard would have her picture too:

> Your loving Father James says, that when his present duties are attended to, and he has a little leisure time, he will send you the picture you so long desired. He intends to draw it on Mother Hannah's fine linen pocket handkerchief, which has now some pretty things on it, and he wants me [Eunice Wyeth] to write a short Hymn, and a few lines of poetry on it for you.[88]

So, thirty-six years after Eunice Wyeth's original vision, Jane Blanchard's star was finally depicted for her. If first generation Eunice Wyeth could experience the visible presence of her deceased Mother Ann, so could third generation Jane Blanchard; for Wyeth this happened in a vision, for Blanchard in an image.

Blanchard's star, as painted on Mother Hannah's handkerchief, represented a vital connection between 1815 and 1850. The "short Hymn" and "few lines of poetry," reportedly commissioned of Wyeth by Father James Whittaker in the spirit world, the instrument dated 1815 and 1850 respectively. Both hymn and poem the instrument included on the reverse side of the gift image (as well as at the end of the manuscript booklet), emphasizing her intention to link the experience of first born and rising generation.[89] The poem, especially, expressed the intimate union between eternity and time, between first generation in heaven and third generation on earth.

> My spirit to earth, with joy takes its flight,
> And there with the faithful can freely unite,
> In thanks and in praise to the God that has given,
> This freedom to souls on earth and in heaven.
> This Holy Communion with the subjects of time,
> Is blest, not express'd, it is pleasure sublime . . .
>
> A recompence greater I never will seek
> Than to feel my relation with the pure and meek
> [living at New Lebanon].
> And to know that I'm owned of my blessed Mother
> [in heaven],
> Is sufficient for me, I wish for no other.[90]

Mother Hannah's Pockethandkerchief was sacramental emblem as well as relic and reliquary. As the poem made clear, the painting was a concrete reminder of a current experience of "Holy Communion" between the inhabitants of eternity and the "subjects of time."[91] Shaker visionary episodes, like the one(s) responsible for this image, collapsed time; they made present a sacred past by recalling to earth the inhabitants of heaven. Gift images, as products of spiritual sight, rendered this recaptured past accessible, *not only as memory but also as experience*, to young as to old within the Shaker community.[92]

Gift images, then, represented what Mircea Eliade might label a "revolt against the irreversibility of time."[93] By creating and beholding these drawings and paintings, members of the rising generation became contemporaries of Mother Ann and her eyewitnesses; time no longer separated first born and rising generation. In the spiritual world envisioned for Shakers by their instruments, people of all generations shared each other's company.[94] In the products of their spiritual imaginations, the instruments of Mother's Work made present a sacred past and made accessible a sacred presence by augmenting memory and by enhancing vision.

Mid-century Shakers were, in fact, poised in time—looking back to recover the visible presence of Ann Lee and looking ahead to fulfill the eschatological reality of Mother Ann.[95] The first movement connected present to past; the second pulled Believers toward the future. In fact, mid-nineteenth-century Shakers employed the past to project their present toward an otherworldly future. According to her followers, Mother Ann, now resident in the heavenly sphere, beckoned to her offspring from their ultimate destination in eternity. The future gift images constituted was not the future on earth. The content of the internal revival called Mother's Work allowed Shakers to participate in the full continuum of sacred time(s), from the establishment of their faith community in the life and ministry of Ann Lee and her earthly companions to the unfolding of Shaker society in the eternal realm. The manifestations of Mother's Work which drew Lee's spiritual descendants into contact with the sect's original charismatic impulses simultaneously pointed this third generation toward a glorious celestial future. Conflating past and present, time and eternity in pictures on paper, gift images not only retrieved the "visible presence" of Mother Ann, but, through visual analogy, demonstrated to faithful young Believers the similarity between their own spiritual appearances and the decorated appearance of their deified founder. This is, then, the "decorating presence," the third mode of restoring visible presence, of dealing visually with the founder's "visible" absence: the paintings and drawings of Shaker instruments recalled the person of Mother Ann by constituting for the individual Shaker a spiritual appearance associated with the appearance of the Shaker founder. The images quite literally provided for Believers a "*self-image,*" a way of conceptualizing their own spiritual appearances in relationship to the "appearance" of Ann Lee. The images provided, in other words, a "*decorated self,*" adorned with emblems symbolic of the celestial virtues of Mother Ann and other early leaders. When contemporary Believers assumed their rightful places in the heavenly sphere, the instruments maintained, these individuals would be able to see first-hand the spiritual ornaments with which deity had decorated them and their celestial habitations throughout their mortal lives. While yet in time, the instruments' pictures provided mortal Believers a preview of their spiritual appearances, showed them how, through faithful living, they had already begun to accumulate a mantle of celestial adornments, had already begun to furnish the beautiful heavenly mansions in which they would one day reside, urged them to press on toward this visible goal.[96]

Visually as well as spiritually, the individual Believer was a work in progress (cf. the notion of the Believer as a work of art, first raised in chapter 4). In fact, the faithful person was a *work of art* in the sense of being drawn upon, being decorated, by a divine artist. The instruments' images established not just visual accessibility to the past and to eternity, but visual similarity in the present and the future. Shaker image-makers created an ornamental (and metaphorical) image for Mother Ann (and for other spiritual forebears) which living Believers might themselves resemble. The instruments' pictures thus visually linked a celestial Mother Ann to the third generation as they provided third generation adherents with novel images of their own spiritual appearances. The fact that the instruments generally chose to represent the spiritual rather than the physical likeness of Ann Lee promoted the opportunity for registering the visible similarity between Lee and her followers.[97] If access to Mother Ann could be gained in religious images, if the self was indeed a religious "image," a work of art, then access to Mother Ann might be gained within the decorated self. The presence of Mother Ann might be suggested (and, ultimately, an internal substitute for her external presence might be provided) by the association of the appearance of the Believer with the appearance of Mother Ann. Mother Ann was indeed the "perfect pattern of piety to all who saw her," the decorated self which each Believer strove to approximate.

While prohibited as superfluity in its earthly form, ornament, like image, played an important role in the spiritual realm. According to the instruments, the inhabitants of the celestial sphere called the gifts of Mother's Work "ornaments."[98] The instruments who spoke for Mother Ann insisted that while "ornaments of Heaven" should not be used to "deck and adorn" the "idols" of the earth,[99] in relationship to Lee's chosen ones, in present time and in their future heavenly state, "beautiful ornaments adorn[ed] the faithful soul," "render[ing] it lovely in the sight of God."[100] The ornaments with which deity decorated the faithful on earth and the inhabitants of heaven represented, of course, heavenly virtues. Adapting the figurative as well as literal meaning of the verb "to decorate," Shakers understood this action to confer heavenly blessing, honor, grace, beauty as well as to embellish.

> So press ye on, increase in gospel virtues, *love, meekness,* charity and condescension: all these gospel graces beautify and adorn the children of the New Creation: they form a garment that is far brighter than the sun: nothing can be compared with its beauty nothing can form so bright a robe.[101]

Clearly Shakers did not regard such heavenly ornamentation as "merely decorative."

The instruments' images, as a genre, *were* spiritual ornaments; they also *depicted* particular spiritual ornaments adorning persons and places in eternity and individuals in the Shaker temporal sphere. On many occasions, as in the quotation just cited, deity "adorned" Shakers, individually and collectively, with splendid spiritual garments, the garments themselves often ornamented with images.

> Then I will crown thee with everlasting Life, and enrobe thee with eternal salvation. Yea, in raiment white as snow, embroidered with artful needle-work and pictured with flowers of shining gold, glowing with my eternal brightness and glory shalt thou then be adorned my blessed child.[102]

The spirit of Ann Lee "made" some of the more elaborate spiritual garments of Mother's Work for her spiritual offspring to wear in celebration of the Passover of Holy Mother Wisdom in 1842. An instrument described some of the items included in this gift:

> A necklace of gold beads to place about the neck.

> A bonnet of silver color, trimmed with white ribband [*sic*]; also a pair of blue silk gloves. These denote holy faith, true honesty, and cheerful cross-bearing.
>
> For both brethren and sisters, there is a fine linnen [*sic*] pocket handkerchief, white as the driven snow and in the middle of them is the picture of the Holy of Holies, the Eternal Throne, and the Eternal Two in One, setting [*sic*] upon it. In One corner is the likeness of Holy and Eternal Wisdom even myself, when descending to earth, in my chariot of brightness and elegancy, with twenty thousand Angels each side of the same; and twenty span of white horses before, which drew the chariot of glittering brightness. In another corner is the likeness of the Holy One, the great *I AM,* holding his sword of wrath in his hand, and words of terror and judgment coming forth from his lips. Upon the other corners are printed the names of all your Heavenly Parents, with each one's seal of love and approbation in the form of a star at the end of their names; and the name of the one that shall receive it under theirs.
>
> These are the garments for my good children, (says Holy Mother Wisdom) prepared by your ever blessed Mother Ann, for her dearly beloved little ones.[103]

Instruments and ministry invested articles of spiritual apparel with a wide ranging content. According to the presence or absence of such attire and to its degree of decoration, gifts of spiritual clothing indicated important spiritual transitions and differences in spiritual status ("you see that they are not all alike but vary according to the degree of travel, and the order in which individuals stand").[104] Spiritual habiliment marked individuals and groups as belongings of Holy Mother Wisdom and Almighty God the Father; it communicated and reinforced "notions of authority, hierarchy, community, and gender" as well as maintaining a constellation of spiritual meanings.[105] As Believers put on mantles of virtue "after the form of" mantles worn by Mother Ann and Jesus, they identified with Mother Ann and Jesus, became more like Mother Ann and Jesus, and they accepted the protection, in spiritual travel, of the heavenly Daughter and Son. Concerning the presentation of these mantles, the instrument wrote about

> some blue velvet mantles lined with white fur, and upon the shoulders were four tostles [*sic*] of gold. These were sent to all over the age of twenty years. The names of each were printed on them in letters of gold; they were also embroidered with gold. These mantles[,] said the Savior[,] belonging to the brethren are made after the form of my own mantle and I want they should receive them from me in sweet love. Mother said the sisters['] were made after the form of hers; and she wanted they should receive them from her with her affectionate love. They are composed of wisdom purity and love, and are to be kept sacred and choice for wearing on journeys.[106]

On 23 September 1842, Holy Mother Wisdom gave a gift of golden medals to all those "who ascended the Holy Mount to receive the blessing of the Ancients." These spiritual medals bore engravings "of the likeness of the lovely virtues of your Mother's first born children." Through the ministry and instruments, Holy Wisdom stipulated that

> ye should wear, and ever be clothed in these lovely virtues . . . And while ye remain faithful this likeness which I now place upon you, shall remain shining brighter and brighter. And know ye, while this likeness I behold upon you, no harm shall come nigh you, for my holy wings of protection shall cover you.
>
> But know ye that the medal with the likeness which I now give unto you shall remain with none, save those who cultivate the lovely virtues thereon inscribed. And to those who are found without this likeness, saith Holy Wisdom, I promise no protection.[107]

Thus the garments maintained both expressive and instrumental significance, communicating blessing and "visualizing" present spiritual condition as well as encouraging individuals in their struggles and urging them to come into their spiritual inheritance, offering ever more brilliant raiment as they neared spiritual maturity.

In each case described, and in many others, the spiritual garments which clothed Believers were visible only to the inspired ones. The ritualized bestowal of mantles, jewels, medals, breastplates, crowns, handkerchiefs, etc., expressed the Shaker visual imagination in a spiritualized form. Gift images, which often represented or included pictures of spiritual vestments, gave concrete, material shape to these parallel but more ethereal experiences (cf. figs. 25, 26, 30 and Pl. V). The text on one visually organized gift identified the image's border as a chain from Mother Ann, inscribed with "Mother's word," to be taken from the recipient's neck and read in times of need (fig. 25). In particular, Shaker image-makers elaborated upon the figure of the spiritual breastplate (Ephesians 6:10-20), which they understood to be inscribed with recognition of righteousness and pursuit of truth and with promises of eternal glory. New Era texts frequently mentioned gifts of elaborate spiritual breastplates given to New Lebanon Shakers. In some earlier instances, while the breastplate was not actually drawn, a figure of the plate was set off in the script through the use of decorative brackets and a change in calligraphic form (fig. 24, verso). The instruments actually depicted many of the recipients' breastplates on the heart cutouts of 1844 (fig. 3, verso) and the breastplate's form became still more pictorial in several colorful gift images of 1848 and 1849 (figs. 26 and 30).

With heavenly garments, the instruments maintained, deity decorated individuals and images. In other cases, God Almighty and Holy Mother Wisdom plied their art directly on human canvases; the very bodies of Shakers became works of art.[108] Returning to *Mother Hannah's Pockethandkerchief* (Pl. V), on this painted field the instrument pictured a celestial image with which deity decorated Jane Blanchard's face.[109] The celestial star, the visible sign sealing Blanchard as a true witness, occupied the entire central portion of the instrument's painting. The circular sunburst of this "very bright Star," with its halo of flaring trumpet-like forms, the image-maker carefully integrated into her larger composition. Yet, in the prominent placement of the star and by the lavish use of bright yellow paint to communicate celestial illumination, she also suggested the star's special significance as divine decoration of a third generation spiritual daughter.

Appealing to a celestial pattern, the instrument located within the luminous yellow and pink star a double symbolic "portrait" of Blanchard (a decorative presence). Blanchard appeared twice, first as the "Lamb of Innocence" at the center of the image, and second (according to the Shaker convention of signifying individuals by the appearance of their hearts) in the heart-shaped floral design below (and around) the lamb.[110] The lamb itself was both emblem of Blanchard (a "lamb of innocence" who came early to the gospel of Ann Lee) and representation of the divine likeness (the Christian "lamb of God") decorating Blanchard. Inside the star and adjacent to the lamb and heart, Holy Mother Wisdom made a special appeal to Blanchard and her companions in the rising generation to respond to such a clear demonstration of divine presence and promise.

> Come unto Me, saith Wisdom in thy infancy. Devote thy whole heart to serve thy Creator in the morning of thy days, and of the beautiful treasures of my Kingdom thou shalt abundantly share. Come at my call thou Lamb of Innocence.

The treasures forming the surrounding wreath of emblems from Mother Hannah's handkerchief (e.g., Jepha's lamp to provide light during periods of tribulation and rejection, Mother Hannah's fan to "blow away buffetings," Moses' trumpet to reveal word to the nations) were not selected at random but underscored the message that steadfast and wholehearted devotion, even in times of great tribulation, ultimately would yield universal salvation.

Stars were not the only configurations "painted" on the followers of Ann Lee. The image of Wisdom's Seal, incorporated into numerous gift drawings and paintings (cf. figs. 28 and 29), marked the faithful individual as Wisdom's own, decorated the faithful individual with an emblem of eternal life. In 1841 and again in 1847, Holy Mother Wisdom descended to "seal" Believers. In both instances, Shakers understood the image Wisdom imprinted on their foreheads to be the spiritually visible badge of a chosen and sanctified people. In 1841, only the inspired could actually make out the visual appearance of the Seal. In 1847, the instrument pictured the Seal for all to see. The ritual context for the giving of Wisdom's Seal, the instruments and ministry adapted from the book of Revelation (especially 7:2-3 and 19:20). The Shaker ritual reconstituted, in particular, the apocalyptic episode in which the Seal of the Living God was placed upon the foreheads of the faithful setting them apart from destruction, the unfaithful receiving instead the mark of the beast. Wisdom's Seal or the Seal of Eternal Life designated true Believers for salvation. Holy Wisdom bestowed this sign in order to identify her chosen, "that I may know who are my people."[111] Each person so ornamented would subsequently carry this spiritual image upon his or her forehead throughout time and eternity. The Seal of Death or the mark of the adversary, on the other hand, identified those who would "share with the wicked the judgments that are ready to burst upon a guilty world."[112] Of the ritual accompanying the distribution of the Seals, one participant noted that no one in attendance "doubted the real presence of Holy Mother Wisdom."[113] In 1841, instruments described in great detail the visual appearance of the marks received (which varied, again, according to the virtue of the individual) but did not picture them.[114]

In contrast, both the original and copies of the November 1847 "Golden Roll or Holy Gift" from Holy Mother Wisdom to the ministry, which specified that Wisdom would again mark her children on Christmas day of that year, included not only a textual description of Wisdom's Seals but also a picture of the Seals and the boxes fashioned to hold them. The image in the original booklet, the instrument painted in watercolors; the copies in booklet form, the instrument drew in pen and ink.[115] The text of the Golden Roll described the appearance of the eternal ornaments Wisdom placed on Believers' faces.

> The Seals are in the form of a Dimond, bearing the likeness of an all-seeing Eye, and these words, "My Seal shall prove a Seal of life or death, to all who receive it." A cross is suspended to one point of the Seals. These shall be placed on the foreheads of my people, never thro' time or eternity to be removed or taken off, but by the hand that placed them.[116]

A letter from the New Lebanon ministry, dated 16 November 1847 and likely intended to circulate among the eastern communities, excerpted major passages from the Roll and included a full-page, multicolor painting of "Holy Wisdom's Seal of Life or Death To all who Receive it" and the "Emblem of the Boxes Containing the Seals" (fig. 27).[117] The 16 November letter and the multiple illustrated copies of the Roll demonstrate that the ministry understood the visual character of the Seal to be central to the sacralizing experience. The diamond shape of the Seal identified it as an emblem of purity.[118] In the center of the diamond, Wisdom placed her eye, quite literally, the instruments said, upon the offspring of Mother Ann. Holy Mother Wisdom could see the faithful; unceasingly she could read their hearts. *And* the faithful could see as with a new spiritual eye, the eye of Wisdom, situated between their own two eyes. The cross appended to the diamond signified the sacrifice required of those who would participate in the New Creation. Like Christian baptism, the placing of Wisdom's Seal represented a ritual of initiation, a ritual concerning the individual's present and future identity. Those who received the Seal became part of an inner group of purified, specially marked and decorated Believers, visibly destined for eternal salvation.[119] Soon after the circulation of the painted picture among the eastern settlements, the image of Wisdom's Seal appeared in several large gift images. Here again the Seal demonstrated visibly the gift of God's saving grace and the promises offered to those who willingly received it. Furthermore, the instruments' pictures of the Seal carried the distilled meaning of the ritual events of 1841 and 1847, evoking the repetition of those sacralizing experiences in Believers' memories.

In their representations of the celestial embellishments decorating individual Believers, gift images suggested that the faithful themselves in fact ornamented heaven, decorating for all eternity the city of God. With striking frequency, gift images (e.g., heart cutouts, depictions of celestial trees and even narrow paths,

Mother Hannah's Pockethandkerchief) included emblematic representations of the believing individual, usually the recipient, sometimes surrounded by visual promises of safe passage and decorated by the heavenly treasures and tokens earned in time. If individuals could see themselves as ornaments of heaven, then, as celestial decorations, these individuals existed in a "future" eternity as well as in "present" time, in "temporal" proximity to heaven's inhabitants and the heavenly sphere as to the earthly community.

One series of large pictures (e.g., figs. 7 and 13) employed the form of a decorated heart within a squared border (a "walled" heart) to signify the promised future union (the heart) of the individual soul with Holy Mother Wisdom within Wisdom's celestial mansion (the bordered area around the heart) in eternity.[120] While the popularity of the ornamented heart motif as an emblem of the individual's own spiritual core remained constant (cf. chapter 1 and heart cutouts), in a parallel development instruments transformed the walled heart into a representation of an "actual" celestial mansion, a symbol of the self's ideal future state and eternal destination. The movement from heart to mansion was not evolutionary in the sense of producing progressively superior replacements for earlier forms. Rather, visual images of hearts and walled hearts and mansions represented the rich ideational association of these images and their meanings in the mid-century Shaker thoughtworld. Instruments continued to promote the content expressed in the heart cutouts even as this central motif attracted additional (*not* replacement) meanings. In the transitional "walled heart" series, the heart was both the individual's and Wisdom's, represented in spiritual union one with the other. The quadrilateral border around the heart suggested the walls of Wisdom's celestial mansion; their strength and beauty would protect and comfort the saved soul. According to Believers, at the time of death each person "put off the earthly tabernacle" and received instead a "place and a mansion according to their travel of soul" or degree of spiritual maturity.[121] Alternatively, the Believer might sojourn in Wisdom's own mansion, the prototype for all other celestial mansions. In this case, the decorative splendor of the virtuous individual's soul ornamented the heavenly home. As with the celestial garden and the holy city, multiple variations on the celestial mansion metaphor added depth and richness to its use. The central idea was that a place in Wisdom's abundantly ornamented residence awaited the faithful individual in eternity.

In each of the horizontally layered images of the "walled heart" series, the lower register contained emblems of sacred history (biblical and Shaker) and the heavenly decorations of a regenerate earth. The upper register represented the celestial regions, ornamented with spiritual treasures and crowned by emblems of Almighty God the Father and Holy Mother Wisdom. Since the natural, biblical, and historical orders were figures or types of the spiritual order, similar heavenly treasures appeared in both realms.[122] The walled heart, centerpiece of each composition, represented the final resting place of the recipient's eternal soul in the celestial mansion of Holy Mother Wisdom.

In *From Holy Mother Wisdom to Eliza Sharp, October* 25, 1845, as in most of these images, the invitation to spiritual union was explicit:

> Come unto me saith Wisdom . . . For within my mansion no evil can enter, but all is quietness and peace. So receive my love saith Wisdom, and be strong in the work of your God; for if you are faithful, you shall yet walk the golden streets of Paradise.[123]

In *From Holy Mother Wisdom to Joanna Kitchell* (fig. 13), too, Wisdom's promises, written and drawn as though inscribed upon the individual's pure heart, adorned this central motif.

> For with mine own hand saith Wisdom, I have prepared a beautiful mansion for all my faithful children when their work on earth is done, and time with them is no more. Blessed Most blessed are the pure in Heart, saith *Wisdom.*

Here, as in most of the images, the walled heart rested on a supporting foundation, extending downward from Wisdom's precinct, straddling the border between eternity and time, the foundation's constituent elements ("lively stones," "firm pillars," bricks, columns) emblematic of faithful Believers on earth, the New Era "pillars" of the Millennial Church. The Eliza Sharp image integrated ladders into this foundational structure, facilitating ascent out of time.[124]

The unbordered central heart in *From Holy Mother Wisdom to Sarah Ann Standish,* an image similar but not technically belonging to the layered series, used images and words to identify the heart with Standish's celestial mansion. In the picture, the heart's apex sprouted rose blossoms; the text encompassed within the heart described the floral decoration of Standish's mansion. "Thy mansion shall be clean and neat, ornamented with heavenly roses that eternally bloom . . . There, dear child, if you will be faithfull, thy joys shall be Eternal, saith Holy Wisdom."[125]

Three other gift images demonstrated the association between the walled heart and the celestial destination of the individual, Holy Wisdom's mansion. First, the New Lebanon instrument of *From Holy Mother Wisdom to Eldress Dana or Mother* (fig. 28) included a central heart, surrounding "Wisdom's Holy Seal," set within concentric circles of image and text. The circle of words (underlined twice in pink watercolor) carried divine reassurances to Hancock's leading eldress, first born Cassandana (Dana) Goodrich (1769-1848), some two months prior to her death.[126] "Thou art sealed with eternal life . . . thine abode shalt be in the Courts of my love; where none but the pure in heart can enter." The instrument represented Goodrich's pure heart, marked for eternal life by Wisdom's Seal, at home in Wisdom's court, within the golden orb of the heavenly sphere. The caption at the bottom of the image informed the beholder that the image-maker copied this emblem "from the picture of her [Goodrich's] Mansion and seal."[127] According to the image, deity dispatched "The Savior's Ship of Safety," flanked by the descending angels of Mother Ann and Holy Mother Wisdom, to escort Goodrich as she departed from time.[128] The sailing ship image Shaker instruments adapted from its conventional nineteenth-century American use in memorial portraiture.[129] For Goodrich the image held promises of a divinely secured future.[130] For members of her Hancock community this painting was also a memorial portrait painted just before Goodrich's death by an inspired one who could see the eldress's decorative spiritual appearance. The painting, then, was both heavenly promise and memorial emblem.[131]

Sometime prior to his death in 1849, Elder Ebenezer Bishop (1768-1849) of New Lebanon received a watercolor painting similar to Goodrich's image, produced by the same hand (fig. 29).[132] After a series of relatively debilitating illnesses, Bishop would likely have taken comfort in the invitation to enter the celestial mansion. *From Holy Mother Wisdom to Elder Ebenezer Bishop* supports the case for interpreting the somewhat earlier walled hearts in the context of spiritual union and the virtuous Believer's destination in eternity. Here, in fact, the heart has disappeared, or rather, the heart has become the mansion. The same symbols (clock, flowers, Seal, doves, angels) adorn the eternal habitation, and its outline still vaguely suggests a heart shape. But the heart itself has been transformed into a house with walls, roof, and floor, a door, and fruit trees flanking the entrance. Itself set within a starry firmament, a beveled inscription formed the roof of this "mansion of the blessed," also identified by the instrument as Bishop's own residence in Wisdom's court. Wisdom decorated Bishop's mansion with emblems of his virtue and marked the New Lebanon elder (like Hancock's eldress) with Wisdom's own Seal of eternal life. As in Goodrich's picture, the instrument of Bishop's image depicted a golden chariot in the lower right-hand corner. Foretelling her own death many years earlier, Ann Lee had described a "golden chariot" which would come to "take [her] home."[133] According to the instrument, a similar vehicle would now bear Bishop to his celestial habitation. In the text that formed the roof of the mansion image, Holy Mother Wisdom recited Bishop's future:

> Thou art sealed with eternal life; a Priest of the Most High God and shall reign with Him Forever. Thou hast found thy salvation through pain and sufferings and now thou shalt have thy reward. So, Come and sit down in the mansion of the blessed to go out no more. Come saith Wisdom for thy mansion is prepared, and the feast made ready; here in my holy Court is thy robe and crown. Come, for thy joy will be full, in my Love.

A Present from Mother Lucy to Eliza Ann Taylor April 8th 1849 (fig. 30) completed the transformation of the central heart (still maintaining its association with the individual's own heart or soul) into heavenly mansion and thus completed the identification of individual Believer and decorative architectural image. In this image, the instrument focused the beholder's attention on a central mansion adorned, above the entrance on the vertical axis, with the all-seeing open eye of Wisdom, more realistic, less emblematic than on Wisdom's Seal or above the walled hearts, referring nonetheless to the same content (cf. figs. 7, 13, 28, 29, 30). In the inscription under the building, Holy Mother Wisdom again repeated her invitation and promise, this time a promise of success in ministry to a relatively young third generation Shaker leader.

> Come saith Wisdom, for I have formed thee a dwelling and placed mine eye upon it. And from thee [*sic,* the] sequestered shades of death, my Angels shall gather many souls, whom I shall call upon thee to feed and clothe, and give them where to lay their heads in peace. . . . You shall be their Shepherd and they shall be my people saith WISDOM.

Eliza Ann Taylor's (1811-1897) time on earth was not yet finished. With her parents and siblings, she had come to the New Lebanon Shakers in 1823 at age twelve. She signed the Shaker covenant in 1833, the same year as Jane Blanchard with whom she was well acquainted. In 1849, when Taylor received this painting, she was an eldress in the Church Family, a position she occupied from 1844 until 1856, when she was called into the parent ministry as junior sister.[134] In *A Present from Mother Lucy,* the image of the mansion was simultaneously the dwelling of Holy Wisdom and the spiritual appearance of the Shaker meeting house, with its double doors and upper floor ministerial residence, where Taylor would one day live as a member of the parent ministry. The mansion here, then, was Taylor's future home on earth as well as her ultimate eternal destination. The tiled floor reiterated the tiling of the celestial mansion in an unfinished image associated with the walled heart series.[135] The heart in this painting, the instrument displaced to the left of the mansion where, once again, the heart represented future spiritual union, here between Taylor and the now-deceased companions of her youth. The words on this heart speak in Taylor's own voice:

> My treasure is not on the Earth, But in the heavens far away, where the cares of time cannot find them. When my work on earth is done, how gladly will I fly to the arms of the saints, who have watch'd over me in the days of my youth, for they love me and I love them and nought can separate us from each other

The relationship between stars, seals, hearts, mansions, and Shaker individuals, between these emblems and the individual's future in eternity, did not rest on a one to one correlation between any one picture or symbol and any one meaning. Rather, Shakers recognized in these generally inanimate ornaments what Freedberg might call "the presence of the living."[136]

Shakers pictured celestial decorations and they pictured themselves as God decorated them. They gave themselves and their communities, as well as heaven and heaven's inhabitants, visible spiritual appearances. At both individual and corporate levels, Believers internalized apparently external image and event. Each Shaker and the Shaker community as a whole became a "work in progress." For these beholders, engagement in this "visioning" was both revealing and transforming. They not only "saw" Mother Ann and her eyewitnesses from a past Shaker era but, by restoring a visible presence, they became eyewitnesses themselves. They not only saw others represented as offspring of the Eternal Parents, decorated with celestial emblems by the Divine Pair, but, by demonstrating the spiritual decoration of the third generation and the similarity between their ornamentation and that of Mother Ann and her first born, they saw their own participation in a "visible" communal family, their own promised place in the familial mansion. Visible spiritual authority, it appeared, rested with the third generation as with the first, could be transferred from Mother Ann to the individual Believer in a later age.[137] Image was ornament, image was presence, was spiritual companion, was evidence of spiritual community. Claiming decorative, sacramental, pastoral content, embodying that content in personally and communally significant ways, visionary images restored relationship and regulated behavior.

The instruments' pictures, interpreted in the context of the understandings about vision, visibility, and likeness which produced them, represented a significant and unique attempt to provide a solution to the central spiritual concern of Mother's Work. Visibly ordering, converging, punctuating, conflating spatial and temporal dimensions, gift images demonstrated the proximity of heaven and earth; past, present, and future; eternity and time, assuring mid-nineteenth-century Shakers of the [visible] presence of Mother Ann.

Epilogue

THE POWER OF AMBIGUITY

The era of Mother's Work in mid-nineteenth-century Shakerism presents many striking paradoxes. Some of the most tantalizing surround the creation of Shaker gift images. In a society which forbade pictures on the walls, ministry and instruments justified elaborate paintings and drawings. In a clearly anti-iconic community, visual experience was absolutely central to religious reality. In this sect where images themselves trespassed the boundaries of traditional sensibility, a familiar visionary vocabulary suggested that the distinction between choosing "vision" and choosing "blindness" constituted the difference between good and evil. In a group which vigorously condemned decoration and ornament, image-makers depicted the rich spiritual jewels and treasures that adorned Believers' souls.

Gift images were the logical visual products of a revival which essentially sought to reproduce a visible presence. The images issued from a common visionary experience, from the need for a communal record of that experience, and from a desire for physical evidence of divine accessibility. New Era Believers adopted several alternative solutions to the problem of Ann Lee's "visible" absence. Most importantly, they created for her a new drawn and painted "presence" and they ornamented themselves to resemble that presence, suggesting that "visible" authority could be passed from one generation to another. In addition, mid- nineteenth-century Shakers dealt with the loss of a visible and corporeal Mother Ann by extending Shaker maternity into the celestial sphere in the figure of Holy Mother Wisdom.[1] Although she had been introduced into the United Society much earlier, mid-century Shakers elaborated and expanded the role and activity of this other heavenly Mother. The direct spiritual experience of Holy Mother Wisdom, whom *no one* had ever encountered in the body, made less important for members of the rising generation the fact that they had never seen the earthly Ann Lee. At least where Holy Mother Wisdom was concerned, the first and third generations stood on common ground.[2] But the significance of vision and visibility did not diminish in relationship to Holy Mother Wisdom. According to her instruments, this mother-god too played a major role in the transmission and production of visionary images. No other heavenly treasures could help individuals to see as clearly as could these spiritual spectacles, these patterns of celestial virtue, these windows on heaven. Gift images made naturally visible the critical objects of spiritual sight.

New Era spirituality revived Mother Ann and her founding circle and, in visions and images, made these leaders personally available to the third generation and to their companions in faith. Mother's Work focused, first and foremost, on providing direct encounter with the Shaker celestial hierarchy and the attributes of heaven. While gift images were not the only means of visibility in a community in which various visionary expressions abounded, these pictures were the most novel, radical, and tangible forms that Shakers used to recreate an experience of vision for the rising generation. The images not only made Mother Ann visible and present, they also revealed the content of her gospel by patterning appropriate ethical order, by embodying the fluid relationship between heaven and regenerate earth, by consoling, challenging, and fortifying Believers with heavenly treasures and celestial food, by representing persuasive family history, and by demonstrating the relationship of first and third generation Believers in a visible ancestral line. Because New Era perceptions of the person of Ann Lee fused the charism of the founder with the institutional structuring accomplished by her immediate successors, a dual desire for contact and order fueled the aspirations of her mid-nineteenth-century followers.

Along the dimensions of space and time, gift images addressed each of the two principal impulses of New Era reform. By challenging conventional notions of spatial and temporal organization, the instruments' pictorial compositions illustrated means for reestablishing order (institution) as they embodied renewed contact (charism) with heaven and its inhabitants, including long-deceased Shaker forebears. Gift images adapted the primitive and charismatic category "gift" and the innovative form "image" to an institutionalizing content which reasserted the authority of the ministry as well as the official order and values of the Millennial Church. In this sense visionary pictures at least partially domesticated a radical construction, decontaminating the image by incorporating it within the framework of the authorized version of Mother's Work. Over time visionary pictures became less experimental, less tentative, less insistently concerned with legitimating themselves by reference to acceptable forms and ideas. The initial threat diminished. Once the category of non-superfluous images had fully established itself in the community (by around 1849 or 1850), the instruments' images began to resemble somewhat more closely the decorative pictures of "the world." Gift images generally became larger, "prettier," more colorful, less prophetic, judgmental, or potentially divisive (e.g., Pls. II–V). Both ministry and instruments recognized the inherent ability of objects to display and to persuade, to depict a particular set of values or beliefs, to make represented values appear true and inevitable. Consciously and unconsciously, ministry and instruments exploited in gift images these characteristics of material goods.[3]

As the months and years passed, Mother's Work, like its pictorial manifestations, changed. Although Believers did not waver in their desire to reestablish contact with Mother Ann and other inhabitants of the celestial sphere, the tone of Mother's Work and its particular tactics shifted. While the tension between charism and order remained unresolved, emphasis moved from one to the other and (at least intermittently) back again. Contemporary interpreters within the Shaker community realized this fact and commented on it. In the early months of spontaneous charism at Watervliet, the spirits attended affectionately to mostly female children and adolescents and to more marginalized members of the Society, encouraging them in their efforts to be good Shakers. According to the official internal interpretation, these early spontaneous manifestations were "refreshing showers" preparatory to the real "cleansing work" that was to be inaugurated at New Lebanon.

> Those gifts [at Watervliet] were remarkably calculated to draw the attention of all; to create love to spiritual things, to stimulate the desire and heighten the prospects of future happiness, and of course to weaken the prejudice of the natural mind against divine things.
>
> Thus the feelings of Believers were universally attracted, and their expectations roused, anxious to see the result, and as it were unconsciously willing to take hold of any requirement that the progress of the work presented.
>
> In this state of things the work broke forth upon the Church at the centre [New Lebanon], and they were prepared as a body, to come directly into the true spirit of the work.; and by this time the true object of the work became apparent, and the gifts seemed directed to some important end.
>
> The wisdom of God and our heavenly Parents was apparent in this work. Had the pruning knife been applied and violent purifying winds been suffered to blow, before some refreshing showers had invigorated the drooping plants in the vineyard, many branches might have been cut off, and much good fruit been blown off, that otherwise were saved.[4]

The approach of the spirits changed as Mother's Work began at New Lebanon, then. For a number of years following the arrival of spirit possession at the Shaker center, spirit communications and gifts focused on confession, purification, and conversion to the gospel of Ann Lee.[5]

> Mother [Ann] seemed to set right about the work of reform. She stated what was the first step towards a reform, and what was the only means that would enable souls to advance off from the old ground and move heavenward; and this was a full and thorough work of cleansing, confession of every sin, diging [*sic*] to the very bottom and bringing to light every secret thing. . . . And such a work of confession, repentance and purification followed, as the present generation never experienced. And what rendered the scene sublime beyond description, was the astonishing display of the external and visible power of God, on the bodies of many of the younger part.[6]

At its outset, this first officially sanctioned phase of the revival (following Victor Turner, I have called this phase "normative charism") depended upon the power of immediate experience and radical expression to remake adherents' behaviors, commitments, and perceptions. As Mother's Work progressed, and more who were disbelieving or lukewarm in their faith left the United Society, the model for revival manifestations moved from purification to edification, from conversion to sanctification. Rather than turning recalcitrant people around, later manifestations sanctified, edified, built up the already faithful. Attention shifted subtly from demanding purification to rewarding purity, from retaining the tempted and thereby maintaining numbers to acknowledging the promise in those who persevered.[7] This was a change of degree, however, not of kind. In sacred communications Shakers incorporated both conversion and sanctification, as modes of expression, throughout the course of Mother's Work. Although the emphasis varied significantly, neither voice ever disappeared completely.[8]

During the second half of the 1840s and throughout the 1850s, gifts and exercises continued.[9] Entirely new forms and rituals, however, became more and more rare.[10] Although the flood of spiritual presents, messages, and visions showed no signs of ceasing, Shakers expressed the opinion that voluntary efforts of individuals increasingly replaced the spontaneous operation of spirits.[11] Mother's Work had reached its pinnacle of institutionalization when a prominent scribe, in 1860, suggested in all seriousness that the guidance of the "Visible Lead" had replaced inspiration by the Heavenly Parents.[12] Almost two decades earlier one instrument had communicated the remark that "gifts of inspiration . . . must diminish, and souls must gather to their Visible Lead, and find an increase in the gospel by strict obedience to the Orders of God, thro' their Lead."[13]

In some ways, gift images were themselves a part of the process of institutionalization and social control. Because tangible and concrete, the careful drawings of the instruments could never be quite as spontaneous and immediate as visions and operations shared or acted out on the spot.[14] Making charismatic experience visible allowed the instruments to impose structure on the experience. The first gift images did not appear until after the beginning of the official New Era programme at New Lebanon in 1838. And many of the earlier drawings fit the conversionary tone of early normative charism. These images intended to shock, to puzzle, to mystify (e.g., figs. 4, 16, 17, 19, 20). From the outset, however, and in increasing proportions, gift images generally participated in processes of sanctification (which, in its later phase—but *not* during spontaneous charism—bore some resemblance to institutionalization, although the two did not always go hand in hand). The instruments began painting relatively late in the revival, with only a few preliminary forms before 1843.[15] Many of the images were predominantly visible demonstrations of blessing and proximity to the divine rather than admonitions or warnings. By the late 1840s the fervor of the New Era proper had diminished; Mother's Work, as a charismatic adventure was about over. Most scholars date the close of the Era to around 1847 or even earlier. But instruments produced gift paintings, in particular, until at least 1859 and instances of spiritual communications and gifts, less frequent but at least outwardly much like those of the early years of Mother's Work, continued into the 1860s and 1870s.[16]

As the community accomplished the transition from a period of spontaneous charism (early spirit possessions among children and more marginalized Believers) and then normative charism (beginning with the first official possessions at New Lebanon) to a period marked increasingly by institution and organization, gift images (which embodied both charism and order) helped to bridge the decade between Mother's Work and the years of consolidation that followed.[17] Gift images institutionalized charism in a permanent mode that sanctified and comforted the faithful as the community entered a period of demographic change and serious numerical decline. The latest visionary pictures of 1858 and 1859 retained only a trace of the tension and ambiguity which marked the instruments' earlier graphic efforts. In addition, as time passed, it appears that the instruments addressed more and more of their images to members of the ministry or to those who would soon enter leadership positions.[18] These images offered certificates of initiation and encouragement to new ministers and consolation and approbation to those with significant tenure in the service of the United Society (e.g., figs. 5, 21, 22, 25, 28, 29, 30). As heaven seemed to offer fewer images and visually organized messages to a comparatively wide variety of Shaker individuals, it gifted more who had contributed, or who had the potential to contribute, significantly to the community. These later pictures intended to participate in the shaping of new communal leaders by holding up established leaders as worthy examples and by reiterating and embodying essential communal values. The later images thus continued to express the Shaker conviction of an ordered universe in which terrestrial and celestial realms enjoyed certain regular and regulated relationships with one another and in which visual and structural characteristics exerted influence for good or for evil. The notions of art as restoration, as pattern, and as memorial were, after all, conservative in the strictest sense. Growing out of the desire to preserve a past and particularly powerful religious resource (a visible and visionary presence), gift images subsequently functioned to retain the moment of Mother's Work, its experiences and values, to deny its passing when the charismatic moment itself was over. Gift images outlasted the more fleeting expressions of Mother's Work precisely because they could represent charism in a tangible, reproducible, and institutionalized form, precisely because they could provide a relatively durable and abiding presence beyond the years of enthusiasm and spiritual immediacy.

The product of seemingly paradoxical impulses (innovation and conservation, charism and order, discontinuity and continuity, modern and primitive, conversion and sanctification), this tension itself had been a principal source of power in gift images. Ambivalence toward images and their producers was an understandable outgrowth of a religious community which so prized spiritual vision and, at least historically and officially, so despised nonessential decoration, which so highly valued spontaneous charism and so desperately avoided disorder and disunion. The ambivalent charge retained by visionary pictures had resulted from the conceptual suspension of gift images somewhere between ecstatic vision and material frippery, between celestial gift and superfluity, between the spiritual and the corporeal (even "carnal"). Once the tension surrounding visionary pictures was sufficiently resolved, once the taint of forbidden extravagance receded, the images no longer communicated as forcefully within the Shaker community. Although they retained sacralizing, memorial, and sentimental significance, the impact of drawings and paintings in the religious experience of the United Society diminished. The sacred and powerful had indeed become too familiar. And, although many carefully retained the images they had been given, gift paintings and drawings ultimately went the way of other manifestations.[19]

Soon different sorts of images (photographs and prints, decorated text and decorative borders in new communal newsletters, illustrated books, and periodicals from "the world") would become more acceptable among the Shakers. To the degree that gift images provided a remedy for the relative visual deprivation of the Shaker domestic environment, the need for this remedy disappeared as Victorian visual comforts found a place in the United Society.[20] Changes in Shaker attitudes toward images reflected changed attitudes in the larger American culture, generally with a time lag of a number of years. Factored through a particular set of religious understandings, Shaker perceptions resembled those of their neighbors, more carefully circumscribed, more subtly modulated. Initially, Shakers became interested in visualizing the spiritual world in tangible form at just the same time that photography and new modes of mechanical reproduction allowed wider distribution of representations of the physical world in American society at large.[21] The 1830s, 40s, and 50s brought changes in the status of "art" both within and without the boundaries of Shakerism. Shaker and non-Shaker, each with their own reasons, became more accepting of pictures, less inclined to view them as necessarily corrupting luxuries. For Shaker and non-Shaker alike, the impulse to image was strong.[22] Perhaps equally strong in both groups were continuing reservations about this impulse.

Like their Shaker contemporaries, other Americans in the middle third of the nineteenth century eschewed anything approaching art for art's sake.[23] Attempting to establish the practical utility of images, these Americans promoted drawing as a general skill akin to writing. Widely disseminated in drawing manuals of the time, this philosophy and approach reinforced linearity, especially in popular forms of American art (e.g., "school girl" images) and in forms which adapted popular techniques (e.g., Shaker gift images). If drawing was like writing, then lines were the essence of form.[24] What Vlach calls the campaign of democratic art instruction[25] and Marzio calls the art crusade resulted in the association of drawing skills and schools, of images with penmanship, mapmaking, geography lessons, literacy, refinement. Inventories of Shaker libraries and accounts of Shaker teaching techniques, not to mention the backgrounds of most Shaker image-makers (cf. chapter 3), demonstrate the influence of such ideas among the followers of Ann Lee.

More importantly, in addition to establishing a practical aura for art, the artist-authors of the popular mid-nineteenth-century drawing manuals, like the general public, expected images to have a moral or religious function.[26] It is one of the great myths of American art history that this nation, in its infancy and youth, had no religious art. In fact, the opposite is more nearly true. Until late in the nineteenth century, citizen and Believer would agree that the aesthetic realm required a religious or at least an ethical rationale. The separation of church and state and the relative disengagement of both from art patronage did not sever connections, especially connections of content, between art and religion.

By 1850 and 1860, however, and certainly by 1870, due principally to the alliance of aesthetic with moral and spiritual objectives, lingering American reservations about the association of art and corrupting luxury had all but disappeared. Clergy became conspicuous patrons of art. In popular literature and in public discourse, prominent Americans represented the minister as an artist and the artist as a minister.[27] Art's mission was indeed moral and spiritual; an appreciation for beauty went hand in hand with spiritual maturity.[28] Not just the painted originals of American and European artists, but mechanically produced prints of these images (as well as of less "elevated" works) enhanced the moral and spiritual environment of American homes. While the view had its critics, and while none yet dared suggest (as some later would) that art might replace religion, many construed art and religion as "alternate routes toward moral improvement."[29] Referring to different forms of pictures, Shakers to their own gift paintings and drawings and their American neighbors generally to the "finer" arts, the two agreed on the idealistic nature of images. Shaker attitudes toward images not only reflected American cultural roots but also shared with American culture the broader Western heritage of the Protestant Reformation. Linking images with words, avoiding illusory means of establishing resemblance between image and prototype, emphasizing the celestial giver of the visionary gift rather than the image itself or its instrument as the essential ingredient, Shakers produced their own particularly Protestant style of visionary record.

So the "edge" cultivated by gift images as a truly alternative and celestial form of picture gradually diminished. Not only did repeated distribution of images at New Lebanon and Hancock lead to greater familiarity and less "danger," but increasing awareness of shifting attitudes in the culture at large legitimated art and made its practice in the service of religion less risky.[30] While Shakers certainly did not adopt images wholesale, and while they maintained a spare visual environment in comparison to the "world," in the years following Mother's Work they expressed fewer and fewer reservations about the presence of many kinds of pictures in their midst.[31]

The average Shaker of this period certainly did know more about the world. While the United Society itself had seen increasing "worldliness" as a principal cause of revival, ultimately this concern did not resolve itself by banishing the world but by adopting a more generous tone in relationship to the world. The world, for its part, beginning decades earlier, had ceased its persecution of Shaker adherents and thus no longer actively assisted Believers in the erection of barriers.[32] After 1850, when Shakers sensed in spiritualism the "commencement of a New Era in religious matters in the world," they recognized God's outside work as parallel in some ways to God's work in their midst and many felt that Shakers too should rethink their relationship with more worldly neighbors. Beginning in 1854, Shakers expressed renewed interest in missions in the world.[33] They also registered genuine excitement over technological advances—for example, the "great Atlantic telegraph cable," steam engines, and the achievements exhibited at the Crystal Palace. And, while Believers turned down an invitation to display their manufactured goods at the Crystal Palace in 1853, they did exhibit their wares at the Centennial Exposition in Philadelphia in 1876.[34] Some perceived this shift in disposition as a faithful response to God's activity among the "children of the world." Some believed it to be a disastrous indication of backsliding among their own.

But even those Believers who most completely shunned the fashions of the world found themselves exposed more and more to the world's influence as the rate of transition in membership continued to increase. In the year 1860, Isaac Newton Youngs lamented, "the sense is continually aspiring after more, becoming more and more tasty, about clothing and articles of fancy, the use of high colors, of paint, varnish, etc. perhaps more than is virtuous or proper."[35] In 1870, at the Poland Spring community in Maine, Philemon Stewart, an official New Lebanon instrument ultimately censured by the ministry, entered his complaint on record:

> For thirty years or more since the days of Mother's manifestation, Believers especially in this place, instead of doing as the Manifestation required, to put their own hands to work, keep more at home, and keep the World out, they have extended trade and traffic four fold, if not more, and let the world in ten fold more than ever before. [36]

Although Shakers continued to integrate within their belief system both restorationism and millennialism, in the 1850s and 1860s they placed increasing emphasis on progressivism in relationship to revelation, universalism in relationship to salvation, and modernity in relationship to material and technological advances.[37]

While many Shakers never doubted the sacrality of the images and other presents they had received from the heavenly sphere, greater exposure to the "world's" pictures and opinions may have led to a growing conviction that the world would not understand gift images, that the images indeed might prove cause for embarrassment if the world knew of them. Increasingly, Shakers concerned themselves instead with the "image" they presented to the world. As the century waned, Shakerism developed a more self-consciously public face, less prophetic and less judgmental, more promotional, more broadly persuasive or appealing. During Mother's Work itself, censorship of images considered inconsistent with the revival's charismatic and ordering content likely accounted for the destruction of some images and other gifts "in the line of writing." Relatively early in the revival, the sect restricted to its own membership access to some manifestations lest they be mistaken for "unadulterated foolishness."[38] As Mother's Work progressed, both celestial beings and Shaker leaders urged Believers not to retain what might prove unseemly later on. On 12 January 1847, speaking through her instrument, Mother Ann delivered these words to the New Lebanon ministry:

> altho' I do not wish to lay more burthen upon you than you are able to bear yet it would be a great comfort to me your Mother to have all that has been written by inspiration throughout Zion examined and inspected (while the present Ministry are able to attend to it) by whoever ye may feel has the greatest gift of understanding for this purpose, if ye are not able to read all yourselves. For ye know not what critic's hand many of these sacred things may fall into . . . therefore I should be glad to have nothing left on record where it can possibly be circulated which can in any way be prooved false, or which does not accord with the faith and practice of my first- born children.[39]

Later in the century, fears about consistency between and within pictures and other messages diminished and then disappeared. But concern that drawings and paintings would be misunderstood by nonbelievers continued, leading Shakers to draw "the veil of oblivion" over more of the "extravagances" of the Era.[40] For the most part, however, later destruction of gift messages and similar materials had less to do with issues of content and ideology and more to do with housekeeping. As images became separated from now-dead recipients who had valued them and as shrinking Shaker communities began to close, survivors sorted and consolidated records and archives, discarding whatever seemed unnecessary to them. Ironically, images that had once narrowly escaped categorization as superfluities now became, in a more mundane sense, superfluous to the Shaker life. Shakers in the remaining communities, concerned with neatness and cleanliness, threw out everything for which they had no use. Many documents from the era of Mother's Work did not survive this inclination toward neatness.[41]

In *Visions of the Heavenly Sphere,* collector and historian Edward Deming Andrews tells how he and Faith Andrews, his wife and partner in both collecting and writing, were among the first outsiders to see Shaker gift images.

> In the retiring-room of the family dwelling of a New England Shaker community we were talking one evening in the 1930's with a sister of that religious order. When the conversation turned to the various modes by which a reticent sect expresses its inner spirit, she grew thoughtful and then said: "I have something to show you which I have kept secret since I was a child of eight. I want your opinion about it." She then opened a chest in a corner of the room and took out an illuminated scroll entitled "An Emblem of the Heavenly Sphere." As we looked at it she was silent and watchful. Our reaction was one of delight and wonder; we did not know, after ten years' acquaintance with this secluded folk, that they ever attempted to depict the signs and objects of the spiritual world. Seeking an explanation for the document's nature and source, we learned that Sister Alice had rescued it from wastepaper con-

signed to an oven, had hidden it away, and as she grew older, had treasured it increasingly as a precious, if somewhat mysterious, expression of the Shaker soul. "My showing it to you was a test," she afterward declared. "If you had shown any evidence of levity in your response, I was prepared to keep it as mine alone. I would have known that the 'world' could not understand."[42]

The Andrewses' encounter with Alice Smith at Hancock demonstrates the danger to gift drawings posed by both the fear of misunderstanding and the desire for neatness. Elsewhere, Faith Andrews recalled that Smith, in 1892, had rescued numerous paintings and drawings from the ovens of Shaker Eldress Mary Frances Hall "whose passion for cleaning drawers and closets resulted in the destruction of scores of Hancock documents."[43]

On the last day of 1856, Isaac Youngs closed his "history of the Spiritual department of the Church" with these comments:

> Much depression of spirit has been felt, and struggling thro' dark and gloomy prospects, on account of apostacies, lifelessness and backslidings of unfaithful members, and scanty ingathering from without.
>
> There have been some efforts to open our testimony to the world, for the last two years, and invite in such as were ready to unite in our faith; but there is such a stupidity of soul, and absence of conviction for sin in the world, that there is rarely one to be found who is willing to submit to the mortifying terms of the gospel.
>
> We gather in many children, but when they come to act for themselves, a large portion of them choose the flowery path of nature, rather than the cross.
>
> Nevertheless there has been, particularly in meetings for worship, many refreshing gifts, much enjoyment of real devotion to God, much consolation administered from soul to soul, and much good faith and integrity manifested; which overbalances the evil influences: insomuch that we can say Zion yet rejoices in her God and gives glory to his name.[44]

In fact, in the decades following Mother's Work, Believers continued to draw heavily upon its "many refreshing gifts." After all, they maintained, the gifts themselves had never gone bad, rather, the forces of evil had led some instruments astray and instilled doubt and disbelief in the hearts of others. While some prominent Shakers had indeed left because of the excesses of Mother's Work, others had been revived by their eyewitness experience of Mother Ann's presence.[45] Even David Lamson, one of the most vocal of mid-century apostates, expressed his conviction that those who stayed genuinely believed in Mother Ann's gifts and took heart in her promises.[46] New Era solutions to the crisis of the third generation did not ultimately solve the problems facing Shakers in the middle third of the century. The instruments of Mother's Work had summoned up the past and represented it to the rising generation as their present and future. But even the most skilled instrument could not bring the realities of mid-nineteenth-century America to match the pattern set in 1790. Ultimately, even a "visible presence" was not enough to mold into an earlier Shaker image the complex and compelling forces reshaping the later nineteenth-century Shaker community.

The modernist tends to view the Shakers as a simple people of the ideal American past, dedicated in the practice of their faith to a spirituality of streamlined aesthetics. In the modernist telling of the story, Shaker restorationism has been persuaded to serve modernist restorationism. Neither the chronology of Shaker experience nor the multivocality of the Shaker spiritual aesthetic fits this portrayal. In the final analysis, mid-nineteenth-century Shaker restorationism ultimately involved reorientation as much as restoration. Attempts to restore a visible presence to Ann Lee, to retrieve the charism and order of the ministries of Lee and her early successors, redirected the gaze of Lee's later followers. Restoration of the past entailed reorientation of the past toward the present and future. Emphasizing Lee as spiritual pattern and guide promoted the successors as patterns and guides, subtly shifting Shaker attention from these earlier ministers to the contemporary ministry and suggesting that later leaders, too, constituted an appropriate pattern and guide for Shakers of the 1860s and 1870s. Though attempts to somehow resurrect Ann Lee gave Mother's Work its rationale and focus, as the revival waned Believers followed Lucy Wright's advice instead: "you need not labor for gifts to dream dreams or see visions, if you keep your union together as good brethren and sisters there will be nothing to separate you from Mother."[47] Union with the contemporary Visible Lead did, in fact, increasingly replace the charism of the founder. As order was, for Shakers, finally inseparable from charism, this drift was, again, a matter of emphasis. But, true to Wright's intentions, the guidance of the contemporary ministry more and more completely replaced the sort of inspiration represented in the person and ministry of Ann Lee. Nevertheless, Mother's Work had met the pressing spiritual needs of many communal adherents. These Believers retained heavenly images and records of celestial gifts to shore them up in times of trial. Shakers who remained (and there were many of them) rededicated themselves to their callings and expected Mother Ann's spiritual presence to lead them toward a new century. More mature Shakers, usually those who had participated in Mother's Work, continued to rejoice that they were surrounded and supported in their daily activities by the inhabitants of the celestial sphere.[48] Their younger, now fourth generation, companions, too, generally believed that the Era's manifestations had been genuine.[49] Believers young and old quietly continued to receive new visions and to collect and copy old ones.[50] And Shakers of each successively smaller generation interpreted and internalized Ann Lee's prophecies of decrease preceding increase in order to give meaning to their own situation in time.[51]

FIGURES

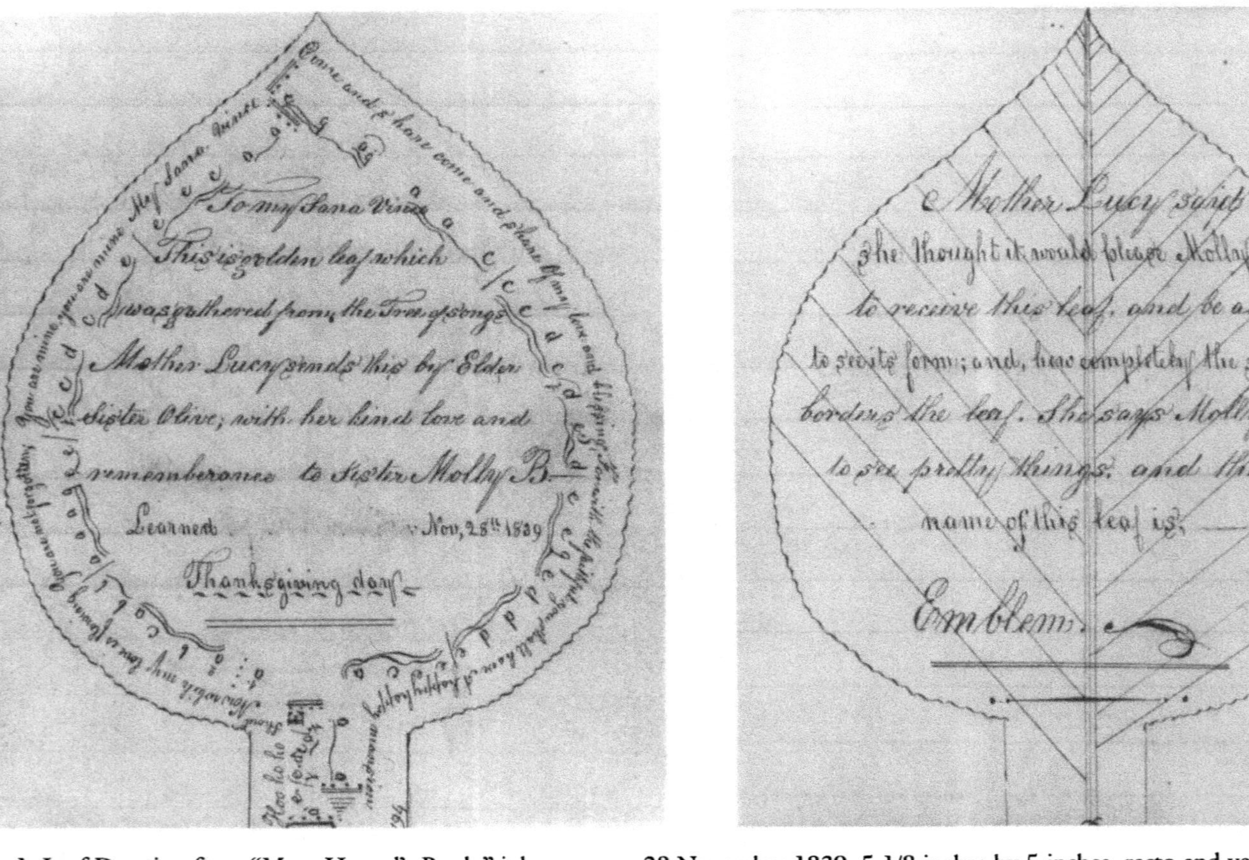

FIG. 1. Leaf Drawing from "Mary Hazard's Book," ink on paper, 28 November 1839, 5 1/8 inches by 5 inches, recto and verso, WML. Courtesy of The Winterthur Library: The Edward Deming Andrews Memorial Shaker Collection, NO. *896*

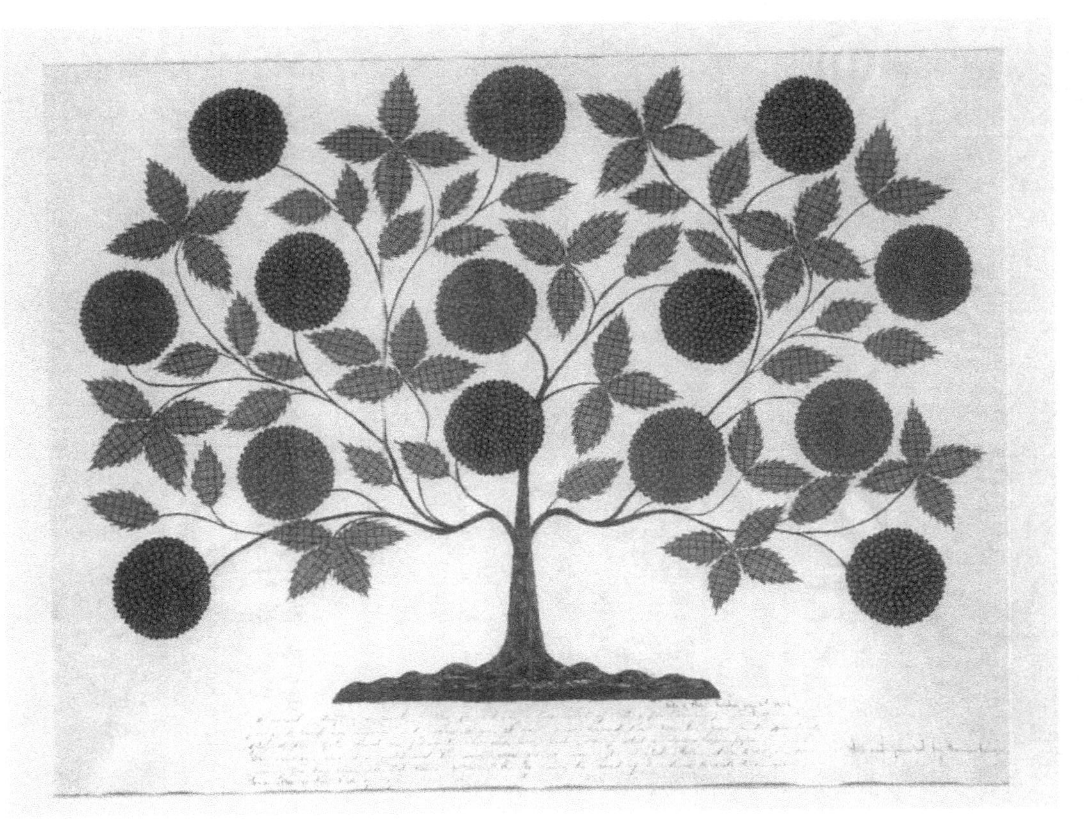

FIG. 2. Hannah Cohoon, *Tree of Life*, watercolor or tempera and ink on paper, 1854, 18 1/8 inches by 23 5/16 inches, HSV.
Courtesy of Hancock Shaker Village, Pittsfield, Massachusetts

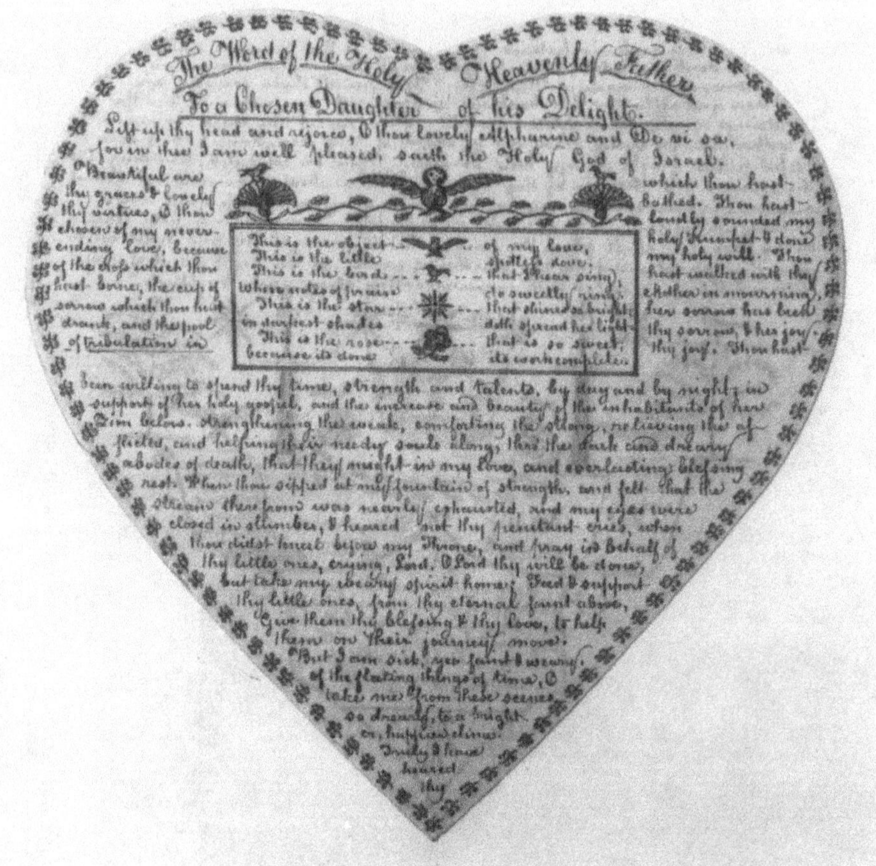

FIG. 3. Heart Cutout, "The Word of the Heavenly Father, To a Chosen Daughter of his Delight," ink on paper, 25 April 1844, 4 3/8 inches by 4 5/8 inches, recto and verso, WRHS.
Courtesy of Western Reserve Historical Society

cries, have listened to thy prayers, and
sent my holy Angels to commune with thee, when sorrows on
sorrows did around thee roll. But thro' all these scenes of sorrow and affliction, thou hast not murmured against me, nor the
doings of my All-righteous hand. Therefore let thy spirit be merry
within thee, for truly thou art a saint of my kingdom, and a beautiful pillar of light in my holy Temple. Yea be comforted, knowing that
thy sorrows are known by thy Eternal Father above, who will not fail of
rewarding thee with a crown of his bright glory, and unfeigned love.
So tune up thy praises and march on thy way, For with my holy Angels
on thy harp thou shalt play, the song of eternal peace, of joy and sweet mirth,
when thou art releas'd from the sorrows of earth, at the right hand of my
Eternal throne, crowned with my everlasting glory and brightness.

Well done my good and faithful Servant.

This is the emblem of my ever-lasting blessing with precious fruit.

Betsy Darrow. April 28th 1844.

A Holy saint of my Kingdom, A Virgin of purity, uprightness and holiness, crowned with my everlasting glory, sitting at my right hand with the redeemed of my glory.

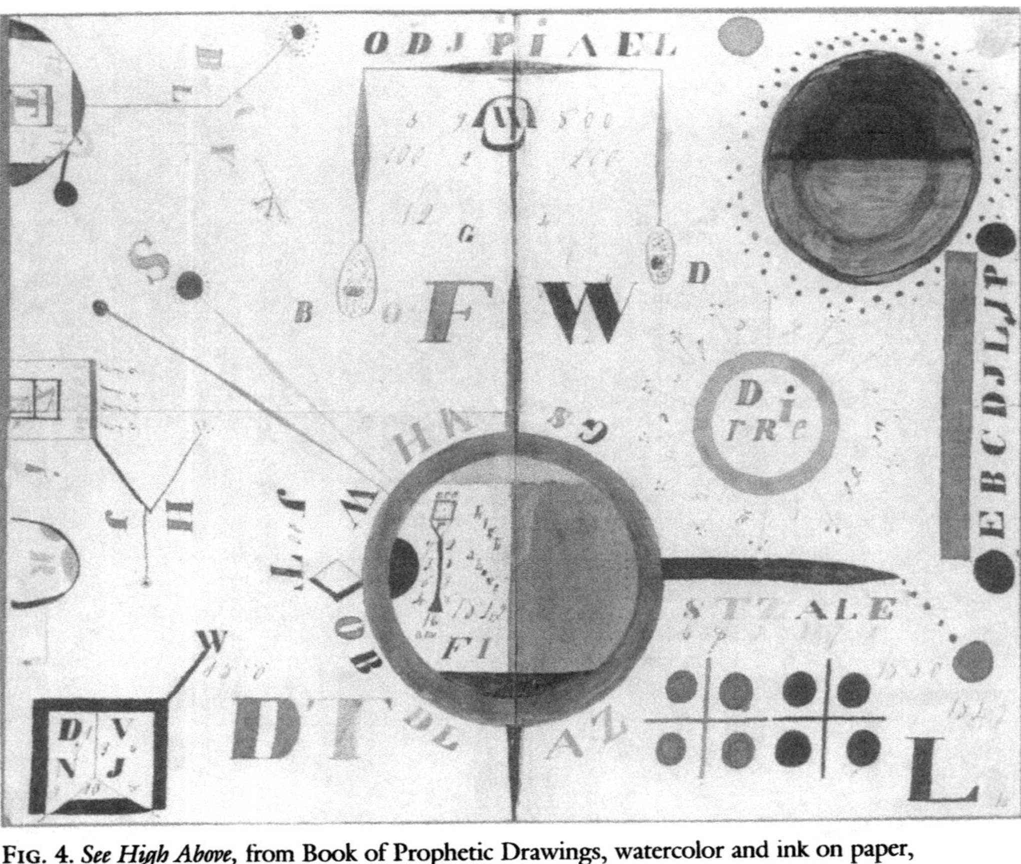

FIG. 4. *See High Above*, from Book of Prophetic Drawings, watercolor and ink on paper, [1843?], 13 inches by 15 3/4 inches, WRHS.
Courtesy of Western Reserve Historical Society

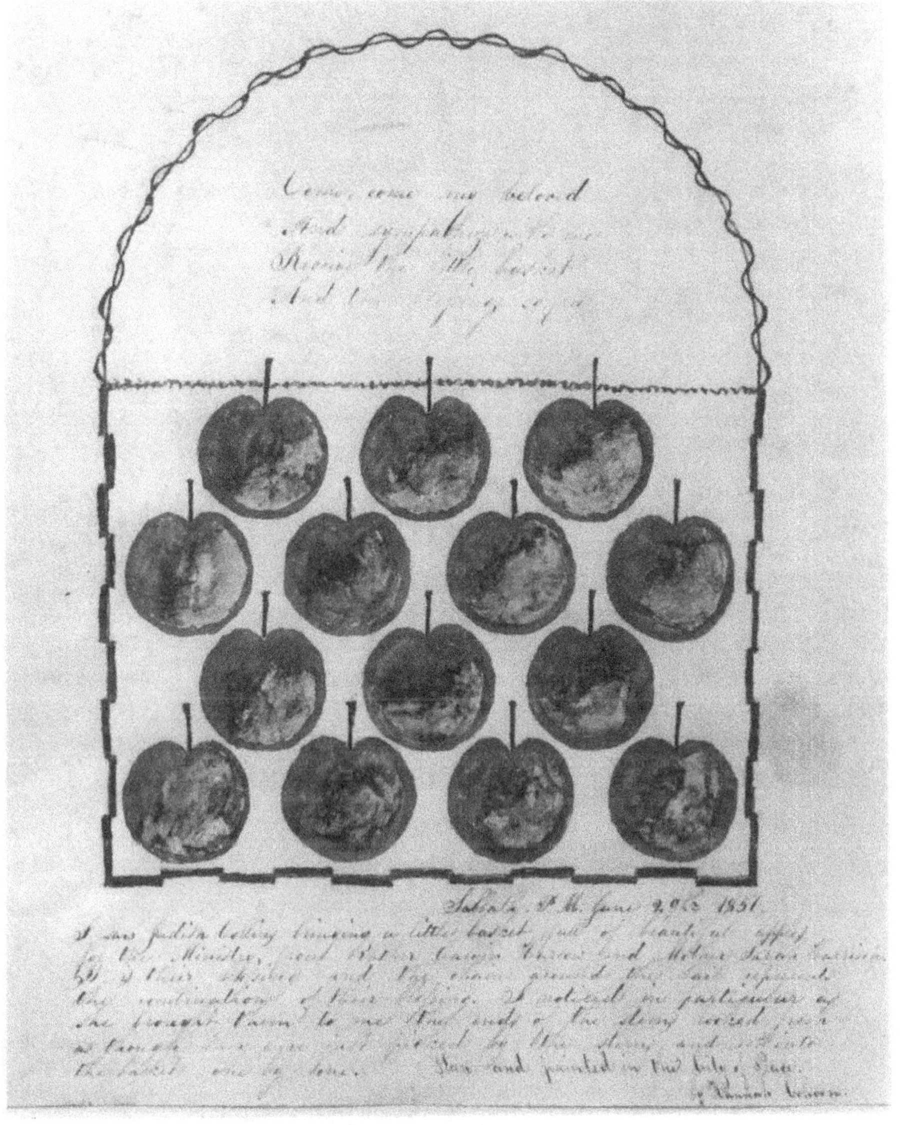

Fig. 5. Hannah Cohoon, *A Little Basket Full of Beautiful Apples,* watercolor and ink on paper, 1856, 10 1/8 inches by 8 1/8 inches, HSV.
Courtesy of Hancock Shaker Village, Pittsfield, Massachusetts

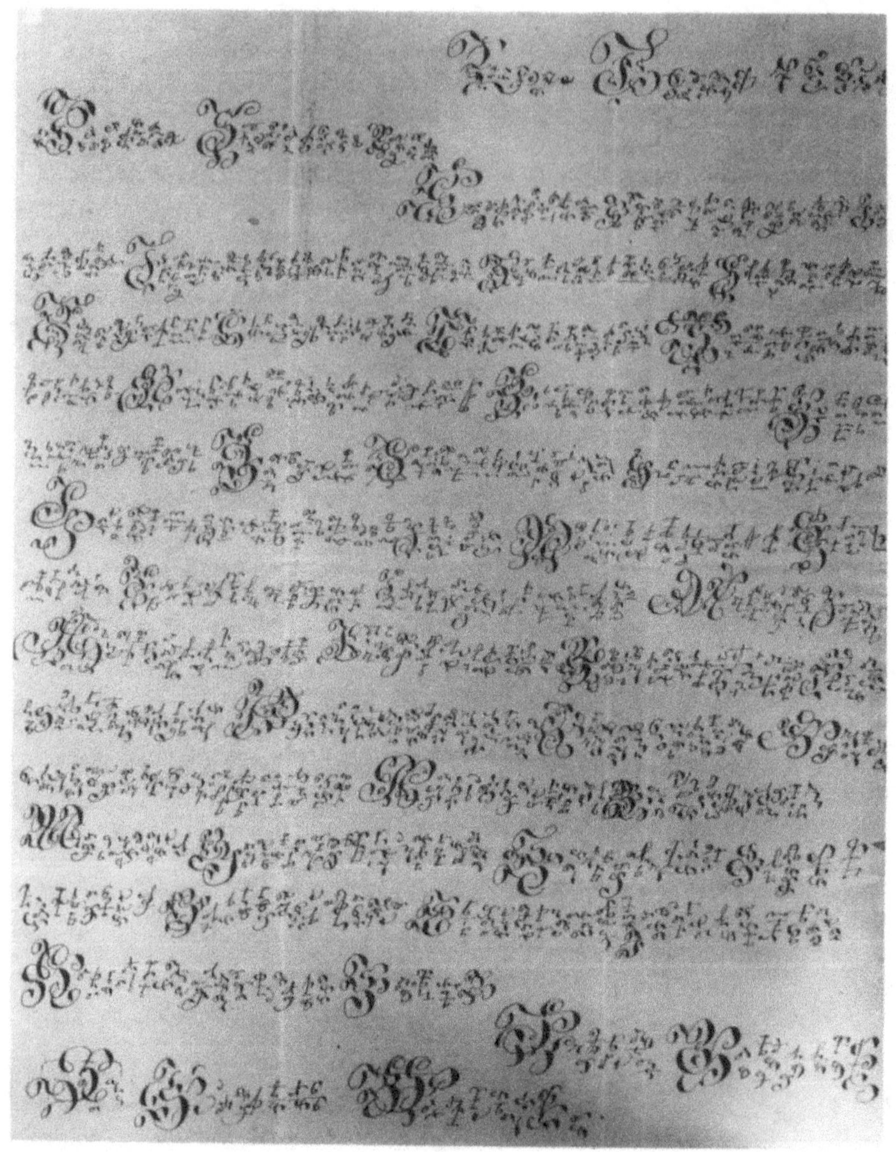

FIG. 6. Page of a Native Spirit Letter, ink on paper, 25 September 1842, approx. 10 inches by 8 inches, WRHS.
Courtesy of Western Reserve Historical Society

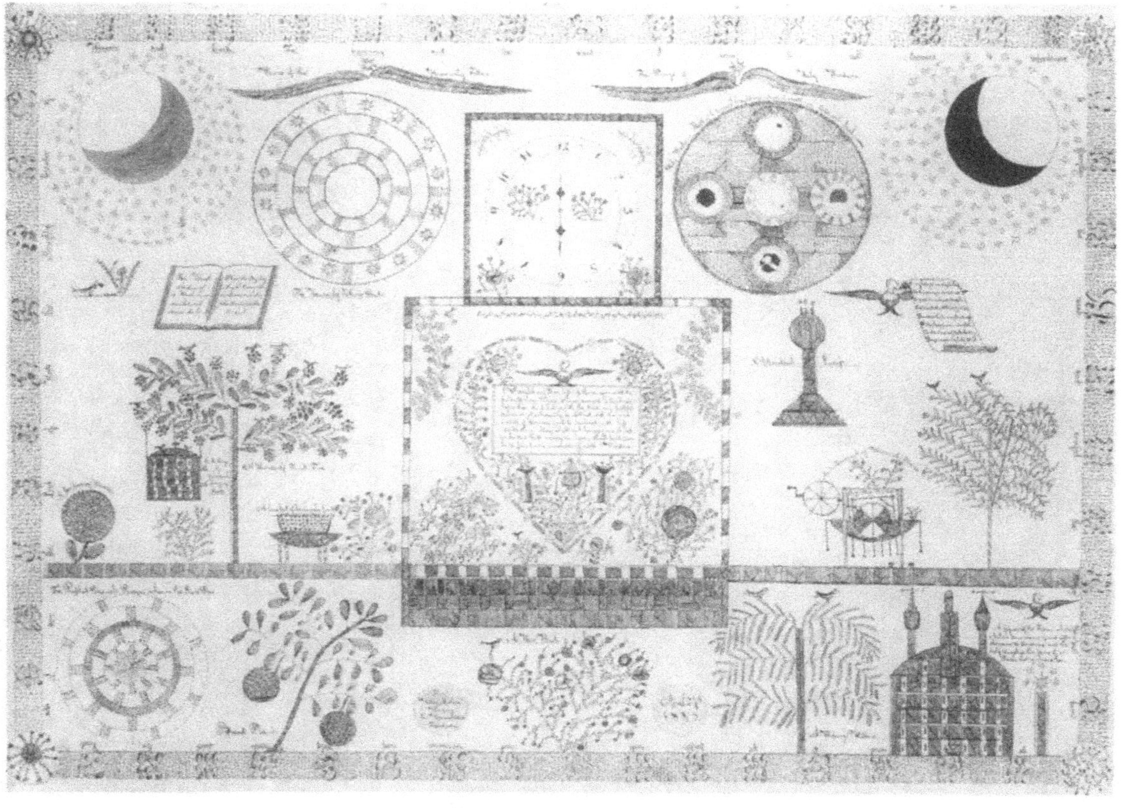

Fig. 7. ***From Holy Mother Wisdom to Hannah Ann Treadway,*** watercolor, ink, and sealing wax on paper, 27 April 1845, 15 inches by 20 1/2 inches, PMA.
Courtesy of Philadelphia Museum of Art: Gift of Mr. and Mrs. Julius Zieget

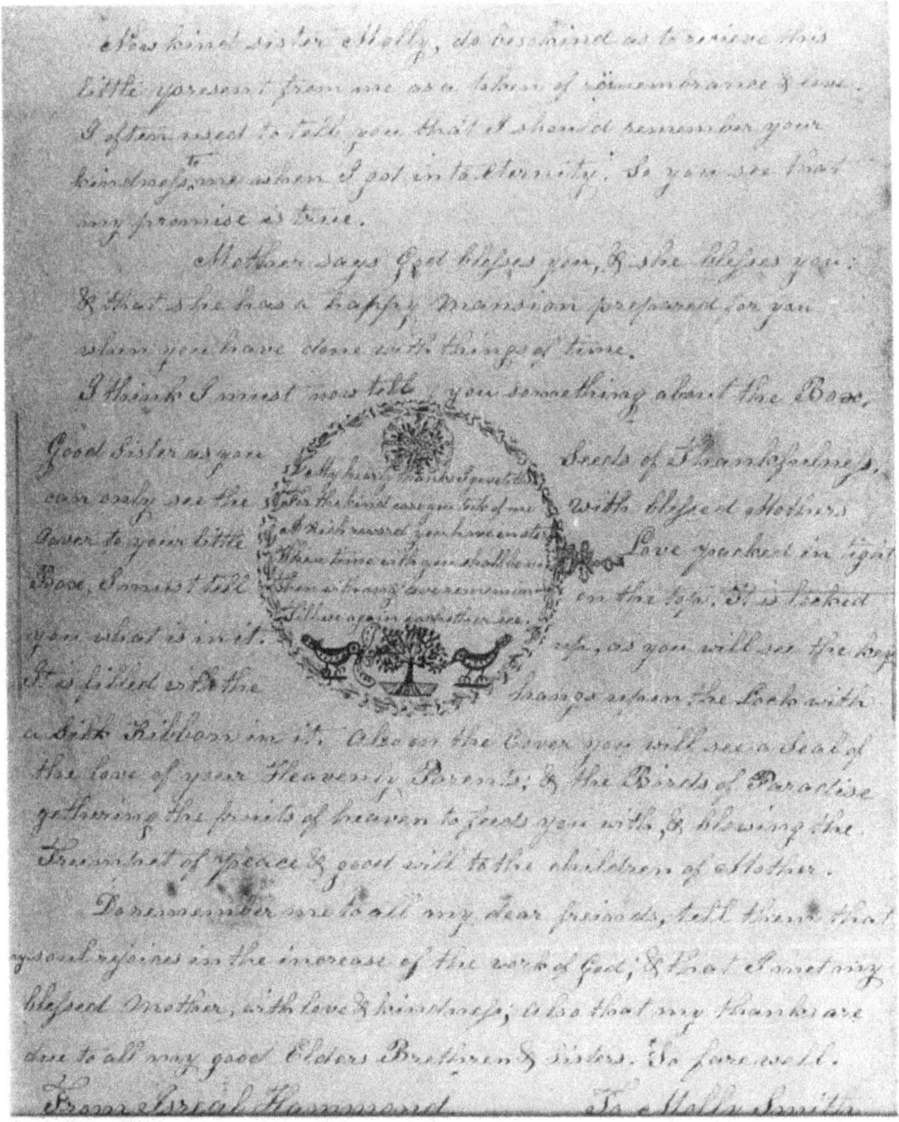

Now kind sister Molly, do be so kind as to receive this little present from me as a token of remembrance & love. I often used to tell you that I should remember your kindness to me when I got into Eternity. So you see that my promise is true.

Mother says God blesses you, & she blesses you; & that she has a happy mansion prepared for you when you have done with things of time.

I think I must now tell you something about the Box. Good Sister as you can only see the cover to your little Box, I must tell you what is in it. It is filled with the Seeds of Thankfulness, with blessed Mother's Love packed in tight on the top. It is locked up, as you will see the key hangs upon the Lock with a Silk Ribbon in it. Also on the Cover you will see a Seal of the love of your Heavenly Parents; & the Birds of Paradise gathering the fruits of heaven to feed you with, & blowing the Trumpet of peace & good will to the children of Mother.

To My heart thanks I give thee
For the kind care you took of me
A rich reward you have in store
When time with you shall be no more
[illegible]
[illegible] again [illegible] see.

Do remember me to all my dear friends, tell them that my soul rejoices in the increase of the work of God; & that I met my blessed Mother, with love & kindness; also that my thanks are due to all my good Elders Brethren & Sisters. So farewell.

From Israel Hammond To Molly Smith

FIG. 8. "A Present Given to Sister Molly Smith at Hancock," watercolor and ink on paper, 25 January 1847 (28 April 1845), 10 inches by 8 inches, verso, SDL. Courtesy of the Collection of the United Society of Shakers, Sabbathday Lake, Maine

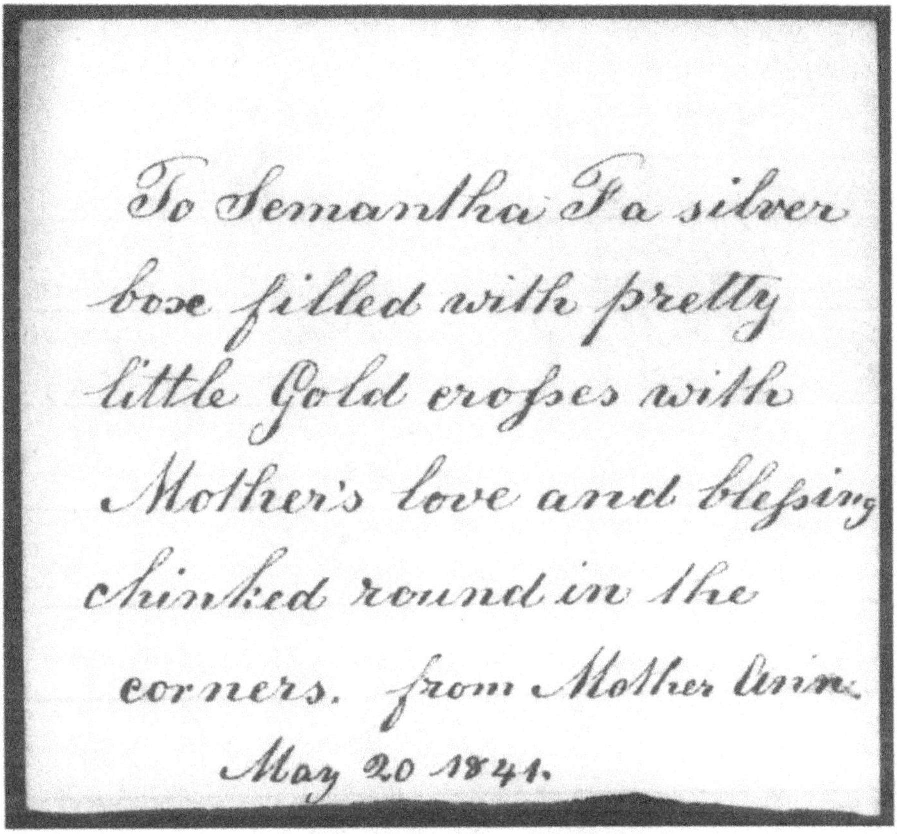

To Semantha F a silver
box filled with pretty
little Gold crosses with
Mother's love and blessing
chinked round in the
corners. from Mother Ann.
May 20 1841.

FIG. 9. "A Silver Box," ink on paper, 20 May 1841, 2 5/8 inches by 2 7/8 inches, WRHS.
Courtesy of Western Reserve Historical Society

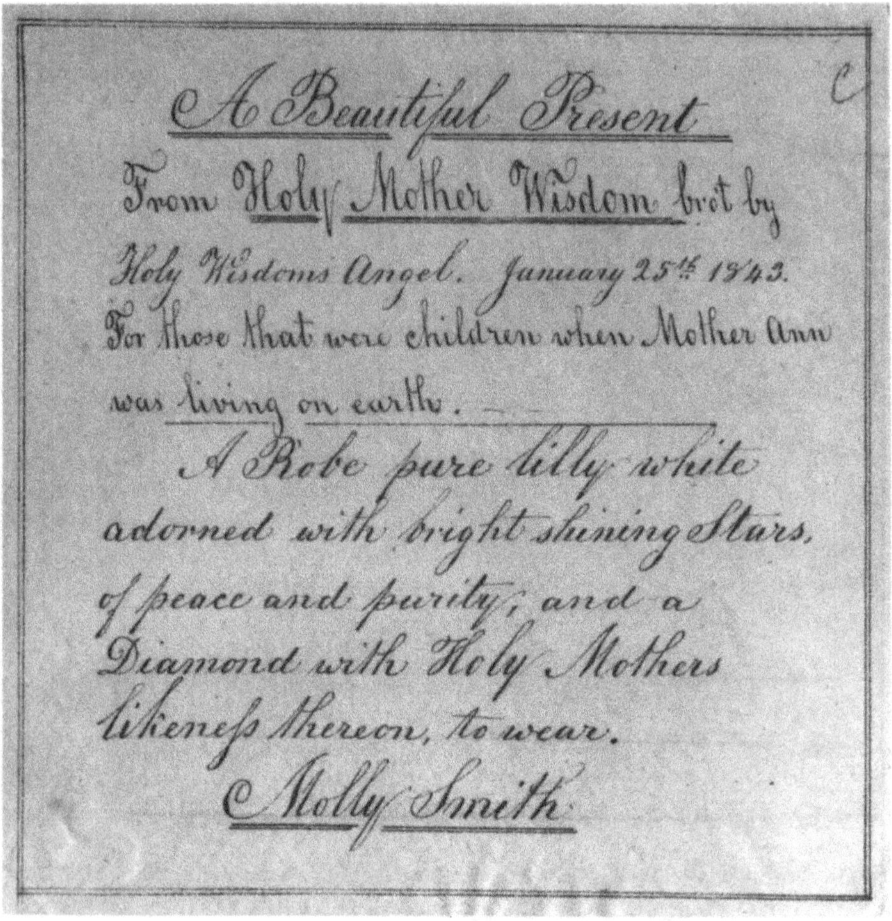

C

A Beautiful Present

From Holy Mother Wisdom brot by
Holy Wisdoms Angel. January 25th 1843.
For those that were children when Mother Ann
was living on earth. —

A Robe pure lilly white
adorned with bright shining Stars,
of peace and purity; and a
Diamond with Holy Mothers
likeness thereon, to wear.

Molly Smith

FIG. 10. "A Beautiful Present," ink on colored paper, 25 January 1843, 4 3/4 inches by 4 3/4 inches, WRHS.
Courtesy Western Reserve Historical Society

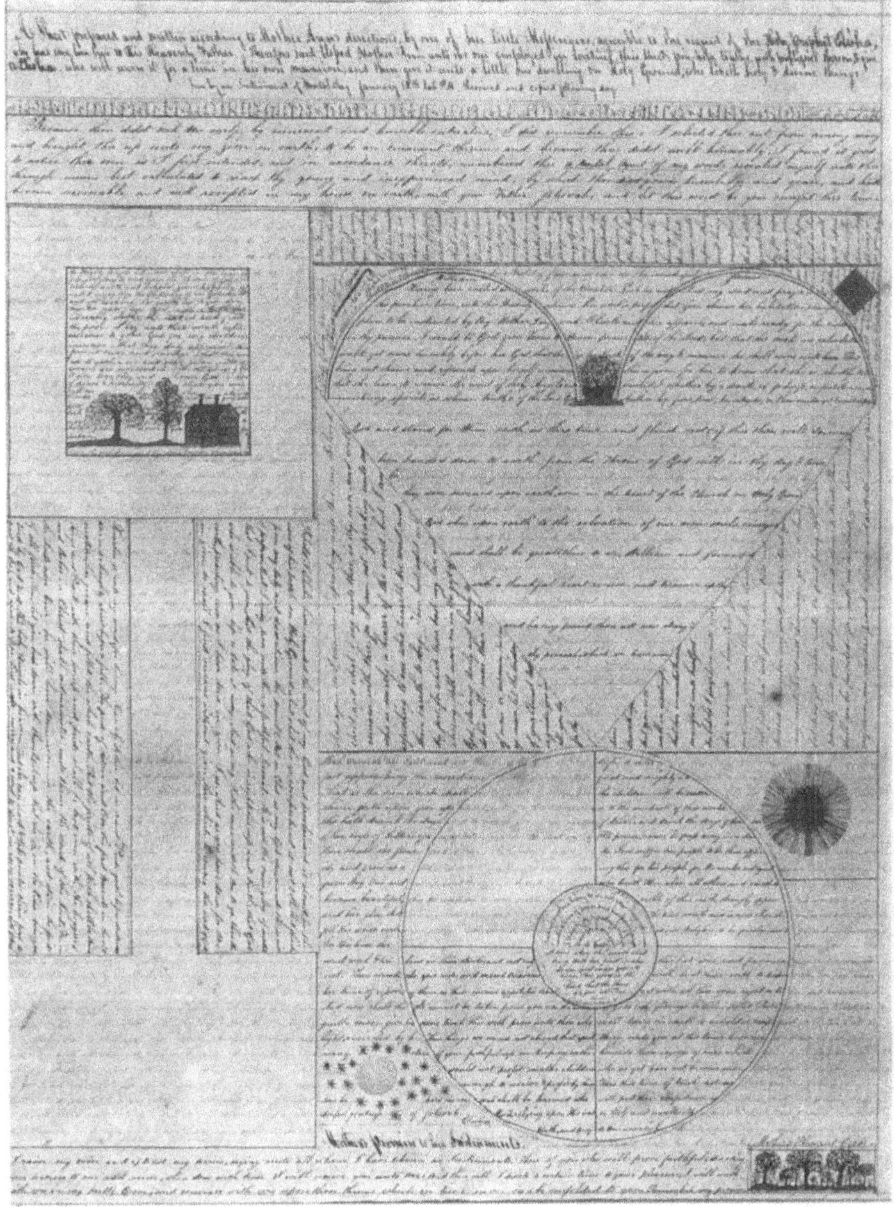

FIG. 11. *A Sheet prepared and written according to Mother Ann's directions,* watercolor and ink on paper, 13 January 1845, 20 1/2 inches by 15 3/4 inches, SDL. Courtesy of the Collection of the United Society of Shakers, Sabbathday Lake, Maine

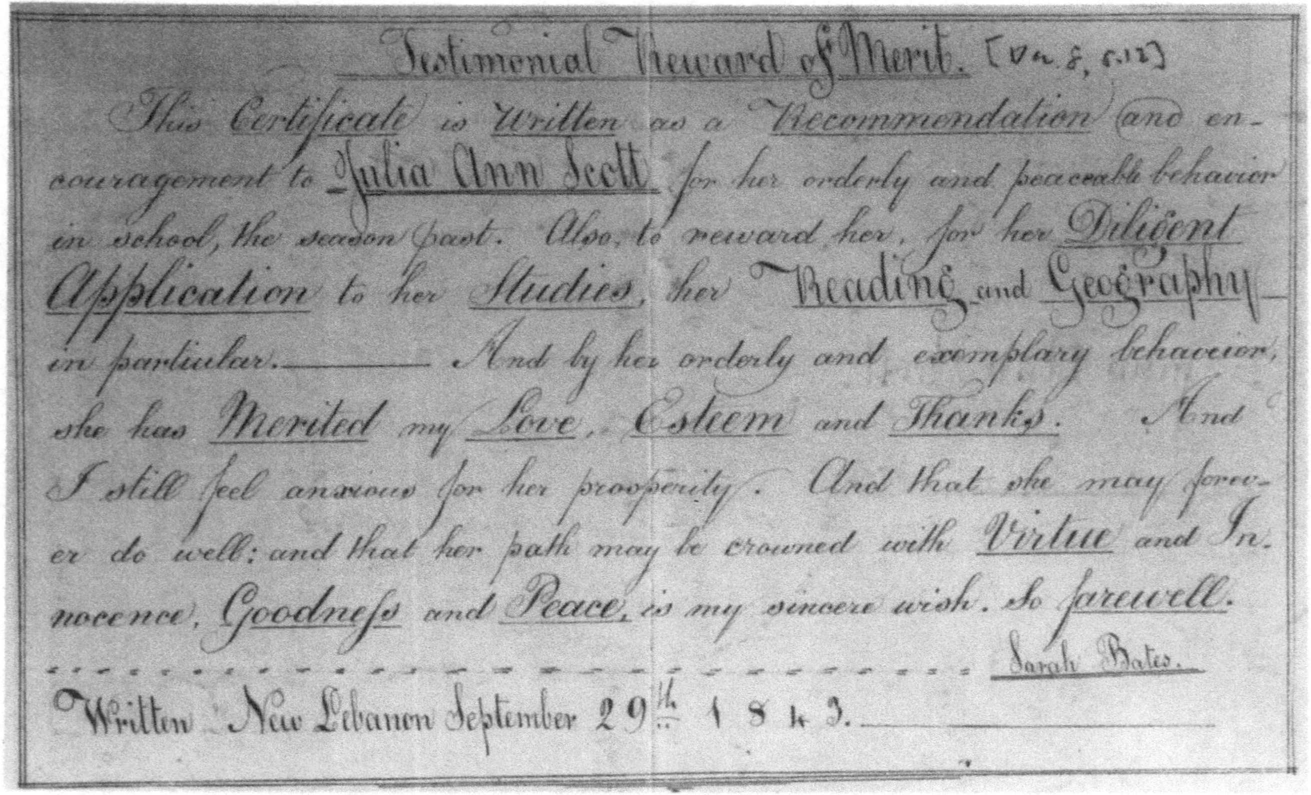

Testimonial Reward of Merit. [Vn. 8, c.12]

This Certificate is Written as a Recommendation and encouragement to Julia Ann Scott for her orderly and peaceable behavior in school, the season past. Also, to reward her, for her Diligent Application to her Studies, her Reading and Geography in particular.——— And by her orderly and exemplary behavior, she has Merited my Love, Esteem and Thanks. And I still feel anxious for her prosperity. And that she may forever do well; and that her path may be crowned with Virtue and Innocence, Goodness and Peace, is my sincere wish. So farewell.

Sarah Bates.

Written New Lebanon September 29th 1843.

FIG. 12. Sarah Bates, “Testimonial Reward of Merit,” ink on colored paper, 29 September 1843, 4 13/16 inches by 7 15/16 inches, WRHS.
Courtesy of Western Reserve Historical Society

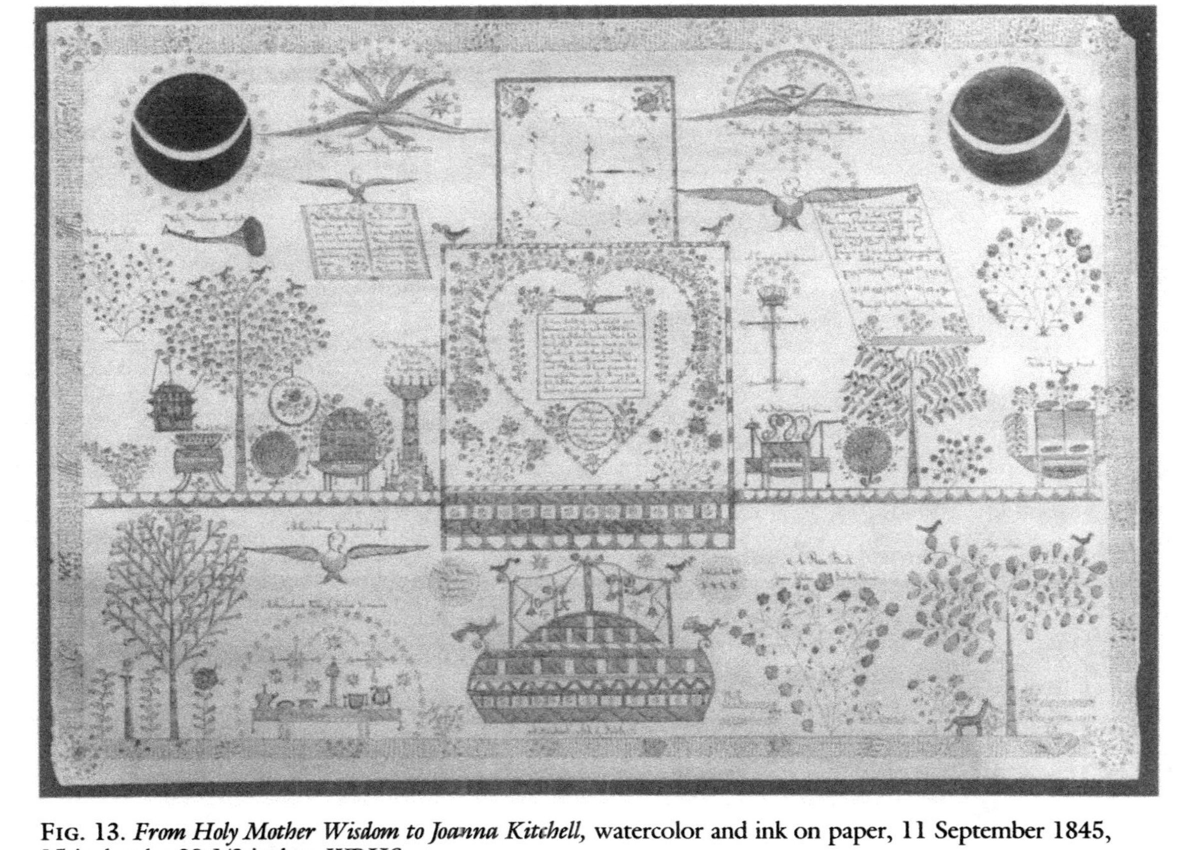

FIG. 13. *From Holy Mother Wisdom to Joanna Kitchell,* watercolor and ink on paper, 11 September 1845, 15 inches by 20 1/2 inches, WRHS.
Courtesy of Western Reserve Historical Society

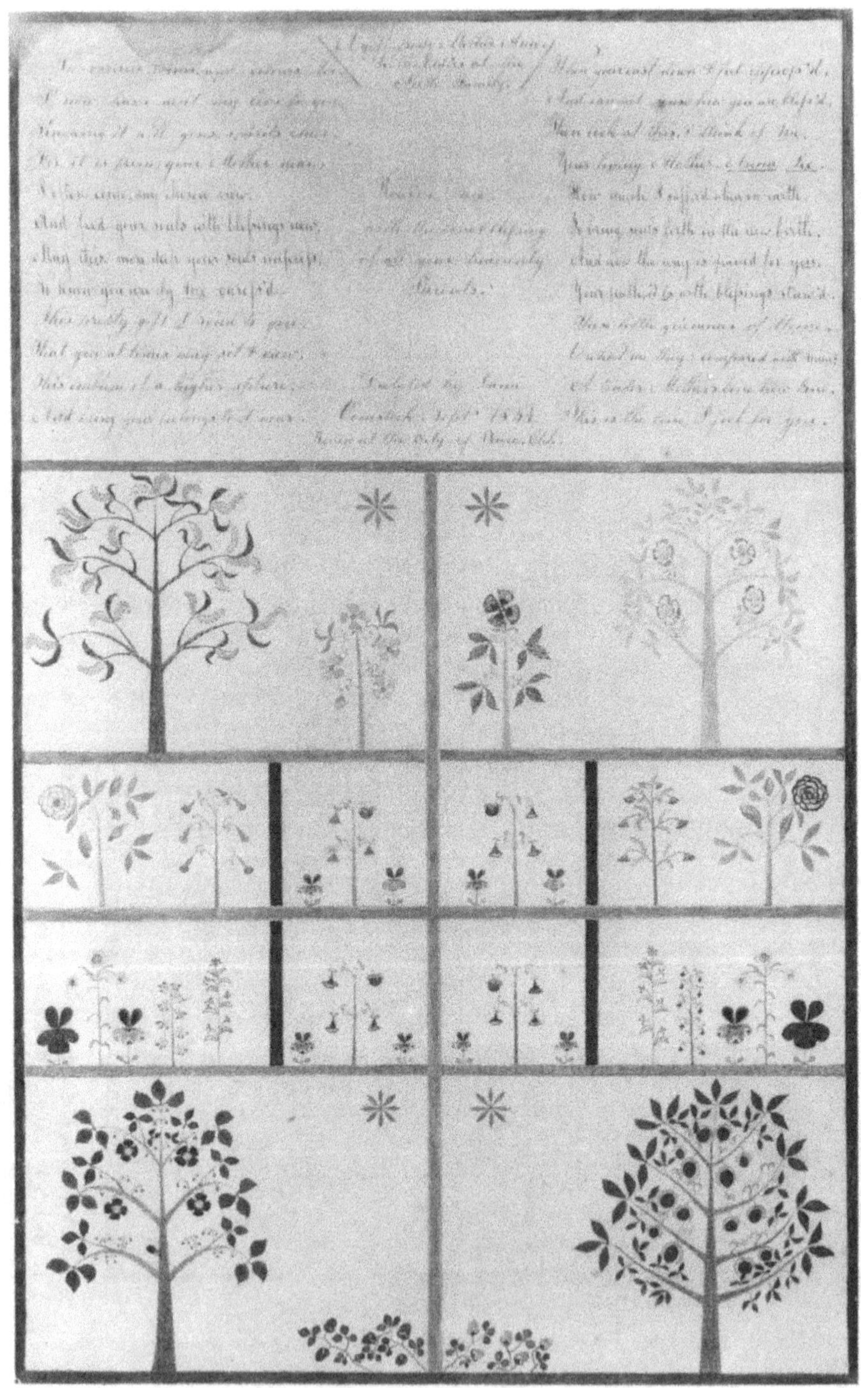

Fig. 14. *A gift from Mother Ann to the Elders at the North Family,* watercolor and ink on paper, September 1854, 19 inches by 12 inches, HSV.
Courtesy of Hancock Shaker Village, Pittsfield, Massachusetts

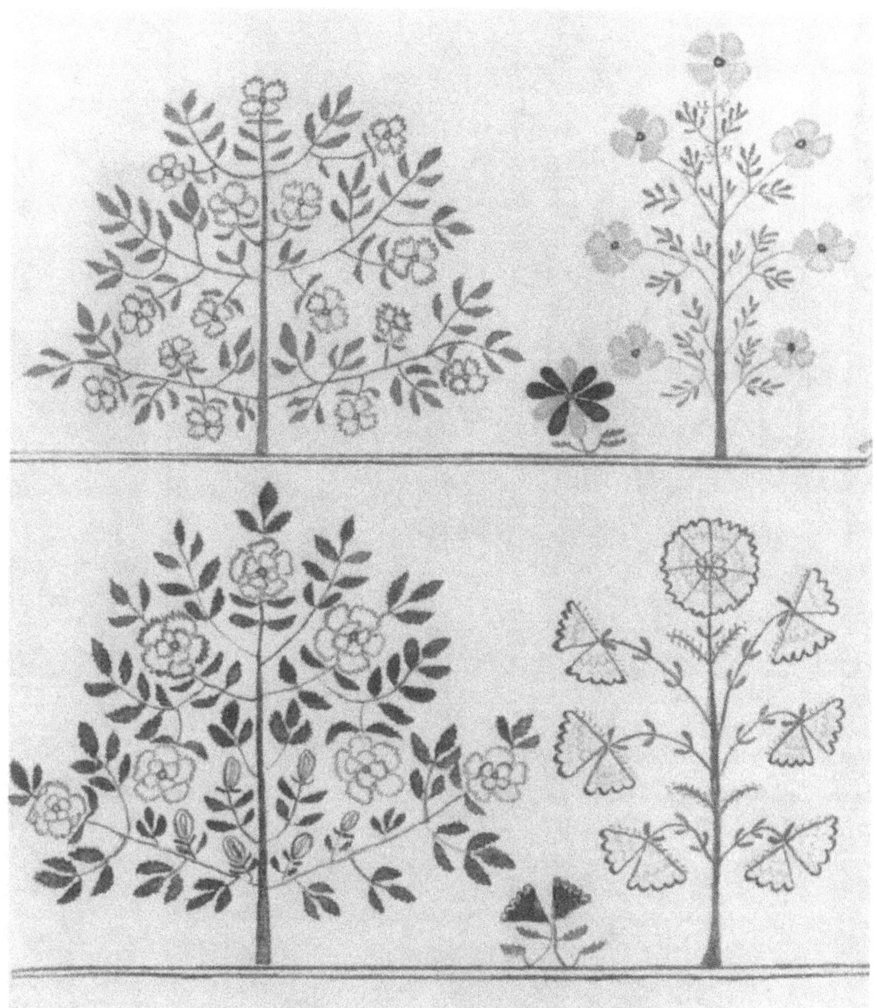

FIG. 15. *Celestial Garden,* from Polly Collins' Book, watercolor or tempera and ink on paper, n.d. (entries in book dated 1840s and 1850s), 7 3/4 inches by 6 3/8 inches, WRHS.
Courtesy of Western Reserve Historical Society

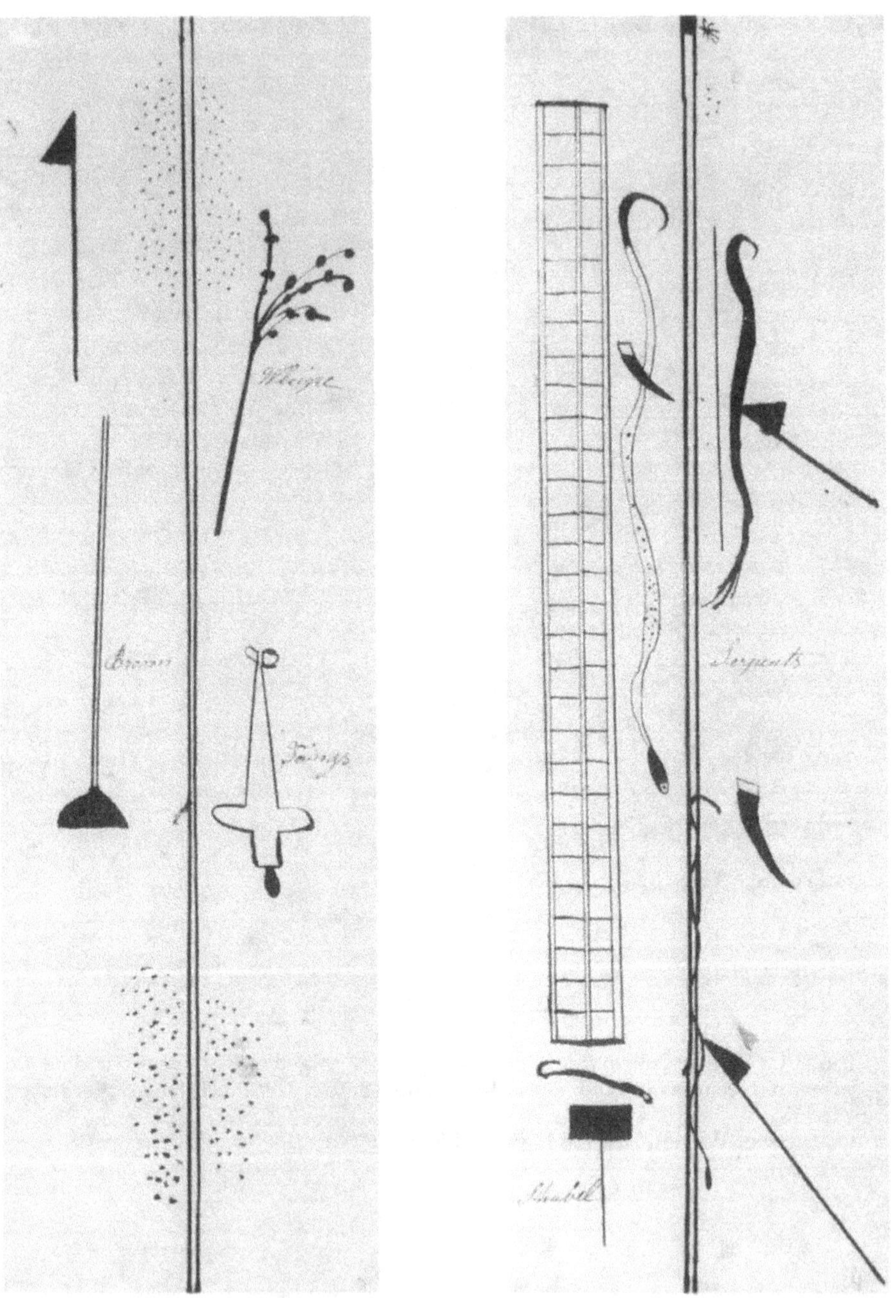

FIG. 16. Narrow Path Segments, ink on paper, [1843?], "Whipe, Broom, Tongs"; and "Serpents, Shubel," 13 inches by 4 inches; "Walls of Zion," 12 3/8 inches by 4 inches, NYPL.
Courtesy of Shaker Manuscripts Collection, Rare Books and Manuscripts Division, The New York Public Library, Astor, Lenox and Tilden Foundations, Photo: Robert D. Rubic, NYC

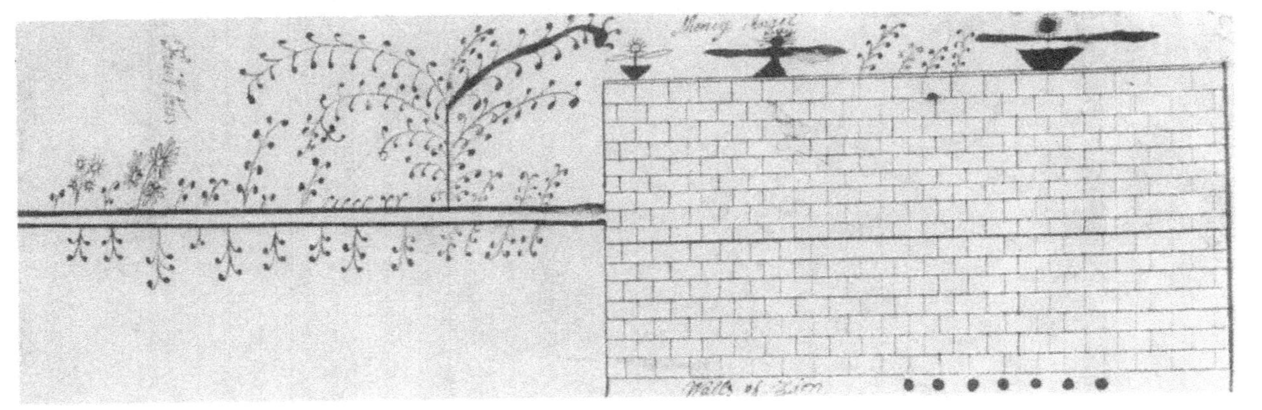
Fruit trees
Mercy Angel
Walls of Zion

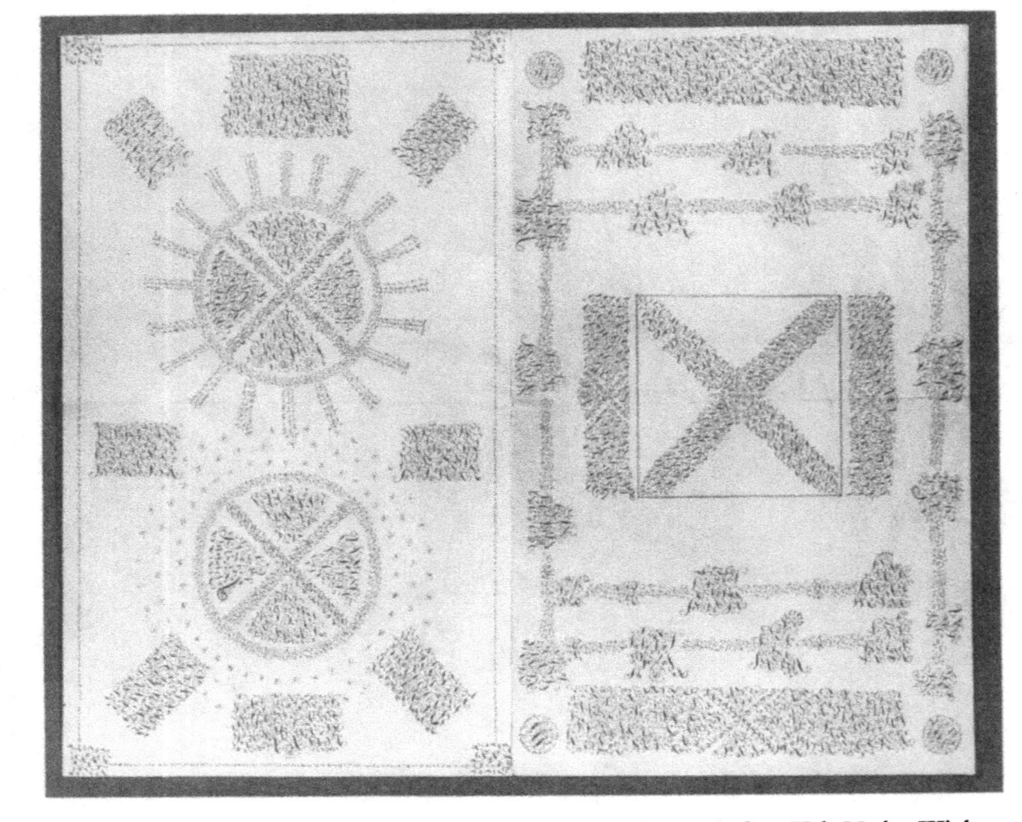

FIG. 17. [Semantha Fairbanks and Mary Wicks], *A Sacred Sheet, Sent from Holy Mother Wisdom, by Her Holy Angel of Many Signs for Daniel Bowler,* ink on paper, 25 January 1843, 15 3/4 inches by 26 inches, WRHS.
Courtesy of Western Reserve Historical Society

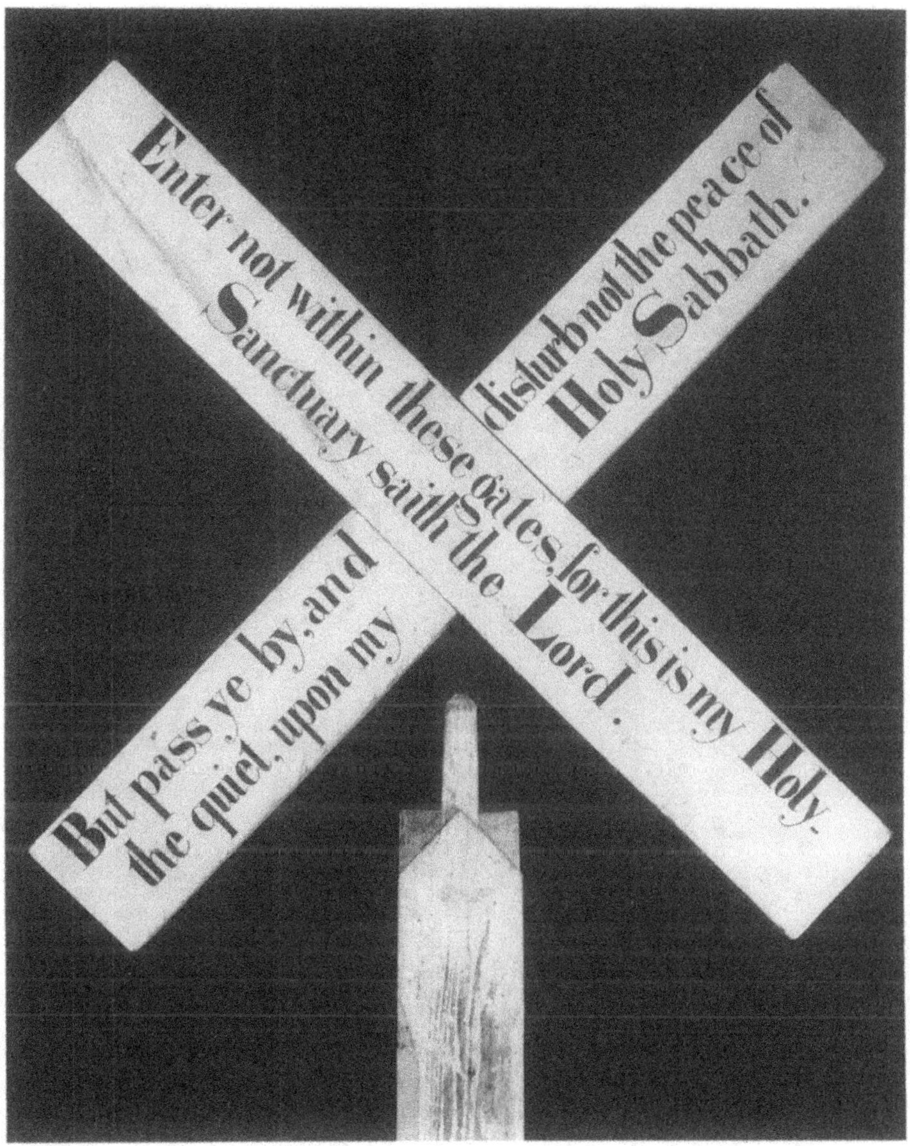

FIG. 18. Meeting House Cross, paint on wood, 1842, 28 3/4 inches by 28 3/4 inches, HSV. Courtesy of Hancock Shaker Village, Pittsfield, Massachusetts, Photo: Paul J. Rocheleau, Richmond, Massachusetts

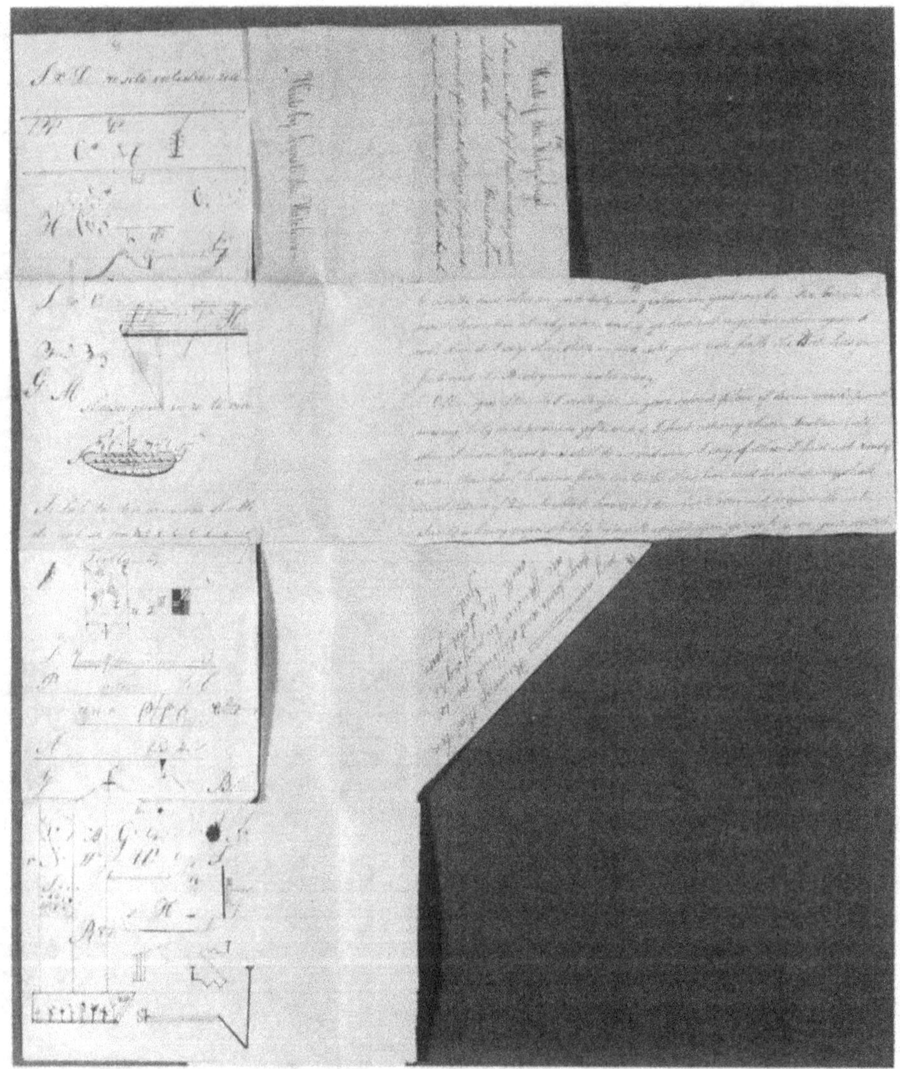

FIG. 19. Cut-and-Fold Booklet, "Words by Signs to the Watchmen," ink on paper, 1843, approx. 3 1/4 inches by 4 1/8 inches closed, NYPL.
Courtesy of Shaker Manuscripts Collection, Rare Books and Manuscripts Division, The New York Public Library, Astor, Lenox and Tilden Foundations, Photo: Robert D. Rubic, NYC

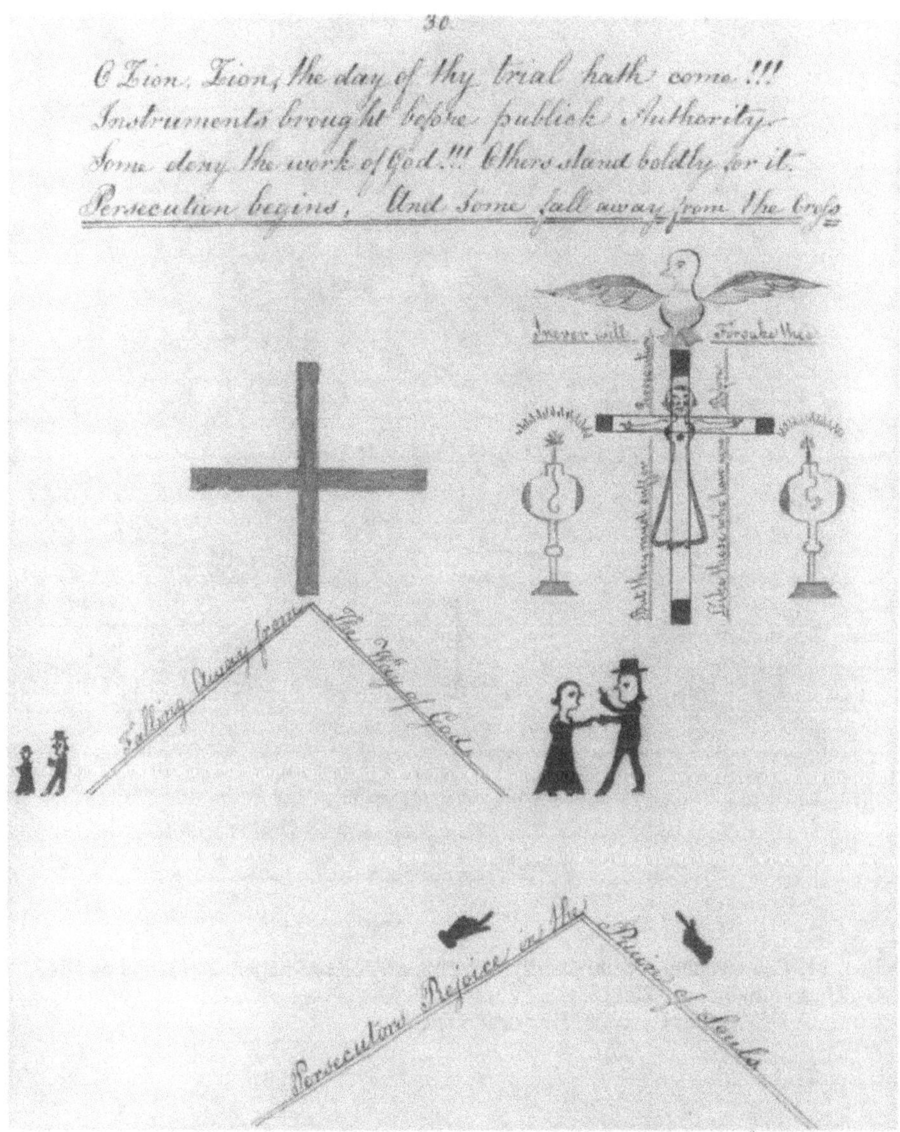

FIG. 20. *Mother Ann's Cross,* from [Miranda Barber and Polly Reed?] Book of Inspired Visions and Messages, watercolor and ink on paper, June 1843, 8 1/8 inches by 6 1/2 inches, WRHS.
Courtesy of Western Reserve Historical Society

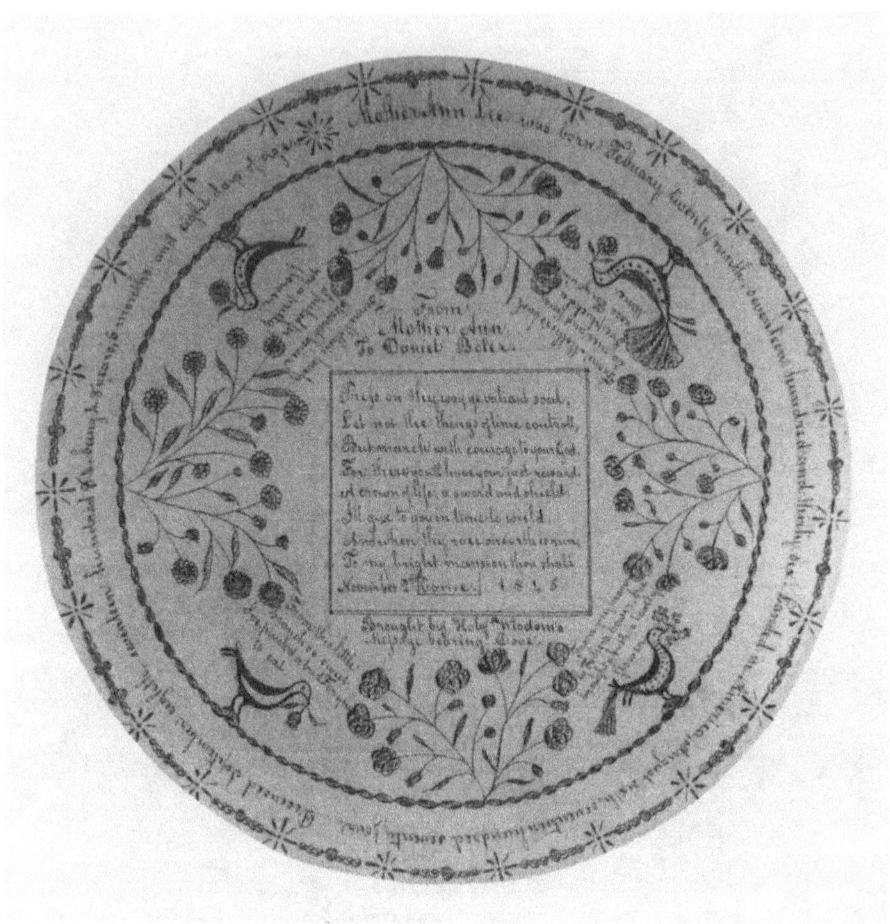

FIG. 21. *From Mother Ann to Daniel Boler,* ink on colored paper, 2 November 1845, 6 inches in diameter, WRHS.
Courtesy of Western Reserve Historical Society

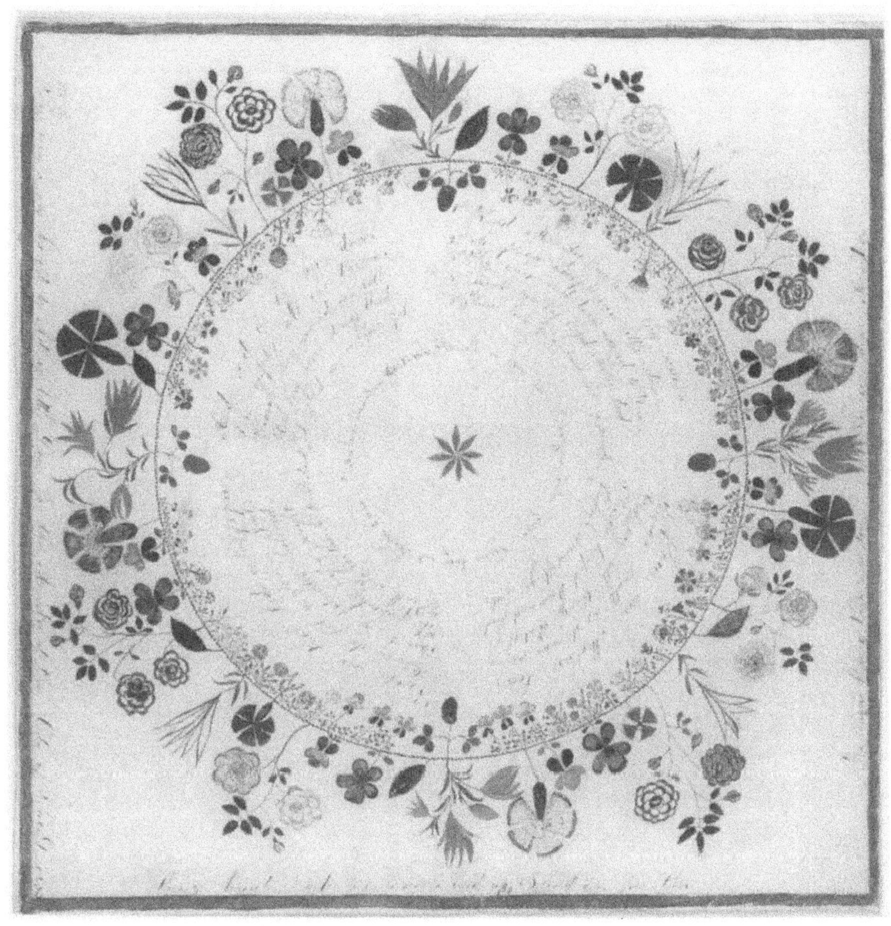

FIG. 22. *Floral Wreath,* watercolor and ink on paper, December 1853, 12 1/16 inches by 11 15/16 inches, HSV.
Courtesy of Hancock Shaker Village, Pittsfield, Massachusetts

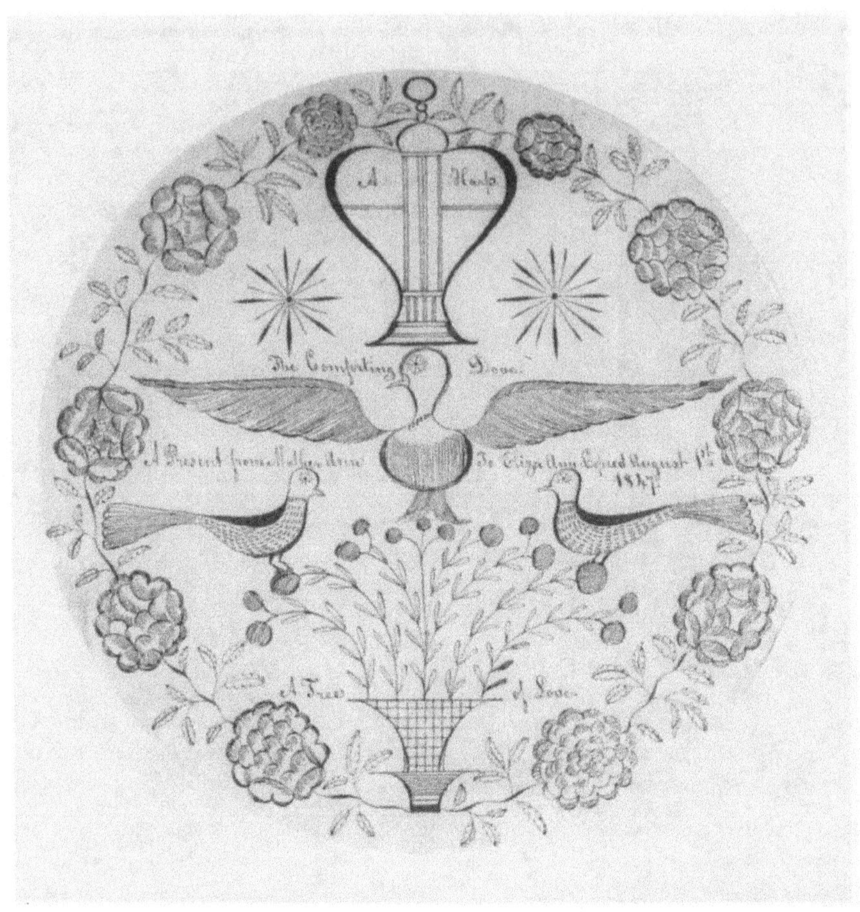

FIG. 23. “A Present from Mother Ann to Eliza Ann [Taylor],” ink on paper, 1 August 1847, 3 3/4 inches in diameter, recto and verso, WRHS.
Courtesy of Western Reserve Historical Society

Words of the Comforting Dove.

I was sent from the Throne on High to dwell
with your blessed Mother, and to comfort her in hours
of tribulation with the love of God. Now she has given
me to you. Why. It's to comfort you with my love,
and strengthen you with my blessing, and my peace you shall
be possessing. So do be lively and cheerful, happy and free, For I shall
forever remain with thee. Stop, says Mother, for I want to
speak to my kind loving Daughter, while she is yet here in the house that
I once inhabited. Here, dear child, have I spent many an hour in
prayer to God, that the way might be opened that my sons and daughters might serve their God in peace; So now rejoice with me your
Mother, that the time has come, that Zion's children are set free. Dear
child. Tell the young and tender plants, to forget not their Mother; think
of their Mother in an icy prison; in health and sickness, heat and cold,
in days of plenty and days of scanty. Tell them I love them &
bless them and my peace shall ever remain with them. Dear
Sister, do you think I have forgotten to give you my love for your-
self and the rest of my faithful crossbearers. Nay but give it
to them freely from your little tree. Just look on the other side
of your paper, and you will know that I have not forgotten you. Now here, dear sister is a book
from Holy Mother Wisdom. She says
when you enter the spiritual world
you shall sit at her right
hand, & read what is contains. So
fare ye well. Mother Ann

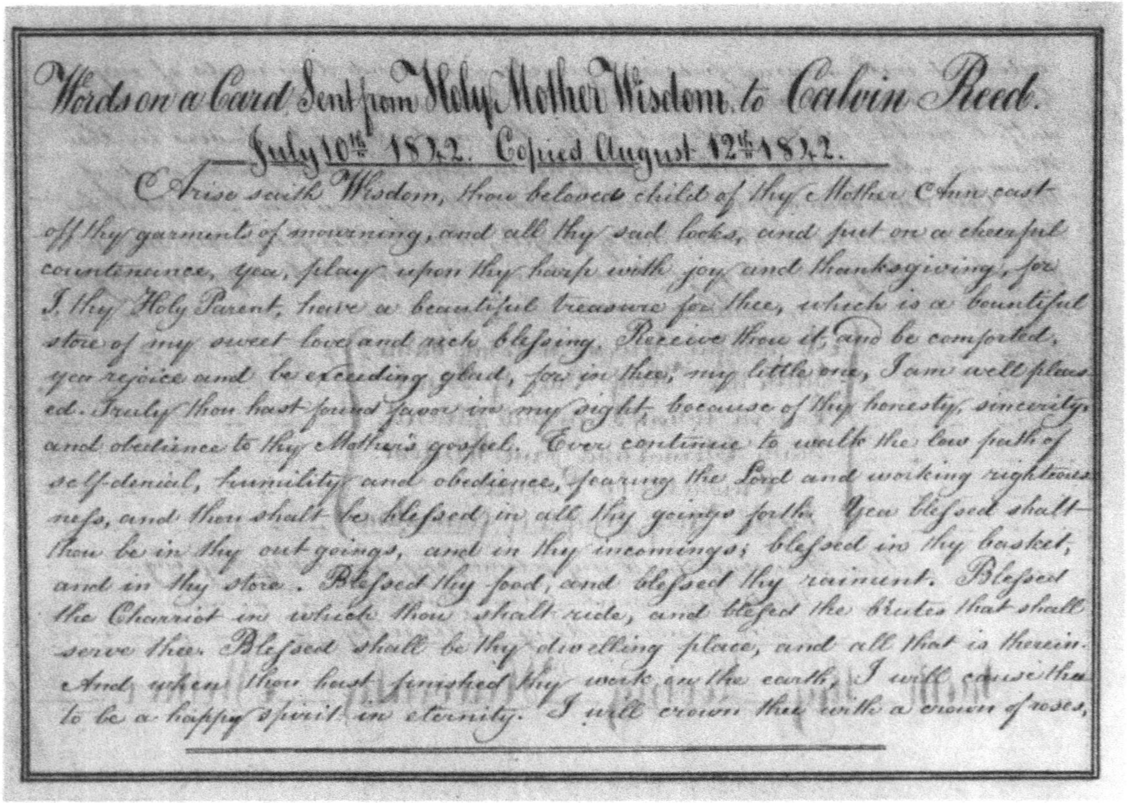

Words on a Card Sent from Holy Mother Wisdom to Calvin Reed.
July 10th 1842. Copied August 12th 1842.

Arise saith Wisdom, thou beloved child of thy Mother Ann cast off thy garments of mourning, and all thy sad looks, and put on a cheerful countenance, yea, play upon thy harp with joy and thanksgiving, for I thy Holy Parent, have a beautiful treasure for thee, which is a bountiful store of my sweet love and rich blessing. Receive thou it, and be comforted, yea rejoice and be exceeding glad, for in thee, my little one, I am well pleased. Truly thou hast found favor in my sight, because of thy honesty, sincerity, and obedience to thy Mother's gospel. Ever continue to walk the low path of self-denial, humility and obedience, fearing the Lord and working righteousness, and thou shalt be blessed in all thy goings forth. Yea blessed shalt thou be in thy outgoings, and in thy incomings; blessed in thy basket, and in thy store. Blessed thy food, and blessed thy raiment. Blessed the Chariot in which thou shalt ride, and blessed the brutes that shall serve thee. Blessed shall be thy dwelling place, and all that is therein. And when thou hast finished thy work in the earth, I will cause thee to be a happy spirit in eternity. I will crown thee with a crown of roses,

FIG. 24. "Words on a Card Sent from Holy Mother Wisdom to Calvin Reed," ink on colored paper, 12 August 1842, 4 13/16 inches by 6 3/4 inches, recto and verso, WRHS.
Courtesy of Western Reserve Historical Society

adorned with many precious jewels, gems and diamonds of my heavenly love, and clothe thee in fine raiment, embroidered with artful needle-work, pictured with the most elegant flowers in the Heavens. And if thou wilt be faithful in time, to stand for the work of thy God, and sound forth his word when it is given thee, should it be before hundreds and thousands of people, I will also place on thee a breast-plate of shining gold, and will write with my own finger,

These words thereon.

A faithful Servant unto my Name,
Saith the Holy One of Israel.
One in whom I am well pleased,
Saith Eternal and True Wisdom.
Crowned to be Prince,
In the Holy Temple of Jerusalem.

There thou shalt dwell my beloved, enjoying every blessing
that thy soul can desire,
thro' a never-ending Eternity.

Saith thy Loving Heavenly Mother.

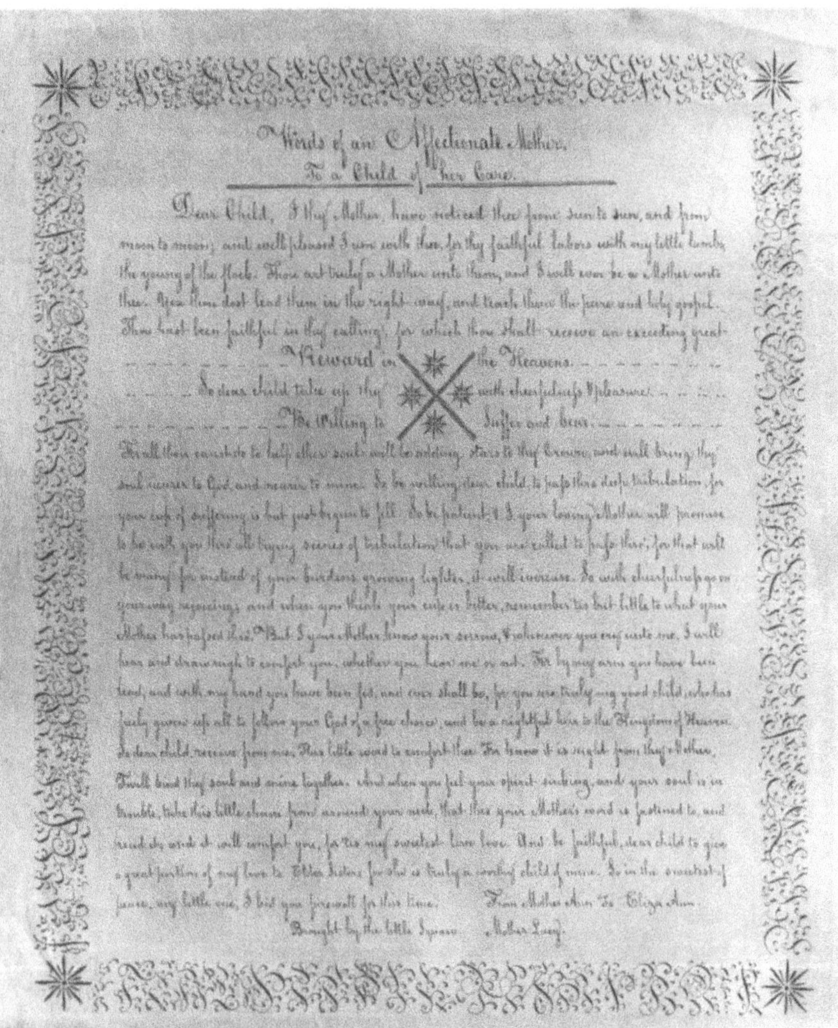

Words of an Affectionate Mother.
To a Child of her Care.

Dear Child, I thy Mother, have noticed thee from [illegible] to [illegible], and from moon to moon; and well pleased I am with thee, for thy faithful labors with my little lambs, the young of the flock. Thou art truly a Mother unto them, and I will ever be a Mother unto thee. [illegible] thou dost lead them in the right way, and teach them the pure and holy gospel. Thou hast been faithful in thy calling, for which thou shalt receive an exceeding great

Reward in the Heavens.

So dear child take up thy [illegible] with cheerfulness & pleasure.

Be willing to suffer and bear.

[illegible]

From Mother Ann to Eliza Ann

Brought by the little Sparrow. Mother Lucy.

Fig. 25. "Words of an Affectionate Mother," ink on colored paper, n.d., 10 inches by 8 inches, WRHS.
Courtesy of Western Reserve Historical Society

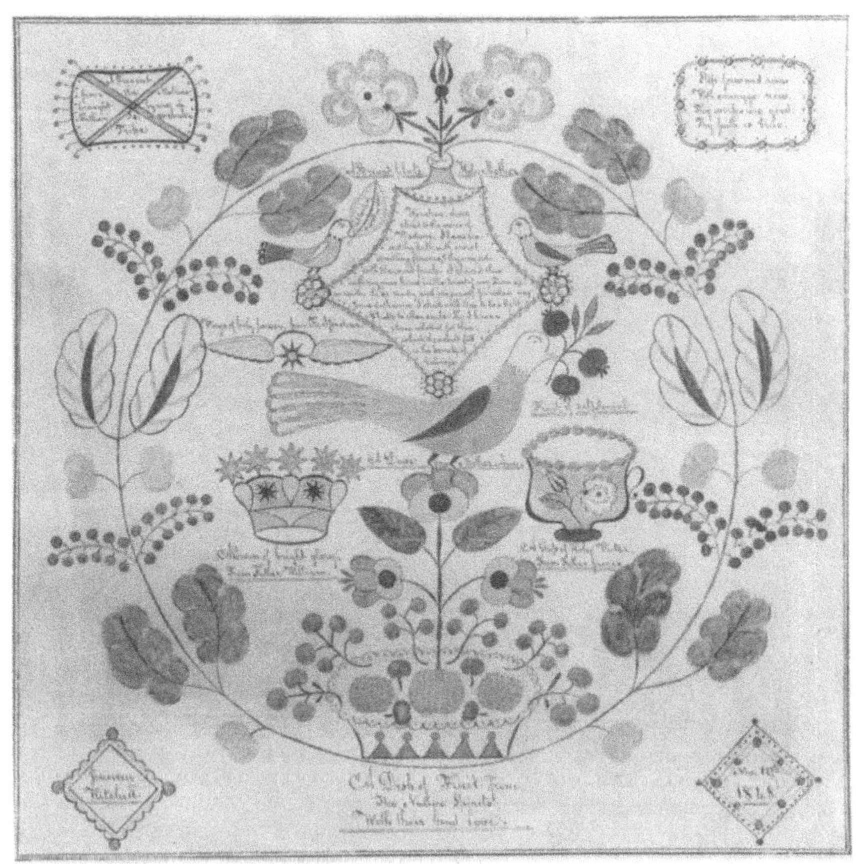

FIG. 26. Square Gift Painting to Joanna Kitchell, watercolor and ink on paper, 1848, 9 5/8 inches by 9 5/8 inches, WRHS.
Courtesy of Western Reserve Historical Society

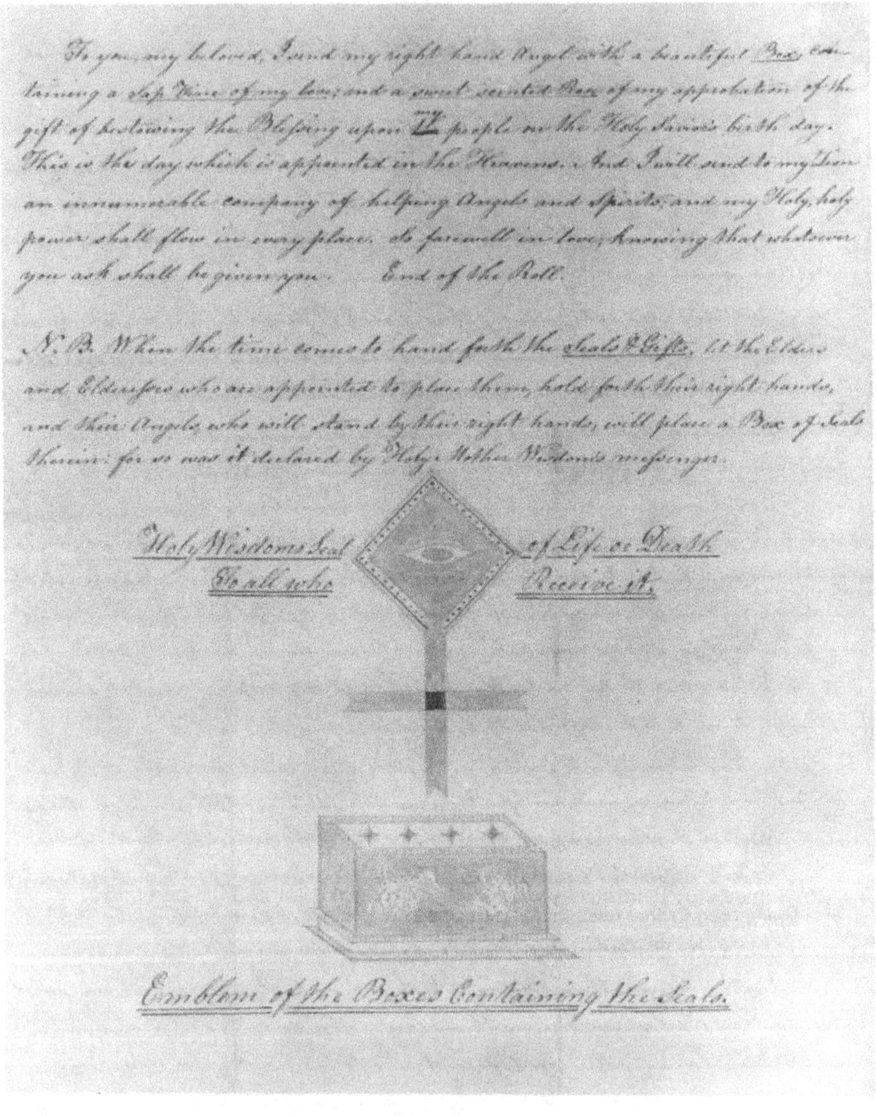

To you, my beloved, I send my right hand Angel with a beautiful Box, containing a Cup Wine of my love; and a sweet scented Box of my approbation of the gift of bestowing the Blessing upon my people on the Holy Savior's birth day. This is the day which is appointed in the Heavens. And I will send to my Zion an innumerable company of helping Angels and Spirits, and my Holy, holy power shall flow in every place. So farewell in love, knowing that whatever you ask shall be given you. End of the Roll.

N. B. When the time comes to hand forth the Seals & Gifts, let the Elders and Eldresses who are appointed to place them, hold forth their right hands, and their Angels, who will stand by their right hands, will place a Box of Seals therein: for so was it declared by Holy Mother Wisdom's messenger.

Holy Wisdoms Seal of Life or Death
To all who Receive it.

Emblem of the Boxes Containing the Seals.

FIG. 27. "Holy Wisdom's Seal" and "Emblem of the Boxes," from a circular letter from "Holy Mount," watercolor and ink on paper, 16 November 1847, 9 7/8 inches by 8 inches, WRHS.
Courtesy of Western Reserve Historical Society

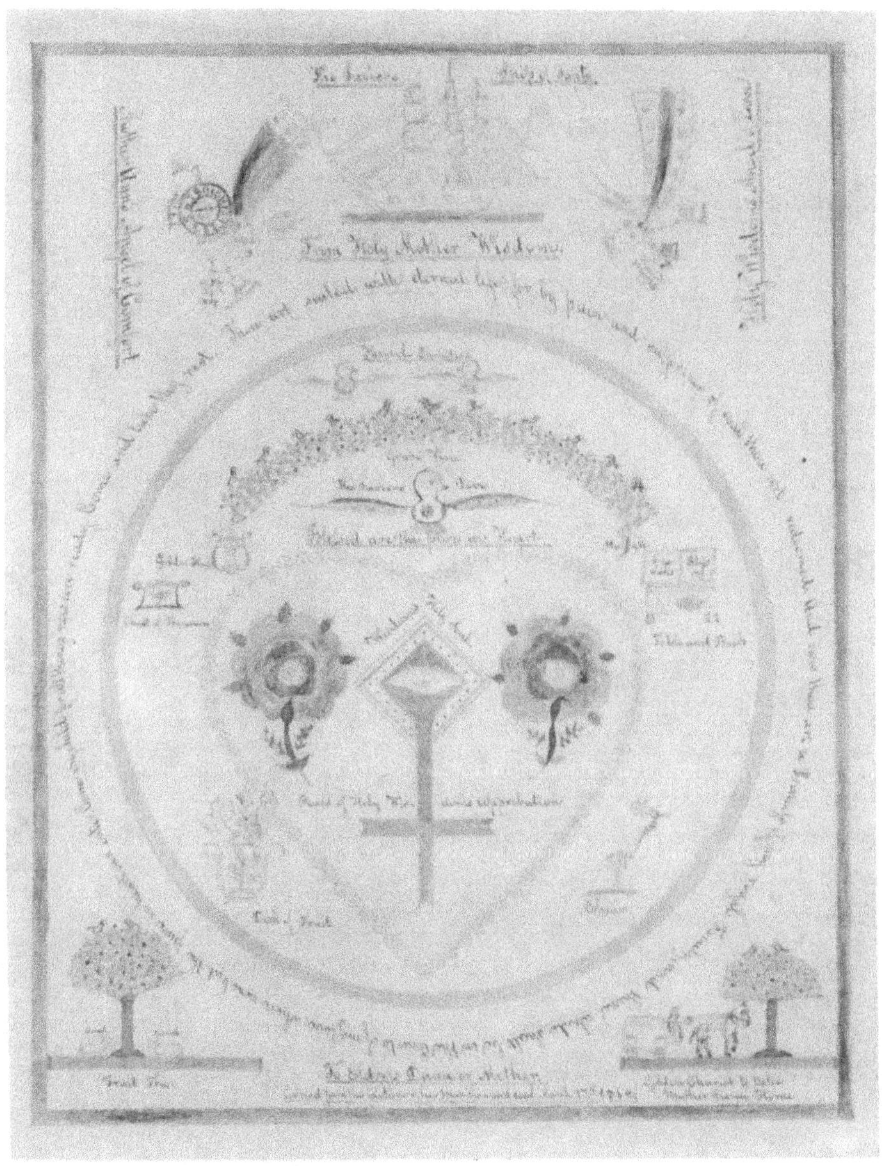

FIG. 28. *From Holy Mother Wisdom. To Eldress Dana or Mother,* watercolor and ink on paper, 27 March 1848, 9 25/32 inches by 7 23/32 inches, HSV.
Courtesy of Hancock Shaker Village, Pittsfield, Massachusetts

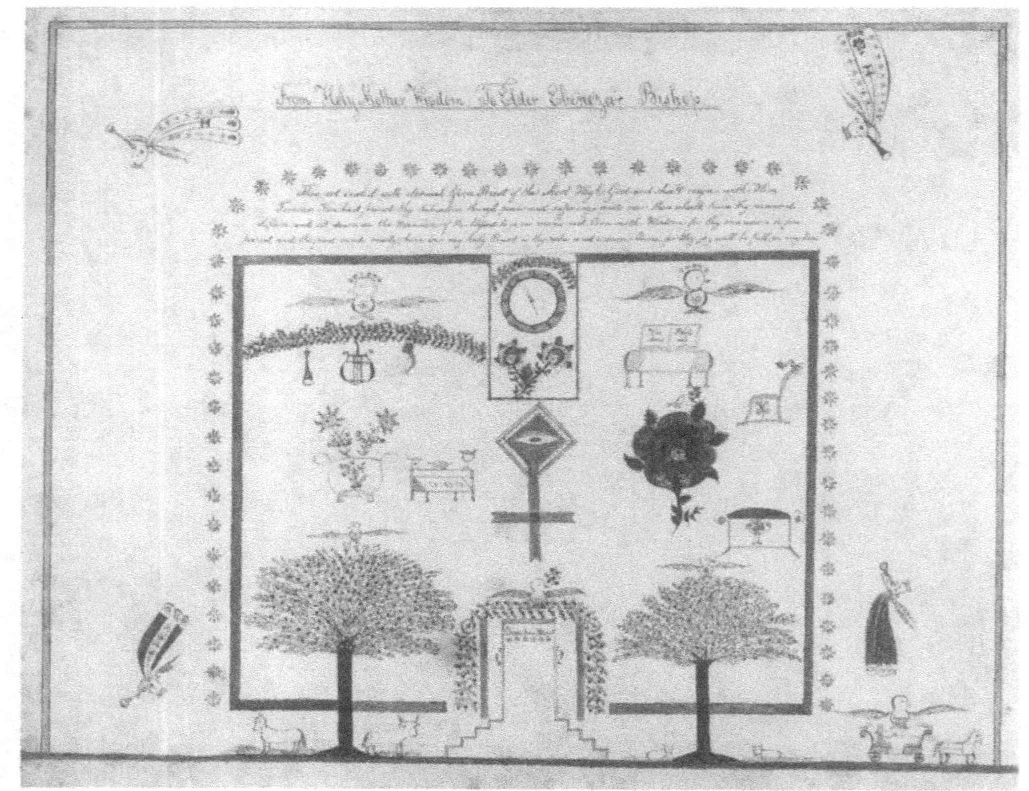

FIG. 29. ***From Holy Mother Wisdom. To Elder Ebenezer Bishop,*** watercolor and ink on paper, [1848 or 1849], 11 3/8 inches by 14 1/2 inches, PMA.
Courtesy of Philadelphia Museum of Art: Gift of Mr. and Mrs. Julius Zieget

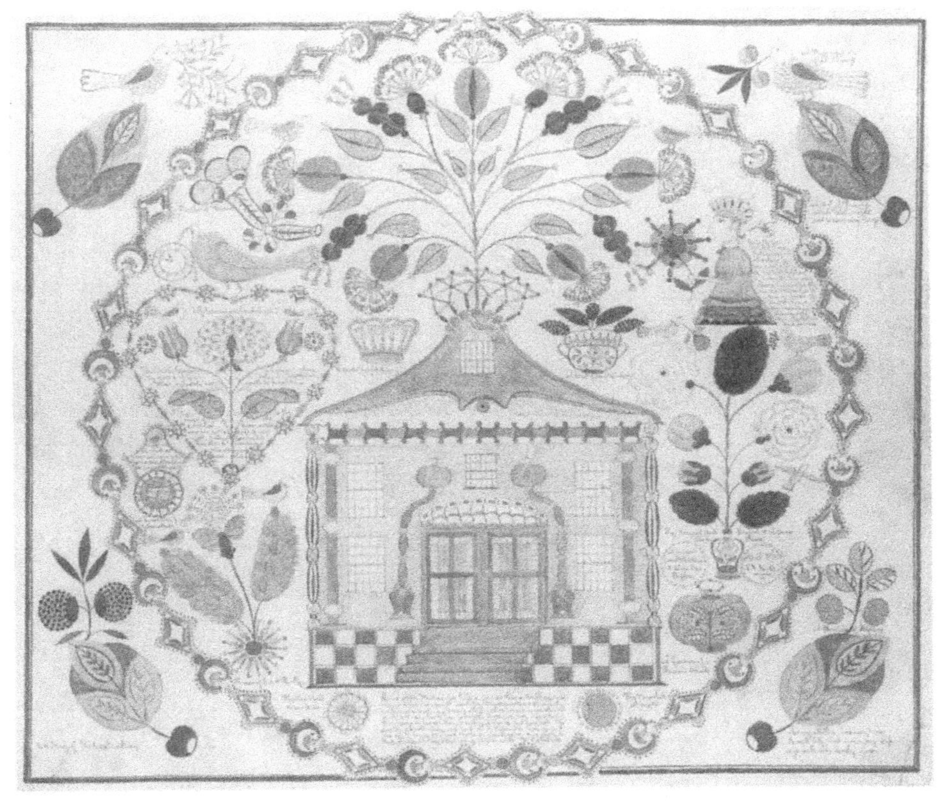

Fig. 30. *From Mother Lucy to Eliza Ann Taylor,* watercolor and ink on colored paper, 8 April 1849, 14 inches by 16 3/8 inches, HSV.
Courtesy of Hancock Shaker Village, Pittsfield, Massachusetts

LIST OF ABBREVIATIONS

BA	Shaker Collection, Berkshire Athenaeum, Pittsfield, Massachusetts
EBK	Shaker Manuscript Collection, Emma B. King Library of the Shaker Museum, Old Chatham, New York
HSV	Shaker Manuscript Collection, Hancock Shaker Village, Pittsfield, Massachusetts
LC	Shaker Collection, Manuscript Division, Library of Congress, Washington, D.C.
NGA	National Gallery of Art, Washington, D.C.
NYPL	Shaker Manuscripts Collection, Rare Books and Manuscripts Division, New York Public Library, Astor, Lenox and Tilden Foundations, New York, New York
PMA	Shaker Collection, Department of Prints, Drawings, and Photographs, Philadelphia Museum of Art, Philadelphia, Pennsylvania
SDL	Shaker Manuscript Collection, Shaker Library, United Society of Shakers, Sabbathday Lake, Poland Spring, Maine
WML	Shaker Manuscript Collection, Henry Francis du Pont Winterthur Museum Library, Winterthur, Delaware
WRHS	Shaker Manuscript Collection, Western Reserve Historical Society Library, Cleveland, Ohio

NOTES

Preface

1. Isaac Newton Youngs at New Lebanon to Joel Shields at Pleasant Hill, 10 February 1850, Shaker Manuscript Collection, Western Reserve Historical Society (hereafter WRHS) 20 IV:A-40. During these two decades and more, Shakers received gifts of spiritual spectacles on numerous occasions. Even outsider John Humphrey Noyes mentioned the Shakers' reception of spiritual spectacles as vehicles of spiritual sight. John Humphrey Noyes, *History of American Socialisms* (Philadelphia: J. B. Lippincott, 1870; repr., New York: Dover, 1966), pp. 599 and 607.

In this text "Believers" (from United Society of Believers in Christ's First and Second Appearings, the formal name of the Shakers) is used as a synonym for "Shakers."

2. New Lebanon Ministry to the South Union, Kentucky, Ministry, 12 August 1839, "Copies of the Principal letters of the Ministry at New Lebanon to other Societies of Believers East and West, written by Rufus Bishop Begun July 2, 1839," WRHS 27 IV:B-9, p. 5.

3. "Records Concerning the Finding of Mount Sinai, the Mount of Olives, and Mount Horeb with the Meetings thereon Beginning June 19, 1842," Shaker Manuscript Collection, Shaker Library, United Society of Shakers, Sabbathday Lake, Poland Spring, Maine (hereafter SDL), p. 62. Accounts of the same meeting appear in at least two other New Era manuscripts. See "A Record of Meetings Held on Mount Sinai," SDL, pp. 5 and 49; and "A Record Kept of the Several meetings held upon Mount Sinai by the Family Orders on Days of the Feasts," Shaker Manuscript Collection, Henry Francis du Pont Winterthur Museum Library, Winterthur, Delaware (WML) 150 SA 787, especially ch. 1. Cf. Edward Deming Andrews, *The People Called Shakers: A Search for the Perfect Society*, new enl. ed. (New York: Dover, 1963), p. 136.

4. Mary Hazard, "Mary Hazard's Book. Received June 15 A.D. 1839 A Collection of Songs of Various Kinds; written and pricked for the purpose of retaining them," WML 481 SA 1119, p. 192, verso of leaf drawing. Inscriptions on other images also made clear the goal of making visible. See "To the Instrument Writers," Shaker Manuscripts Collection, Rare Books and Manuscripts Division, New York Public Library, Astor, Lenox and Tilden Foundations, New York, New York (hereafter NYPL) 103, pp. 6 and 15; and David R. Lamson, *Two Years' Experience Among the Shakers* (West Boylston, Mass: David R. Lamson, 1848; repr., New York: AMS Press, 1971), p. 74, where Lamson describes how drawing and writing made spiritual objects visible to all.

5. Spirits had warned community members not to judge the gifts of God inadequate because only a few could see them. "Records Concerning the Finding," SDL, p. 185.

6. New Lebanon Ministry to South Union Ministry, 12 August 1839, "Copies of letters, Begun 1839," WRHS 27 IV:B-9, p. 5. This citation refers generally to the "gifts" of the New Era and not to the drawings in particular.

7. The tiny company who booked sea passage to America with Ann Lee aboard the *Mariah* included William Lee (Ann Lee's natural brother), James Whittaker, John Hocknell, Richard Hocknell (John Hocknell's son), James Shepherd, Mary Partington, Nancy Lee (Ann Lee's niece), and Abraham Stanley (Ann Lee's husband). Stanley left his wife and the company relatively soon after their arrival in New York. In 1775, John Hocknell returned to England to bring his wife Hannah, daughter Mary, and others to join the American Shakers. [Benjamin S. Youngs], *Testimony of Christ's Second Appearing, Exemplified by the Principles and Practice of the True Church of Christ*, 4th ed. (Albany: Van Benthuysen, 1856), pp. 616 and 621. The first (1808, p. 24), second (1810, p. xxix),

and third (1823, p. xxvii) editions of this text contain only partial listings of these "English" Shakers. The third edition, however, is almost as complete in this regard as the fourth.

8. Stephen Stein's use of the word "commotion" in relationship to this period of Shaker history captures both the turbulence and the excitement expressed in contemporary Shaker descriptions. See Stephen J. Stein, "Shaker Gift and Shaker Order: A Study of Religious Tension in Nineteenth-Century America," *Communal Societies* 10 (1990): 110.

9. Shakers generally used the term "New Era" to describe rather than to label or name the period. New Lebanon Ministry to Sodus Elders, 19 December 1837, "Copies of the Principal letters of the Ministry at New Lebanon to other Societies of Believers East and West, written by Rufus Bishop. Begun July 16, 1833," WRHS 27 IV:B-8, p. 231; Isaac Newton Youngs, "A Concise View of the Church of God and of Christ on Earth. Having its foundation in the faith of Christ's first and second appearing. New Lebanon, 1856," WML SA 760, p. 175; and [Philemon Stewart], *A Holy, Sacred and Divine Roll and Book* (hereafter *Sacred Roll and Book*) (Canterbury, N.H.: United Society, 1843), p. 216.

10. Edward Deming Andrews and Faith Andrews, *Visions of the Heavenly Sphere: A Study in Shaker Religious Art* (Charlottesville: University Press of Virginia, 1969), p. 4. The Andrewses carefully transcribed the textual portion of each gift image included in their book on the pages adjacent to the illustration. As the inscriptions on some of the original images have faded almost to the point of illegibility, this resource has become especially valuable.

11. Nineteenth-century documents indicate that Shakers understood the popular appeal of the sort of religious spectacle created by worship during the Era. Believers hoped that this spectacular spirituality would draw members of the United Society and potential converts closer to God rather than creating an occasion for ridicule and disbelief. Contemporary descriptions of the "spectacle" of New Era Shaker spirituality abound. See, for example, "Meetings on Mount Sinai," SDL, pp. 122–23. Cf. Clarke Garrett, *Spirit Possession and Popular Religion: From the Camisards to the Shakers* (Baltimore: Johns Hopkins University Press, 1987), pp. 93 and 162, for his discussion of the "spectacular" body language of earlier participants in Shaker spiritual theatre.

12. New Era manuals, with directions for making paints, stains, inks, dyes, etc., indicate a sophisticated knowledge of color. These books provide information on the colors preferred by Shakers, on mixing colors, and on the properties of color. See, for example, "Receipt Book, Concerning Paints, Stains, Cements, Dyes, Inks, etc.," WRHS 117 XI:B-14, especially pp. 58–59 and 79.

13. See, for example, Polly Collins' Book and Hannah Cohoon's paintings (figs. 15, 2, 5, and Pl. IV). The use of opaque watercolor, liberally applied, probably accounts for the appearance of tempera in at least some of these images.

14. Daniel W. Patterson, *Gift Drawing and Gift Song: A Study of Two Forms of Shaker Inspiration* (Sabbathday Lake, Maine: United Society of Shakers, 1983), p. xi. Patterson's term also appears frequently in this text. One advantage of his "gift drawings" is that it highlights the linear quality of the images. This visual emphasis on line tied gift images to the work of other "amateur" artists of the mid-nineteenth century and especially to the work of those young women and "school girls" who learned to draw from popular drawing manuals. On the content and character of the drawing manuals, see Peter C. Marzio, *The Art Crusade: An Analysis of American Drawing Manuals, 1820–1860* (Washington, D.C.: Smithsonian Institution Press, 1976), especially pp. iv and 7.

15. In contrast, historical studies of western Christianity generally have been dominated by the examination of written texts. In recent years, however, scholars of religion have demonstrated increasing interest in the relationship between religious experience and visual imagery. See, for example, Margaret Miles, *Image as Insight: Visual Understanding in Western Christianity and Secular Culture* (Boston: Beacon Press, 1985); John

Dillenberger, *The Visual Arts and Christianity in America: From the Colonial Period to the Present* (New York: Crossroad, 1988); Diane Apostolos-Cappadona, ed., *Art, Creativity, and the Sacred: An Anthology in Religion and Art* (New York: Crossroad, 1984); and Wilson Yates, *The Arts in Theological Education: New Possibilities for Integration*, Studies in Religious and Theological Scholarship, 3 (Atlanta: Scholars Press, 1987).

16. By analyzing Shaker images in their religious contexts, I do not mean to suggest that the Shaker experience of images in relationship to religion is normative. The nature of the relationship between image and belief shifts with each particular application across time and across a variety of religious experiences and institutions. Processes and content of representation vary as well.

17. See Roger B. Stein, exhibition review, "Winslow Homer in Context," *American Quarterly* 42 (March 1990): 76.

18. With few exceptions, extant drawings were made by women at New Lebanon and Hancock between 1839 and 1859. A proportionately small number of drawings and paintings survive from the Western (Ohio and Kentucky) and other Eastern Societies. Perhaps images were more of an anomaly in other communities, especially those farther from the seat of authority at New Lebanon. What is less likely but possible is that other communities initially had comparable numbers of drawings relatively more of which were subsequently destroyed. Each community's involvement in the Era exhibited some unique features as well as variations on New Lebanon's theme. In any case, a somewhat different situation pertained in the region that was then the "West" because of its status as a mission field, its lack of direct historical contact with Ann Lee and her early circle, and land disputes which plagued Shakers there.

Unfortunately, in assessing the period of Mother's Work, twentieth-century researchers must depend principally on the numerous and detailed official documents of this time. Surviving manuscripts of the average Shaker adherent are much rarer. While a relatively complete picture is possible given the number of surviving documents, interpretation is significantly influenced by the official nature of this material.

19. On a common cultural obsession with social geography and behavior and a shared sense of dislocation as well as crisis, see, for example, Karen Halttunen, *Confidence Men and Painted Women: A Study of Middle Class Culture in America, 1830–1870* (New Haven: Yale University Press, 1982), especially chs. 1, 2, and 4.

20. Edward and Faith Andrews began collecting objects of American material culture even before their marriage in 1921. In 1923 they made their first visit to the Shakers at Hancock. A. D. Emerich, "A Conversation with Faith Andrews," *Shaker: Furniture and Objects from the Faith and Edward Deming Andrews Collection* (Washington, D.C.: Smithsonian Institution Press, 1973), pp. 23–24.

21. Daniel J. Singal, "Towards a Definition of American Modernism," *American Quarterly* 39 (Spring 1987): pp. 7–26. Miles Orvell describes as the goal of the Index of American Design the desire to link objects from the American past with modernist functionalism. See Miles Orvell, *The Real Thing: Imitation and Authenticity in American Culture, 1880–1940* (Chapel Hill: University of North Carolina Press, 1989), p. 196; see also p. 167.

In modern American religious history the appeal of the restorationist impulse can be accounted for, in part, by the tendency to see restorationism as one response to the confusions and ambiguities of modernity. In this context, Shaker artifacts attract attention because of aesthetic and theological primitivism as well as aesthetic simplicity. Cf. Richard T. Hughes and C. Leonard Allen, *Illusions of Innocence: Protestant Primitivism in America, 1630–1875* (Chicago: University of Chicago Press, 1988).

22. Robert Bishop as quoted in Kenneth L. Ames, *Beyond Necessity: Art in the Folk Art Tradition* (Winterthur, Delaware: The Henry Francis du Pont Winterthur Museum, 1977), p. 63. For a history of the folk art movement within the fine art world, see Beatrix

T. Rumford, "Uncommon Art of the Common People: A Review of Trends in the Collecting and Exhibiting of American Folk Art," in *Perspectives on American Folk Art,* ed. Ian M. G. Quimby and Scott T. Swank (New York: W. W. Norton, 1980), esp. pp. 25, 30, 48, and 52. See also Henry Glassie, "Folk Art," in *Material Culture Studies in America,* ed. Thomas J. Schlereth (Nashville: American Association for State and Local History, 1982), p. 131.

23. Jean Lipman, *American Primitive Painting* (New York: Dover, 1942), p. 18. See also the descriptive page of contents, "The Cover," *Antiques* 40 (September 1941): preliminaries, celebrating the Museum of Modern Art's "recognition of the relationship between American primitives and American modern art."

24. Ames, *Beyond Necessity,* p. 63. See also John Michael Vlach's problematic and provocative *Plain Painters: Making Sense of American Folk Art* (Washington, D.C.: Smithsonian Institution Press, 1988), p. 162, for mention of what Vlach calls the "modernist view of folk art"; Orvell, *The Real Thing,* p. 168 on Lewis Mumford's desire to demonstrate America's "maturity and independence from Europe"; and David McCracken, "Seeds of the Future," *Chicago Tribune,* Friday 17 March 1989, Section 7, p. 52 on the search by artists of 1920s for "home-grown antecedents for new artmaking."

25. Guy Eglington, "Art and Other Things," *International Studio* 80 (February 1925): 418.

26. For example, in *By Their Fruits: The Story of Shakerism in South Union* (Chapel Hill: University of North Carolina Press, 1947), p. 269, Julia Neal asserts that "functionalism, as practiced by the modern designer, is merely a contemporary application of an old Shaker idea." See also Alice Winchester, "Antiques for the Avant Garde," *Art in America* 51, no. 4 (1963): 53–59; Faith and Edward D. Andrews, "Sheeler and the Shakers," *Art in America* 53, no. 1 (1965): 90–95; and Eugene Merrick Dodd, "Functionalism in Shaker Crafts," *Antiques* 98 (October 1970): 588–93. Significant in this regard, Beatrix Rumford ("Uncommon Art," p. 15) mentions a painting by modernist Wood Gaylor titled *Picnic at Shaker Lake* (1923); artists working for the Index of American Design (a project rooted in assumptions about similarities between modern and folk) produced renderings and photographs of many Shaker objects, a large number of these from the Shaker collections of Edward and Faith Andrews and of modernist artist Charles Sheeler.

More recently, in 1973–74, a major Shaker exhibition at the Renwick Gallery commemorated the bicentennial of American Shakerism. The catalogue for this show included a piece by Janet Malcolm titled "The Modern Spirit in Shaker Design"; see *Shaker: Furniture and Objects from the Faith and Edward Deming Andrews Collection,* pp. 18–22. In 1988, the Charles Sheeler exhibit at the Whitney Museum of American Art demonstrated the attraction of Shaker design for this American modernist painter and photographer. Sheeler not only collected but also photographed and painted things Shaker. See Theodore E. Stebbins, Jr., and Norman Keyes, Jr., *Charles Sheeler: The Photographs* (Boston: Little, Brown, 1987). Some time later, an unnamed print journalist went so far as to refer to Shaker "minimalist candlestands." See "Shaker Inflation," *Chicago Tribune,* 19 February 1989, Section 15, p. 17.

27. Carol Vogel, "The Shakers' Simple Grace," *The New York Times Magazine,* 11 May 1986, pp. 70–72. See also the beautifully produced exhibit catalogue, June Sprigg, *Shaker Design* (New York: Whitney Museum of American Art in association with W. W. Norton, 1986); and Carol Vogel, "Simple Beauty of Shaker Design Showcased," *Chicago Tribune,* 22 June 1986, Section 15, p. 12 which quotes June Sprigg, the exhibit's guest curator: "We decided early on not to create period room settings but rather to let the pieces stand on their own, like works of sculpture."

28. Orvell, *The Real Thing,* pp. 215, 219, 226, 241–42.

29. R. Stein, "Winslow Homer in Context," pp. 76 and 89.

30. See Wanda Corn's discussion of decontextualization and the "master myth" of proto-modernism in American folk art in Corn, "Coming of Age: Historical Scholarship

in American Art," *The Art Bulletin,* 70 (June 1988): 206. See also Johannes Fabian and Ilona Szombati-Fabian, "Folk Art from an Anthropological Perspective," in *Perspectives on American Folk Art,* ed. Quimby and Swank, pp. 289–90; Vlach, *Plain Painters,* p. 173 ("When critics, collectors, and curators make folk [read Shaker] art the equivalent of modern art, they dismiss the actual conditions of its creation"); and Simon J. Bronner, "The Idea of the Folk Artifact," in *American Culture and Folklife: A Prologue and a Dialogue* ed. Bronner (Ann Arbor: UMI Research Press, 1984), pp. 18, 24–25.

31. See, for example, the photographs in Edward Deming Andrews, "Shaker Design," *Art in America* 51, no. 4 (1963): 60–63.

32. In addition, collectors with a modernist bent have generally considered Victorian Shaker furnishings and Western Shaker furnishings less typically "Shaker" than earlier, and especially Eastern, forms. Out of more than 200 years of Shaker history, scholars as well as collectors have concentrated attention on only the first 80 years.

33. For an excellent color reproduction of this image see Sprigg, *Shaker Design,* p. 211.

34. Writers have frequently overstated the distinctions between Cohoon's images and other Shaker visionary pictures. In fact, this visual "similarity" to modernist images (including simplification and geometric design) and Cohoon's inclusion of her name on her images constitute the principal differences. Some other Shaker images include the name of the instrument as well. And the "modernist" visual characteristics of Cohoon's paintings are likely a result of her use of quilt patterns and appliqued emblems as sources rather than the more intricate embroidery designs and schoolgirl pictures from which other instruments drew visual inspiration.

Introduction

1. Isaac Newton Youngs, Personal Journal (1837–1859), entries for March 1837 and 14 May 1837, Shaker Manuscript Collection, Emma B. King Library of the Shaker Museum, Old Chatham, New York (hereafter EBK), 10,509, pp. 13 and 17. Isaac Newton Youngs was a particularly colorful and prolific scribe of the New Era. In response to Mother's Work and the crisis which produced it, he shared the feelings of a large number of Shakers. He was, however, more strikingly and consistently pessimistic than most others. His writings indicate an erratic emotional character. In 1867 he jumped from a third story window to a slow and agonizing death. The degree to which his personal perspective has influenced interpretations of the period of Mother's Work is difficult to determine but other documents usually corroborate the general tone and content of his reports.

In this manuscript, I have taken care to reproduce quotations exactly as they appear in the original text without, in most cases, noting inconsistencies, archaisms, or errors in spelling and punctuation.

2. Priscilla J. Brewer, *Shaker Communities, Shaker Lives* (Hanover, N.H.: University Press of New England, 1986), p. 204; and [Isaac Newton Youngs], "A Preface, or Introduction to the Records of Sacred Communications, Given by Divine Inspiration, In the Church at New Lebanon" [1842], WRHS 75 VIII:B-109, pp. 1–13. (In Isaac Newton Youngs, Journal [1839–1858], entry for November 1842, WRHS 35 V:B-134, Youngs reveals that he wrote the "Preface, or Introduction" to the spiritual writings, finishing it sometime around December 1842.)

3. [Youngs], "Preface, or Introduction," WRHS 75 VIII:B-109, pp. 11–12. See also "Remarks, On the necessity of reforming the morals, and improving the religious condition of our Youth and Children: with some propositions for the same. Approved by the Church. New Lebanon. 1830," WRHS 56 VII:B-66A.

4. Brewer, *Shaker Communities,* p. 141 and Table A.2, Appendix A, p. 210.

5. Ibid., p. 141. For additional information on Shaker demographics during these years see Lawrence Foster, *Religion and Sexuality: The Shakers, the Mormons, and the*

Oneida Community (New York: Oxford University Press, 1981; Urbana: University of Illinois Press, 1984); William Sims Bainbridge, "Shaker Demographics 1840–1900: An Example of the Use of U.S. Census Enumeration Schedules," *Journal for the Scientific Study of Religion* 21, no. 4 (December 1982): 352–65; and Michael Barkun, *Crucible of the Millennium: The Burned-Over District of New York in the 1840s* (Syracuse: Syracuse University Press, 1986). Barkun uses Bainbridge's statistics to build his argument that *overall* population size remained relatively stable through 1860 but that variations between different communities and the rate of transition in membership increased markedly (p. 81). Barkun also notes (p. 87) that antebellum Shakers were demographically fairly typical of the general American population. Extremes in sex and age ratios did not become obvious until later in the century. See also Stephen A. Marini, *Radical Sects of Revolutionary New England* (Cambridge, Mass.: Harvard University Press, 1982), p. 100, on earlier Shakers' demographic similarity to non-Shakers in the same region.

6. Marini, *Radical Sects,* pp. 112–14. See also material on this period in Foster, *Religion and Sexuality*; Brewer, *Shaker Communities*; and Garrett, *Spirit Possession.*

7. "Domestic Journal. 1847" (1847–1855), entries for 20, 21, 24, and 26 May 1853, WRHS 32 V:B-70.

8. Marini, *Radical Sects,* p. 94.

9. In this manuscript, I capitalize "Society" when it refers to the United Society of Believers in Christ's Second Appearing as a whole, but not when it refers to an individual community of Believers.

10. Foster, *Religion and Sexuality,* p. 56.

11. New Lebanon Ministry to Sodus Elders, 19 December 1837, "Copies of letters, Begun 1833," WRHS 27 IV:B-8, p. 231.

12. "A true Record of Sacred Communications; Written by Divine Inspiration, By the Mortal Hands of Chosen Instruments; In the Church at New Lebanon," vol. 8 (10 November 1841–8 December 1841), WRHS 76 VIII:B-123, p. 87. "A Roll, written by Father Joseph to the Elders of the first Order: February 5th 1841," castigated the young generation for their materialism, see "A true Record of Sacred Communications; Written by Divine Inspiration, By the Mortal Hands of Chosen Instruments; In the Church at New Lebanon," vol. 4 (28 November 1840–16 February 1841), WRHS 75 VIII:B-119, pp. 125–26.

13. Youngs, Personal Journal, EBK 10,509, p. 52.

14. Brewer, *Shaker Communities,* p. 93 and [Youngs], "Preface, or Introduction," WRHS 75 VIII:B-109, p. 8. See also New Lebanon Ministry at Watervliet to South Union Ministry, 29 September 1832, Copies of Letters from New Lebanon Ministry to other Ministries (17 June 1823-5 July 1833), WRHS 26 IV:B-7, p. 329; New Lebanon Ministry to Pleasant Hill Ministry, 21 May 1833, ibid., p. 342; and New Lebanon Ministry to Union Village Ministry, 9 October 1838, "Copies of letters, Begun 1833," WRHS 27 IV:B-8, p. 271.

15. Brewer, *Shaker Communities,* p. 115.

16. Bainbridge, "Shaker Demographics," p. 359. See also Marjorie Procter-Smith, *Women in Shaker Community and Worship: A Feminist Analysis of the Uses of Religious Symbolism* (Lewiston, N.Y.: Edward Mellon Press, 1985), pp. 177–80.

17. Marini, *Radical Sects,* p. 100; Garrett, *Spirit Possession,* p. 194. Both of these authors discuss briefly the influence of admitting extended biological families into the Shaker community.

18. The example of David Lamson at Hancock is a case in point. See Lamson, *Among the Shakers.*

19. Bainbridge, "Shaker Demographics," pp. 361–63.

20. Cf. Brewer, *Shaker Communities,* pp. 101–103.

21. Hannah Kendal [sometimes spelled Kendall] of the Harvard Ministry to Elders John [Warner] and Rufus [Bishop] of the New Lebanon Ministry, 5 May 1813, WRHS

18 IV:A-21. Lucy Wright was the last member of the parent ministry understood by Believers to have been so designated by Ann Lee herself.

22. New Lebanon Ministry to Father David, Mother Ruth, Elder Solomon, and Eldress Rachel [at Union Village], 2 October 1821, WRHS 20 IV:A-34.

23. [Benjamin S. Youngs], *The Testimony of Christ's Second Appearing* (Lebanon, Ohio: Press of John M'Clean, Office of the Western Star, 1808).

24. [Rufus Bishop and Seth Y. Wells], eds., *Testimonies of the Life, Character, Revelations and Doctrines of Our Ever Blessed Mother Ann Lee, and the Elders with Her* (Hancock, Mass.: J. Tallcott and J. Deming, Jrs., 1816), p. iii. This text was intended only for the "regenerate," that is, for use within the Society. Shakers printed a limited number of copies which were distributed among Shaker leaders, reaching the general membership through oral readings by the elders. For this reason, Shakers called the document "The Secret Book of the Elders."

25. [Seth Y. Wells and Calvin Green], *Testimonies Concerning the Character and Ministry of Mother Ann Lee and the First Witnesses of the Gospel of Christ's Second Appearing* (Albany, N.Y.: Packard and Van Benthuysen, 1827).

26. New Lebanon Ministry at Watervliet to Elder David Spinning at North Union, 22 April 1834, "Copies of letters, Begun 1833," WRHS 27 IV:B-8, p. 34. See also New Lebanon Ministry to South Union Ministry, 10 April 1834, ibid., pp. 25–29.

27. "A true Record of Sacred Communications; Written by Divine Inspiration, By the Mortal Hands of Chosen Instruments; In the Church at New Lebanon," vol. 2 (4 August 1839–20 June 1840), WRHS 75 VIII:B-117, pp. 185–86. See also Derobigne Bennett and Isaac Newton Youngs, "Journal of Inspired Meetings at New Lebanon Begun by Derobigne Bennett and continued by Isaac Newton Youngs. 1840–1841," entry for 3 May 1840, WRHS 77 VIII:B-138; and "A true Record," vol. 4, WRHS 75 VIII:B-119, pp. 106–7.

28. New Lebanon Ministry to Harvard Ministry, 20 March 1850, WRHS 20 IV:A-40. See also Hancock Ministry to Harvard Ministry, 3 June 1848, WRHS 18 IV:A-39.

Not only journals and correspondence but also products of Shaker poets and hymnists narrated the passing of the beloved first Believers. For examples of hymns, see "First Believers" in "Hymns and Poems by Eunice Wyeth, Copied by Eunice Bathrick in 1865," WRHS 89 IX:B-11, pp. 94–95; "First Founders," in Collection of Hymns, WRHS 100 IX:B-180, pp. 8–9; and "Home of Rest" in Sarah Bates, "A Collection of Hymns and Extra Songs," WRHS 89 IX:B-16, pp. 28–30. For examples of poems, see Giles B. Avery, "A Journal of Domestic Events and Transactions In a brief and conclusive form, Commenced February 7th 1838," entry for 15 August 1842, WRHS 34 V:B-107.

29. "A true Record of Sacred Communications; Written by Divine Inspiration, By the Mortal Hands of Chosen Instruments; In the Church at New Lebanon," vol. 10 (2 January 1842–2 March 1842), WRHS 76 VIII:B-125, p. 149.

30. New Lebanon Ministry and Elders to [?] Ministry, 19 March 1822, WRHS 20 IV:A-34. The first and third terms here, Shakers used with great frequency. "Second crop," on the other hand, they used only rarely.

31. Cf. linguistic usage in David E. Stannard, *The Puritan Way of Death: A Study in Religion, Culture, and Social Change* (New York: Oxford University Press, 1977), pp. 61 and 130; and Garrett, *Spirit Possession,* pp. 128, 134, and 224.

32. New Lebanon Ministry and Elders to [?] Ministry, 19 March 1822, WRHS 20 IV:A-34.

33. Alonzo Giles Hollister, compiler, Collection of Messages and Visions, WRHS 81 VIII:B-201, p. 113.

34. Cf. [Bishop and Wells], *Testimonies,* 1816, p. 220, where Ann Lee claims Joseph Meacham as her "first born son in America."

35. See, for example, "Mother's Closing Address to Her Children upon Earth April

11th 1841," NYPL 29; "A true Record of Sacred Communications; Written by Divine Inspiration, By the Mortal Hands of Chosen Instruments; In the Church at New Lebanon," vol. 6 (12 March 1841–16 May 1841), WRHS 76 VIII:B-121, p. 156; "A true Record," vol. 8, WRHS 76 VIII:B-123, pp. 101–102; Bennett and Youngs, "Journal of Inspired Meetings," entries for 6 December 1840, 11 April and 19 December 1841, and Review of 1841, WRHS 77 VIII:B-138; "A true Record of Sacred Communications; Written by Divine Inspiration, By the Mortal Hands of Chosen Instruments; In the Church at New Lebanon," vol. 11 ("Promiscuous Dates"), WRHS 76 VIII:B-126, p. 6; and Miranda Barber, "A Collection of Various Interviews and Visionary Scens [*sic*] Witnessed by Miranda Barber," EBK 12,316, pp. 12–13.

36. See "A true Record," vol. 2, WRHS 75 VIII:B-117, p. 65; "A true Record," vol. 4, WRHS 75 VIII:B-119, p. 9; and Bennett and Youngs, "Journal of Inspired Meetings," entry for 6 December 1840, WRHS 77 VIII:B-138; and "A true Record of Sacred Communications; Written by Divine Inspiration, By the Mortal Hands of Chosen Instruments; In the Church at New Lebanon," vol. 9 (10 December 1841–5 January 1842), WRHS 76 VIII:B-124, p. 176.

37. While still maintaining association with the more specifically generational terminology, the designations "old" and "young" Believer provided a somewhat more elastic alternative. The "young Believer" usage appeared as early as 1808 in [B. Youngs], *Testimony,* 1808, p. 587, for example.

38. Mircea Eliade suggests that "the term initiation . . . denotes a body of rites and oral teachings whose purpose it is to produce a decisive alteration in the religious and social status of the person to be initiated." Mircea Eliade, *Myths, Rites, Symbols: A Mircea Eliade Reader,* ed. Wendell C. Beane and William G. Doty, vol. 1 (New York: Harper and Row, 1976), p. 164. Jerald C. Brauer first alerted me to the possible fruitfulness of examining mid-nineteenth-century Shaker revivalism as a rite of initiation. In his essay, "Changing Perspectives on Religion in America," in *Reinterpretation in American Church History,* ed. Jerald C. Brauer (Chicago: University of Chicago Press, 1968), p. 26, Brauer notes that the ritual process of initiation sought "to put people through a particular kind of experience, one could call it a trial or test, in order that they might emerge as reborn or new." In this process, the initiate died to an old self and subsequently "stood in an utterly new relation to the center of the universe and thus [acquired] a new understanding of . . . self and . . . fellow human beings (p. 27)." Foster, *Religion and Sexuality,* p. 64, comments on the need among Shaker initiates for a "powerful, direct, and personal experience of the truth of the Shaker message."

39. "Divine Inspiration containing Explanations of the manner in which the inspired gifts have been given in the marvelous display of divine manifestations which have been in operation for several years past; together with the effects thereof upon different Instruments and members of the body at large, etc. Given by inspiration from the holy Prophet Elijah, at the Holy Mount, in the Church, first order N. Lebanon. 11th month 29. 1844," in a Book of Miscellaneous New Era Writings, WRHS 78 VIII:B-143, section I, paragraphs 8–9, n.p.

40. "A Record of Messages and Communications given by Divine Inspiration in the Church at Hancock, Commencing in 1840," WML 428 SA 1066, p. 4. Cf. second copy of the same manuscript in "A Record of Messages and Communications given by Divine Inspiration in the Church at Hancock. Commencing in 1840," (19 July 1840–5 March 1843), second page of introduction, WRHS 71 VIII:B-20; "A Record of Divinely Inspired Communications and Messages," (Hancock 1841–43), WML 430 SA 1068, p. 20; New Lebanon Ministry to Enfield (New Hampshire) Ministry, 28 February 1838, "Copies of letters, Begun 1833," WRHS 27 IV:B-8, p. 249; and "A true Record," vol. 6, WRHS 76 VIII:B-121, p. 251.

41. "Divine Inspiration Containing Explanations," WRHS 78 VIII:B-143, section I, paragraph 16, n.p.

42. New Lebanon Ministry to Groveland Ministry, 25 April 1840, WRHS 20 IV:A-38; see also Youngs, "Concise View," WML SA 760, pp. 120–21.

43. See "Inspired Communications and Messages," WML 430 SA 1068, p. 63; New Lebanon Ministry to North Union Ministry, 4 January 1839, "Copies of letters, Begun 1833," WRHS 27 IV:B-8, p. 292; Daniel Boler at New Lebanon to Abner Bedell at Union Village, 8 April 1838, WRHS 20 IV:A-37; and "Holy Orders of God," First Church, New Lebanon, 30 November 1840, WRHS 78 VIII:B-150, p. 112.

44. Canterbury's Record of Celestial Messages Received at New Lebanon and Watervliet, EBK 12,787, p. 3.

45. Ibid., p. 7. See also "A true Record of Sacred Communications; Written by Divine Inspiration, By the Mortal Hands of Chosen Instruments; in the Church at New Lebanon," vol. 3 (1 July 1840–14 November 1840), WRHS 75 VIII:B-118, pp. 73–75; and Bennett and Youngs, "Journal of Inspired Meetings," entry for October 1840, WRHS 77 VIII:B-138.

46. Still, for some Shakers of 1784, the initial crisis at the time of Ann Lee's death had much to do with expectations concerning Lee's immortality, a characteristic generally associated with divinity. Though Lee herself had not encouraged such expectations, this view regarding immortality nonetheless influenced some followers.

47. [Bishop and Wells], *Testimonies,* 1816, p. vi.

48. [Calvin Green and Seth Y. Wells], *A Summary View of the Millennial Church, or United Society of Believers, Commonly Called Shakers,* 2nd ed., rev. (Albany: C. Van Benthuysen, 1848; repr., New York: AMS Press, 1973), pp. 258–71.

49. Bennett and Youngs, "Journal of Inspired Meetings," entry for 1 March 1841, WRHS 77 VIII:B-138.

50. Cf. Hughes and Allen, *Illusions of Innocence,* pp. 136–38 on pluralism and authority.

51. Historically, Shakers have differed in opinion about the precise status of Ann Lee. Different individuals at different times have emphasized different qualities in her character and nature. During the era of Mother's Work, most Believers portrayed Mother Ann as the female manifestation of the Christ spirit. The millennial age began, then, with Ann Lee and her immediate precursors.

52. The contrast between the ministry's reaction to the visionary episode of 7 August 1837, involving the mature Gideon Kibbee, and their reaction to the episodes beginning 16 August of the same year, involving fourteen-year-old Ann Mariah Goff, is particularly noteworthy. See Rufus Bishop, "A Daily Journal of Passing Events, Begun January the 1st 1830," entries for 17 January and 1 February 1832, 14 and 21 February 1835, 2 October 1836, and (especially) 7 August 1837, NYPL 1.

53. "Divine Inspiration containing Explanations," WRHS 78 VIII:B-143, "Introduction," n.p. See also New Lebanon Ministry to Sodus Elders, 19 December 1837, "Copies of letters, Begun 1833," WRHS 27 IV:B-8, p. 232.

54. "A true Record of Sacred Communications; Written by Divine Inspiration, By the Mortal Hands of Chosen Instruments; in the Church at New Lebanon," vol. 1 (22 April 1838–6 July 1839), WRHS 75 VIII:B-116, p. 164. See also "A true Record," vol. 8, WRHS 76 VIII:B-123, pp. 10–12.

55. Of the period of Ann Lee's ministry, Stephen Marini writes, "The picture that emerges from the Niskeyuna community is that of a fluid and continuous social process of religious communication that the Shaker leaders controlled by a kind of ensemble improvisation. . . . The varied gifts displayed by the worshippers . . . [gave] prospective converts easy access to the group. In these moments of high group emotion a person who had become intellectually convinced of the Shaker gospel could abandon himself or herself to a relatively fluid form of ritual self-expression" (Marini, *Radical Sects,* pp. 89–90). The Watervliet (New York) community, during Ann Lee's lifetime, had been called by its Native American name, "Niskeyuna."

56. Ibid., pp. 109–12, 127–34. As Shakerism became more institutionalized, "the charismatic gifts of the spirit were still sought, but now they descended through the mediation and authority of a hierarchy of elders and eldresses." Garrett, *Spirit Possession,* p. 149.

57. Victor Turner, *The Ritual Process: Structure and Anti-Structure* (Chicago: Aldine Publishing Company, 1969; Ithaca, New York: Cornell University Press, Cornell Paperbacks Edition, 1977), pp. 107, 128–29, 131–32; Stein, "Shaker Gift and Shaker Order," pp. 104–105.

58. Cf. Foster, *Religion and Sexuality,* pp. 44–48, 64. Among Believers, too much reliance on spiritual enthusiasm carried with it the joint risks of extremism and fragmentation as individuals followed their own lights. Too much dependence on structure carried the risk of alienating Shakerism from its own motivating source in the spirit and, consequently, of stifling both freshness and power.

59. Garrett, *Spirit Possession,* pp. 152, 156–58.

60. For biographical information on William Lee and James Whittaker, see Marini, *Radical Sects,* pp. 109–14.

61. Garrett, *Spirit Possession,* p. 153.

62. New Lebanon Ministry to North Union Ministry, 4 January 1839, "Copies of letters, Begun 1833," WRHS 27 IV:B-8, p. 287.

63. Alternatively Ann Maria Goff. Mid-nineteenth-century Shakers frequently used multiple spellings of a single individual's name. It is not unusual to find several spellings within a single document.

64. [Isaac Newton Youngs], "Visions Seen by Elleyett Gibbs and Ann Mariah Goff," entry for 1 December 1837, EBK 3270.

65. New Lebanon Ministry to Union Village Ministry, 6 August 1837, "Copies of letters, Begun 1833," WRHS 27 IV:B-8, p. 205.

66. New Lebanon Ministry to Sodus Elders, 19 December 1837, ibid., p. 231.

67. New Lebanon Ministry at Watervliet to Groveland Ministry, 30 October 1838, ibid., pp. 276–77.

68. [Youngs], "Preface, or Introduction," WRHS 75 VIII:B-109, p. 3.

69. Daniel Boler at New Lebanon to Abner Bedell at Union Village, 8 April 1838, WRHS 20 IV:A-37.

70. [Youngs], "Preface, or Introduction," WRHS 75 VIII:B-109, pp. 15–16.

71. For descriptions of several instruments under inspiration, see Isaac Newton Youngs, "Sketches of Visions and various spiritual gifts of which I obtained Information in various ways," 1838, WRHS 75 VIII:B-113, pp. 52–60. At least two of these instruments (Miranda Barber and Mary Wicks) would later produce gift images.

72. Youngs, "A Concise View," WML SA 760, pp. 97–111.

73. The Church Family was the central family at the New Lebanon community. New Lebanon was the seat of the parent ministry and exercised authority over all other Shaker societies.

74. [Youngs], "Preface, or Introduction," WRHS 75 VIII:B-109, p. 56.

75. Youngs, "Concise View," WML SA 760, pp. 121–22.

76. "Sequel, to the Holy Orders of God," WRHS 78 VIII:B-150, p. 112.

77. See, for example, New Lebanon Ministry to Pleasant Hill Ministry, 4 December 1837, "Copies of letters Begun 1833," WRHS 27 IV:B-8, p. 222.

78. Richard T. Hughes, "Introduction: On Recovering the Theme of Recovery," in Hughes, ed., *The American Quest for the Primitive Church* (Urbana: University of Illinois Press, 1988), p. 1. See also p. 3 which distinguishes between restoration ("chronological primitivism") and primitivism ("cultural primitivism").

79. Hughes and Allen, *Illusions of Innocence,* pp. 2, 20–21. See also the Hughes and

Allen discussion of restorationism as fundamentally American and shaping of American character and identity (pp. 20–21).

80. Ibid., p. 139. Cf. the Mormons.

81. "The Holy Word of God Almighty," 5 March 1843, WRHS 79 VIII:B-170, "Contents," last page.

82. William Leonard, "The Life and Sufferings of Jesus Anointed, our Holy Savior and of our Blessed Mother Ann," written at Harvard, Massachusetts, October 1841 (New Lebanon, New York: n.p., 1904), EBK 3226–105, pp. 7–9, 40–42, and 60–61.

83. Youngs, "Concise View," WML SA 760, pp. 132–36; and Youngs, "Sketches of Visions," WRHS 75 VIII:B-113, p. 5.

84. Bennett and Youngs, "Journal of Inspired Meetings," entry for 21 November 1841, WRHS 77 VIII:B-138.

85. "Holy Laws of Zion," SDL, pp. 4, 57, and 62.

86. "Domestic Journal of Important Occurrences. Kept for the Elder Sisters. Begun January 1842 New Lebanon," entries for 14 August 1848, 6 May 1854, 1 and 3 July 1854, WRHS 32 V:B-61; [Seth Y. Wells and Isaac Newton Youngs], "Records Kept by Order of the Church," entry for March 1844, NYPL 7, p. 224; and Giles B. Avery to Hervey Eads, Summer 1856, WRHS 21 IV:A-41.

87. Garrett, *Spirit Possession,* p. 201.

88. Ibid., pp. 235–37. The idea of a select youth order had to be abandoned because by 1795 the pressure of the spiritual discipline began to cause a significant number of promising young Believers to leave the United Society.

89. These differences can be overstated; because of negative reactions of varying degrees, Shakers eventually abandoned many New Era regulations as well.

1. From Vision to Image

1. [Bishop and Wells], *Testimonies,* 1816, p. 231.

2. [Wells and Youngs], "Records Kept by Order of the Church," entry for 2 June 1844, NYPL 7, p. 228. See also Youngs, "Concise View," WML SA 760, p. 166; and Rufus Bishop, "A Daily Journal of Passing Events begun May the 19th 1839, at Watervliet," entry for 2 June 1844, NYPL 2, p. 224. Entries for April and May 1844 in the same volume record the visits of the "Heavenly Father" and the "Blessed Savior" to the New Lebanon community, see especially pp. 222–25.

3. "Antionett" Belknap was 12 years old; "L. B." (probably Lovina Belknap) was 10 years old. See Patterson, *Gift Drawing,* p. 9.

4. Patterson counts sixty-six women, forty-four men, twenty girls, and eighteen boys in New Lebanon's First Order. Patterson, *Gift Drawing,* p. 9.

5. Of the surviving hearts, eleven are dated sometime in April 1844, as early as the second day of the month. It is likely, then, that the initial "promise" described by the recordkeeper was given in April and that the instruments had two months in which to "write" the hearts.

6. Bishop, "Daily Journal begun 1839," entry for 2 June 1844, NYPL 2, p. 224. Cf. the practice of ritual blessing among the French Prophets discussed in Garrett, *Spirit Possession,* p. 49.

7. [Alonzo G. Hollister, compiler?] Messages, Songs and Anthems, WRHS 75 VIII:B-115, pp. 231–32; see also p. 230.

8. [Hollister, compiler?] Messages, Songs and Anthems, WRHS 75 VIII:B-115, p. 187.

9. [Paulina Bates], *The Divine Book of Holy and Eternal Wisdom* (hereafter *Holy Wisdom's Book*) (Canterbury, N.H.: United Society, 1849), p. 12.

10. "A Book of Wisdom and Sacred Truth" (New Lebanon, 16 February 1841), WRHS 78 VIII:B-153, p. 45.

11. [Hollister, compiler?] Messages, Songs and Anthems, WRHS 75 VIII:B-115, p. 184.

12. [Bishop and Wells], *Testimonies,* 1816, pp. 230, 232–33.

13. "A true Record," vol. 1, WRHS 75 VIII:B-116, p. 106.

14. See, for example, [Bishop and Wells], *Testimonies,* 1816, p. 230; [Wells and Green], *Testimonies,* 1827, p. 90.

15. "Solemn and Sacred Word," WRHS 78 VIII:B-152, p. 97. On faith producing sight, see "A Report of the General proceedings of the Second and Hill Families Passover on the Holy Mount. May 8th 1842," WRHS 79 VIII:B-165, p. 37.

16. [Bates], *Holy Wisdom's Book,* p. 427.

17. "Divine Inspiration containing Explanations," WRHS 78 VIII:B-143, quotation is from "Notice" on final page of document, n.p.

18. New Lebanon Ministry at Watervliet to Groveland Ministry, 30 October 1838, "Copies of letters, Begun 1833," WRHS 27 IV:B-8, p. 277. See also New Lebanon Ministry to Some Members of the New Lebanon Ministry visiting at Enfield, New Hampshire, 8 November 1837, ibid., pp. 218–19.

Drawings were *internal* evidence of divine reality and grace. Shakers did not intend these images to convert the world. Other sorts of evidence, like healings, testified of the second appearance of Christ to the world. See [B. Youngs], *Testimony,* 1808, pp. 467–86. This material was repeated, with some changes to incorporate responses to the New Era, in the fourth edition of the *Testimony,* 1856, pp. 416–26.

19. "A true Record," vol. 1, WRHS 75 VIII:B-116, pp. 140–42. For a similar account, probably of the same visit, see [Hollister, compiler?], Messages, Songs, and Anthems, WRHS 75 VIII:B-115, p. 165. This second account is dated 18 March 1839. For an example of spiritual "pictures" being interpreted as revelatory of an otherwise invisible reality, see [Miranda Barber and Polly Reed?] Book of Inspired Visions and Messages, WRHS 87 VIII:C-1, pp. 121–22.

20. A contemporary seeker who visited the Shakers during the New Era made some interesting observations about spiritual manifestations and natural and spiritual visibility. See Noyes, *American Socialisms,* pp. 608–609. Here Noyes is quoting his source, Macdonald, who is quoting the unidentified seeker.

21. [Youngs], "Preface, or Introduction," WRHS 75 VIII:B-109, p. 15.

22. For example, the use of captions in gift drawings served not only to identify elements of a drawing, but also to reproduce more faithfully the character of objects in some Shaker visions. As early as 2 December 1837 Ann Mariah Goff had a vision that included a very large bird which sat on a golden seat belonging to Jesus and sang for the Savior's pleasure. As Goff related in her account of the vision, "this bird had Jesus' name written on its back" ([Youngs], "Visions Seen," entry for 2 December 1837, EBK 3270). See also "A true Record of Sacred Communications; Written by Divine Inspiration, By the Mortal Hands of Chosen Instruments; In the Church at New Lebanon," vol. 7 (18 May 1841–14 November 1841), WRHS 76 VIII:B-122, pp. 115–16 where angels seen in a vision wear garments and jewelry (a breastplate and a gold neck band) with their "name[s] painted thereon."

23. See [Bates], *Holy Wisdom's Book,* p. 95; and [Stewart], *Sacred Roll and Book,* p. 38.

24. "A true Record," vol. 8, WRHS 76 VIII:B-123, pp. 200–201; and New Lebanon Ministry to Groveland Ministry, 26 April 1844, WRHS 20 IV:A-38. Confession of sin, as a central rite of the Shaker church, was intimately related to the examination of one's own heart. The heart gifts, by materializing this usually interior process in a manner that simultaneously spiritualized a popular material form of keepsake (the valentine), presented an interesting variation on the more general mid-nineteenth-century sentimental ideal of transparency and self-revelation, see Halttunen, *Confidence Men,* pp. 40, 60, 89–90, and 154–55.

25. Bennett and Youngs, "Journal of Inspired Meetings," entry for 25 December

1841, WRHS 77 VIII:B-138. Ann Lee herself possessed powers of discernment: she could *see* people's sins. See, for example, [Bishop and Wells], *Testimonies,* 1816, p. 63; [Wells and Green], *Testimonies,* 1827, p. 90.

26. Bennett and Youngs, "Journal of Inspired Meetings," entry titled "Review of 1841," WRHS 77 VIII:B-138; and Giles B. Avery, "A Record of Presents," entry for 13 June 1841, in Compilation of Messages and Anthems, WRHS 65 VIII:A-26.

27. "A Heart of Purity Given by Father James Whereon is the Likeness of the Eternal Two in One. This Token of Remembrance, from Father James, is given with his Blessing and his Love, To Brother Rufus Bishop Wisdom's Valley March 20 1842," EBK 13,525, n.p. Rufus Bishop was among those who received a heart cutout in June 1844. The text of the cutout did not duplicate the text of the booklet. Eldress Ruth Landon (and, therefore, perhaps also the other two members of the parent ministry, Asenath Clark and Ebenezer Bishop) received a "Heart of Purity" very similar to Rufus Bishop's heart of 1842. See "A Heart of Purity: Given by Father James. Whereon is the Likeness of the Eternal Two in One. This token of Remembrance, from Father James, is given with his Love and Blessing, To Eldress Ruth. Wisdom's Valley. Mar. 20th 1842," WRHS 69 VIII:A-69.

28. Cf. Shaker leaf and star gifts. On 12 June 1844, ten days after the reception of the heart cutouts, eight women between the ages of forty-six and eighty-one received messages of comfort and blessing in the form of leaf-shaped cutouts, e.g., "A Word of Love and Blessing, from Abraham of Old, the Father of the Faithful. To Ursula Bishop, June 12, 1844," Shaker Collection, Department of Prints, Drawings, and Photographs, Philadelphia Museum of Art, Philadelphia, Pennsylvania (hereafter PMA) 63-160-199-(3). In preparing these gifts, instruments hand-colored one side of a sheet of white paper with an unusually bright and vibrant green paint. When the papers dried, the instruments cut them into shapes resembling olive leaves and added, on both sides of the cutouts, text, miniature images of choice jewels or shining stars, and intricate border designs, often resembling the characters of Shaker sacred script. Inscribed leaves were a very popular gift of Mother's Work. Like most other gift forms, some leaf gifts were visible only to the spiritual eye. Others, like those described above, took material form. In addition to the eight leaf cutouts of 12 June 1844, at least six similar leaf cutouts survive. Many of the leaf gifts, spiritual and material, Shakers understood to have been sent through the mediation of the biblical Abraham. See, for example, "Good Father Abraham's Present ['an *Olive Leaf* to everyone that is numbered in Zion']," 1 January 1842, Hancock, WRHS 65 VIII:A- 22. Multiple references for this date, describing a gift from Abraham of inscribed leaves in a treasure box, survive from several communities. It is possible that the instruments did not produce material versions of these gifts until mid-June 1844, after the favorable reception of the heart cutouts.

29. "A Word of Elder Sister Olive, March 3, 1867," EBK 12,107. This beautifully calligraphed message was written in blue ink on both sides of a white paper, 7 inches by 12 inches. The text here employs the images of Proverbs 25:11 (KJV): which reads "A word fitly spoken is like apples of gold in pictures of silver." In *A Little Basket Full of Beautiful Apples* (fig. 5) Hannah Cohoon pictures the golden apples of Proverbs. Here the apples represent the gracious words of heaven to the ministry ("a word fitly spoken").

30. Some of the known instruments of images were also among the most prominent instruments of gift texts and aural manifestations as well.

31. [Wells and Youngs], "Records Kept by Order of the Church," entry for 30 January 1842, NYPL 7, p. 191.

32. Seldom did a Shaker scribe write an explicit interpretation of a particular image; only slightly more frequently did a scribe offer even the briefest comment on a painting or drawing. But scribes did take down, in writing, visions and messages (as well as records of visions and messages) which help viewers in other times and places to under-

stand the context and content of gift images. Shakers themselves would not have deemed inconsistent the use of texts to interpret images.

33. [Wells and Youngs], "Records Kept by Order of the Church," entry for 30 January 1842, NYPL 7, p. 191. It is unlikely that these particular "likenesses" were ever executed in material form.

34. Youngs, "Concise View," WML SA 760, p. 166. See also p. 165.

35. [Wells and Youngs], "Records Kept by Order of the Church," entry for 2 June 1844, NYPL 7, p. 228.

36. It was not the case that Shakers made no distinctions between word and image. Distinctions could be and were made if that was desirable and necessary for clarity within the community. A shared vocabulary existed, however. For the twentieth-century researcher, ambiguity in terminology sometimes blurs differences that would have been much clearer to Believers in possession of the original documents.

37. Patterson, *Gift Drawing,* pp. 4–5.

38. Canterbury's Record, EBK 12,787, p. 14; "Records Concerning the Finding," SDL, Table of Contents; Eunice Bathrick, compiler, "Sermons and public discourses, choice poetry, curious discoveries and remarkable facts, sketches, etc., collected and recorded by Eunice Bathrick, commencing in the year 1865," WRHS 54 VII:B-28, p. 82; Isaac Newton Youngs and his New Lebanon Companions to the Parent Ministry Visiting in the Western Communities, 26 July 1852, WRHS 20 IV:A-40; Bennett and Youngs, "Journal of Inspired Meetings," entry for 10 March 1841, WRHS 77 VIII:B-138. Bates, "Hymns and Extra Songs," WRHS 89 IX:B-16, p. 4, demonstrates that the melody and words of a gift song could be received in a visual format.

39. [Wells and Youngs], "Records Kept by Order of the Church," entry for 1 March 1843, NYPL 7, p. 206 comments on sacred script.

40. "By Mother Dana this is given, But Polly Laurance aids in drawing," 1 July 1853, Shaker Collection, Manuscript Division, Library of Congress, Washington, D.C. (hereafter LC), Container 9, Item 135, #2. This sheet retained the stationer's imprint at the top.

41. "The Word of the Holy Heavenly Father To a Saint of his Eternal Glory," 21 April 1844, Berkshire Athenaeum, Pittsfield, Massachusetts (hereafter BA), V289.8, Un 1.

42. Marcel Maus, *The Gift: Forms and Functions of Exchange in Archaic Societies,* trans. Ian Cunnison (New York: W. W. Norton, 1967), especially pp. 10, 25–26, 37, and 56–57.

43. In addition to the content of form itself, the content of the historical understanding of image (in Protestant Christianity in general and Shakerism in particular—see ch. 2), and the content of the overall formal characteristics of gift images (the clarity of form, strict organization in composition, use of captions, etc.—see especially ch. 4) contributed to the impact of these pictures in the Shaker community.

44. Cf. Bronner, "Idea of the Folk Artifact," p. 16, on the use of "vision and touch to verify reality."

45. Grant McCracken, *Culture and Consumption: New Approaches to the Symbolic Character of Consumer Goods and Activities* (Bloomington: Indiana University Press, 1988), pp. 26, 132. McCracken's work deals with the broader visual cultural field of "material objects" rather than with the subcategory "images." See also Glassie, "Folk Art," p. 134, on the permanence of material objects; and Bronner, "Idea of the Folk Artifact," pp. 14–16, 20.

46. The principal images of this "visual language" Shakers often derived from the bible.

47. Procter-Smith, *Women in Shaker Community,* pp. 125–26.

48. [Wells and Youngs], "Records Kept by Order of the Church," entry for 30 January 1842, NYPL 7, p. 191.

49. "A Little Book, Written by Father James, Containing the word of Mother Ann,

Father William, Father James, Father Joseph and Mother Lucy, Placed upon the head of Lydia Mathewson, by Mother Ann, while she received her blessing, from Holy Mother Wisdom. Dec. 28th 1841," WRHS 66 VIII:A-37, p. 6.

50. "A Little Book, Containing a short word from Holy Mother Wisdom, concerning the Robes and Dresses which are prepared for all such as go up to the Feast of the Lord; or attend to Her Holy Passover. Holy Mount July 21st 1842," WRHS 67 VIII:A-42, pp. 12–15.

51. "A Short Word of Notice from Father James to Jane Blanchard," January 1841, EBK 12,113. See also the very similar "A Short Word of Notice from Father James to Eliza Ann Taylor. With a Present gathered from the Heavens by Father William," 1 January 1842, PMA 63-160-190-(9); and "A Record of Spiritual Presents," received by Seth Blanchard, WRHS 72 VIII:B-55, pp. 31–32.

52. New Lebanon Ministry to Union Village Ministry, 6 April 1840, "Copies of letters, Begun 1839," WRHS 27 IV:B-9, p. 35.

53. By the time this passage was written, Governor George Clinton was dead. According to mid-nineteenth-century Shaker belief, he had been converted to Shakerism in the spirit world by Mother Ann. Shakers remembered Clinton as the person responsible for the release of Ann Lee from an Albany prison in 1780. See [B. Youngs], *Testimony,* 1808, p. 28.

54. "Presents Received in Our Meetings from our Heavenly Parents. Commencing 1838," WRHS 75 VIII:B-114, p. 34. See also Record of Spiritual Gifts Received at Harvard and Shirley, WRHS 72 VIII:B-52; and "Record of Spiritual Presents," WRHS 72 VIII:B-55.

55. Mary Hazard, "Mary Hazard's Book," WML 481 SA 1119, pp. 191–92. Other early New Era leaf drawings in hymnals or song books can be found in "Hymns Improved in the Worship of Believers," WRHS 99 IX:B-169, p. 120; and Rhoda Blake, "A Collection of Anthems and Spiritual Songs Improved in the Worship of Believers," WRHS 102 IX:B-218, p. 50; Collection of Hymns, WRHS 109 IX:B-316, p. 63; and "A Collection of Anthems and Spiritual Songs Improved in Sacred Devotion," WRHS 109 IX:B-318, p. iv. Some Shaker hymnals dating from the 1840s and 1850s included even more elaborate pictorial decoration. See "Amelia Lyman's Book, Commenced November 18, 1855," WRHS 103 IX:B-231, pp. 10 and 12; and [D. A. Buckingham?], Collection of Hymns, WRHS 103 IX:B-239, pp. 84, 100, 103, 112, 156, 163.

56. Natural phenomena like storms, famines, or floods, seen or foreseen with the spiritual eye, were signs. However, official Shaker opinion usually counseled against interpreting *actual* natural phenomena as spiritual events. As Giles B. Avery insisted, natural phenomena belonged to the world of natural women and men; spiritual phenomena belonged to the world of spiritual women and men. "A Record of the Communications, Gifts, and Spiritual Exercises of the day of Christmas 1845," WRHS 80 VIII:B-179, p. 48; Giles B. Avery, "A Journal of Domestic Events and Transactions, In a brief and conclusive form, Commenced February 7th 1838," entry for 21 May 1842, WRHS 34 V:B-107; and "Domestic Journal," WRHS 32 V:B-70, entry for 11 August 1854. For a contrary view, see Bishop, "Daily Journal; Begun 1830," note at conclusion of entry for 24 December 1833, NYPL 1; and Bennett and Youngs, "Journal of Inspired Meetings," entry for 2 November 1840, WRHS 77 VIII:B-138.

57. In Giles B. Avery, "Historical Sketches or a Record of Remarkable events with Remarks and Illustrations" (January 1834–February 1843), entry for 25 January 1843, LC Container 4, Item 53, p. 149, celestial beings spoke in "many strange and incomprehensible signs."

58. Ibid., especially pp. 147–49. In this case, the symbolic objects used ritually (sheets of cloth, paper, clothing, lamps, etc.) were "real" in a material sense.

59. Here a "*facsimile* [in sealing wax and ink] of the word and seals written upon the red wrapper" was included in the log.

60. Avery, "Historical Sketches," entry for 29 January 1843, LC Container 4, Item 53, pp. 166–70.

61. See "Second and Hill Families Passover," WRHS 79 VIII:B-165, p. 38.

62. Cf. [Wells and Youngs], "Records Kept by Order of the Church," entry for 1 March 1843, NYPL 7, p. 206, on sacred sheets.

Although the record on the actual drawing of figures and images during Shaker meeting is sparse, the documentation for the ritual use of the finished products of instrument/artists is somewhat more substantial. During a service at Watervliet, instruments spread out on benches a "Roll about 17 feet in length, written by Inspiration, and in hiragliphics." This "Roll" had been "drawn by the spirit of God" a year earlier and carefully preserved to be read aloud in a worship setting. Shakers interpreted the manifestations accompanying this reading as evidence of the hand of God in such material phenomena. See Bishop, "Daily Journal begun 1839," entry for 28 July 1844, NYPL 7, p. 227. See "A Church Meeting Journal" (Watervliet 1844), entry for 4 April 1844, WRHS 48 V:B-327, pp. 31–32, for another instance of the ritual use of such a roll. Note the difference between these two rolls at Watervliet in which the signs were likely visible to the natural eyes of all present and other similarly described phenomena which were visible only to the spiritual eye of the instrument. See Barber, "Collection of Visionary Scens [*sic*]," EBK 12,316, pp. 60–73 and 124–26.

63. Calvin Green, "Biographic Memoir of the Life and Experience of Calvin Green," copied and expanded by Alonzo G. Hollister, vol. 3, WRHS 51 VI:B-31, p. 567. See also "A Roll from Mother Ann to her Anointed and Appointed Ministers," WRHS 67 VIII:A-47, pp. 12–13, and 28–29; Record of Spiritual Gifts, WRHS 72 VIII:B-52, p. 43; [Hollister, compiler?] Messages, Songs, and Anthems, WRHS 75 VIII:B115, pp. 166, 177, and 268.

64. See, for example, Avery, "Historical Sketches," entry for 25 January 1843, LC Container 4, Item 53, pp. 150–54, where Believers used white, red, and black sheets of cloth, four feet square, in a complex ritual performance with prophetic content. During the course of this dramatic service of worship, "The angel spake, saying the white [sheet of cloth] is truly the most pleasant, but the black and the red must be passed thro before the white is obtained. . . . The Holy Angel now spake a few words, saying the clouds of darkness [black] hover over Zion and blood to blood [red] doth run, yet shall she never be entirely overcome by her enemies [p. 152]." See also pp. 160–61 of this document as well as [Stewart], *Sacred Roll and Book*, p. 302; and "A true record," vol. 11, WRHS 76 VIII:B-126, p. 2. Barber, "Collection of Visionary Scens [*sic*]," EBK 12,316, pp. 103–106 has red ink as blood, signifying the commitment of self to God.

2. Image and Iconoclasm

1. In Kenneth L. Ames, "Material Culture as Nonverbal Communication: A Historical Case Study," in Edith Mayo, ed., *American Material Culture: The Shape of Things Around Us* (Bowling Green, Ohio: Bowling Green State University Popular Press, 1984), p. 38, Ames comments on "society's ability to tolerate contradictions" and on "objects' capacity to perform widely varied and seemingly opposing functions."

2. Cf. David Freedberg, *The Power of Images: Studies in the History and Theory of Response* (Chicago: University of Chicago Press, 1989), pp. 388, 405, 427 on love and fear of images as "two sides of one coin" (p. 405).

3. See Garrett, *Spirit Possession,* p. 200 for evidence from 1783. Cf. New Light James Davenport and 1743 in New London, Ct.

4. [Wells and Youngs], "Records Kept by Order of the Church," entry for March/April 1840, NYPL 7, pp. 178–79.

5. "A true Record," vol. 2, WRHS 75 VIII:B-117, p. 134.

6. While the material culture of Victorian Shakerism appeared worldly by compari-

son with early Shaker furnishings, the artifacts of Victorian Shakerism were simple and relatively unadorned versions of Victorian America as the artifacts of early Shakerism had been for the early national period.

7. Cf. "A true Record," vol. 4, WRHS 75 VIII:B-119, p. 125.

8. Robert Emlen concurs on this point. See Robert P. Emlen, *Shaker Village Views: Illustrated Maps and Landscape Drawings by Shaker Artists of the Nineteenth Century* (Hanover, N.H.: University Press of New England, 1987), p. viii. Potential converts brought decorated and illustrated materials into the Society with them. Believers had at least limited access to newspapers, books, writing tablets, and almanacs which contained illustrations. Some of these were censored, but others were not. In addition to New Era texts which document provision for the disposal of images, later Shaker sources record the removal of pictures from rooms in response to reinforced regulations during the period of Mother's Work. See Henry C. Blinn, *The Manifestation of Spiritualism Among the Shakers, 1837–1847* (East Canterbury, N.H.: United Society, 1899), p. 36; and Anna White and Leila Sarah Taylor, *Shakerism, Its Meaning and Message* (Columbus, Ohio: Fred J. Heer, 1905), pp. 233–34. (White and Taylor probably relied on Blinn for information regarding this period.)

9. "A true Record," vol. 2, WRHS 75 VIII:B-117, p. 92.

10. "Milenial [*sic*] Laws, or Gospel Statutes and Ordinances, adapted to the day of Christ's second Appearing; Given and established in the Church, for the protection thereof: By the Ministry and Elders. New Lebanon, August 7th 1821," WRHS 3 I:B-37, pp. 38–39.

11. "Millennial Laws, or Gospel Statutes and Ordinances adapted to the Day of Christ's Second Appearing. Given and established in the Church for the protection thereof by Father Joseph Meacham and Mother Lucy Wright the presiding Ministry, and by their Successors the Ministry and Elders. Recorded at New Lebanon August 7th 1821. Revised and re-established by the Ministry and Elders Oct. 1845," WML 121 SA 757, part II, section X, paragraph 7. This Hancock copy of the Millennial Laws varies only slightly from a New Lebanon version which reads, "No maps, charts, and no pictures or paintings shall ever be hung up in your dwelling rooms, shops, or Office, (but modest advertisements, may be put up in the Trustees Office when necessary)" ("Millenial [*sic*] Laws, or Gospel Statutes and Ordinances adapted to the Day of Christ's Second Appearing. Given and established in the Church for the protection thereof by Father Joseph Meacham and Mother Lucy Wright the presiding Ministry, and by their Successors the Ministry and Elders. Recorded at New Lebanon August 7th 1821. Revised and reestablished by the Ministry and Elders Oct. 1845," WML 121 SA 758, p. 46).

Earlier New Lebanon codes offered prototypes for these restrictions on images. Almost identical rules (each including the sentence on framing from the Hancock version) can be found in the 1841 "Holy Orders of the Church," WRHS 78 VIII:B-154, p. 39; and in "An Extract from the Orders Rules and Counsels for the People of God, Written by Father Joseph to the Elders of the Church at New Lebanon, Copied agreeable to Father Joseph's Word. February 18, 1841," WRHS 79 VIII:B-155, p. 36. Some early codes, like the 1841 Holy Orders, seem to have been tested at New Lebanon and then, somewhat later, sent out to all Believers in the form of the Millennial Laws.

The 1860 version of the Millennial Laws, "Rules and Orders for the Church of Christ's Second Appearance. Established by the Ministry and Elders of the Church. Revised and Reestablished by the Same. New Lebanon New York May 1860," WRHS 3 I:B-52, especially p. 45, was even more stringent and specific. "No Maps, Charts, and pictures or paintings should ever be hung up in the retiring rooms; and no pictures paintings or likenesses, as Dauguerrotypes etc., set in frames or otherwise should ever be kept by Believers. Modest adversisements [*sic*] may be put up in the Trustees Office, when necessary."

12. [Miranda Barber and Polly Reed?] Book of Inspired Visions and Messages, WRHS 87 VIII:C-1, p. 104; and "Holy Laws of Zion," SDL, pp. 5, 13, 27.

13. New Lebanon Ministry to Groveland Ministry, 25 April 1840, "Copies of letters, Begun 1839," WRHS 27 IV:B-9, pp. 41–42.

14. "Holy Laws of Zion," SDL, p. 32; and "Solemn and Sacred Word," WRHS 78 VIII:B-152, p. 82. On durabilty and utility as goal of all products made by Believers, see Jonathan Woods, Edward Fowler, and Giles B. Avery at New Lebanon to Theodore Sedgewick and William Whetter representing the Directors and Secretary of the New York Association for the Exhibition of the Industry of all Nations (at the Crystal Palace), 7 June 1853, WRHS 20 IV:A-40. See also Woods, Fowler, and Avery to the New Lebanon Ministry, 13 June 1853, WRHS 20 IV:A-40, in regard to the above letter.

15. [The spirit of] Mother Hannah to the Harvard Ministry, 25 March 1844, WRHS 19 IV:A-24.

16. "Millennial Laws, or Gospel Statutes and Ordinances, adapted to the Day of Christ's Second Appearing: Given and established in the Church for the protection thereof, by Father Joseph Meacham and Mother Lucy Wright the presiding Ministry, and by their Successors the Ministry and Elders. Recorded at New Lebanon August 7th, 1821. Revised and re-established by the Ministry and Elders. Oct. 1845," WRHS 2 I:B-17, pp. 103–105. Other codes of the New Era were just as specific. See almost identical regulation given at New Lebanon in "Holy Orders of the Church," WRHS 78 VIII:B-154, pp. 43–44.

17. Youngs, "Concise View," WML SA 760, p. 126.

18. Copies and Extracts of Messages, WRHS 75 VIII:B-112, p. 8.

19. "A true Record," vol. 2, WRHS 75 VIII:B-117, p. 52. See also [Barber and Reed?] Book of Inspired Visions and Messages, WRHS 87 VIII:C-1, p. 61. Cf. this position of the Shakers with that of St. Bernard and the Cistercians (noted, for example, in Freedberg, *Power of Images*, p. 301).

20. Some pictures remained, for example, Believers used picture books in teaching children to read. But: "Ye shall not buy picture books, with large, flourished, and extravagant pictures in them; the little primers now in use, have pictures sufficient in them" ("Holy Orders of the Church," WRHS 78 VIII:B-154, p. 26).

21. "Holy Orders of the Church," WRHS 78 VIII:B-154, p. 50.

22. New Lebanon Ministry to Groveland Ministry, 25 April 1840, "Copies of letters, Begun 1839," WRHS 27 IV:B-9, p. 42.

23. Emlen, *Shaker Village Views,* p. 114.

24. Hervey Elkins, *Fifteen Years in the Senior Order of Shakers: A Narration of Facts, Concerning that Singular People* (Hanover, N.H.: Dartmouth Press, 1853; repr., New York: AMS Press Inc., 1973), p. 26; see also p. 29.

25. "Solemn and Sacred Word," WRHS 78 VIII:B-152, pp. 48–50.

The spirits sometimes considered waste to be worse than superfluity, sometimes the reverse. A spirit communication encouraged deacons to "purchase that which is plain, as far as you can, even if the meterial is not quite so good, rather than to get that which is covered with superfluous flowers and pictures" ("A true Record," vol. 2, WRHS 75 VIII:B-117, p. 92). But, when products already owned by Believers were judged superfluous, the ministry sometimes sanctioned continued use of these products to avoid waste. See New Lebanon Ministry to Groveland Ministry, in care of J. Tallcott, 22 July 1842, WRHS 20 IV:A-38. Prohibitions of waste, like prohibitions of superfluity, appear in the earliest Shaker documents.

26. "Holy Laws of Zion," SDL, pp. 87–88. This regulation says nothing about images on paper that were not hung from the walls.

27. "Solemn and Sacred Word," WRHS 78 VIII:B-152, p. 48.

28. "A true Record," vol. 3, WRHS 75 VIII:B-118, p. 2. See also Bennett and

Youngs, "Journal of Inspired Meetings," entry for 16 August 1840, WRHS 77 VIII:B-138.

29. Bennett and Youngs, "Journal of Inspired Meetings," entry for 19 April 1840, WRHS 77 VIII:B-138.

30. See Neil Harris, *The Artist in American Society: The Formative Years, 1790–1860* (New York: G. Braziller, 1966; Chicago: University of Chicago Press, Phoenix Books, 1982), especially pp. 30–36. On page 32, in a chapter titled "The Perils of Vision," Harris notes that for Americans during these years "luxury was a disease of virtue itself." Shakers adapted the category of superfluity from contemporary American culture and infused the terminology with a peculiarly Shaker content. In the 1780s, New Light converts to Shakerism brought with them their own already well formed opposition to superfluity.

31. For relationship of virtue and simplicity to republican form of government, see Halttunen, *Confidence Men,* p. 67.

32. Harris, *Artist in American Society,* p. 33. Shakers, then, resembled other Americans in their need to subordinate art to "higher" aims.

33. Ibid., pp. 30–31. See also Freedberg, *Power of Images,* pp. 25, 63, and 65 on the Western dualistic bias that the material corrupts the spiritual, the senses corrupt the intellect.

34. See Freedberg, *Power of Images,* pp. 318 and 375 for a discussion of "arousal by image." Because of the relationship between form and sensuality Freedberg argues that images are generally subversive in Western culture which, historically, has valued mind over body and the spiritual over the material.

See [Hollister, compiler?], Messages, Songs, and Anthems, WRHS 75 VIII:B-115, p. 199 for New Era testimony against lust and the "nasty," "cursed" flesh.

35. When an image refers to the spiritual, it does so in and through the treatment of physical form. If an image strives to overcome or deny the physical, the very physicality of the material object and its enmeshment in a physical context reminds the beholder of the tension and ambiguity between material and spiritual. As long as religion is ambivalent about the material world, religion will be ambivalent about art. Cf. Samuel Laeuchli, *Religion and Art in Conflict: Introduction to a Cross-Disciplinary Task* (Philadelphia: Fortress Press, 1980).

36. "A true Record," vol. 4, WRHS 75 VIII:B-119, p. 147. On the dangers of private property as a threat to uniformity, see New Lebanon Ministry at Watervliet to the Union Village Ministry, 29 May 1845, "Copies of letters, Begun 1839," WRHS 27 IV:B-9, p. 184; Bennett and Youngs, "Journal of Inspired Meetings," entry for 15 April 1840, WRHS 77 VIII:B-138; "A true Record," vol. 2, WRHS 75 VIII:B-117, pp. 94–99; and "Holy Orders of the Church," WRHS 78 VIII:B-154, pp. 41–43, and 45–47.

37. For a discussion of the relationship between luxury and destructive social divisions in a mid-nineteenth-century American context, see Halttunen, *Confidence Men,* pp. 65–67.

38. For the significance of red as a "fine" color, see Instructions on Wearing Apparel, NYPL 113, i. Shakers used red, especially in prophetic drawings, to signify blood and commitment.

39. Along these lines, Emlen points out that Shaker maps and village views were "intended to be documents, not decorations." Emlen, *Shaker Village Views,* p. 4. Underscoring their nondecorative function, maps like drawings generally were not hung. In fact, Shaker maps frequently assumed odd and irregular shapes which would have made framing or hanging difficult. Instead of displaying their maps, Shakers carefully rolled and stored them, taking them out when someone needed to look at one (p. 27).

40. Volume containing the Word of Holy Wisdom and the Word of God Almighty (1843 and 1844), WRHS 79 VIII:B-170d, pp. 84–85.

41. "A true Record," vol. 1, WRHS 75 VIII:B-116, p. 138.

42. See David Morgan's comments on Shaker images and the "management of desire," in "Response to Sally Promey, 'Shaker Visionary Images: Restoring a Visible Presence'" (Response to Paper delivered at the Chicago Art History Colloquium, Chicago, Ill., 15 May 1991), p. 2.

Not only did gift images offer compensation for the limited number of earthly goods allowed to Shaker individuals, but these spiritual gifts provided a clever way around newly reinforced restrictions on gift-giving within the United Society. See, for example, "Holy Orders of the Church," WRHS 78 VIII:B-154, pp. 26 and 31.

43. "A Closing Roll, from Holy and Eternal Wisdom, Mother Ann, Father William, and Father James, to the Children of Zion," 1843, EBK 12,027, p. 23.

44. Cf. a gift of roses to *smell* when feeling "peevish or cross," Bennett and Youngs, "Journal of Inspired Meetings, entry for 14 November 1840, WRHS 77 VIII:B-138.

45. Copy of "Holy Orders of the Church" (18 February 1841), WRHS 78 VIII:B-154a, p. 37.

46. "Copy of a card of true comfort from Father William for his little one Augustus Blace," 23 March 1842, WRHS 69 VIII:A-69.

47. The inscriptions on or accompanying some images plainly cited the permission of the spirits or described the nature of divine collaboration in the production of the image. See, for example, *A Type of Mother Hannah's Pockethandkerchief* (Pl. V).

48. See "A true Record," vol. 1, WRHS 75 VIII:B-116, pp. 140–43; and "A Short Word of Notice from Father James to Jane Blanchard," EBK 12,113.

49. For a relevant gift message on superfluous earthly treasure in relationship to heavenly treasure see "A true Record of Sacred Communications; Written by Divine Inspiration, By the Mortal Hands of Chosen Instruments; In the Church at New Lebanon," vol. 10 (2 January 1842–2 March 1842), WRHS 76 VIII:B-125, pp. 115–16.

50. Photograph of Peter Foster, "Diagram of the South Part of Shaker Village, Canterbury," 1849, SDL. In the inscription on the map, Foster referred to himself as "the Artist who drew this Diagram."

Although the vocabulary was foreign to the Shakers, this study will occasionally use the words "art" and "artist" in order to distinguish drawings from texts and instruments of images from instruments of other Shaker visionary products and experiences.

51. The early drawings of some Shaker instruments, then, bore a formal and conceptual resemblance to Hasidic micrography. Hasid and Shaker offered a similar solution to a similar problem. In response to somewhat different religious proscriptions, each drew with letters and words to avoid creating images. For an additional Shaker example, see "The Word of God written on a Sheet of Iron, and hung up in the meeting room on the night of the 19th Aug. 1844," WRHS 69 VIII:A-78. W. J. T. Mitchell, "What Is an Image," *New Literary History* 15, no. 3 (1984): 518, discusses writing, generally, as the "translation of speech into a visible code." See Norman L. Kleeblatt and Gerard C. Wertkin, *The Jewish Heritage in American Folk Art* (New York: Universe Books, 1984), pp. 54–55. Also Freedberg, *Power of Images,* pp. 56–59.

52. Curiously, there seems to have been something of an inverse relationship between the number of gift images and the number of village views produced in a Shaker community. If the numbers of surviving documents can be taken as an indicator (a very big "if"), Shakers at New Lebanon and Hancock made many gift images and few village views, while Believers in other communities made more village views and few gift images, see Emlen, *Shaker Village Views,* p. 18.

53. For example, Isaac Youngs ("Concise View," WML SA 760, pp. 164–65) claimed that Believers received "many drawings, signs and figures" in 1843 and in the preceding years. Only a handful of these early pictorial gift messages survive.

54. Ames, "Material Culture as Nonverbal Communication," p. 26, discusses continu-

ity and change as social constants, conservation and innovation as "relative terms rather than fixed measurements."

55. Form is the structure of content; content is communicated in and through form.

56. Garrett, *Spirit Possession,* p. 222.

57. In one spirit communication, Mother Ann repeatedly promised that the "doors and windows of heaven should never again be shut as they had been for some years previous." She went on to say that even after the work of the renewal itself was complete, an angel would take up residence with Believers at New Lebanon and would make known God's will through an instrument. Bennett and Youngs, "Journal of Inspired Meetings," entry for 28 February 1841, Sabbath morning meeting, WRHS 77 VIII:B-138. In another communication, the spirit of an early Shaker leader insisted that she did not know "why the gift of inspiration should be suffered to die away among you, unless you stiffle [*sic*] it." "A Book Containing Mother Hannah's Bequest to her Middle Aged Children in Lovely Vineyard and Pleasant Garden," WRHS 75 VIII:B-102, p. 46.

58. "Holy Orders of God," First Church, New Lebanon, 30 November 1840, WRHS 78 VIII:B-150, pp. 16–17.

3. Production and Regulation of Images

1. See Barber, "Collection of Visionary Scens [*sic*]," EBK 12,316, p. 35; and New Lebanon Ministry to North Union Ministry, 4 January 1839, "Copies of letters, Begun 1833," WRHS 27 IV:B-8, pp. 288–90.

2. [Barber and Reed?] Book of Inspired Visions and Messages, WRHS 87 VIII:C-1, pp. 59–60.

3. Ibid., pp. 6–7; Barber, "Collection of Visionary Scens [*sic*]," EBK 12,316, p. 35; [Wells and Youngs] "Records Kept by Order of the Church," NYPL 7, p. 190. Not only were the official instruments anointed for their task, they were also given special celestial names, they played a part in the designation of other instruments, and they often preceded the ministry on marches to the holy feastgrounds. See Barber, "Collection of Visionary Scens [*sic*]," EBK 12,316, pp. 32–33; [Miranda Barber?] Record of Wisdom's First Visit and Preparations for her Second Visit (1842), WRHS 79 VIII:B-159, pp. 11–12; and "Finding of Mount Sinai," SDL, p. 25.

4. See, for example, Bennett and Youngs, "Journal of Inspired Meetings," entry for 24 December 1841, 8:00 p.m. meeting, WRHS 77 VIII:B-138.

5. In [Stewart], *Sacred Roll and Book,* pp. 370–71, six instruments recounted their experience of God's power at work in them. See also Eunice Bathrick's testimony in Eunice Bathrick, Autobiography and Testimony, WRHS 49 VI:A-5, pp. 27–30. For veiled criticism of the ministry in an early gift message, see [Youngs], "Preface, or Introduction," WRHS 75 VIII:B-109, p. 54–55; and "A true Record," vol. 1, WRHS 75 VIII:B-116, p. 4.

6. Turner, *Ritual Process,* p. 95; see also pp. 94, 102–103, 108, 116–17, 145.

7. "Closing Roll," EBK 12,027, pp. 9–10.

8. See "The Word of Holy and Eternal Wisdom Directed to the beloved Ministry at Wisdom's Valley, to be dealt with according as their wisdom may direct Written by Inspiration, commencing May 3d 1844," WML 454 SA 1092, pp. 38–39.

9. Some official instruments (Semantha Fairbanks, for example) rose in community ranks to become members of the ministry. Once they assumed ministerial responsibility, however, they generally ceased to function as instruments.

10. Turner, *Ritual Process,* pp. 108–11, 128–29.

11. See Freedberg, *Power of Images,* pp. 41–42, and p. 46 on the "aura" of magic and/or divinity associated with image-makers in Western culture. See also Simon J. Bronner on the ability of images to "create" another world, in Bronner, "Visible

Proofs: Material Culture Study in American Folkloristics," in Thomas J. Schlereth, ed., *Material Culture: A Research Guide* (Lawrence: University of Kansas Press, 1985), especially p. 130 where Bronner claims that "objects are tangible references people use to outline the worlds they know, the ones they try to cope with, and those they aspire to or imagine. Arts, crafts, architecture, clothing, and food become markers for the physical and intellectual surroundings with which people identify. Such objects reify intangible, abstract human and spiritual relations in those surroundings."

12. Turner, *Ritual Process,* p. 132. Turner uses this terminology in reference to his "communitas," a model for society that emerges in a liminal period and contrasts with "structure" (pp. 96–97).

13. [Youngs], "Visions Seen by Gibbs and Goff," entry for 31 August 1837, EBK 3270. See also [Youngs], "Preface, or Introduction," WRHS 75 VIII:B-109, p. 35. The degree of Goff's marginality is reiterated in an account which suggests that she was likely sickly as well as young, female, and a member of the gathering order. New Lebanon Ministry to Groveland Ministry, 6 December 1842, "Copies of Letters, begun 1839," WRHS 27 IV:B-9, p. 99 recounts Goff's death on 30 November 1842 of "consumption."

14. Turner, *Ritual Process,* p. 132. In the case of spontaneous charism, charismatic experience was, to a large extent, an end in itself. In the case of normative charism, charismatic experience became a persuasive means to an end. Turner argues that "the spontaneity and immediacy of communitas . . . can seldom be maintained for very long. Communitas itself soon develops a structure, in which free relationships between individuals become converted into norm-governed relationships between social personae." Here "communitas" is an unmediated relationship between concrete individuals, a "direct, immediate, and total confrontation of human identities." Turner continues that "it is the fate of all spontaneous communitas in history to undergo what most people see as a 'decline and fall' into structure and law" (pp. 131–32, also 107 and 128–29).

15. For Turner, charism and liminality are both characteristics of the social "structure" of communitas.

16. Despite attempts to create a structure for the institutionalization of all instruments (see Barber, "Collection of Visionary Scens [*sic*]," EBK 12,316, p. 34 for message designating every Shaker as an instrument who would be called to serve at some particular but unspecified point in time), to a degree, at least, spontaneous liminality continued for some years in the persons of "unofficial" instruments.

17. On girls performing as early instruments at New Lebanon, see Youngs, "Sketches of Visions," WRHS 75 VIII:B-113, pp. 59–60.

18. [Youngs], "Preface, or Introduction," WRHS 75 VIII:B-109, pp. 56–57.

19. Emlen, *Shaker Village Views,* pp. 16–18.

20. Mary C. Black, "American Primitive Watercolors," *Art in America* 51, no. 4 (1963): 81.

21. See, for example, Halttunen, *Confidence Men,* p. 57 on women's "superior sensibility"; Marzio, *The Art Crusade,* p. 9 on women and drawing; and Peter C. Marzio, *The Democratic Art: Pictures of a Nineteenth-Century America, Chromolithography 1840–1900* (Boston: David R. Godine, in association with Amon Carter Museum of Western Art, Fort Worth, 1979), p. 125 on the nineteenth-century association of art with things feminine.

22. See "A Book of Records, kept by Order of the Deacons, or Trustees of the Church at New Lebanon," WRHS 3 I:B-30, pp. 47–57. "A true Record," vol. 8, WRHS 76 VIII:B-123, p. 7, claims that all of the instruments were gathered into Zion in the days of their childhood and therefore had "unstained hands and hearts." This was the official position, even if it was not true in every case.

23. See Miranda Barber at New Lebanon to Isaac Newton Youngs at New Lebanon, 14 August 1833, WRHS 20 IV:A-36.

24. Beginning around 1808, probably because of the larger numbers of children entering their communities, Shakers reversed their earlier neglect of, and even hostility toward, education (cf. Garrett, *Spirit Possession*, pp. 198–99, 235). In 1817, the United Society established a "public school" at the Church Order, New Lebanon. In 1821, Shaker Seth Y. Wells, who had experience as a teacher in the non-Shaker public schools of the surrounding region, was appointed superintendent of the Shaker school. Shaker records document the expenditure of public money on materials and equipment for these schools and the participation of Wells and others in the public administration of this "Shaker" institution. For a brief secondary source summary of this history see Andrews, *People Called Shakers*, pp. 186–94.

25. See White and Taylor, *Shakerism, Its Meaning and Message*, pp. 156–57; and "A Record of a Visit made by the Ministry at the City of Peace, to Holy Mount June 23rd 1849," WML 153 SA 790. In 1869 Polly Reed was elected to the parent ministry.

26. The association between image-makers and schools held for the mostly male producers of maps and village views as for the mostly female producers of gift images. See Emlen, *Shaker Village Views*, p. 18.

27. Seth Wells to Elders, Deacons, and Trustees of the United Society, 1 October 1844, WRHS 20 IV:A-38, p. 2.

28. M. Barber to I. Youngs, 14 August 1833, WRHS 20 IV:A-36; and "The Holy Orders of the Church" (18 February 1841), WRHS 78 VIII:B-154, pp. 26–27. The Holy Orders also encouraged teachers to discard extravagantly illustrated picture books.

29. One New Era document contains a writing specimen from fourteen-year-old Polly Reed at New Lebanon to Isaac Newton Youngs at New Lebanon, 7 September 1832, WRHS 20 IV:A-36. It is likely that Polly Reed was the instrument of many images. See, for example, "A Star of Approbation," to Eliza Ann Taylor, 1 January 1845, WRHS 87 VIII:C-2.

30. Nancy F. Cott, *The Bonds of Womanhood: "Woman's Sphere" in New England, 1780–1835* (New Haven: Yale University Press, 1977), p. 101.

31. The border of a map of the state of New York, made by young Eliza Maria Manning in 1853, is almost identical to the borders on many gift images. This close visual similarity likely demonstrates the influence of Sarah Bates, teacher and instrument of drawings. See Eliza Maria Manning, "New York the Empire State," WRHS 121 XIV:12. See also maps made in 1829 by J. C. Buckingham (probably Joseph Chapman Buckingham, Jr., 1797–1880, the brother of Watervliet instrument David Austin Buckingham, 1803–1885, both of whom were sons of Joseph Chapman Buckingham, Sr., 1761–1832), WRHS 121 XIV:12; and numerous maps, mostly from 1852, penned by pupils, ibid.

32. "School Instructions. A short Communication from Mother Ann concerning the Instruction of Children in School, principally designed for the School Teachers in Zion. Given by Inspiration in the Church of the Society at Holy Mount, in New Lebanon, November 22nd 1840, and written the 23rd," WRHS 78 VIII:B-145, p. 23. See also "School Record for District No. 12. Town of New Lebanon," entry for 9 May 1839, WRHS 3 I:B-32.

33. "School Instructions," WRHS 78 VIII:B-145, p. 24.

34. For a mid-nineteenth century description and sketch of a Shaker type board see ibid., p. 25. Teachers drilled pupils on the letters of the alphabet using these wooden boards approximately seven inches wide and eighteen inches long. Thin strips of wood placed at even intervals across the boards created lines and spaces. Letters painted on "small wooden types" could be moved from one space to another in the course of a classroom exercise. In addition, Believers mounted alphabet boards on the front walls of their schoolrooms. In contrast to the smaller type boards, alphabet boards

consisted of a single, large, flat expanse of wood, painted white, with the letters of the alphabet inscribed in high contrast black. As early as 1825, teachers at the New Lebanon school used an alphabet board to teach reading and writing. A board, dated 1825, from the New Lebanon school was included in the recent exhibit on Shaker design at the Whitney. See Sprigg, *Shaker Design,* p. 216.

35. Seth Wells at New Lebanon to James Prescott at North Union, 15 November 1845, WRHS 20 IV:A-39.

36. It is probable that expert calligrapher and instrument Polly Reed, a pupil and then a colleague of Sarah Bates, penned some rewards of merit as well. The earliest extant reward of merit is dated 1843 (WRHS 121 XIV 15); similar extant gift drawings bear dates between 1842 and 1843. Mutual influence is thus likely.

37. Cf. the "Werkzeuge" of the Community of True Inspiration, with which community in America the Shakers established some contact.

38. "A true Record," vol. 1, WRHS 75 VIII:B-116, p. 3.

39. Hannah Cohoon, at Hancock, clearly stated her own involvement with visionary images.

40. See, for example, "A General Statement of the Holy Laws of Zion," SDL, p. 54; "A Closing Roll," EBK 12,027, p. 10; Canterbury's Record, EBK 12,787, pp. 13–20; "A true Record," vol. 2, WRHS 75 VIII:B-117, p. 64; "A true Record," vol. 11, WRHS 76 VIII:B-126, p. 17; Bennett and Youngs, "Journal of Inspired Meetings," entry titled "Review of 1840," WRHS 77 VIII:B-138; and Communication from Father James on Recording Celestial Messages, 27 February 1841, WRHS 65 VIII:A-20.

41. Cf. more general regulations concerning private property, initialing belongings, etc., "Holy Orders of the Church," WRHS 78 VIII:B-154, pp. 46–47.

42. See Stein, "Winslow Homer in Context," p. 76, for a discussion of such issues in relationship to the "new art history."

43. Several of the images known as Sacred Sheets identify two women, Semantha Fairbanks and Mary Wicks, as instruments of each image, see, for example, fig. 17 of this book; and "A Sacred Sheet sent from Holy Mother Wisdom by her Holy Angel of many signs, for Sister Asenath Clark" received 9 March 1843 and written 21 March 1843, National Gallery of Art, Washington, D.C. (hereafter NGA), 1971.83.26.

While one New Era text separates the "prophets" or instruments as those who see and speak from the "scribes" as those who witness and write suggesting that some image-makers may have been scribes rather than instruments, as a general rule this seems unlikely. Barber, "Collection of Visionary Scens [*sic*]," EBK 12,316, pp. 32–34, lists Miranda Barber as an instrument and Polly Reed as a scribe but both produced images. If the instruments "saw" and the scribes witnessed in paint, instruments and scribes (both divinely anointed and ordained) would have worked together to produce a visionary image. But the same text which separates and defines instruments and scribes also requires that the names of both be affixed to gifts and to records, and no images include the names of both instrument and scribe (though Hannah Cohoon notes that she both "saw" and "painted" her images). In most cases, too, manuscript evidence demonstrates that known image-makers were also known instruments. And in all cases, the images represent the visionary experience of an instrument.

44. Garrett, *Spirit Possession,* pp. 4–5; see also pp. 10, 12, 21, 25, 44, and 95.

45. Benjamin S. Youngs, Copy of an Article from the *New York Journal of Commerce,* 3 July 1839, WRHS 24 IV:A-71.

46. Daniel W. Patterson, *The Shaker Spiritual* (Princeton: Princeton University Press, 1979), p. 322.

47. Bishop, "Daily Journal begun 1839," entry for 11 September 1846, NYPL 2, p. 274, also entry for 12 September 1846. The keeper of a "Domestic Journal of Important Occurrences," entry for 11 September 1846, WRHS 32 V:B-61, called this apostasy "an astonishing and awful event."

48. Barber, "Collection of Visionary Scens [*sic*]," EBK 12,316, pp. 32–33. For other relevant material see "Domestic Journal of Important Occurrences," entries for 24 August 1846 and 22 August 1851, WRHS 32 V:B-61. In the latter entry, Derobigne Bennett and Mary Wicks return as husband and wife to visit New Lebanon. Believers attached to the back cover of Bennett and Youngs, "Journal of Inspired Meetings," WRHS 77 VIII:B-138, three pages by Shaker M. C. [Mary Catherine?] Allen examining Derobigne Bennett's character and activities prior to and after leaving the Shakers.

49. See Michael B. Taylor, "'Try the Spirits': Shaker Response to Spiritualism," *Journal of Religious Studies* 7 (Fall 1979): 30–38 on the case of Richard McNemar. McNemar's connections with the "Christian" movement and with the Churches of Christ have been documented elsewhere. See, for example, Hughes and Allen, *Illusions of Innocence,* pp. 103, 104, 110–11, 114, 119.

50. New Lebanon Ministry to the Union Village Ministry, 23 February 1839, "Copies of letters, Begun 1833," WRHS 27 IV:B-8, p. 309. See also "Divine Inspiration containing explanations," WRHS 78 VIII:B-143, section III, paragraphs 31–36; Ebenezer Bishop, "Farewell Address of Elder Ebenezer Bishop, of New Lebanon, to the inhabitants of Zion. Written at Holy Mount, December 29, 1842" (Canterbury, N.H.: United Society of Shakers, 1850), EBK 13,341, p. 12; and "A true Record," vol. 7, WRHS 76 VIII:B-122, pp. 192–93.

51. See also Bennett and Youngs, "Journal of Inspired Meetings," entry for 5 April 1840, WRHS 77 VIII:B-138; and "A true Record," vol. 2, WRHS 75 VIII:B-117, p. 62.

52. "A true Record, vol. 1, WRHS 75 VIII:B-116, p. 72.

53. Bennett and Youngs, "Journal of Inspired Meetings," entry for 5 April 1840, WRHS 77 VIII:B-138.

54. Communication of 22 March 1840 at the conclusion of a Journal of the Travels made by the Harvard Ministry to other Shaker Communities, WRHS 30 V:B-37, n.p.

55. Ibid.

56. "Closing Roll," EBK 12,027, p. 10.

57. E. Bishop, "Farewell Address," EBK 13,341, p. 9.

58. New Lebanon Ministry at Watervliet to Pleasant Hill Ministry, 6 November 1839, "Copies of letters, Begun 1839," WRHS 27 IV:B-9, p. 16.

59. Frederick W. Evans, *Autobiography of a Shaker and Revelation of the Apocalypse* (New York: American News Company, 1869), p. 60. Gideon Cole was another Believer "converted" "out of heresy" by the spiritual manifestations of the New Era. See Youngs, "Sketches of Visions," entries for 13 and 24 February 1838, WRHS 75 VIII:B-113, pp. 14 and 16.

60. This was not the first, though certainly the most spectacular, appearance of spiritual gifts among Believers. See Garrett, *Spirit Possession,* p. 238, for comments on the reception of spiritual gifts in 1796 following the death of Joseph Meacham and in 1808 accompanying the beginning of the process of deification of Ann Lee.

61. Blinn later maintained that the Era was genuine precisely because it began with the children. See Blinn, *Spiritualism,* pp. 21–22.

62. Bishop, "Daily Journal; Begun 1830," entry for 8 October 1837, NYPL 1.

63. Giles B. Avery, "A Journal of Times, Rhymes, Work, and weather, Very much mixed up together. Commenced February 11th, 1836," entry for 29 December 1837, WRHS 34 V:B-106; and New Lebanon Ministry to Elder Brother Joseph Hodgson at Watervliet, 20 November 1837, "Copies of letters, Begun 1833," WRHS 27 IV:B-8, pp. 219–21.

64. Youngs, "Sketches of Visions," WRHS 75 VIII:B-113, pp. 6–7. During his visit to New Lebanon, Elder Brother Joseph Hodgson introduced a "new manner of labor" that had been taught to Ann Mariah Goff in the spirit world. See [Wells and Youngs], "Records Kept by Order of the Church," entry for 2 December 1837, NYPL 7, p. 140.

65. Daniel Boler at New Lebanon to Isaac Newton Youngs at Watervliet, 12 December 1837, WRHS 20 IV:A-37. Daniel Boler was an elder in the First Order at New Lebanon when he wrote this letter.

66. Avery, "Journal of Times," entries for 1 January 1838 and 7 January 1838, WRHS 34 V:B-106.

67. Youngs, "Sketches of Visions," entry for 6 February 1838, WRHS 75 VIII:B-113, p. 11. This entry reads "Sarah Bates and others were at Hancock today and heard considerable of the visions there. Elizabeth Oaks there has seen considerable." Sarah Bates, of the First Order, New Lebanon, was to become an instrument of gift images.

68. Ibid., entries for January–March 1838, pp. 7–20.

69. "A true Record," vol. 1, WRHS 75 VIII:B-116, p. 2; see also p. 4.

70. [Youngs], "Preface, or Introduction," WRHS 75 VIII:B-109, p. 35.

71. Ibid., p. 55.

72. Ibid., p. 28. See also Youngs, "Concise View," WML SA 760, pp. 109–11; and [Youngs], "Preface, or Introduction," WRHS 75 VIII:B-109, p. 28.

73. [Wells and Youngs], "Records Kept by Order of the Church," entry for March/April 1840, NYPL 7, p. 178. See also WRHS 75 VIII:B-109, p. 21, for the scribe's claim that "It was plainly shown that Believers had fallen back from their former rectitude; that the Church order had been greatly trampled upon, and the life and spirit of the gospel in a great measure lost."

74. The phrase "Millennial Church" suggests some tension as well.

75. [Youngs], "Preface, or Introduction," WRHS 75 VIII:B-109, p. 55.

76. Ibid., pp. 23–24.

77. Cf. Brewer, *Shaker Communities,* p. 122, on the "redirection" of the revival in 1838.

78. During Mother's Work, Shakers appealed to early Shakerism more often than to early Christianity but Shakers also noted the "degeneracy of primitive christianity," with "primitive christianity" representing the third dispensational model for their own fourth dispensational times. [Youngs], "Preface, or Introduction," WRHS 75 VIII:B-109, p. 59.

79. Among the Shakers, the gifts of Mother's Work reiterated the sacramental character of authority; those who constituted the "visible lead" functioned as visible signs of an invisible and divine grace and presence.

80. Record of Spiritual Gifts, entry for 4 July 1841, WRHS 72 VIII:B-52, p. 6.

81. Blinn, *Spiritualism,* pp. 49–50. See also J. P. MacLean, "Spiritualism Among the Shakers of Union Village, Ohio," *Shakers of Ohio* (Columbus: F. J. Heer Printing Company, 1907; repr., Philadelphia: Porcupine Press, Inc., 1975), pp. 391–94.

82. New Lebanon Ministry to Pleasant Hill Ministry, 4 December 1837, "Copies of letters, Begun 1833," WRHS 27 IV:B-8, p. 221. Grove Wright was a member of the ministry at Hancock.

83. Ibid., p. 228.

84. Record of Spiritual Gifts, entries for 6 July and 4 August 1839, WRHS 72 VIII:B-52, pp. 2–3.

85. See, for example, "Holy Laws of Zion," SDL and WRHS 77 VIII:B-140; "Holy Orders of God," WRHS 78 VIII:B-150, especially p. 14; and "A true Record," especially vol. 11, WRHS 76 VIII:B-126, pp. 9–11.

The separation of Believers from the world (and their simultaneous unification with one another) was a second major theme of these codes.

86. Institutionalizing tendencies represented a response to this crisis of authority as charismatic tendencies represented a response to the crisis of remoteness.

87. Halttunen, *Confidence Men,* pp. 21 and 25. On a "general crisis in *religious* authority" (italics added) in America as a result of democratizing tendencies, see Philip L. Bar-

low, "Before Mormonism: Joseph Smith's Use of the Bible 1820–1829," *Journal of the American Academy of Religion* LVII (Winter 1989): 743–44.

88. See Brewer, *Shaker Communities,* p. 47 for her reflections on the impact of the rise in the adult apostasy rate upon the Shaker leadership pool.

89. Barlow, "Before Mormonism," p. 744.

90. [Wells and Youngs], "Records Kept by Order of the Church," entry for November 1842, NYPL 7, pp. 200–201; see also entry titled "Review of 1843," p. 219.

91. "Holy Orders of God," WRHS 78 VIII:B-150, pp. 17–18. See also "Solemn and Sacred Word," WRHS 78 VIII:B-152, p. 36 on the character of members of the ministry.

92. "Holy Orders of God," WRHS 78 VIII:B-150, p. 17.

93. Elkins, *Fifteen Years,* pp. 126–27.

94. Record of Visions and Celestial Messages, Beginning 1 April 1840, WRHS 65 VIII:A-24, pp. 10–17; and "A Little Book of the Holy Word of God Written in Three Parts," Watervliet Church Family, 6 January 1843, WRHS 69 VIII:A-73, pp. 8–9.

95. "A Sacred Covenant of our Heavenly Parents Sent forth upon Earth to their children at the close of their late Manifestation for the purification of Zion and the Inhabitants thereof: Given by Inspiration in the Church of the Holy Mount of God at New Lebanon, December 31st 1841," WRHS 79 VIII:B-164, pp. 16–37.

96. "Solemn and Sacred Word," WRHS 78 VIII:B-152, p. 65.

97. Ibid., pp. 65–66. In practice, this was perhaps less severe than it sounds. "Eventually" left quite a bit of leeway. And, for the most part, Shakers left enforcement to God.

98. "A true Record," vol. 1, WRHS 75 VIII:B-116, p. 56. See also first official message of 22 April 1838 on spirits coming to help the ministry in Copies and Extracts of Messages, WRHS 75 VIII:B-112, p. 2.

99. New Lebanon Ministry to North Union Ministry, 4 January 1839, "Copies of letters, Begun 1833," WRHS 27 IV:B-8, p. 291.

100. "Divine Inspiration containing Explanations," WRHS 78 VIII:B-143, section II, paragraph 13, n.p. On the appropriate distribution of attention with regard to instrument and gift, see New Lebanon Ministry to South Union Ministry, 7 January 1839, "Copies of letters, Begun 1833," WRHS 27 IV:B-8, p. 303. See also New Lebanon Ministry to North Union Ministry, 4 January 1839, ibid., p. 291; and New Lebanon Ministry at Watervliet to Enfield, N.H. Ministry, 28 April 1837, ibid., p. 196.

101. Representative of New Lebanon Community to New Lebanon Ministry at Enfield, N.H., 8 November 1837, "Copies of letters, Begun 1833," WRHS 27 IV:B-8, p. 218.

102. New Lebanon Ministry to Sodus Elders, 19 December 1837, ibid., p. 233. See also ibid., p. 232; and New Lebanon Ministry to New Hampshire Ministry, 3 February 1836, ibid., p. 116.

103. [Youngs], "Preface, or Introduction," WRHS 75 VIII:B-109, pp. 52–53. The admonition to "try the spirits" placed attention on the gift rather than on the instrument.

Disputes about spiritual gifts and enthusiasm were not unique to Shakers. Others (e.g., John Wesley, Jonathan Edwards, Separate and Baptist leaders like Isaac Backus) also looked to I John 4:1 for guidance on "trying the spirits." See Garrett, *Spirit Possession,* pp. 78–79, 117–18, 133–34. Different individuals and groups applied slightly different tests of validity.

104. New Lebanon Ministry at Watervliet to Harvard Ministry, 21 February 1838, "Copies of letters, Begun 1833," WRHS 27 IV:B-8, p. 237. See Youngs, "Concise View," WML SA 760, p. 105 on efforts to "prevent those gifts from tending to wildness."

105. See, for example, New Lebanon Ministry at Watervliet to Sodus Elders, 11 January 1836, "Copies of letters, Begun 1833," WRHS 27 IV:B-8, pp. 99–101; New Lebanon Ministry at Watervliet to Harvard Ministry, 21 February 1838, ibid., p. 236; New Lebanon Ministry to Harvard Ministry 7 December 1838, ibid., pp. 283–85; New Lebanon Ministry to North Union Ministry, 4 January 1839, ibid., pp. 285–94;

New Lebanon Ministry to Union Village Ministry, 9 January 1839, ibid., pp. 295–99; New Lebanon Ministry to South Union Ministry, 12 August 1839, "Copies of Letters, Begun 1839," WRHS 27 IV:B-9, p. 5; and New Lebanon Ministry at Watervliet to Pleasant Hill Ministry, 6 November 1839, ibid., p. 15.

106. New Lebanon Ministry to Union Village Ministry, 17 November 1841, "Copies of letters, Begun 1839," WRHS 27 IV:B-9, p. 73. See also New Lebanon Ministry to Union Village Ministry, 11 July 1840, ibid., pp. 42–44; "A true Record," vol. 3, WRHS 75 VIII:B-118, p. 13; and "Divine Inspiration containing Explanations," WRHS 78 VIII:B-143, especially section III, paragraphs 29–30, n.p. The "Wisdom" referred to, of course, was Holy Mother Wisdom.

107. For example, Isaac Newton Youngs and some of the Watervliet Elders recorded the first New Era visions and communications at Watervliet. See Bishop, "Daily Journal, Begun 1830," entry for 23 October 1837, NYPL 1; Daniel Boler at New Lebanon to Isaac Youngs visiting at Watervliet, 12 December 1837, WRHS 20 IV:A-37; and New Lebanon Ministry to North Union Ministry, 4 January 1839, "Copies of letters, Begun 1833," WRHS 27 IV:B-8, p. 287.

108. The original message containing this requirement was given on 27 February 1841 ("A true Record," vol. 11, WRHS 76 VIII:B-126, pp. 7–25). Scribes copied and sent a version of this message to all Shaker Societies (Communication on Recording Celestial Messages, 27 February 1841, WRHS 65 VIII:A-20). See also [Youngs], "Preface, or Introduction," WRHS 75 VIII:B-109, pp. 25 and 30; and Canterbury's Record, EBK 12,787.

A "Confidential" note in a letter from New Lebanon to Union Village, 16 March 1841, "Copies of letters, Begun 1839," WRHS 27 IV:B-9, p. 57, set forth new requirements for annual visits to New Lebanon (or to the western lead at Union Village for those in that region) by "at least one of each lot of Ministry in the house of Israel" (p. 61). See also "Solemn and Sacred Word," WRHS 78 VIII:B-152, p. 87. The spirits also asked that all instruments formally declare their complete faith in the celestial messages they transmitted. See, for example, Canterbury's Record, EBK 12,787, p. 19; and "A true Record," vol. 11, WRHS 76 VIII:B-126, pp. 23–25.

109. Believers also recorded celestial visions and messages that they and their successors might better understand and remember the work of God in the New Era. See [Wells and Youngs], "Records Kept by Order of the Church," general remarks by Youngs and entries for 1 January 1840 and 31 March 1841, NYPL 7, pp. 157, 176–77, 182–83.

110. Seth Wells was particularly concerned with internal, historical, and scriptural consistency in gift messages. See Seth Y. Wells at New Lebanon to the Harvard and Shirley Ministry and Elders, 12 November 1842, WRHS 20 IV:A-38, especially p. 1. This letter was recast as a bulletin and sent to all the societies. See Seth Y. Wells, "Remarks upon inspired Writings," WRHS 80 VIII:B-173.

111. New Lebanon Ministry to Union Village Ministry, 17 November 1841, "Copies of letters, Begun 1839," WRHS 27 IV:B-9, p. 72. See Marini, *Radical Sects,* p. 132 on required visits to New Lebanon in the 1790s.

112. See "A true Record," vol. 11, WRHS 76 VIII:B-126, pp. 17–18.

4. Ethics and Aesthetics

1. See, for example, Linda Seidel, " 'Jan van Eyck's Arnolfini Portrait': Business as Usual?," *Critical Inquiry* 16 (Fall 1989): 54–86.

2. Seeking "an alternative to ahistoricality," Samuel S. Hill, Jr., coined the term "compression" as "a means of refining the category of 'ahistorical' on which Mircea Eliade, Sidney Mead, and Richard Hughes have relied." Hill, "Comparing Three Approaches to Restorationism: A Response," in Hughes, ed., *The American Quest for the Primitive Church,* p. 233. For Hill, "compression" refers to the drawing together of

heaven and earth and has both "horizontal" and "vertical" expressions (pp. 233–35), where horizontal and vertical bear some relationship to my temporal (Part III) and spatial (Part II) division of the content of gift Shaker religious images.

My spatial/temporal division is an arbitrary device employed in the service of analysis. To Shakers, of course, Mother Ann and the early Elders were, by 1840, both the inhabitants of heaven and the heroes of a glorious and meaningful past.

3. [Bates], *Holy Wisdom's Book,* pp. 220–21.

4. "Explanation of the Holy City, with its various parts and appendixes pointed out. Drawn and partly written March 16th, 1843. [Completed March 21]," PMA 63-160-5a, pp. 5–8, and 16. The map of the Holy City is numbered PMA 63-160-5.

5. The consistent direction of the numbering on the central section of the map establishes that Shakers intended the map to hang vertically, with dowels at top and bottom, rather than to be read horizontally, with dowels at the sides as a scroll. Shaker maps and village views were frequently oriented other than conventionally (i.e., with north at the top) and the Holy City map was, in this sense, no exception. Cf. Emlen, *Shaker Village Views,* pp. 56–57.

6. While the Millennial Laws forbade the hanging of maps as well as pictures and paintings in most parts of the community, Shaker legal codes were less specific about the use of maps in Shaker schools. The unglazed, wooden dowel format was relatively common in "secular" maps used by Shakers for educational purposes. A photo of a school library cupboard from the 1974 Renwick exhibition notes that the features of the cupboard include "two pegs at the top from which maps or charts were hung" (*Shaker: Furniture and Objects,* exhibit catalogue photo No. 5, p. 52). Hervey Elkins, who taught in the Shaker school at Enfield, New Hampshire, described the environment in which he taught: "The books were choice; and globes, celestial and terrestial, maps and diagrams adorned the apartment" (Elkins, *Fifteen Years,* p. 77). Nonetheless, many Shaker maps were intended to be read while laid out on flat surfaces and there is no evidence that even those which were hung had glass in front of them. See Emlen, *Shaker Village Views,* pp. 56–57.

7. For insight into the New Era understanding of Adam and Eve, see [Bates], *Holy Wisdom's Book,* pp. 601–622, esp. p. 621; and Volume Containing the Word of Holy Wisdom and the Word of God Almighty (1843–44), typescript copy produced by NYPL (1904–05), WRHS 79 VIII:B-170C, pp. 6–8.

8. For a discussion of Shaker dispensationalism, see ch. 6.

9. New Lebanon Ministry to Harvard Ministry, 22 March 1843, "Copies of letters, begun 1839," WRHS 27 IV:B-9, p. 115.

10. Especially Revelation 21 and 22.

11. "A true Record," vol. 2, WRHS 75 VIII:B-117, pp. 132–33; and "Book of Wisdom and Sacred Truth," WRHS 78 VIII:B-153, p. 15. The journey visions of the early instruments of Mother's Work encouraged the spread of Holy City imagery in Shaker imagination. See [Isaac Newton Youngs], "Visions Seen by Elleyett Gibbs and Ann Mariah Goff," entries for Goff, 1 and 2 December 1837, and Gibbs, 2 and 3 December 1837, EBK 3270, n.p.

The development of an elaborate spiritual geography supported the identity of the Shaker Zion with the New Jerusalem. Information included in the index to the Holy City map not only established New Lebanon as the Holy City but also identified the land occupied by the Shakers at Groveland as the site of Adam's creation and the "valley at Watervliet" as the Garden of Eden. "Explanation," PMA 63-160-5a, pp. 56–60.

12. For Mormons, as for Shakers, the City of Zion linked heaven and earth, the former times and the latter days. Shakers patterned their earthly Zion after a heavenly original. For Mormons the connection was less figurative: the "city literally would descend from heaven itself," as the New Jerusalem on earth, the "center of the millennial kingdom." Hughes and Allen, *Illusions of Innocence,* pp. 147–48.

13. "Explanation," PMA 63-160-5a, pp. 19–20.

14. Ibid., pp. 20–21.

15. Garrett, *Spirit Possession,* p. 227.

16. This idea of a "primitive pattern" to which faithful churches ought to conform had seen earlier expression on the North American continent, particularly in the thought of Puritan John Cotton. See Hughes and Allen, *Illusions of Innocence,* pp. 40, 46, 57–59, 96, and 100. Later, Henry Ward Beecher would describe the Protestant minister as "pattern man," Milton C. Sernett, "Behold the American Cleric: The Protestant Minister as 'Pattern Man,' 1850–1900," *Winterthur Portfolio* 8 (1973).

17. "Mother Hannah's Bequest," WRHS 75 VIII:B-102, p. 11; and "The Youth's Guide in Zion, and Holy Mother's Promises," Mother's Work Series No. 1 (Canterbury, N.H.: United Society, 1842; repr., n.p.: United Society, 1974), p. 13. Cf. p. 16. The notion of order as "heaven's first law" did not originate with Shakers. The Shakers, however, refashioned and promoted this idea (elsewhere attributed to Alexander Pope) as though it were their own. See *Roget's International Thesaurus,* 4th ed., revised by Robert L. Chapman (New York: Harper and Row, 1977): 59.1.

18. "A true Record," vol. 4, WRHS 75 VIII:B-119, p. 153.

19. "A true Record of Sacred Communications; Written by Divine Inspiration, By the Mortal Hands of Chosen Instruments; In the Church at New Lebanon," vol. 5 (17 February 1841–11 March 1841), WRHS 75 VIII:B-120, p. 5. See also "Solemn and Sacred Word," WRHS 78 VIII:B152, p. 85.

20. While Shakers offered their own variation on the theme, the notion that the universe was engaged in a struggle between order and chaos was certainly not peculiar to them. In New England in the early and mid-nineteenth century, Federalist perceptions (which outlived the Federalist party by several decades at least) supported this sense of universal division and duality. Washington Allston (1779–1843), who continued to paint images influenced by his Federalist American vision into the early 40s, in the 1830s diagrammed the "Ideas of the Deity and Sin." His diagram, in both form and content, strongly resembles similar dualistic graphics in Shaker theological and doctrinal manuscripts. See David Bjelajac, *Millennial Desire and the Apocalyptic Vision of Washington Allston* (Washington, D.C.: Smithsonian Institution Press, 1988), p. 92 for diagram, pp. 165–66 for discussion. See also Peter Dobkin Hall, *The Organization of American Culture 1700–1900: Private Interests, Elites, and the Origins of American Nationality* (New York: New York University Press, 1982).

21. Lawrence Foster has pointed out that three different mid-nineteenth-century religious societies, Mormons, Oneidans, and Shakers, formed three very different constellations of sexual practice based on different interpretations of this single passage. Foster, *Religion and Sexuality.*

22. Heavenly order was of two varieties. There was, first, the celestial order that was similar in appearance to regenerate earthly order. This was an order in which everything had its divinely ordained place and shape. Then there was an ultimate celestial order, an order of the highest heavens, an order so fundamental that it required no conscious bounds. This order was total freedom made possible by the pervasiveness of the underlying divine pattern. Dolores Hayden's *Seven American Utopias* (Cambridge, Mass.: MIT Press, 1976), pp. 64–103, encouraged me to consider Shaker arrangement and division of space. But her schema contrasts ordered (regenerate) earthly space with disordered heavenly space (what I call ultimate celestial order) and therefore fails to capture the complexity of the Shaker spatial system. My chapter focuses on heavenly order because of its greater impact on gift images and visual order in Shaker society.

23. "Youth's Guide," p. 13.

24. Calvin Green, "Discourses on various subjects calculated to illustrate the existence,

omnipotence, wisdom and justice of the Great first Cause, and the united and correspendent [*sic*] relation of all his works," LC Container 6, Item 76, p. 35.

25. "A true Record," vol. 8, WRHS 76 VIII:B-123, pp. 99–100. Mother's Work instituted a vigorous campaign to dispel disorder among Shakers, "A true Record," vol. 2, WRHS 75 VIII:B-117, pp. 92, and 110–11.

26. [Bates], *Holy Wisdom's Book,* p. 86. See also p. 161. Because likeness was figurative, instruments cautioned Believers to interpret prophetic fulfillment spiritually and expressively rather than literally. See "Mother Hannah's Bequest," WRHS 75 VIII:B-102, pp. 26–29.

27. Seth Y. Wells at New Lebanon to William Leonard at Harvard, October 1834, WRHS 20 IV:A-36.

28. New Lebanon Ministry at Watervliet to New Lebanon Elders, 8 March 1842, "Copies of letters, Begun 1839," WRHS 27 IV:B-9, p. 81.

29. Cf. Suzanne Youngerman, " 'Shaking Is No Foolish Play': An Anthropological Perspective on the American Shakers—Persons, Time, Space, and Dance Ritual" (Ph.D. diss., Columbia University, 1983), pp. 387–88, on Shaker ritual.

30. Book of Prophetic Drawings, WRHS 87 VIII:C-6, n.p.

31. The divine original here, the one whose "likeness" suggested the pattern for Believers, was, alternately, "Almighty God the Father" and "Holy Mother Wisdom." The Shaker sense of "likeness" thus drew upon and reflected both masculine and feminine aspects of godhead. Cf. "A Collection of Sacred Writings at the Second Family New Lebanon," SDL, p. 47 and "Holy Mother Wisdom's Warning and Seal, Unto her people who she has marked in their foreheads with the name of Almighty God," NYPL 38, n.p.

32. Freedberg, *Power of Images,* pp. 161–64, 174, and 179.

33. "Remarks," WRHS 56 VII:B-66A, p. 22.

34. Ibid.

35. Ibid., p. 21.

36. Ibid., pp. 22–23.

37. If, as Webster notes, physical symmetry is characterized by a correspondence in size, shape, and position of opposite parts then theological symmetry exists when such a balance of parts or persons is established in the concept of deity. *Webster's New World Dictionary of the American Language,* 2d college edition (1970), s.v. "symmetry."

38. [Bates], *Holy Wisdom's Book,* p. 505. For an excellent discussion of this sort of theological symmetry, see Marini, *Radical Sects,* pp. 148–53.

39. See *Millennial Praises, Containing a Collection of Gospel Hymns, in Four Parts; Adapted to the Day of Christ's Second Appearing* (Hancock, Mass.: Josiah Tallcott, Jr., 1813), section V, pp. 16–17; and David Benedict, *A History of All Religions* (Providence: John Miller, 1824), p. 262; see also p. 263.

40. "A true Record," vol. 7, WRHS 76 VIII:B-122, p. 140.

41. [Miranda Barber?], Record of Holy Mother Wisdom's First Visitation and Preparations for her Second Visitation, 1842, WRHS 79 VIII:B-159, p. 92.

42. Appendix of "A true Record," copy 2, vol. 11, WRHS 77 VIII:B-137, pp. 176–77. In many of the same documents, however, Believers qualified Wisdom's role to some extent. Holy Mother Wisdom was indeed one with Almighty Power. Like God the Father, she was omniscient. But she also assumed more culturally feminine roles, becoming the Father's witness, the mediator through whom the Father sent messages to earth, and an intercessor for humans before the Father. In terms of her official status during Mother's work and her impact on visual symmetry in gift drawings, however, Holy Mother Wisdom assumed a role equal and parallel to Almighty Power. In the images, perhaps even more emphatically than the texts, Holy Mother Wisdom emerges as the equal of God the Father.

43. In fact, they established and justified their concept of a dual God, male and female according to the ideal of likeness.

44. "Solemn and Sacred Word," WRHS 78 VIII:B-152, p. 83.

45. "The Prince and the Princess of Peace" (n.d.), WRHS 116 X:A-2(P). This Christmas poem also referred to Jesus and Ann Lee as the "Christ and Christess."

46. [Bates], *Holy Wisdom's Book,* editorial note at bottom of p. 689.

There were different ways of expressing the parallelism of Ann Lee and Jesus Christ. William Leonard wrote to Hervey Eads in defense of Frederick Evans' formulation on the "preexistence of Christ and the mediumship of Jesus." According to Leonard's apologia, Evans claimed that Jesus and Ann were both mediums of the Christ. "Jesus is not the Christ but a Medium, like our Mother Ann" (William Leonard of Harvard to Hervey Eads of South Union, n.d., WRHS 18 IV:A-21). This letter was probably written ca. 1850–55 judging from the knowledge of and interest in spiritualism demonstrated by the author and the writer he defends. Evans here made a clear distinction between Jesus and the Christ. Evans was not alone in making this distinction. But Shakers also used the words "Christ" and "Jesus" interchangeably. Context must be examined in each case to determine whether the "Christ" referred to is the Christ spirit (appearing in both Jesus and Ann Lee) or the equivalent of the incarnate Jesus.

Shaker doctrine on Mother Ann was in a fairly constant state of flux throughout the nineteenth century. Usually subtle, and sometimes not so subtle, differences of opinion were common. As with Holy Mother Wisdom, inconsistencies frequently appeared in a single document. Again, however, a symmetrical relationship between Jesus and Mother Ann best represents the predominant official (i.e., New Lebanon) New Era point of view. This version of Ann Lee's status also best fits both the form and the content of gift images.

The construction of the "Spiritual Parents," "the parents in Church relation, such as *Father Joseph, Mother Lucy, and others,*" came just below that of the Heavenly Parents in the Shaker hierarchy. According to Believers, these ancestors in faith, by their perfection and their humanity, helped to bridge the gap between heavenly and earthly spheres. See Youngs, "Concise View," WML SA 760, pp. 110–11. On many, generally less formal, occasions, however, Shakers included Mother Lucy and other Spiritual Parents in the category of Heavenly Parents.

47. Giles B. Avery referred to the reception of these "tickets of notice" in Avery, "Historical Sketches," entry for 25 January 1843, LC Container 4, Item 53, especially pp. 155–56. See also New Lebanon Ministry to Union Village Ministry, 6 April 1840, "Copies of letters, Begun 1839," WRHS 27 IV:B-9, p. 35.

48. The cards from Mother Ann and Jesus were, in most respects, very similar to the cards of July and August 1842 from Holy Mother Wisdom (fig. 24). In contrast to the notices from the two Shaker messiahs, however, the message on Holy Wisdom's cards of July and August 1842 read continuously from one side to the other. The instrument clearly designated the front side of the cards with the beginning of Wisdom's message.

49. Lamson, *Among the Shakers,* p. 53.

50. The parent ministry as well as the eldership and the diaconate included a senior female, a senior male, a junior female, and a junior male. See [Bates], *Holy Wisdom's Book,* pp. 240–42, for a detailed Shaker exegesis of the significance of the number four.

51. The "Explanation" (PMA 63-160-5a, p. 21) to the Holy City map declared that the "streets of the Holy City run due East and West, North and South" at right angles to one another.

52. "A Book of Wisdom and Sacred Truth—New Lebanon, February 16, 1841," WRHS 78 VIII:B-153, p. 15.

53. Ibid., p. 27.

54. "Holy Laws of Zion," SDL, p. 62.

55. "Millennial Laws," 1845, WRHS 2 I:B-17, p. 96.

56. Calvin [Reed? or Green?] at New Lebanon to the New Lebanon Ministry and Elders visiting "in the east," 9 July 1861, WRHS 21 IV:A-43.

57. Cf. Garrett, *Spirit Possession,* p. 227 for a 1791 statement by Joseph Meacham regarding the necessity of planting Shaker gardens and fields in straight rows as a visual demonstration of celestial order.

58. "A true Record," vol. 11, WRHS 76 VIII:B-126, p. 52.

59. "Millennial Laws," 1845, WRHS 2 I:B-17, p. 60. See "Holy Orders of the Church," WRHS 78 VIII:B-154, p. 36; on not obstructing the straight flow of traffic in hallways, see also p. 9.

60. "Short Account of the Death of Polly Lawrence," in "Remains of Joseph A. H. Sampson, who died at New-Lebanon, 12 mo. 14, 1825 aged 20 years. Published by the request of his friends, for the benefit of youth" (Rochester, N.Y.: E. F. Marshall for Procter Sampson, 1827), EBK 274, pp. 55–56. Polly Lawrence was born 24 July 1792 and died 2 August 1826.

61. Youngerman, " 'Shaking Is No Foolish Play,' " p. 467, argues that Shaker instruments, ever concerned with order and ordering, with separation and categorization, "made visually accessible a preoccupation with classifying." See also p. 466.

62. [Youngs], "Visions Seen by Gibbs and Goff," entry for Gibbs, 2 and 3 December 1837, EBK 3270. Cf. Shaker dances, which include in their names as in their movements the same intense interest in "order," and especially in the "square," the "straight," and the "circular."

63. Avery, "Journal of Times," entry for 2 February 1838, WRHS 34 V:B-106. Like the early Islamic "circular" city of Baghdad (aligned, as was the Shaker City, with the center of the universe), the shape of the Shaker circular city was important not so much for the "physical character of its forms, as . . . [for] the ideas suggested by the forms," Oleg Grabar, *The Formation of Islamic Art* (New Haven: Yale University Press, 1973), p. 69; see also p. 71.

64. "Mother Hannah's Bequest," WRHS 75 VIII:B-102, p. 64.

65. Shakers made this orientation explicit when they called New Lebanon "Zion's Centre." See "Solemn and Sacred Word," WRHS 78 VIII:B-152, p. 150; "Preface, or Introduction," WRHS 75 VIII:B-109, pp. 35 and 36; and "A true Record," vol. 1, WRHS 75 VIII:B-116, pp. 9–10.

66. "Holy Orders of God," WRHS 78 VIII:B-150, p. 91.

67. See, for example, "Records Concerning the Finding," SDL, pp. 102–103 and 127.

68. Eleanor Potter, "Supplement to the Holy Laws of Zion" (1840), EBK 3335, p. 2. See also "A true Record," vol. 2, WRHS 75 VIII:B-117, p. 53; and "A true Record," vol. 7, WRHS 76 VIII:B-122, pp. 91–111.

69. "Explanation," PMA 63-160-5a, p. 51. Revelation, chs. 21 and 22, in contrast to this Shaker text, has the twelve gates represent the twelve tribes of Israel.

70. See "Explanation," PMA 63-160-5a, p. 24. See also p. 20.

71. On the symbolism and "prestige" of the center, see Mircea Eliade, *The Myth of the Eternal Return or, Cosmos and History,* trans. Willard R. Trask (Princeton: Princeton University Press, 1974), pp. 12, 16–17.

72. Early references to the preparation of the lot appear in accounts of the month of April 1842 and following; see, for example, "Domestic Journal of Important Occurrences," WRHS 32 V:B-61.

73. See, for example, "Meetings on Mount Sinai," SDL, pp. 46 and 91–92.

74. "Words of a Sacred Roll Concerning the Feast Ground," New Lebanon, 1 August 1842, WRHS 67 VIII:A-43, p. 33.

75. "Records Concerning the Finding," SDL, p. 27.

76. "Words of a Sacred Roll Concerning the Feast Ground," WRHS 67 VIII:A-43, pp. 10, 15–18, 30–32. After work was underway on the New Lebanon feastgrounds, word went out to other communities regarding the discovery or "finding" of their own feast grounds. See, for example, New Lebanon Ministry to Groveland Ministry, 6 De-

cember 1842, WRHS 20 IV:A-38; and Groveland Ministry to New Lebanon Ministry, 28 January 1843, WRHS 18 IV:A-17.

77. Barber, "Collection of Visionary Scens [*sic*]," EBK 12,316, p. 26. See also p. 31.

78. "The striving for resemblance marks our attempts to make the absent present and the dead alive," Freedberg, *The Power of Images,* p. 201.

79. Volume Containing the Word, WRHS 79 VIII:B-170D, pp. 126–27. For a similar metaphorical use of the language of "drawing" and "picturing," see Bennett and Youngs, "Journal of Inspired Meetings," entries for 10 and 11 March 1841, WRHS 77 VIII:B-138.

80. Bennett and Youngs, "Journal of Inspired Meetings," entry titled "Review of 1841," WRHS 77 VIII:B-138.

81. The fact that it is difficult to count precisely twelve kinds of fruit on the tree is not significant in this context. Elsewhere (Andrews and Andrews, *Visions,* Figure 17) an instrument drew a tree with ten kinds of fruit and titled it specifically the "Tree of Life, spoken of in Revelations, which bore twelve manner of fruits." The number seems to be understood symbolically but not literally.

82. Catherine Albanese, *America: Religions and Religion* (Belmont, Calif.: Wadsworth Publishing Company, 1981), p. 293, notes that trees, because they are rooted in the ground and tower upwards toward the sky, have long been symbols of the relationship between heaven and earth. In Shaker society, trees bridged the gap between the terrestrial and the celestial spheres because of the heavenly and spiritual patterns upon which all figures of trees were based.

83. Branches from the Hancock union tree (the tree represented in the painting) spread "from one society to another throughout all Mother's children" ("Meetings on Mount Sinai," SDL, p. 42).

84. The instrument who copied one gift song noted that it was "Sung by Mother Ann and the Holy Angel that guards the tree of Life in the Holy Sanctuary" (Henry DeWitt, A Choice Selection of Songs of the best Quality" [song dated 27 March 1843], WRHS 90 IX:B-28, n.p.).

85. The inscription accompanying the drawing notified beholders that "This heavenly Tree standeth in the center of the meeting room of the Church. City of Peace."

Because of its relatively large size it is likely that Hancock Church Family Believers shared *The Gospel Union, fruit bearing Tree* during a meeting for worship. The text indicates that the intended recipients were either the members of the Church Family or the Ministry of that Family.

86. Bathrick, comp., "Visions. Addresses, Extracts," WRHS 75 VIII:B-108, pp. 215–16; see also p. 193.

87. Avery, Compilation of Messages and Anthems, WRHS 65 VIII:A-26, n.p. See also Collection of Miscellaneous Inspired Writings, WRHS 80 VIII:B-175, pp. 73–79. For New Era regulations concerning actual flowers, see "A true Record," vol. 10, WRHS 76 VIII:B-125, pp. 115–16, where the possession of flowers was permissable if used appropriately and not "Idolized." The flowers described here ("flower pots, nosegays, rosebushes, and pink posies") resembled those depicted, in celestial form, in Polly Collins' Book.

88. "Words on a Card Sent from Holy Mother Wisdom, to Jonathan Wood. July 10th 1842. Copied August 8th 1842," PMA 63-160-197-(20), blue ink on pink paper.

89. Cf. Freedberg, *Power of Images,* p. 59. It was not a problem that the tree here was also identified by the instrument as an image of heaven because individuals and communities, like trees, contained the image of heaven.

Although instruments relatively seldom drew images of people, choosing instead to represent individual persons through their virtues and characteristics and through analogy to other images, numerous textual references indicate that Shakers certainly understood the idea of likeness to include portraiture. Two visionary messages of 1839 described Isaiah, the prophet, as an artist who drew likenesses or portraits of each member of the Shaker community to show to his companions in the celestial sphere. See [Hollister], Messages, Songs, Anthems, WRHS 75 VIII:B-115, p. 165; and "A true Record," vol. 1, WRHS 75 VIII:B-116, pp. 140–42.

90. If Polly Collins indeed compiled and illustrated this book, as Patterson (*Gift Drawing,* pp. 51–53) claims, it is a unique record of visions directed to an artist and recorded by that artist for her own use. Collins was well liked by the brothers and sisters at Hancock and it is possible that the many named instruments relayed these messages to her while she served as scribe and illustrator. Although there are some attractive arguments in favor of Patterson's conclusions, I am not convinced that Collins was artist and compiler because variant spellings (Polly and Polley) of her name exist in several entries. While it is the case that Shakers frequently employed multiple spellings of names, it seems unlikely that Collins would have repeatedly offered two different spellings of her own name. Collins was, however, the instrument for at least one of the initialed messages in her book, an 1851 notice from the spirit of Benjamin Collins (Polly Collins' natural father, who died a Shaker in 1850). On Benjamin Collins and his family, see Lamson, *Among the Shakers,* pp. 71–74; and Patterson, *Gift Drawing,* p. 52.

In addition, a genre of gift books like Polly Collins' Book, though usually unillustrated, existed at Hancock. At least three of the four members of the Hancock ministry in the early 1840s received similar books. It is entirely improbable that these three different people, Cassandana Goodrich, Nathaniel Deming, and Grove Wright, would have kept such very similar books—and equally improbable that members of the ministry would have had time to transcribe their own books. If they did not write their own books, might not someone else have written and illustrated a book for instrument Polly Collins?

91. Polly Collins' Book, WRHS 71 VIII:B-21, n.p.

92. New Lebanon Ministry at Watervliet to Union Village Ministry, 23 January 1840, "Copies of letters, Begun 1839," WRHS 27 IV:B-9, p. 30.

93. For a revealing discussion of a similar phenomenon in Puritan society see Ann Kibbey, *The Interpretation of Material Shapes in Puritanism: A Study of Rhetoric, Prejudice, and Violence* (New York: Cambridge University Press, 1986). Here people are images and icons and this notion exerts ethical force.

94. God created Shakers in God's own likeness; Almighty Power was a Shaker. (Journal of Meetings on the Mount of Olives, Mount Horeb, and Mount Sinai, SDL, p. 85). See also "Closing Roll," EBK 12,027, p. 21 in which Shakers were "baptised into the spirit and image of God's eternal brightness." In Barber, "Collection of Visionary Scens [*sic*]," EBK 12,316, p. 35, God referred to instruments as "images of my likeness." The "very sight" of Believers' faces revealed that they were of God and gave others cause to believe ("A true Record," vol. 6, WRHS 76 VIII:B-121, p. 188).

95. [Bates], *Holy Wisdom's Book,* pp. 7–8. On the splendor of being adorned with "gospel graces," see Compilation of Messages to Individuals, WRHS 78 VIII:B-151, p. 34.

96. "A true Record," vol. 2, WRHS 75 VIII:B-117, p. 190.

97. "A Heart of Purity," EBK 13,525, n.p. See also "Communications to Cassandana Goodrich," SDL, p. 163, where Goodrich, an eldress at Hancock, was a "safe pattern for all to follow."

98. The pictures declared Bishop "an anchor to the weak, a pillar of light to the strong."

99. "A Short Communication from John Robbinson to the Holy Anointed given at Lovely Vineyard and copied by mortal hand March the 14th 1846," in Collection of Communications, WRHS 75 VIII:B-104, n.p. The inscribed text of *The Gospel Union, fruit bearing Tree* (Pl. III) refers to the drawn likeness of the tree as "A faint resemblance of the home/That Mother giveth you." The fact that the tree was both heaven and the individual was not a problem for Shakers, who, in fact, patterned their own lives after the order of heaven.

Ultimately, Shakers conceived of all "good" likeness in relationship to God and in relationship to the heavenly sphere, by virtue of its proximity to God. For Believers, an emblem was but an approximation of the original—and the deity was the only true original. Shakers, Shaker drawings, and Shaker communities, while true likenesses, were but "faint emblems" of the Eternal Parents and the glory and beauty of their celestial habitations.

100. Brewer, *Shaker Communities,* pp. 93, 115, and especially 147–48.

101. The family and youth functioned, historically, as fundamental foci for social anxiety. Shaker leaders like Frederick Evans were familiar with the works of Henry Ward Beecher, Horace Bushnell, etc.

102. Halttunen, *Confidence Men,* p. 10.

103. Ibid., p. 40; see also pp. 21–23, 96–97, 114–15.

104. Ibid., p. 60—cf. discussion of heart cutouts in my ch. 1. A Shaker ideal took shape in relationship to and was reinforced by a cultural ideal. Shaker life was, in many ways, the perfect expression of a sentimental ideal which "reinterpret[ed] submission as a discovery of the power to master one's inner nature as well as the world." Donald E. Pease, "Introduction," Walter Benn Michaels and Donald E. Pease, eds., *The American Renaissance Reconsidered* (Baltimore: Johns Hopkins University Press, 1985), pp. viii–ix. See also the essay in this same publication by Jane P. Tompkins, "The Other American Renaissance," pp. 34–57, esp. pp. 34, 47, and 48.

105. Halttunen, *Confidence Men,* p. 40, also pp. 71 and 89.

106. Ibid., p. 158.

107. Cf. McCracken, *Culture and Consumption,* p. 132.

108. [D. A. Buckingham], "Little Book of the Holy Word of God," WRHS 69 VIII:A-73, p. 36.

5. Image as Threshold of Heaven

1. Green, "Prophetic Revelations," WRHS 78 VIII:B-147, pp. 6–7. See also Bishop, "Farewell Address," EBK 13,341, p. 8.

The windows metaphor appeared with striking frequency, particularly in the official records of Mother's Work. See, for example, "A true Record," vol. 2, WRHS 75 VIII:B-117, p. 182; "A true Record," vol. 6, WRHS 76 VIII:B-121, p. 213; "A true Record," vol. 9, WRHS 76 VIII:B-124, p. 2; Bennett and Youngs, "Journal of Inspired Meetings," entry for 5 July 1840, WRHS 77 VIII:B-138; [Bates], *Holy Wisdom's Book,* p. 70; and Youngs, "Concise View," WML SA 760, pp. 97–98. In addition, though somewhat less frequently, God opened heaven's door. In 1842, on a visionary journey to Holy Wisdom's mansion, instrument Phebe Ann Smith of the 2nd Order, Watervliet, identified the celestial door "thru which the gifts of heaven come so freely to Mother's children here" (Compilation of Messages to Individuals, WRHS 78 VIII:B-151, pp. 72–73).

When they chose not to use the windows and doors metaphor, Shakers referred to the "showers from heaven" descending upon them. See New Lebanon Ministry to Pleasant Hill Ministry, 4 December 1837, "Copies of letters, Begun 1833," WRHS 27 IV:B-8, p. 228. Sometimes Believers used these two images together. See, for example, "Gifts and Spiritual Exercises of Christmas 1845," WRHS 80 VIII:B-179, p. 47; and Avery, "Journal of Times," entry for 30 November 1837, WRHS 34 V:B-106.

2. See, for example, "Records Concerning the Finding," SDL, pp. 59 and 88–93.

3. Because the instruments did not intend their religious pictures to be framed, only the painted border physically separated the picture from the actual world of its beholders.

4. Hannah Cohoon may have been acquainted with a similar sacred leaf form, drawn in 1842 by Joseph Wicker, an instrument and leader in her Hancock home. Wicker's representation showed four leaves coming together in a (here smaller) circular center. Describing the sacred fountain on the Hancock feast ground, Wicker commented: "The

waters of this fountain spout up several feet above the surface of the basin of the Pool, and in the center the waters stand level. In the center of this level spot is a beautiful plant haveing four leaves lying flat on the surface of the water. The following sketch will give some idea of the form of the beautiful Lavilla that lies upon the Fountain. The leaves of this plant are perpetually green and point exactly to the four cardinal points. The stem does not rise above the leaves, but appears level with them. Each leaf is about fourteen inches long" ("Records Concerning the Finding," SDL, pp. 17–18).

5. In addition to other aspects of the image which imply the representation of volume, this incorporation of two simultaneous views suggests a third dimension. For an example of similar features in other Shaker graphic modes, see Emlen, *Shaker Village Views,* p. 15, on "simultaneous representation of two-and three-dimensional features" in Shaker maps and village views.

6. In Shaker visionary paintings text often tells about time and place; text locates the image for the beholder.

7. It cannot be convincingly argued that the figures are spirits and therefore not visible to the human eye. If this were the case, the beholder would see nothing, for the bower itself is a spiritual bower visible only to one gifted with spiritual sight.

8. The "stage set" composition is common in gift drawings. See also *The Gospel Union, fruit bearing Tree* (Pl. III) in which four angels mentioned in the inscription go undepicted.

9. Garrett defines spirit possession itself as a sort of sacred theater, suggesting that Shaker communities become stage sets for the coming together of heaven and earth. The action of Believers was scripted for them by the organization and expectations of their community and, I would add, of their images. Garrett, *Spirit Possession,* pp. 227–28.

10. Hannah Cohoon's *The Tree of Life* (fig. 2) accomplishes a similar inclusion of the spectator in a different fashion. Here the brilliant red, orange, and green of the tree's fruits create an optical oscillating effect. The warm advances, the cool recedes. The spectator is drawn into this reverberating pull and push and held now and again in earthly and heavenly space. The millennial status of the living regenerate Shaker, participant in the heavenly sphere, yet still of the earth, is underscored in this movement. The play of warm and cool colors in a *Bower of Mulberry Trees* reverses the movement into the painting suggested by other compositional elements, implying that the table moves forward into the viewer's space as it invites the viewer under and into the bower. The intermingling of spaces that results reiterates the picture's theme of the convergence of heavenly and earthly spheres.

11. The bower's shape associated it with an expressive form of venerable history: the Roman arch and its derivatives in monumental and triumphal art and architecture. Nineteenth-century Believers were familiar with the formal significance and power of the arch. The Great Temple of the Eternal Father and Mother, in the Holy City Map, boasted "great and noble arches" ("Explanation to the Holy City," PMA 63-160-5a, p. 26, also pp. 21 and 53). Shakers used bowers, in drawings and texts, as spiritually powerful forms.

12. It is possible that the two smaller trees "inside" the bower were intended to constitute the third and fourth trees of a "four square" bower. However, Cohoon clearly designated the bower as a "Bower of *Mulberry* Trees [italics added]" and she just as clearly stated that the two smaller trees were a different sort of tree, "bearing the fruit of the tree of Paradise."

13. Genesis 9:8-17.

14. The boundary concerns of Mother's Work can be understood as a revival of an earlier response to crisis. In 1780, following the deaths of William Lee and Ann Lee, the Shakers also separated themselves from the world, turning inward to organize and regulate the Society, see [B. Youngs], *Testimony,* 1808, p. 31.

15. See Bennett and Youngs, "Journal of Inspired Meetings," entry for 12 December 1841, WRHS 77 VIII:B-138.

16. See Youngs, "Concise View," WML SA 760, pp. 152–53, 169; and "Domestic Journal of Important Occurrences," entry for 27 July 1845, WRHS 32 V:B-61. There may have been some interim breaks in the prohibition, however. For example, [Wells and Youngs], "Records Kept by Order of the Church," entry for 18 June 1843, NYPL 7, p. 213, noted a public meeting attended by families of Believers on 18 June 1843. For the text of the "advertisement" publishing the closing of the gates, see Bennett and Youngs, "Journal of Inspired Meetings," entry for 12 December 1841, WRHS 77 VIII:B-138. The New Lebanon ministry notified other communities about the reception of this "gift"; a letter from the New Lebanon Ministry to the Union Village Ministry, 26 July 1842, "Copies of letters, Begun 1839," WRHS 27 IV:B-9, p. 88, dealt largely with "the gift that was made known, at Watervliet, for them to suspend their public meeting and close their gates against the world." This gift had consequences for all Shakers: "It appears evident that a great change, a great cutting off and seperation from the world is called for" (ibid.).

17. New Lebanon Ministry at Watervliet to New Lebanon Church Family Elders, 9 February 1842, "Copies of letters, Begun 1839," WRHS 27 IV:B-9, p. 77. It might be suggested that some of the smaller gift images, especially, were like the calling cards that became so indispensible to social etiquette in the broader American culture during this period. These tokens of celestial visitation reiterated social boundaries in crossing cosmological boundaries.

18. [Youngs], "Preface, or Introduction," WRHS 75 VIII:B-109, p. 57, paragraph headed "Some notes omitted thro' mistake." See also Foster, *Religion and Sexuality,* pp. 63–4; and Brewer, *Shaker Communities,* p. 86.

19. [Wells and Youngs], "Records Kept by Order of the Church," entry titled "Review of 1845," NYPL 7, p. 251.

20. "Holy Laws of Zion," SDL, p. 58.

21. Potter, "Supplement to the Holy Laws of Zion," EBK 3335, p. 3. Separation was the central theme of the "Supplement." Through the instrument, the divine world urged Shaker communities to cease hiring labor from outside their borders or, if this was not possible, to keep hired help separated from members at all times. Ibid., p. 4; and [Stewart], *Sacred Roll and Book,* pp. 4, 7, 112, 114, and 119.

22. "Solemn and Sacred Word," WRHS 78 VIII:B-152, p. 79.

23. After the "office deacons" or "trustees," the "family deacons" (also called simply "deacons" or "deaconesses") acted as a second level buffer between the "world" and the "church." This organization of Shaker society Believers often likened to Solomon's temple: "The established order of the lot of Deacons and Deaconnesses, is to be the door through which all things must pass to, and from the heart of the Church; for as the Office, and Trustees, are as the Outer Court of the temple, even so, the family Deacons, stand as the door which openeth into the inner court, and the most holy place" ("Holy Orders of the Church," WRHS 78 VIII:B-154, pp. 8–9). Cf. discussion of the *Holy City,* Pl. I.

24. "Holy Orders of the Church," WRHS 78 VIII:B-154, p. 18. These notions of travel etiquette appear excessive in relationship to late twentieth-century conceptions of appropriate public behavior. As suggested in ch. 4, however, in comparison to the restrictive etiquette promoted in the manuals of mid-nineteenth-century American sentimental culture, Shaker behavior, though still extreme, seems less bizarrely regimented. See Halttunen, *Confidence Men,* especially pp. 114–15.

While many historians claim that only male Believers served as trustees, the "Holy Laws of Zion" (SDL, p. 38) specified that "the lot or order of Trustees may be composed of two or more of each sex."

25. See, for example, "Solemn and Sacred Word," WRHS 78 VIII:B-152, pp. 77,

123, and 128; "Messages of Warning, admonition, and instruction," WRHS 75 VIII:B-111, p. 37; and "Holy Orders of God," WRHS 78 VIII:B-150, p. 23. One Narrow Path drawing depicts the watchmen on the walls (fig. 16). See also "Communications to Grove Wright," WML 431 SA 1069, p. 1.

26. *Mother's Banner of Love and Comfort,* 16 March 1845, blue ink with red wash, 23 5/8 inches by 17 11/16 inches, NGA 1971.83.29.

27. See Eliade, *Myths, Rites, Symbols,* vol. 1, p. 156, on walls and fences as boundaries against disorder. See Hayden, *Seven American Utopias,* p. 43; and [Benjamin T. Lossing], "Visiting the Shakers in 1857," *Harpers New Monthly Magazine* no. 86 (July 1857; facsimile repr., n.p.: Shaker Museum Foundation, 1975): 166, on the visibility of Shaker border crossings.

28. Garrett, *Spirit Possession,* p. 227.

29. "Presents Received," WRHS 75 VIII:B-114, pp. 168–69. The golden chain had been used by Shakers years earlier as a figure for spiritual union between two individuals, e.g., Ann Lee and James Whittaker. Here Lucy Wright extended the figure to apply to the community. Cf. [Bishop and Wells], *Testimonies,* 1816, pp. 354–55.

30. New Lebanon Ministry to South Union Ministry, 14 February 1821, WRHS 20 IV:A-34. Similar letters sent to all societies of Believers contained word of Mother Lucy's death and extracts of her golden chain address.

31. "A true Record," vol. 1, WRHS 75 VIII:B-116, p. 126.

32. Seth Wells for the New Lebanon Ministry and Church Elders to Union Village Ministry and Community, 16 March 1836, WRHS 20 IV:A-37. See also "A true Record," vol. 3, WRHS 75 VIII:B-118, p. 151; "Mother Hannah's Bequest," WRHS 75 VIII:B-102, pp. 60 and 63–64; and New Lebanon Ministry and Elders to Union Village Ministry, 9 April 1836, "Copies of letters, Begun 1833," WRHS 27 IV:B-8, p. 125. See Suzanne Youngerman's discussion of the chain of safety (" 'Shaking Is No Foolish Play,' " pp. 379–81).

33. Copies of 1845 "Millennial Laws," for example, WML 121 SA 757 and WML 121 SA 758.

34. In "A true Record," vol. 1, WRHS 75 VIII:B-116, p. 74, Mother Ann, acting on behalf of Almighty Power and Holy Mother Wisdom, "drew" a "separating line" between her children and the evil "forms and fashions of the world." Elsewhere (e.g., "Mother Hannah's Bequest," WRHS 75 VIII:B-102, pp. 66–67 and 72) Almighty God drew the line. Note the role of Mother Ann and of God as "artist" here, *drawing* a separating line of distinction. For a more specific citation on the moral component of this "art," see Bennett and Youngs, "Journal of Inspired Meetings," entry for evening meeting, 4 April 1841, WRHS 77 VIII:B-138. See also "Report of the General Proceedings," WRHS 79 VIII:B-165, pp. 15–16, and p. 39, where "the Savior" had "drawn a line around" Shakers, "encircl[ing]" them in the safety of his blessing.

35. New Lebanon Ministry at Watervliet to Groveland Ministry, 8 August 1840, "Copies of letters, Begun 1839," WRHS 27 IV:B-9, p. 46; New Lebanon Ministry to Shirley Ministry, 22 March 1843, ibid., pp. 117–18; New Lebanon Ministry at Watervliet to Union Village Ministry, 23 January 1840, ibid., p. 30; and New Lebanon Ministry to Harvard Ministry, 31 March 1842, ibid., p. 86. The ministries of different communities hesitated even to send sacred communications by mail and often dispatched a Shaker messenger to carry them instead.

36. [Stewart], *Sacred Roll and Book,* p. 373.

37. Arnold van Gennep, *The Rites of Passage,* trans. Monika B. Vizedom and Gabrielle L. Caffee (Chicago: University of Chicago Press, 1960), pp. 11, 21, and 191–92.

38. Ibid., p. 20.

39. Turner, *Ritual Process,* pp. 108–11 and 128–29.

40. "Millennial Laws," WRHS 2 I:B-17, pp. 96–97 and 108. See also "Holy Orders of the Church," WRHS 78 VIII:B-154, pp. 56–57, 61, and 77–78.

41. [Youngs], "Preface, or Introduction," WRHS 75 VIII:B-109, p. 35.

42. "Solemn and Sacred Word," WRHS 78 VIII:B-152, p. 95. The inscription to *A Gift from Mother Ann to the Elders at the North Family* (fig. 14) included this verse: "This pretty gift I send to you, / That you at times may sit and view, / This emblem of a higher sphere, / And bring your feeling to it near."

43. Cf. Freedberg, *Power of Images,* pp. 65, 77, and 165. See especially p. 165 on the role of images as aids in the "ascent from the visible to the invisible."

44. Joanna Kitchell at Union Village to Sarah Bates at New Lebanon, 11 October 1835, LC Container 40, Item 367.

45. Mid-nineteenth-century Shakers recognized that both distance and proximity were involved in correspondence. In one instance, an instrument's message had Mother Ann comforting Father James in regard to a Shaker brother who would soon leave his mortal body, "James don't feel bad about that, for he will soon be so near, you will not need to write to him" (Eleanor Potter, "A Short Word of Notice from the Heavenly Father and Holy Mother; also, from all the Heavenly Parents, Given to Elder Ebenezer Bishop Holy Mount March 23, 1845 Brought by a Native Spirit, Electa Blanchard," blue and red ink on white paper, EBK 13,495, n.p.).

46. Unlike Shaker songs, which existed in the years before the New Era, when they were sometimes gifts or messages from one living community member to another, gift images belonged exclusively to the Era and always, according to the instruments, came from the heavenly sphere.

47. Barber, "Collection of Visionary Scens [*sic*]," EBK 12,316, p. 92; see also pp. 94–5.

48. A gift booklet of March 1845 to Elder Ebenezer at New Lebanon contained a representation of a Narrow Path in red and blue ink which included these words, "This lovely path in which thou hast ever traveled is straight and beautiful; and will stand as a lasting memorial of thee; that none need to fear, to travel in" (Potter, "Short Word of Notice to Ebenezer Bishop," EBK 13,495, n.p.). A booklet, of the same date by the same hand, to Rufus Bishop depicted a Narrow Path at the conclusion of this sentence: "Thy feet have trodden the straight path of self denial" (Eleanor Potter, "A Short Notice from the Heavenly Father, from Holy Mother Wisdom, and all the Heavenly Parents, with their seals of approbation and blessing. Brought by a Native Spirit called Electa Blanchard; for Br. Rufus Bishop. Holy Mount," [23 March 1845], EBK 13,494, n.p.). And several heart drawings of 1844 included pictures of the Narrow Path. See Amy Reed and Emma Jane Blanchard hearts, Shaker Manuscript Collection, Hancock Shaker Village, Pittsfield, Massachusetts (hereafter HSV). Other gift drawings and visually organized messages included textual references to the Narrow Path even when the path itself was not depicted.

49. In a telephone conversation of June 1991, Mary B. Bowling, Curator of Manuscripts at the Research Libraries of the New York Public Library, observed that the end of the strip in blue ink which depicts the terminal point of the path has no trace of adhesive.

50. Patterson, *Gift Drawing,* p. 92; see also pp. 90–94.

51. Although eight diverse drawings survive by the same hand (ibid., pp. 90–94), the identity of the instrument has not been established conclusively. Patterson's argument in favor of Emily Babcock of the Second Family, New Lebanon, is not entirely convincing. He bases his case on the fact that Emily Babcock was the most frequently named gift recipient in a collection of song manuscripts by the hand of the Narrow Path strip drawing instrument. In most cases, however, the recipients of gift songs and gift drawings were not also the instruments of those songs and drawings.

52. Blue Paper-bound Manuscript Booklet, entry cited here (first entry) begins, "Mother came here, March the 25, 1815 on Saturday," SDL, n.p.

53. "Record of Messages and Communications at Hancock," WRHS 71 VIII:B-20, p. 149. Shakers did not believe in the resurrection of the physical body because "man's pro-

bation extends into eternity" (Frederick W. Evans, "Memorial to the late Henry Ward Beecher," ed. Edward W. Bok [n.p., n.d.], EBK 16,677, p. 6).

54. *Youth's Guide in Zion,* p. 15. Clarke Garrett notes that "for both the Methodists and Shakers sinlessness was a possibility, but one that could be achieved only within a framework of social structures, moral discipline, and spiritual hierarchy." Garrett, *Spirit Possession,* p. 84. See also Marini, *Radical Sects,* pp. 131, 133, and 152–53.

55. New Lebanon Ministry to Elder Freegift Wells at Union Village, 10 October 1838, "Copies of letters, Begun 1833," WRHS 27 IV:B-8, p. 274. Shakers opposed any doctrine of predestination because it violated the progressive, unfolding nature of God's revelation. [Bates], *Holy Wisdom's Book,* pp. 3, 9, 66.

56. Like the idea of spiritual travel, the concept of the Narrow Path itself was not new to the 1840s. Occasional scattered references survive from earlier years. An 1824 book by non-Shaker David Benedict mentioned a Shaker march that was a "figure of marching the heavenly road, and walking the streets of the New Jerusalem" (Benedict, *History of All Religions,* p. 261). A "Circular Epistle" explicitly used the Narrow Path metaphor to describe the proper lifestyle of Believers. See "Circular Epistle, The Ministry and Elders of the Church at New Lebanon, to all who feel an interest in the prosperity of Zion, and claim a relation to the only gospel of salvation, in this day of Christ's second appearing," 1 September 1829, WRHS 20 IV:A-35, p. 4. It was not until the early 1840s, however, that the Narrow Path assumed ritual and graphic form.

57. Youngs, "Concise View," WML SA 760, p. 113.

58. Bennett and Youngs, "Journal of Inspired Meetings," entry for 1 November 1840, WRHS 77 VIII:B-138. See also ibid., all entries for 1 November through 6 December 1840. For other accounts of the initial gift of the Narrow Path ritual see "A true Record," vol. 3, WRHS 75 VIII:B118, pp. 97–188; "A true Record," vol. 7, WRHS 76 VIII:B-122, pp. 180–83; and Youngs, "Concise View," WML SA 760, pp. 128–29. Youngermann, "'Shaking Is No Foolish Play,'" p. 440, comments on the relationship between bodily movement and the ritual of the Narrow Path. As in Shaker dance ritual, here social control was enforced through physical (self) control.

59. Bennett and Youngs, "Journal of Inspired Meetings," entries for 1 November 1840 through 15 November 1840, WRHS 77 VIII:B-138.

60. "A true Record," vol. 11, WRHS 76 VIII:B-126, pp. 26–45 records an extended narrow path vision.

61. Roll to Daniel Boler, 8 January 1842, EBK 13,483, p. 12.

62. "A true Record," vol. 7, WRHS 76 VIII:B-122, p. 187; and "A true Record," vol. 8, WRHS 76 VIII:B-123, p. 6. Spiritual travel could also be accomplished on the part of others. This practice was known as giving birth to souls.

63. "Holy Laws of Zion," SDL, p. 24.

64. "School Instructions," WRHS 78 VIII:B-145, p. 18. See also Roll to Daniel Boler, 8 January 1842, EBK 13,483, p. 13.

65. Compilation of Messages to Individuals, WRHS 78 VIII:B-151, pp. 72–73.

66. "A true Record," vol. 6, WRHS 76 VIII:B-121, p. 222; and 1844 heart cutout to Samuel White, "The Word of the Holy Heavenly Father, To a little one of his fold," BA V289.8, Un 1, verso. Instruments repeatedly emphasized the restrictive size of the path. See "A true Record," vol. 4, WRHS 75 VIII:B-119, pp. 82–83. The spirits used the case of Joseph Sampson to make explicit the relationship between the straight and narrow path and the need for separation from the world. See Bennett and Youngs, "Journal of Inspired Meetings," entry for 8 November 1840, WRHS 77 VIII:B-138.

67. "A letter from Mother Lucy to Polly Collins, March 6, 1841," in Polly Collins' Book, WRHS 71 VIII:B-21, n.p.

Eliade discusses a "difficult road" leading to the Center. The similarities to the Narrow

Path are striking. "The road is arduous, fraught with perils, because it is, in fact, *a rite of passage,* from the profane to the sacred, from the ephemeral and illusory to reality and eternity, from death to life, from man to divinity." Eliade, *Myth of Eternal Return,* p. 18.

68. Leonard, "Life and Sufferings," EBK 3226-105, p. 61.

69. "A Book of Rolls, letters, Messages, and Communications to the Ministry and Elders and Individual Members. Given by Divine Inspiration at New Lebanon—Not Recorded on the Public Record Transcribed 1843," EBK 12,332, p. 27.

70. "A true Record," vol. 11, WRHS 76 VIII:B-126, p. 48.

71. Potter, "Short Notice to Rufus Bishop," EBK 13,494, n.p.

72. Bennett and Youngs, "Journal of Inspired Meetings," entries for 10 April and 15 May 1841, WRHS 77 VIII:B-138.

73. "A true Record," vol. 5, WRHS 75 VIII:B-120, p. 23.

74. Because the dating of the drawings is uncertain, it is difficult to tell whether visions or drawings came first.

75. The evidence suggests that Shakers may have stored many of their drawings and paintings rolled. See Emerich, "Conversation with Faith Andrews," p. 39.

76. Bennett and Youngs, "Journal of Inspired Meetings," entry for 6 December 1840, WRHS 77 VIII:B-138. See also "Rolls, letters, Messages, and Communications," EBK 12,332, pp. 26–28.

77. [Hollister], Copies of Messages, Songs, and Anthems, WRHS 75 VIII:B-115, pp. 209–10 details the gift of these "little paths our heavenly Parents had rolled up and put in [a box] to send to us." The ritual of the Narrow Path and the use of the figure as a metaphor for Shaker life continued, with varying frequency, until at least 1859. See Giles B. Avery at New Lebanon to Daniel Sering at Union Village, 12 September 1859, WRHS 21 IV:A-42.

78. "A true Record," vol. 10, WRHS 76 VIII:B-125, pp. 1–31.

79. Ibid., page inserted at p. 28.

80. [William Deming], "A Short and interesting account of a beautiful Temple, and glorified Spirits in Heaven, Seen in Vision, Tuesday evening January 24th and written the 28th, 1843," WML 436 SA 1074, pp. 2–3.

81. Compilation of Messages, entry beginning "South House. April 28th 1842," WRHS 79 VIII:B-158, n.p.

82. [Barber and Reed?] Book of Inspired Visions and Messages, WRHS 87 VIII:C-1, pp. 121–34.

83. [Wells and Youngs], "Records Kept by Order of the Church," entry for 26 June 1842, NYPL 7, p. 196. On p. 198 the scribe noted that Believers removed the cross signs on July 3 because the signs "had a tendency to lead astray the world, to other dwellings, when they should call at the Office." See also Youngs, "Concise View," WML SA 760, pp. 152–53.

84. [Stewart and Crossman], "Confidential Journal," entry for 25 July 1842, WRHS 35 V:B-136, p. 2.

85. See, for example, Susan K. Myrick, "A Discription of the Sign on the Holy Hill of Zion," 14 May 1843, WRHS 64 VIII:A-10; and Minerva L. Hill, "A Book Containing Solemn promises and weighty instructions, from Holy Mother Wisdom. Also, a Description of a Sign that stands over the Fountain, on the Feast Ground, at Lovely Vineyard and Pleasant Garden," 31 May 1843, WRHS 64 VIII:A-16, pp. 1–3, 24, 27–30, and 41.

86. Hill, "A Book Containing Solemn promises," WRHS 64 VIII:A-16, p. 24.

87. Meetings on Mount of Olives, Mount Sinai, and Mount Horeb, SDL, p. 37. One visionary painting has a figure similar to the diagonal cross representing "gaits [*sic*]" guarded by angels in Shaker spiritual territory, see Book of Prophetic Drawings, WRHS 87 VIII:C-6.

88. "Collection of Sacred Writings at the Second Family New Lebanon," SDL, pp.

17–18. See also, for example, "A true Record," vol. 9, WRHS 76 VIII:B-124, pp. 86–97.

89. "Closing Roll," EBK 12,027, p. 7.

90. "A Beautiful Present," 1 January 1843, EBK 11,547. Cf. figure 25; see also the picture of a diagonal cross given to Ebenezer Bishop as a sign of sacrifice and salvation in EBK 13,495 (a picture of his Narrow Path appears in the same booklet); a large, colorful gift painting with a central image of a diagonal cross in red inside a large star representing the celestial markings on a young Shaker woman, "A Reward of True Faithfulness from Mother Lucy to Eleanor Potter. July 22nd 1848," reproduced in Sprigg, *Shaker Design,* p. 202; and the gift of a double diagonal cross, given through instruments Semantha Fairbanks and Betsy Bates in a vision of "Mother Ann and the Savior." This double cross, diagrammed in the record, represented a mark of sacrality and sacrifice, in "Confidential to the Ministry," New Lebanon, 23 December 1842, EBK 13,491.

91. [Wells and Youngs], "Records Kept by Order of the Church," entry for 1 March 1843, NYPL 7, p. 206.

92. Patterson, *Gift Drawing,* p. 68, concurs with this hypothesis.

93. William J. Samarin, *Tongues of Men and Angels: The Religious Language of Pentecostalism* (New York: Macmillan Company, 1972), pp. 88–89, 185.

94. See, for example, the borders of Figures 7 and 13.

95. Patterson, *Gift Drawing,* pp. 92–93, deciphers one such text.

96. Seth Wells at New Lebanon to Matthew Houston at Watervliet (Ohio), 5 June 1838, WRHS 20 IV:A-37.

97. [D. A. Buckingham], "A Little Book of the Holy Word of God," WRHS 69 VIII: A-73. Just within the border of her drawing, the instrument of *From Holy Mother Wisdom to Hannah Ann Treadway* (fig. 7) translated into English the sacred script that constituted the border itself. The script edging several series of images strongly resembled the script on Sacred Sheets.

6. [Re]collecting History

1. Hughes and Allen, *Illusions of Innocence,* pp. xiii and 2–7. For Hughes, at least, ahistoricity involves an "aversion to history and tradition," Hughes, "Introduction: On Recovering the Theme of Recovery," *American Quest,* p. 4.

2. In introductory remarks to a book of essays on restorationism, Hughes maintains that "primitivism and a commitment to the contents of history are not necessarily mutually exclusive categories." Ibid., p. 5.

3. Natalie Zemon Davis and Randolph Starn, "Introduction," *Representations* 26 (Spring 1989): 5.

4. Hughes and Allen, *Illusions of Innocence,* p. 14.

5. Cf. ibid., p. 2.

6. Hill, "Comparing Three Approaches to Restorationism," *American Quest,* p. 233. In this essay, Hill suggests "refining the category of 'ahistorical' on which Mircea Eliade, Sidney Mead, and Richard Hughes have relied" (p. 233). Hill goes on to discuss the phenomenon of "compression" in restorationism: horizontal compression of past and present, the ancient and the current," and vertical compression of heaven and earth. He sees the first as subordinating "historical process" (p. 234) "to the will and work of God," as repudiating "all intervening history, rarely as fact, but as holding any theological significance" (p. 233). The second he understands as a "penetration of the eternal into the temporal [which] simply outflanks the issue of history" (p. 235). My organization of the content of images and other manifestations of Mother's Work into issues relative to the dimensions of space and time parallels, in some respects, Hill's division of compression. Further, Hill connects horizontal compression with institution, with "propriety over power" (234) and vertical compression with "dynamic personal experience" (charism) and theophany (p. 235). In Hills terms, Shakers based their New Era schema on both

horizontal (time) and vertical (space) compression. But both forms of compression, for Shakers, involved both institution and charism. Horizontally, Shakers appealed to past charismatic experience as well as to past behavioral norms. Vertically, they appealed to God's Law as well as to the gifts of the spirit.

7. His understanding of prophecy enabled Shaker Calvin Green to make sense of the Era and to place it within the broader scope of God's plan for the world.

> Several years before the late extraordinary out-pouring of the Divine Spirit and heavenly gifts among the children of Zion, it was revealed to me by the spirit of prophecy, that the most wonderful work of God would take place, in many ways, among his chosen people, that ever had been on Earth; that it would commence in the year 1837, and like the Jubilee in ancient Israel, it would operate by the influence of the Divine Spirit, until all things should be set in their proper order, in his spiritual Israel.
>
> I also saw that when this should be accomplished, according to his Divine purpose, the work would then go forth into the world, and prepare its inhabitants for that work which God had determined to bring to pass, and for a great gathering of souls to the gospel.

Calvin Green, "Prophetic Revelations from the Ancient Prophets," 13 November 1843, vol. 1, WRHS 78 VIII:B-147, pp. 5–6.

8. "Words of a Sacred Roll Concerning the Feast Ground, New Lebanon, August 1, 1842," WRHS 67 VIII:A-43, p. 29; and Barber, "Collection of Visionary Scens [*sic*]," EBK 12,316, pp. 32–35.

9. See, for example, "A true Record," vol. 6, WRHS 76 VIII:B-121, p. 234; "A true Record," vol. 3, WRHS 75 VIII:B-118, pp. 5–6; and Canterbury's Record, EBK 12,787, p. 13. Cf. Abraham J. Heschel, *The Prophets* (New York: Harper and Row, 1962), p. xiv.

10. Book of Prophetic Drawings, WRHS 87 VIII:C-6, n.p.

11. Cf. a reference of 14 August 1839 (also at New Lebanon) to a "book that opens four ways." Here the instrument implies that the contents were oriented from the center outward, "A true Record," vol. 2, WRHS 75 VIII:B-117, pp. 1, and 6–7.

12. Cf. Emlen, *Shaker Village Views,* p. 29 on Shaker maps constructed in a sinilar fashion, with no "right side up."

13. For a statement on the role of the prophet as seer and speaker, see Barber, "Collection of Visionary Scens [*sic*]," EBK 12,316, pp. 32–35.

14. On the significance of red ink, see ibid., p. 105, where red, as blood, represents commitment and sacrifice; also Avery, "Historical Sketches," entry for 25 January 1843, LC Container 4, Item 53, p. 152.

15. Book of Prophetic Drawings, WRHS 87 VIII:C-6, n.p.

16. "To the Instrument Writers," NYPL 103; and "Words by Signs to the Watchmen," NYPL 104B. Although these two component parts are numbered and stored separately by the archive—and although a third piece of a *different* booklet, "Words to the Watchmen," NYPL 104A, has been catalogued with "Words by Signs to the Watchmen"—it is clear, on examination, that the pairing of "To the Instrument Writers" and "Words by Signs to the Watchmen" is the correct match.

17. "The Word of the Savior by Signs," NYPL 102. Only this one of the original two pieces of this work survives. This booklet recorded a "parable or sign" about the Savior's vineyard in Zion. Many of the intricate black ink images depict the crop that is planted in this vineyard, the vicissitudes that befall these "lovely vines," and the vinedressers called to care for them. Typical of the eschatological and apocalyptic tone of Shaker prophecy

and prophetic drawings, this surviving segment of the booklet emphasizes the importance of being prepared for imminent judgment, of "making strong the walls" of Zion and "fastening the gates" against the evil of the still unregenerate world.

18. "Words to the Watchmen," NYPL 104A; and "To the Instrument Writers," NYPL 103.

Other prophetic pamphlets carried images and messages similar to the cut-and-fold booklets. See, for example, Illustrated Booklet of 30 April 1843, NYPL 47; and Sayings of the Prophetesses Anna, Miriam, and Deborah (21 June 1843), NYPL 96. An artist working for the Index of American Design produced a rendering (circa 1936) of one elaborate large scale prophetic image (NGA, Index of American Design, 1943.8.13460, location of original unknown) similar in conception and stylistic execution to a number of pages in the Book of Prophetic Drawings (WRHS 87 VIII:C-6) and to certain features of both the Narrow Path drawings (see ch. 5) and the cut-and-fold booklets.

19. Calvin Green, "Prophetic Revelations," vol. 1, WRHS 78 VIII:B-147, p. 9.

20. Compilation of Messages to Individuals, WRHS 78 VIII:B-151, p. 79; Andrew D. Barrett, "A Collection of Sacred Writings," WRHS 80 VIII:B-192, title page; "Divine Inspiration containing Explanations," WRHS 78 VIII:B-143, section II, paragraphs 19–37, n.p.; Seth Wells at New Lebanon to Elder David Spining at North Union, 16 October 1838, WRHS 20 IV:A-37; and Giles B. Avery, compiler, "Prophetic Warnings of the Judgments of God about to come upon the Earth," delivered at New Lebanon, 1840–44, collected 1846–47, WRHS 78 VIII:B-146, p. 151.

21. Walter Brueggemann, *The Prophetic Imagination* (Philadelphia: Fortress Press, 1978), p. 13, claims that "*The task of prophetic ministry it to nurture, nourish, and evoke a consciousness and perception alternative to the consciousness and perception of the dominant culture around us*" (italics in original). See also *The Interpreter's Dictionary of the Bible: An Illustrated Encyclopedia,* supplementary volume (1976), s.v. "Apocalypticism," by P. D. Hanson; and ibid., s.v. "Prophecy in Ancient Israel," by M. J. Buss.

22. [Calvin Green and Seth Y. Wells], *A Summary View of the Millennial Church, or United Society of Believers, Commonly Called Shakers,* 2d ed. rev. (Albany: C. Van Benthuysen, 1848; repr., New York: AMS Press, 1973), p. 223. For an excellent secondary source account, see Marini, *Radical Sects,* pp. 148–53. See Frank Kermode, *The Sense of an Ending: Studies in the Theory of Fiction* (New York: Oxford University Press, 1967), pp. 8–11 for a relevant discussion of apocalyptic/prophetic thinking and its projection onto history of fundamentally arbitrary chronological divisions in order to affirm a pattern to life.

23. [Green and Wells], *Summary View of the Millennial Church,* p. 226–30. The quoted material is from p. 226.

24. Alan Richardson, ed., *A Theological Word Book of the Bible* (New York: Macmillan Publishing Co., 1950), pp. 178–82, discusses these two senses of prophecy.

25. Kermode, *Sense of an Ending,* p. 101. Mid-nineteenth-century Believers lived in a permanent transitional state, a liminal period of time. The beginning and the ultimate conclusion of their religious life story Believers knew; everything in between constituted an uncertain "middest."

26. [Barber and Reed?] Book of Inspired Visions and Messages, WRHS 87 VIII:C-1, pp. 14–16.

27. Cf. Brueggemann, *Prophetic Imagination,* p. 14.

28. [Barber and Reed?] Book of Inspired Visions and Messages, WRHS 87 VIII:C-1, pp. 38 and 29, respectively.

29. See [Bates], *Holy Wisdom's Book,* pp. xix–xx. The millennium, literally interpreted, would last one thousand years. In practice, Shakers sometimes expected a more immediate fruition of God's plan.

30. New Lebanon Ministry to South Union Ministry, 12 August 1839, "Copies of letters, Begun 1839," WRHS 27 IV:B-9, p. 4.

31. See Miscellaneous Inspired Writings, WRHS 80 VIII:B-175, pp. 73–76, for notation on Shaker response to the postponement of time.

32. See Andrews and Andrews, *Visions,* Figure 17. The scriptural sources are Joel 2:20-32, Acts 2:19-21, and Revelation 6:12. Shaker prophets made frequent use of the passage from Joel. See "A true Record," vol. 6, WRHS 76 VIII:B-121, p. 246; Avery, comp., "Prophetic Warnings," WRHS 78 VIII:B-146, p. 149; and [Bates], *Holy Wisdom's Book,* p. 355. See Canterbury's Record, EBK 12,787, p. 83, which quotes Joel 2:28-32 (KJV).

33. Quoted from the inscription on *Holy Mother's Wings. The Heavenly Father's Wings,* watercolor and ink on paper, n.d., 19 and 1/2 inches by 27 inches, WRHS 87 VIII:C-6. See Andrews and Andrews, *Visions,* Figure 13. The history of the use of clocks and watches within the Shaker community probably influenced the way images of clocks were perceived by Shakers. Believers placed restrictions on the use and availability of clocks and, especially, watches. A clock was not introduced into the New Lebanon meeting house until 1855. See Youngs, "Concise View," WML SA 760, pp. 455, 475, and 506; and Youngs, Journal (1839–1858), entry for 23 February 1856, WRHS 35 V:B-134.

34. [Barber and Reed?] Book of Inspired Visions and Messages, WRHS 87 VIII:C-1, p. 27. The instrument left this series of drawings unfinished. The fifteenth drawing (p. 42), an image of a heavenly mansion crowned with Wisdom's all-seeing eye, the instrument sketched in pencil but did not paint. Watercolor images fill pp. 28–41; pp. 43–49 are left blank. The text picks up again on p. 50 indicating that perhaps the pages were left purposely blank by a scribe who assumed that ultimately all twenty-two pages would be filled with prophetic pictures.

35. [Youngs], "Preface, or Introduction," WRHS 75 VIII:B-109, p. 55; and Journal of Meetings held in the Church Order, New Lebanon, Beginning 1846, entry for 7 March 1847, EBK 12,339. Since the 1860s, each successively smaller generation of Shakers has seen itself as the faithful remnant prophesied by Mother Ann. Cf. Brewer, *Shaker Communities,* p. 135.

36. New Lebanon Ministry to Harvard Ministry, 18 November 1853, WRHS 20 IV:A-40; and Giles Avery at New Lebanon to William Reynolds at Union Village, 1 February 1865, WRHS 21 IV:A-43.

37. Bennett and Youngs, "Journal of Inspired Meetings," entry for 19 December 1841, WRHS 77 VIII:B-138.

38. "Records Concerning the Finding," SDL, p. 99. See also Hancock Ministry to Harvard Ministry, 15 July 1854, WRHS 18 IV:A-20.

39. New Lebanon Ministry at Watervliet to Union Village Ministry, 27 January 1843, "Copies of letters, Begun 1839," WRHS 27 IV:B-9, pp. 102–106. At the time that this letter was written, Shakers claimed that more than 150,000 spirits, mostly natives of North and South America, were present with them at Watervliet. In addition to "native spirits," New Lebanon entertained spirits of "Arabians," "Mahomitans," "Moors," "Hindoos," "Icelanders," "Laplanders," and "Polanders" as well as English, French, and many others. In New Lebanon Ministry at Watervliet to Groveland Ministry, 15 February

1843, ibid., p. 109, one correspondent wrote that "all the inhabitants of Sodom, that were overthrown at that time, are now at the South Family receiving an offer of salvation." The writer of New Lebanon Ministry to Harvard Ministry, 22 March 1843, ibid., pp. 116–17, remarked that thirty thousand French spirits had arrived at New Lebanon. Shakers were directed to keep "suitable Information" in the French language in every society so that French spirits might be converted.

40. Avery, "Historical Sketches," entry for 1 February 1843, LC Container 4, Item 53, p. 211. Instrument Avery claimed that gathering the spirits gave Believers practice for gathering the nations. Moreover, the converted spirits swelled the numbers of those available to hear confessions and to assist in the converting of others. In addition, if Shakers neglected the conversion of spirits, those same spirits would "stir up opposition and persecution against Zion."

41. Excepting [Barber and Reed?] Book of Inspired Visions and Messages, WRHS 87 VIII:C-1 and the prophetic series with the clock symbols.

42. See Green, "Prophetic Revelations," vol. 3, WRHS 78 VIII:B-149, pp. 173–74; and Avery, comp., "Prophetic Warnings," WRHS 78 VIII:B-146, pp. 159–61.

43. Cf. Barkun, *Crucible of the Milliennium,* pp. 47 and 90; and Brewer, *Shaker Communities,* p. 151.

44. See Lawrence Foster, "Had Prophecy Failed? Contrasting Perspectives on the Millerites and Shakers," in Ronald L. Numbers and Jonathan M. Bulter, eds., *The Disappointed: Millerism and Millenarianism in the Nineteenth Century* (Bloomington: Indiana University Press, 1987), pp. 173–88; and Barkun, *Crucible of the Millennium,* p. 96.

45. See Youngs, "Concise View," WML SA 760, p. 161; and Giles B. Avery, "Notes Taken by Giles B. Avery when he with Philemon Stewart went to the Eastern Societies relative to publishing the Sacred Roll," EBK 12,744, pp. 3 and 9–10. See also [Wells and Youngs], "Records Kept by Order of the Church," entries for February and March 1843, and entry titled "Review of 1843," NYPL 7, pp. 204–206, 218–19.

46. In this text, the feminine aspect of the deity revealed herself "more fully than heretofore." Youngs, "Concise View," WML SA 760, p. 162. Although not the subject of this book, it would be instructive to investigate this period as an episode in Shaker gender constructions. Unlike the *Sacred Roll and Book, Holy Wisdom's Book* circulated primarily among Shakers. Though it was available in manuscript form, Believers did not actually publish this text until 1849. The notion of a female God speaking through a female instrument may have been judged by Shakers as too controversial for a broad public audience.

47. [Barber and Reed?] Book of Inspired Visions and Messages, WRHS 87 VIII:C-1, pp. 56–57; see also pp. 51–52; and "A true Record," vol. 7, WRHS 76 VIII:B-122, pp. 66–69.

48. "Domestic Journal of Important Occurrences," entries for 27 December 1849, 13 February, 22 July, 19 August, and 13 September 1850, WRHS 32 V:B-61. See also, for example, New Lebanon Ministry to Harvard Ministry, 20 March 1850, WRHS 20 IV:A-40; "Domestic Journal of Daily Occurances," entries for 30 January, 22 July, 13 September, and 27–30 September 1850, WRHS 32 V:B-70; and New Lebanon Ministry to Groveland Ministry, 22 December 1851, WRHS 20 IV:A-40.

49. Youngs, "Concise View," WML SA 760, pp. 174–75.

50. By 1872, Shakers recorded an occasion on which Elder John Whiteley and Elder William Leonard attended a "Shaker and Spiritualist Convention" in Troy, New York, "Record of the Succession in Ministry at Harvard and Shirley and Journies performed by

them," entries for 22–24 March 1872, WRHS 32 V:B-59. For an early mention of "a mysterious knocking at Rochester which commenced two or three years ago," see "Domestic Journal of Important Occurrences," entry for 27 December 1849, WRHS 32 V:B-61; see also entries for 13 March, 23 July, 19 August, and 13 September 1850 as well as 27–30 September 1851. Shakers apparently traveled outside the community to see spiritualist mediums and they invited mediums to demonstrate their talents at Hancock and New Lebanon as well as in other Shaker habitations. A letter from New Lebanon to Rufus Bishop and the Ministry visiting at New Gloucester, Maine, of 21 July 1850 (WRHS 20 IV:A-40) remarks on an invitation issued to the Fox sisters to visit New Lebanon. City of Peace to Ministry at Lovely Vineyard (Hancock to Harvard), 11 November 1850, WRHS 18 IV:A-20, noted the lengthy visit of spirit rappers from Springfield at Hancock and New Lebanon. See also "An account of a journey to the spiritual Telegraph Office with Brother Seth Wells, March 25th, 1850, By A.Z.P. [Adah Zillah Potter], Chh. first Order Holy Mount," WRHS 67 VIII:A-46; Youngs, "Concise View, WML SA 760, pp. 179–81; and Bennett and Youngs, "Journal of Inspired Meetings," entries for 12 and 14 May and 12 November 1841, WRHS 77 VIII:B-138. Cf. Ernest Isaacs, "The Fox Sisters and American Spiritualism" in Howard Kerr and Charles L. Crow, eds., *The Occult in America: New Historical Perspectives* (Urbana: University of Illinois Press, 1986), pp. 79–110.

51. [Giles B. Avery], "Rappings" (1851), EBK 12,143, p. 13.

52. Ibid., p. 63. See also Youngs, "Concise View," WML SA 760, pp. 170–81.

53. See Blinn, *Spiritualism,* especially pp. 53–54. For other points of view see Calvin Green, "Biographic Memoir of the Life and Experience of Calvin Green," copied and expanded by Alonzo G. Hollister, vol. 3, WRHS 51 VI:B-31, p. 637; and "Extract from a Vision seen in the First Order's afternoon meeting, Sabbath October 12th 1851 [recto]," and "Concerning rapping, spoken by Mother [verso]," WRHS 69 VIII:A-78.

As historians look for manifestations of the occult in American religion before 1848, the Shakers would seem a natural group for consideration, cf. Jon Butler, "The Dark Ages of American Occultism, 1760–1848," in Kerr and Crow, eds., *The Occult in America,* pp. 58–78, esp. p. 59.

54. See [Barber and Reed?] Book of Inspired Visions and Messages, WRHS 87 VIII: C-1, p. 42, for unfinished pencil sketch of Wisdom's celestial mansion.

55. In *The Past Is a Foreign Country* (Cambridge: Cambridge University Press, 1985), p. 197, David Lowenthal emphasizes the relationship between identity and knowledge of one's past. "Remembering the past is crucial for our sense of identity . . . to know what we were confirms who we are."

56. Green, "Biographic Memoir," vol. 1, WRHS 51 VI:B-29, p. 153. Rufus Bishop of the New Era parent ministry was among those who first decided to record the faith history of the sect and its founder.

57. Youngs, "Concise View," WML SA 760, preface.

58. See, for example, "Holy Orders of the Church," WRHS 78 VIII:B-154, p. 153; "A Heavenly Prize from Mother Ann to Her Little Son, Alonzo Hollister, New Lebanon. January 1st, 1842," WRHS 66 VIII:A-38; and *A Concise Shaker Catechism* (Canterbury, N.H.: n.p., 1850), EBK 10,105, especially pp. 22–33.

59. Cf. Youngerman, " 'Shaking Is No Foolish Play,' " p. 528 where Youngerman notes that Grosvenor, a leader of some prominence, left the Shaker community after forty-six years to study mesmerism.

60. See, for example, Susan Ann Lewis, Travel Diary, entries for 16, 17, and 25 August 1849, EBK 10,484, pp. 1, 4, and 23–24.

61. Avery, "Notes relative to publishing the Sacred Roll," EBK 12,744, pp. 30–32. Avery was by no means the only Believer moved to poetry while visiting the sites of historic Shakerism. John Hobart, an Ohio Shaker, found himself so inspired by the shrines of Shaker history in the Eastern societies that he composed a series of poems based on his "thoughts" and "reflections" while visiting Shakers in New England. See Bathrick, "Visions. Addresses, Extracts," WRHS 75 VIII:B-108, pp. 36–43.

62. New Lebanon Ministry to Hervey [Eads?], 2 November 1845, WRHS 20 IV:A-39.

63. Ibid. "Mother's Sayings" here probably referred to Roxalana Grosvenor's manuscript, which she completed during this year.

64. Joseph Parker of Harvard to J. S. Tillinghast, 8 March 1852, WRHS 19 IV:A-25.

65. See, for example, "A Short account of the rise of Believers and a few of the most interesting occurrences that have taken place since that time," WRHS 32 V:B-60, p. 215; "Domestic Journal of Important Occurrences," entries for 29 February 1844 and 1 March 1845, WRHS 32 V:B-61; "Holy Laws of Zion," SDL, pp. 104–105; and Bishop, "Daily Journal begun 1839," entry for 1 March 1846, NYPL 2, pp. 262–63. Participants in the first celebration of Mother Ann's birthday in 1835 felt that the observance united those on earth with those in heaven. See Bishop, "Daily Journal; Begun 1830," entry for 1 March 1835, NYPL 1.

66. For a note on Mother Lucy's birthday celebration, 5 February 1843, see Record of Spiritual Gifts, WRHS 72 VIII:B-52, p. 35.

67. "The Holy Word of the Lord God Almighty, the Holy One of Israel, To His Chosen People Throughout Zion's Habitations. Given at Wisdom's Valley, And written by Inspiration at the Holy Mount March 5th 1843," WRHS 79 VIII:B-170, ch. 9, vss. 3–4, n.p.; and Bishop, "Daily Journal begun 1839," entries for 6 August 1844 and 6 August 1846, NYPL 2, pp. 228 and 271.

68. "Holy Laws of Zion," WRHS 77 VIII:B-140, pp. 138, 142.

69. Testimony of Elizabeth Wood, WRHS 49 VI:B-1.

70. Lowenthal lists memory, history, and relics as three sources of knowledge about the past. Lowenthal, *The Past,* p. 187. New Era Shakers utilized these three and added a fourth: spiritual vision.

71. This "Last Remains of Mother's Wardrobe" was "Careffully preserved by Jennet Angus, who was born in the year 1810, and came to lovely Zion, 1820. Watervliet, Albany Co. N.Y.," WRHS 116 X:A-1 (L). See also "Fragment of Mother Anns Apron ERS," SDL; and "A fragment of cloth from a dress belonging to Mother Ann Lee, founder of the Shaker faith," stored with PMA 63-160-196.

72. Bishop, "Daily Journal; Begun 1830," entries for 11 and 12 May 1835, NYPL 1. See also New Lebanon Ministry at Watervliet to Whitewater Elders, 22 May 1835, "Copies of letters, Begun 1833," WRHS 27 IV:B-8, pp. 76–77.

73. The Shaker interest in tangible mementos of deceased ancestors reflected, in some ways, the "sentimental cult of mourning" broadly subscribed to by middle class antebellum Americans. According to a contemporary text cited by Karen Halttunen in her study of mid-nineteenth-century middle class culture in America, participants in this sentimental mode of mourning cherished personal items (including portraits and other images) associated with the dead, "because they could be handled and wept over." Halttunen, *Confidence Men,* p. 133. Shaker death and mourning patterns, however, retained the

communal dimension that Halttunen demonstrates was lost to other Americans for whom death became a more private matter (pp. 146–48).

74. For a recent provocative study on Veronica's Veil, see Ewa Kuryluk, *Veronica and Her Cloth: History, Symbolism, and Structure of a "True" Image* (Cambridge, Mass.: Basil Blackwell, 1991).

75. "Holy Orders of the Church," WRHS 78 VIII:B-154, p. 33.

76. Ibid., p. 66.

77. Potter, "Short Notice to Asenith C.," EBK 13,493 (this is a *pictured* pocket handkerchief); and "Communications to Cassandana Goodrich," SDL, p. 132.

78. "Presents Received," WRHS 75 VIII:B-114, pp. 46 and 50.

79. Avery, "Historical Sketches," LC Container 4, Item 53, p. 214—here as a sign of the "thin veil" between this world and the next—see also pp. 162, 178, 188.

80. "A true Record," vol. 11, WRHS 76 VIII:B-126, p. 2; and Bennett and Youngs, "Journal of Inspired Meetings," entry for evening of 24 October 1840, WRHS 77 VIII:B-138.

81. See Lucius Southwick to Jonathan Wood, 2 February 1846, WRHS 20 IV:A-39.

82. Bennett and Youngs, "Journal of Inspired Meetings," entry for 22 November 1841, WRHS 77 VIII:B-138. See also Collection of Miscellaneous Inspired Writings, WRHS 80 VIII:B-175, pp. 44–45 and 73–79; "A true Record," vol. 11, WRHS 76 VIII:B-126, p. 103; Miscellaneous Visions and Communications, WRHS 65 VIII:A-21, n.p.; and "These lines were coppied from a roll of pink silk, wrapped in an orange coulered paper, and laid on Sister Asenath's head, while in meeting. Saturday evening. November 26, 1842," PMA 63-160-196 (8).

83. This uncatalogued booklet was, in August 1984, in the possession of Eldress Bertha Lindsay at Canterbury, New Hampshire.

84. "A Little Box of presents," 5 February 1854, NGA, Index of American Design, 1943.8.13493. This "Little Box," though catalogued with Index renderings of gift images, is an original Shaker visionary image.

85. Collection of HSV.

86. [Bishop and Wells], *Testimonies,* 1816, p. 66.

87. On blazing tree story see "A true Record," vol. 6, WRHS 76 VIII:B-121, p. 38; and Compilation of Messages to Individuals, WRHS 78 VIII:B-151, pp. 75–76.

88. Leonard, "Life and Sufferings," EBK 3226-105, p. 58. Elsewhere, Volume Containing the Word of Holy Wisdom and God Almighty, WRHS 79 VIII:B-170C, pp. 20, 37–40, records a litany of praise for the first born and specifies their crucial role in God's plan for the universe.

89. See, for example, Bishop, "Daily Journal; Begun 1830," entry for 11 September 1833, NYPL 1; New Lebanon Ministry to Union Village Ministry, 18 October 1833, "Copies of letters, Begun 1833," WRHS 27 IV:B-8, pp. 8–11; Journal of Meetings, entry dated 25 January 1847, EBK 12,339; and Joseph W. Babe, Journal of Meetings held in the Church Order, New Lebanon, beginning 1840, entry for 5 May 1841, WRHS 77 VIII:B-139, n.p.

90. On the other hand, indications of friction between young Shakers and the elderly exist. The first born appeared old-fashioned and outdated to some. A few felt the elderly were irrelevant to modern Shakerism. Shaker leaders and spirits intervened and admonished the young to look up to the first born. Some New Era regulations seem to have been designed to prevent ridicule and abuse of the "old-fashioned" first born. See "A true Record," vol. 6, WRHS 76 VIII:B-121, pp. 90–91; and New Lebanon Ministry to

North Union Ministry, 4 January 1839, "Copies of letters, Begun 1833," WRHS 27 IV:B-8, p. 292.

91. The first born were the first "pillars" of the Millennial Church.

92. See Bennett and Youngs, "Journal of Inspired Meetings," entry for 19 December 1841, WRHS 77 VIII:B-138.

93. "A true Record," vol. 1, WRHS 75 VIII:B-116, p. 162.

Because the first born were intimately connected to Mother Ann and therefore holy, Wisdom called upon these ancient children to ritually bless Zion's inhabitants and lands. [Barber and Reed?] Inspired Visions and Messages, WRHS 87 VIII:C-1, pp. 16–17. See also [Stewart and Crossman], "Confidential Journal," entry for 22 September 1842, WRHS 35 V:B-136, p. 10: "there is about 430 Souls including the Ancients of the people, Asscend [*sic*] the Holy Mount this day, to receive the Blessing of Mother's first Born, none under 15 years of age, are permited [*sic*] to go."

94. "Collection of Sacred Writings in the Second Family at New Lebanon," SDL, p. 52. Also [Barber and Reed?] Inspired Visions and Messages, WRHS 87 VIII:C-1, pp. 147–51.

95. For example, Thankful Goodrich, converted at age ten by Mother Ann and Father James, died at age 87 in 1858.

96. At just about this time, other antebellum Americans, too, began to project a *Christian* history onto their past, claiming as their own some of the same heroes as the Shakers. See Jon Butler, *Awash in a Sea of Faith: Christianizing the American People* (Cambridge, Mass.: Harvard University Press, 1990), pp. 285–86.

97. In 1845 the First and Second Order libraries at New Lebanon included biographies of Washington, Columbus, Penn, and Franklin. "School Record," entry for 1845, WRHS 3 I:B-32, n.p. Incidentally, less than two months after Ann Lee's death, Shakers at Niskeyuna had received some historically distinguished visitors, among them, one James Madison and the Marquis de Lafayette.

98. "A true Record," vol. 1, WRHS 75 VIII:B-116, p. 190, also pp. 188–190. Communications from and about Columbus, too, often began with a statement of assumed familiarity between Columbus and the reader. See, for example, "A true Record," vol. 3, WRHS 75 VII:B-118, p. 38.

99. Avery, "Prophetic Warnings," WRHS 78 VIII:B-146, pp. 90– 98.

Some years after the close of Mother's Work, Shakers interpreted the Civil War as an extension of the struggle for moral and political freedom.

> The gospel of the New Creation can never spread to much extent among any people who do not enjoy a national freedom of natural rights . . .
>
> . . . Therefore, whether the people be white or black, whether civilized or savage, God regardeth them as creatures of his peculiar care, and his judgments and providential work shall never cease, until all souls shall be set at liberty. (Ibid., p. 91)

Because of slavery, if it were not for God's Shaker Zion, "the glory of this nation would sink to rise no more." Notwithstanding, heavy judgements would be levied upon the American people.

> For know, . . . that it is not a light thing to cry unto God in distress, and appeal to him under oppression, and when he hath heard, and wrought deliverance, then to abuse that deliverance by inflicting greater distress upon others. Nay, it is the greatest moral sin and rebellion which any people can commit. (Ibid., p. 97)

See also [Bates], *Holy Wisdom's Book,* pp. 105–109; [Barber and Reed?] Inspired Visions and Messages, WRHS 87 VIII:C- 1, pp. 107–117.

100. [Bates], *Holy Wisdom's Book,* p. 330.

101. Mark 1:1-4. Cf. [Bates], *Holy Wisdom's Book,* pp. 331–32.

102. "A true Record," vol. 3, WRHS 75 VII:B-118, p. 41; see also p. 38.

103. Ibid., p. 42. Columbus spoke of his conversion using the conventions of mid-nineteenth century Shaker testimony.

104. Ibid., pp. 38–40. Pages 43–44 comprise a note added by an instrument describing the physical appearance and demeanor of Christopher Columbus and some words on beloved Shaker spirits who appeared with him. Bennett and Youngs, "Journal of Inspired Meetings," entries for 21 and 23 September, WRHS 77 VIII:B-138, record the reading of this Roll regarding Columbus. A Collection of Hymns, WRHS 103 IX:B-239, p. 95, preserves a hymn titled "Christopher Columbus March," given at New Lebanon 25 August 1840. It is legitimate to assume a relatively wide audience for the Columbus roll. New Lebanon Believers included the entire text in correspondence with other communities. See, for example, "Extract of a Letter to the Ministry at Alfred in the state of Maine" (from the New Lebanon Ministry), 6 October 1840, "Copies of letters, Begun 1839," WRHS 27 IV:B-9, p. 49.

105. "Records Concerning the Finding," SDL, p. 12. See also [Bates], *Holy Wisdom's Book,* pp. 332–35, and "A true Record," vol. 3, WRHS 75 VIII:B-118, pp. 40–41.

106. New Lebanon Ministry to Canterbury Ministry, 28 September 1840, "Copies of letters, Begun 1839," WRHS 27 IV:B-9, p. 48.

107. New Lebanon Ministry to Groveland Ministry, 25 April 1840, WRHS 20 IV:A-38.

108. See, for example, "Records Concerning the Finding," SDL, pp. 11–13; New Lebanon Ministry to Groveland Ministry, 25 April 1840, "Copies of letters, Begun 1839," WRHS 27 IV:B-9, pp. 39–40; New Lebanon Ministry to Canterbury Ministry, 28 September 1840, ibid., p. 48; Harvard Ministry to New Lebanon Ministry, 1 March 1844, WRHS 19 IV:A-24; and "A true Record," vol. 1, WRHS 75 VIII:B-116, pp. 188–90.

109. New Lebanon Ministry to Groveland Ministry, 25 April 1840, WRHS 20 IV:A-38.

110. Ibid.

111. For examples of Shaker understandings of the significance of other historic figures see: (on Lafayette) Seth Wells to Rufus Bishop and Isaac Newton Youngs, 1 July 1834, WRHS 20 IV:A-36; and "A Notice from the Marquis Lafayette to Br. Seth Blanchard," Record of Spiritual Gifts, WRHS 72 VIII:B-55, insert, next to last pages; (on Governor Clinton) [Hollister] Messages, Song, and Anthems, WRHS 75 VIII:B-115, pp. 175–76; and (on Benjamin Franklin) ibid., p. 257. For Believers in the mid-nineteenth century, not only American history but, somewhat less frequently, world history found its "true" meaning as part of the Shaker story. See "Calvin's Confession. A Communication given in the name of John Calvin, the Geneva Reformer in the Shaker Community, Shakers, Albany County, New York in 1842. Medium J. Lafume. Reprinted from Progressive Thinker, with additions from the original, August 1904," EBK 3586-1; (on Napoleon) "Records Concerning the Finding," SDL, pp. 83–84; (on Isaac Newton and Isaac Watts) "An account of a journey to a spiritual Telegraph office with Brother Seth Wells, March 25th 1850. By AZP Church first Order Holy Mount,"

WRHS 67 VIII:A-46; and (on Martin Luther and many others) [Avery] "Rappings," EBK 12,143.

112. New Lebanon Ministry at Watervliet to Groveland Ministry, 15 February 1843, "Copies of letters, Begun 1839," WRHS 27 IV:B-9, p. 108. See also New Lebanon Ministry to Harvard Ministry, 22 March 1843, ibid., pp. 114–15.

113. See Volume Containing the Word, WRHS 79 VIII:B-170D, p. 131, on "God's figurative Israel." Mother Ann was the "true representation," the "literal" pattern for the appropriate role of woman and the appropriate relationship between male and female: "and if this is not the true representation, and this order [the female] does not exist in the spiritual heavens, why did not We create and send forth, all living upon earth, in the male order?" [Stewart], *Sacred Roll and Book,* p. 105.

114. Spirit of Father William Lee to New Lebanon Community, 1 April 1843, WRHS 20 IV:A-38; and Lucy Doply, an Indian woman in the spirit world, to "de Shiny Mudder Betty [Betsy Bates]," 26 September 1842, WRHS 20 IV:A-38. Native American spirits appeared to Shaker visionists early in the New Era. For a description of an April 1838 visitation, see Draft of a Letter from Seth Wells at New Lebanon to the Canterbury Ministry, 3 April 1838, WRHS 20 IV:A-37.

115. Instruments for native spirits were usually under thirty years of age. [Wells and Youngs], "Records Kept by Order of the Church," note following entry for 28 July 1842, NYPL 7, p. 198.

116. For examples of native spirit letters denouncing specific cruelties shown to Native Americans, see Spirit of Father William Lee to New Lebanon Community, 1 April 1843, WRHS 20 IV:A-38; Lucy Doply to Betsy Bates, 26 September 1842, WRHS 20 IV:A-38; "Lucy Doply de quaw" at "De Lebanon New" to "De Lovey Shiny Moder Cena [Ascenath Clark]," 25 September 1842, WRHS 65 VIII:A-22; and A "poor red sister" at "Holy Mountain" to "Holy Mother Ruth [Landon]," 25 September 1842, WRHS 65 VIII:A-22.

117. New Lebanon Ministry to Union Village Ministry, 3 November 1842, "Copies of letters, Begun 1839," WRHS 27 IV:B-9, pp. 94–95.

118. Ibid., p. 93. See also [Wells and Youngs], "Records Kept by Order of the Church," entry titled "Review of 1844, NYPL 7, p. 236, for another explicit reference to the "singular characters" of "indian writing," here pertaining to the large number of such documents received in 1844.

119. Potter, "Short Notice to Asenith C.," EBK 13,493, n.p.; Potter, "Short Word of Notice to Ebenezer Bishop," EBK 13,495, n.p.; Potter, "A Short Notice to Ruth Landen," EBK 13,496, n.p.; and Potter, "A Notice to Br. Rufus," EBK 13,494, n.p.

120. Native script bears a striking similarity to sacred script; one might easily be mistaken for the other. Even the instruments of the two overlapped. Semantha Fairbanks was a principal instrument of sacred script and she also penned a 2 February 1845 native spirit message. See New Lebanon Elders to New Lebanon Ministry at Watervliet, 2 February 1845, WRHS 20 IV:A-39.

121. Evans, "Memorial to Beecher," EBK 16,677, pp. 6 and 15; and Collection of Inspired Writings, SDL, p. 84.

122. Cf. Roger Williams in Hughes and Allen, *Illusions of Innocence,* p. 58.

123. "Explanation," PMA 63-160-5a, pp. 56–57.

124. Bathrick, "Visions. Addresses, Extracts," WRHS 75 VIII:B-108, p. 157.

125. New Lebanon Ministry to Harvard Ministry, 31 March 1842, "Copies of letters, Begun 1839," WRHS 27 IV:B-9, p. 84.

126. "Collection of Sacred Writings at the Second Family New Lebanon," SDL, p. 70.

127. Cf. Freedberg, *Power of Images,* pp. 192–97.

128. Butler, *Awash in a Sea of Faith,* p. 242.

129. Marini, *Radical Sects,* p. 129. On the early Shaker practice of converting entire (even extended) biological families, and on the impact of this practice on communal stability in early Shakerism, see p. 100.

As evidence of the necessity of somehow integrating feelings about families of biological origin into conceptions of the Shaker "family," see a gift drawing to Sarah Ann Standish (1809–1895) addressing this orphan's continuing concerns about the early loss of her parents. The gift drawing of 1847 assured Sarah Ann Standish that Holy Mother Wisdom was her "loving Parent." Unlike her earthly parents, this Mother would never leave her desolate and lonely. "I well know the sorrowful path you have traveled for many years, and have often sent my holy Angels to comfort your drooping soul." See *From Holy Mother Wisdom to Sarah Ann Standish July 15th 1847,* ink on paper, 9 and 3/4 inches by 7 and 7/8 inches, HSV. We know something of Standish's history as an orphan from "Domestic Journal of Important Occurrences," entry for 17 July 1851, WRHS 32 V:B-61. For other examples of similar messages allowing orphans and those abandoned in childhood to work out relationships with families of origin and of other messages to a child from a natural parent in the spirit world, see [Isaac Newton Youngs], "Visions Seen by Elleyett Gibbs and Ann Mariah Goff" (9 January–16 February 1838), EBK 3329, pp. 44–46; "An Account of the Meetings Held in the City of Peace, City of Union, and City of Love. On the 25th of December 1845," WML 151 SA 788, p. 35; "A piece of advice delivered by an unbodied Parent, to her youngest daughter who having lost her Mother, when she was five years of age; the Parent feeling a responsibility resting upon her, and a duty to do, she therefore appeared to her on Wensday evening in the year 1838," NYPL 101; and Messages to Eliza Babbit, Beginning 6 August 1841, WRHS 79 VIII:B-160, pp. 10–13, 30–31, and 36–37.

Other gift messages brought words and images of consolation directly from beloved natural family members. In a communication dated 28 September 1841, for example, Issachar Bates, a first born Believer, relayed his love for his daughter Betsey and offered her a meaningful interpretation of his death, his afterlife, and his continuing relationship with her ("Rolls, letters, Messages, and Communications," EBK 12,332, pp. 11–13). The instrument for this fatherly message was the orphaned Sarah Ann Standish. In addition, "A Little Roll from Louisa Blanchard to Seth Blanchard her Natural Father" ("Record of Spiritual Presents," WRHS 72 VIII:B-55, pp. 17–20) conveyed a message of pastoral concern and affection from a deceased child to the parent who, some years later, sought meaning in her death.

130. [Hollister], Messages, Songs, and Anthems, WRHS 75 VIII:B-115, p. 175. See also New Lebanon Ministry at Watervliet to Groveland Ministry, 15 February 1843, "Copies of letters, Begun 1839," WRHS 27 IV:B-9, pp. 108–109.

131. New Lebanon Ministry to Groveland Ministry, 25 April 1840, WRHS 20 IV:A-38. See also Sarah Bates, "Hymns and Extra Songs," WRHS 89 IX:B-16, pp. 28–30.

132. Foster, *Religion and Sexuality,* pp. 12–13.

133. "Holy Laws of Zion," WRHS 77 VIII:B-140, p. 84.

134. Cott, *Bonds of Womanhood,* pp. 64, 65, 68. "The central convention of domesticity was the contrast between home and the world" (p. 64).

135. Cf. Halttunen, *Confidence Men,* pp. 58–59.

136. Symmetry and compartmentalization within the smaller units of the drawing jux-

tapose groupings of Believers with vegetal designs generally representing Shaker virtues. Patterson, *Gift Drawing,* pp. 25 and 31, and Ruth Wolfe, "Hannah Cohoon: Shaker Spirit Painter," *Art and Antiques* 3 (May–June 1980): 94, suggest the domestic needlework of New England (particularly family quilts and embroidered samplers) as sources for this and similar Shaker compositions.

137. Leonard, "Life and Sufferings," EBK 3226-105, p. 59. See Vlach, *Plain Painters,* pp. 74–75 on portraiture and domesticity.

138. If the heavenly sphere was a genealogical garden, it was also a family home. Believers described heaven as a communal celestial mansion as well as a holy city of many mansions housing and representing individual souls. See, for example, Polly Collins' Book, WRHS 71 VII:B-21, n.p.; "Communication from Mother Ann to Amy Reed," EBK 12,087; and "Communications to Cassandana Goodrich," SDL, p. 25. Cf. Ann Douglas, *The Feminization of American Culture* (New York: Avon Books, 1977), pp. 265–72, and the general nineteenth-century theological shift from heaven as kingdom to heaven as home.

139. McCracken, *Culture and Consumption,* pp. 45, 46; also Lowenthal, *The Past,* pp. 257–58, discusses the role of images of past people and events in connecting children with their familial history and with the past in general. Family photo albums did not become popular until after 1861 but women, especially, made keepsake albums and scrapbooks well before this time.

140. Cf. Wolfe, "Hannah Cohoon."

141. See, for example, figure 66 (David Lane–Hannah Marchent family record by William Saville, Gloucester, Mass., 21 Decemeber 1772) and figure 67 (Olive Clark–Andrew Bickford family record by J. Pool, New England, nineteenth century) in Cynthia V. A. Schaffner and Susan Klein, *Folk Hearts: A Celebration of the Heart Motif in American Folk Art* (New York: Alfred A. Knopf, 1984), pp. 56 and 57.

142. George R. Stewart, *American Given Names: Their Origin and History in the Context of the English Language* (New York: Oxford University Press, 1979), cover.

143. Cf. these gift drawings to Staffordshire ceramics of 1750s through 1800s and nineteenth-century Pennsylvania German commemorative plates. See, for example, Henry Kauffman, *Pennsylvania Dutch American Folk Art* (New York: Dover, 1964). Many Shakers were of English extraction. And, after the Shaker Pennsylvania mission of 1828, eighty Pennsylvania residents, some Pennsylvania Germans, came to observe the Shaker way of life. Some twenty to thirty of these, including at least one prominent New Lebanon instrument, Anna Dodgson, stayed and cast their lot with Shakers. See Green, "Biographic Memoir," copied and expanded by Hollister, vol. 2, WRHS 51 VI:B-30, pp. 464–72.

144. A dove on the Eliza Ann Taylor plate bears a "ball of love."

145. See "Communication from Mother Ann to Amy Reed," EBK 12,087; and "Presents Received," WRHS 75 VIII:B-114, p. 44.

146. "A true Record," vol. 4, WRHS 75 VIII:B-119, esp. pp. 105–18.

147. See "A true Record," vol. 5, WRHS 75 VIII:B-120, p. 172; and Avery, "Historical Sketches," LC Container 4, Item 53, pp. 196–98.

148. For a discussion of the normative role of "narratives preserved by collective memory," of their ability to "provide criteria, implicit or explicit, by which contemporary models of action can be shaped or corrected," see Steven Knapp, "Collective Memory and the Actual Past," *Representations* 26 (Spring 1989): 123.

149. Pierre Nora, "Between Memory and History: Les Lieux de Mémoire," *Representations* 26 (Spring 1989): 21.

150. Nora might well add images to his discussion. Images as well as "history books and historical events" can function as "sites of memory"; images too can "inscribe a neat border around a domain of memory," ibid.

151. Davis and Starn, "Introduction," *Representations* 26 (Spring 1989): 3–4.

7. Restoring Relationship

1. Garrett, *Spirit Possession,* p. 207, comments on Ann Lee's ability, during her lifetime, to send "spiritual gifts" into those present with her. New Era manifestations replicated this experience in relationship to the spirit of Ann Lee.

2. [Youngs], "Preface, or Introduction," WRHS 75 VIII:B-109, p. 16.

3. Ibid., p. 14.

4. Copies and Extracts of Messages, WRHS 75 VIII:B-112, pp. 2 and 10; [Youngs], "Preface, or Introduction," WRHS 75 VIII:B-109, p. 20; see also p. 21. In a letter from the New Lebanon Ministry to the North Union Ministry, 4 January 1839 ("Copies of letters, Begun 1833," WRHS 27 IV:B-8, pp. 285–86), the correspondent referred to the New Era as the "mighty work of Mother Ann among you." See also "A true Record," vol. 1, WRHS 75 VIII:B-116, p. 4.

5. "Divine Inspiration containing Explanations," WRHS 78 VIII:B-143, section I, paragraphs 8–9, n.p.

6. Visible presence was not the only issue. It was often in these terms, however, that mid-nineteenth-century Shakers expressed their sense of loss in the face of Lee's absence, encoded their discouragement.

7. [Bishop and Wells], *Testimonies,* 1816, p. 318; see also pp. 289–90.

8. Ibid., pp. 316–17. See also [Wells and Green], *Testimonies,* 1827, pp. 90, 92–93.

9. "A Choice Selection of Heavenly Communications Given by Inspiration, and Words Spoken by our First Parents and Elders, when they were upon Earth. Recollected by Thankful Goodrich," May 1857, WRHS 80 VIII:B-188, entry titled "A Short Sketch," n.p. This New Lebanon sister died on 30 July 1858 at the age of eighty-seven.

10. [B. Youngs], *Testimony of Christ's Second Appearing,* 1808, p. 30.

11. Ibid.

12. "A Large Square Containing Solemn Warnings and Precious Instructions for the Young, Written by Father James in the Holy City January 1st 1841. Read to the Church in Alfred March 6 1842," SDL, n.p.; "Inspired Communications and Messages," WML 430 SA 1068, p. 20; and Copies and Extracts of Messages, WRHS 75 VIII:B-112, p. 2.

13. "Presents Received," WRHS 75 VIII:B-114, p. 174. This document records or copies, at a later date, Mother Lucy's words of 1815. See also "Sayings of Mother Lucy, Spoken at Different Times and Under Various Circumstances," WRHS 56 VII:B-60.1, entry for 5 February 1815 at Watervliet, n.p. "Betsy Bate's [*sic*] Book," WRHS 56 VII:B-61, entry for 25 March 1815 at New Lebanon, n.p. describes the importance of being "joined to the present work of God."

14. "Sayings of Mother Lucy," WRHS 56 VII:B-60.1, entry for July 1816, n.p. In this quotation it is difficult to discern when "Mother" is Wright and when "Mother" is Lee. In this case, it is most likely that Lucy Wright is the "Mother" in question. Cf. ibid., entry for 21 January 1820, n.p., where Wright claims that "union is more valuable than all earthly things."

15. "Collection of Sacred Writings at the Second Family New Lebanon," SDL, p. 2.

16. "A Church Meeting Journal. Kept by request of the Elders, Wisdom's Valley. February 25th 1844," WRHS 48 V:B-327, p. 1.

17. "Divine Inspiration containing Explanations," WRHS 78 VIII:B-143, section II,

paragraph 35, n.p. The original wording, "*Where* there is no vision" (KJV), appears in [Youngs], "Preface, or Introduction," WRHS 75 VIII:B-109, p. 55.

18. "Book of Wisdom and Sacred Truth," WRHS 78 VIII:B-153, p. 17, also pp. 18–21, 30.

19. New Lebanon Ministry at Watervliet to Harvard Ministry, 21 February 1838, "Copies of letters, Begun 1833," WRHS 27 IV:B-8, pp. 236–37.

20. William Leonard to Hervey Eads, n.d., WRHS 18 IV:A-21. Technically, Leonard here refers to God the Father and to Holy Mother Wisdom rather than to the Heavenly Parents (Ann Lee and Jesus Christ) or Spiritual Parents (Lucy Wright, Joseph Meacham, James Whittaker, etc.). Within the context of Leonard's letter to Eads and in relationship to New Era spirituality, however, my extrapolation is fair.

21. [Youngs], "Preface, or Introduction," WRHS 75 VIII:B-109, p. 58.

22. New Lebanon Ministry at Watervliet to Pleasant Hill Ministry, 6 November 1839, "Copies of letters, Begun 1839," WRHS 27 IV:B-9, p. 15.

23. "A true Record," vol. 6, WRHS 76 VIII:B-121, p. 251.

24. "Meetings on Mount Sinai," SDL, p. 99. See also New Lebanon Ministry to Pleasant Hill Ministry, 4 December 1837, "Copies of letters, Begun 1833," WRHS 27 IV:B-8, p. 224; and New Lebanon Ministry to Sodus Elders, 19 December 1837, ibid., p. 232) in which the correspondent noted, "It seems that these youth and children can name and describe almost any of our departed friends, and can give a description of their attainments and degrees of glory; altho' they never saw many of them in the body, if they ever heard their names." Eunice Bathrick's autobiographical testimony reveals one prominent instrument's interpretation of Mother's Work as a phenomenon concerned with Mother Ann's corporeal presence (Eunice Bathrick, Autobiography and Testimony, WRHS 49 VI:A-5, especially pp. 26–27 and 30).

25. "A true Record," vol. 1, WRHS 75 VIII:B-116, p. 4. Underscoring the importance of visual access, Shakers consistently described the first born as "eyewitnesses." In the "various forms and colours" of gift drawings and paintings, third generation Shakers without spiritual vision could see Mother Ann for themselves, could become "eyewitnesses" too (cf. inscription on *A gift from Mother Ann to the Elders at the North Family,* fig. 14).

26. Record of Spiritual Gifts, WRHS 72 VIII:B-52, pp. 41–42. The recorded gift-giver in this case was "Mother Hannah," first female leader at the Harvard community.

27. The inscriptions on several images make explicit not just the association of image with the love of the deified founder, but the *identity* of image and Mother Ann's love. See also, for example, "Words of an Affectionate Mother, To a Child of her Care," WRHS 87 VIII:C-5 (fig. 25).

28. Leonard to Eads, n.d., WRHS 18 IV:A-21. Shakers escaped the problem of the fusion of image and prototype by not depicting the bodily appearance of Ann Lee while simultaneously understanding their images to signify her presence.

29. See [Youngs], "Preface, or Introduction," WRHS 75 VIII:B-109, p. 17: "Much was . . . done in writing and recording the visions, trances, and interviews in the spiritual world, that those who were not eyewitnesses and those who came after, might know in some measure the truth of these things." Cf. "A Closing Roll From Holy and Eternal Wisdom, Mother Ann, Father William and Father James, To the Children of Zion," (Canterbury, N.H.: n.p., 1843), EBK 12,027, p. 30, where, the instrument claimed, henceforth, sacred writings would recall to mind the "reappearance" of Lee and her first generation during Mother's Work as well as the appearance of Ann Lee to her first born years earlier.

30. For evidence of an ongoing ministry of pastoral care among Believers, see, for example, Book of Miscellaneous Lists, WRHS 13 II:B-126, n.p., which includes lists of those with special needs, as well as an appended note specifying that "cards were made"

in response to one item in particular; and Journal of Meetings Held in the Church Order at New Lebanon Beginning 1846, entry for 17 October 1847, EBK 12,339.

31. See, for example, "A Communication or word of Notice and Comfort from Mother Ann to Amy Reed. Monday Evening Sept. 25th 1848," EBK 12,087; *A gift from Mother Ann To Eldress Eunice,* August 1859, SDL; and *Mother Ann's Word to her little child Elizabeth Cantrell,* 14 August 1848, HSV.

32. Cf. Isaacs, "The Fox Sisters," esp. p. 96.

33. New Lebanon Ministry to Pleasant Hill Ministry, 4 December 1837, "Copies of letters, Begun 1833," WRHS 27 IV:B-8, p. 223. See also New Lebanon Ministry to Sodus Elders, 19 December 1837, ibid., p. 233; New Lebanon Ministry to Union Village Ministry, 9 October 1838, ibid., p. 266; and New Lebanon Ministry to North Union Ministry, 4 January 1839, ibid., p. 288.

34. New Lebanon Ministry to Enfield, N.H. Ministry, 28 February 1838, ibid., p. 239.

35. New Lebanon Ministry to Union Village Ministry, 19 May 1852, "Copies of letters, Begun 1839," WRHS 27 IV:B-9, p. 424. See also New Lebanon Ministry to Canterbury Ministry, 27 March 1852, ibid., p. 422; "A Record of Communications from the Spiritual World to Eldress Cassandana Goodrich. Given by Divine Inspiration," SDL, p. 147; and "Sister Semantha Fairbanks Parting Address to the Beloved Ministry," 20 March 1852, WRHS 20 IV:A-40.

36. New Lebanon Ministry to Enfield, N.H. Ministry, 3 March 1839, "Copies of letters, Begun 1833," WRHS 27 IV:B-8, p. 317.

37. "A Roll from Elizeth [*sic*] Babbit to Sarah Hammond," 2 August 1842, WRHS 64 VIII:A-14, n.p. counseled Hammond not to fear death. For, according to the instrument, Babbit testified, "I have thought many times, of the happy hours we spent together in our little terestial [*sic*] paradise; and of the many precious gifts which used to be bestowed on us in those days. But I can tell you, dear Sister, that we did not then, know but little of the joys of the New Jerusalem; for what we then enjoyed, was but a foretaste, and a very small one too, compared with what my eyes have beheld, since my spirit joined the happy numbers of Mother's first-born in heaven. . . . you will be astonished when you behold the beauty and glory of the heavenly order." See also "Comforting Words from Father Calvin to Sister Hannah Munsel. They were written on a little Stone by him, on the holy Mount of Olives. It was Copied off by an inspired Instrument Sabbath P.M. September 25, 1842" (LC Container 1, Item 13); and "A true Record," vol. 10, WRHS 76 VIII:B-125, p. 61. Elkins, *Fifteen Years,* p. 60, vividly describes the consolation provided by New Era manifestations in times of illness.

38. Perhaps Smith was visiting at Hancock when she received this gift; perhaps the gift was delivered through a Hancock instrument for this New Lebanon sister. Like Israel Hammond, Molly Smith was a member of the New Lebanon Church. This was true at least as late as 1 May 1841 when both Molly Smith and Israel Hammond signed the testimony of "Ancient Brethren and Sisters at the New Lebanon Church." Smith received another pictorial gift, "A Little Box of presents," on 5 February 1854, NGA, Index of American Design, 1943.8.13493.

39. For accounts of Hammond's injury and death, see Bennett and Youngs, "Journal of Inspired Meetings," remarks following entry for 10 August 1841, WRHS 77 VIII:B-138; and New Lebanon Ministry at Watervliet to Sodus Elders, 26 January 1833, Copies of Letters, Begun 1823, WRHS 26 IV:B-7, p. 334.

40. Israel Hammond to Molly Smith, given 28 April 1845, recorded 25 January 1847, SDL.

41. Ibid. The instruments produced similar messages to faithful caretakers from other deceased Shakers and from both Heavenly and Spiritual Parents. A visually organized sheet, sent "to Jane [Blanchard] and Amy [Reed], Jan'y 18th 1868," offered heavenly comfort to these two caretaking Shakers. The instrument made two copies of this mes-

sage, one copy for each sister, see "Word of Love, from Mother Lucy; to the Physician Sisters, Jane B. and Amy R. Jan'y 18th 1868," EBK 12,128; and "Words of Love from Mother Lucy; to the Physician Sisters; Jane B. and Amy R. Jan'y 18th 1868," EBK 12,094. For a visually organized text, see "A Short Word from Eldress Betsy, To Sisters Maria Stewart and Amy Reed. March 5th 1869," EBK 12,112.

In addition to relaying gift drawings and other communications from the heavenly sphere, the instruments of Mother's Work also sought answers from the spirits for the ministry and other members of the community on questions regarding the day-to-day care of the sick. See Sally Loomis at Harvard to Asenath Clark and Semantha Fairbanks at New Lebanon, 11 February 1851, WRHS 19 IV:A-25; and Sally Loomis at Harvard to Samuel Myrick at Harvard, 28 December 1851, WRHS 19 IV:A-25. Furthermore, instruments comforted the sick and dying by mediating conversations between them and the spirits and by communicating gifts and blessings from the spirits to victims of grave diseases. See "A short sketch of the illness, and death of Almira Thomson," SDL, n.p. Finally, instruments participated in complex symbolic rites of healing and reassurance. In practice, Shaker pastoral, prophetic, and sacramental ministries overlapped. Instruments used prophetic skills and signs and sacralizing activities in attending to the needs of the sick and dying. See, for example, Giles B. Avery, "Historical Sketches or a Record of Remarkable events With Remarks and Illustrations" (January 1834–February 1843), entries for 5 February 1843 and 30 January 1843, LC Container 4, Item 53, pp. 192–93 and 197–98.

42. "Closing Roll," EBK 12,027, p. 14; see also pp. 15 and 22–23.

43. Instruments of images associated with one another and traveled frequently between New Lebanon and Hancock, see, for example, "Domestic Journal of Important Occurrences," entry for 24 October 1854, WRHS 32 V:B-61. Perhaps the most convincing evidence for contact between artists of different communities is the appearance of a highly idiosyncratic symbol in drawings from both Hancock and New Lebanon. Hannah Cohoon, in *A Bower of Mulberry Trees* (1854), employed the same peculiar convention for a fresh-water spring that a New Lebanon artist used in the early 1840s in a book of prophetic images and signs. Cf. Plate IV and *The Word of the Lord,* in Book of Prophetic Drawings, WRHSmf 87 VIII:C-6, n.p. It is possible, though in this case I think unlikely, that a third outside source may have influenced the iconography.

44. The public record differed from the private gift and Shakers clearly noted this distinction. See [Youngs], "Preface of Introduction," WRHS 75 VIII:B-109, pp. 60–61.

45. Patterson, *Gift Drawing,* esp. pp. 35–42.

46. Cf. Halttunen, *Confidence Men,* pp. 56–57, on the mid-nineteenth-century assumption of the moral superiority of private experience and personal emotion in sentimentalist fiction and ideology. The more "private" function of Shaker images fit with a "sentimental reverence for the personal" (ibid., p. 133) in the larger culture. Gift images thus participated in the reconciliation of a powerful cultural message and a pervasive communal content. In addition, though the millennium was to be lived out collectively, and though the efforts of the very righteous might have some impact on the destiny of the unregenerate, salvation was ultimately an affair of the individual will.

47. Cf. Garrett, *Spirit Possession,* pp. 4–6; and Patterson, *Gift Drawing,* pp. 40–42.

48. These are the words of a nineteenth-century observer of the Shakers, recorded in Carl Bode, *American Life in the 1840s* (Garden City, N.J.: Doubleday and Co., 1967), p. 195.

See the words of Mother Ann in the last paragraph of a communication of 22 March 1840 from Elder Sister Olive Spencer, in an unnumbered entry added to the back of Journal, WRHS 30 V:B-37, n.p., on the private storage of personal gifts; see also "A true Record," vol. 4, WRHS 75 VIII:B-119, p. 118, in a reference to gift plates, on making personal copies of gifts for those who desire them.

49. Freedberg, *Power of Images,* p. 161.

50. This movement predictably reversed the initial introduction of gift images in the Shaker community when spiritual and mental images paved the way for material ones.

51. Gerardus van der Leeuw, *Sacred and Profane Beauty: The Holy in Art* (New York: Holt, Rinehart and Winston, 1963), p. 325. See also George Steiner, *Real Presences* (Chicago: University of Chicago Press, 1989).

52. E. H. Gombrich, *Art and Illusion: A Study in the Psychology of Pictorial Representation,* Bollingen Paperback ed. (Princeton: Princeton University Press, 1972), p. 113.

53. Freedberg, *Power of Images,* p. 404. Cf. pp. 41–44.

54. "To be present, let us not forget, is primarily to be physically present, that is, to have one's senses engaged." Miles, "Formation by Attraction," p. 5. Cf. Freedberg, *Power of Images,* p. 281.

55. John Dunlavy, *The Manifesto, or a Declaration of the Doctrine and Practice of the Church of Christ* (New York: Edward O. Jenkins, 1847), p. 246. Cf. Procter-Smith, *Women in Shaker Community,* pp. 159–60.

56. "Closing Roll," EBK 12,207, p. 14. See also "A true Record," vol. 2, WRHS 75 VIII:B-117, p. 138.

57. "Holy Wisdom's Word," PMA 63-160-196-(21); [Barber and Reed?] Book of Inspired Visions and Messages, WRHS 87 VIII:C-1, pp. 80–98; Roll to Daniel Boler from Mother Ann and Holy Mother Wisdom, EBK 13,483, p. 11; and "Collection of Sacred Writings at the Second Family New Lebanon Commencing December 1840," SDL, pp. 69–71.

58. In addition to "A Present from Mother Ann To Eliza Ann [Taylor]," 1 August 1847, WRHS 87 VIII:C-2 (fig. 23 here), see, for example, "A Collection of Sacred Writings at the Second Family," SDL, pp. 11–12; [Barber and Reed?] Book of Inspired Visions and Messages, WRHS 87 VIII:C-1, pp. 80–98; "A Book Containing Mother Hannah's Bequest to her Middle Aged Children in Lovely Vineyard and Pleasant Garden," WRHS 75 VIII:B-102, pp. 4–5, and 55–57; and "A true Record," vol. 9, WRHS 76 VIII:B-124, p. 49.

59. Orvell, *The Real Thing,* p. 73. In the decades following the New Era, as the production of gift images ceased and sacramental associations of image-making gradually diminished, Shakers began to use photographs and stereoscopic images to record the appearance of individual members and communities and to advertise and promote Shaker life. By 1871, following by some years the actual introduction of photographs into the Society, communal laws made allowances for the possession of photographs among Shakers. Cf. Gus Macdonald, *Camera: Victorian Eyewitness, A History of Photography: 1826–1913* (New York: Viking Press, 1980), especially pp. 13 and 22.

60. Orvell, *The Real Thing,* p. 75.

61. Youngs, "Concise View," WML SA 760, p. 151.

62. [Stewart and Crossman], "A Confidential Journal Kept in the Elder's Lot," entry for 21 August 1842, WRHS 35 V:B-136, p. 5. According to *The Compact Edition of the Oxford English Dictionary,* s.v. "peach blow," peach blow is a "delicate purplish-pink colour."

63. "Word of a short Roll sent from Holy Mother Wisdom to the Ministry concerning the Cards she had sent unto those in the First and Second Orders of the Church August 20, 1842," PMA 63-160-198, pp. 7–8. For a second copy of the text of this booklet, see Barber, "Collection of Visionary Scens [*sic*]," EBK 12,316, pp. 48–51. See also "Words of a Shining Roll, Sent from Holy Mother Wisdom, To Eldress Ruth Landen. July 10th 1842. Copied from the Original, August 16th 1842," WRHS 67 VIII:A-42. Pages 10–14 of this document reiterate the primary content of the PMA booklet, "Concerning the Cards." Other New Lebanon leaders received similar gift booklets bearing approximately the same dates.

64. "Roll concerning the Cards," PMA 63-160-198, pp. 10–12.

65. Collection of Miscellaneous Inspired Writings, WRHS 80 VIII:B-175, p. 86; "An

Account of the Meetings Held in the City of Peace, City of Union, and City of Love. On the 25th of December 1845," WML 151 SA 788, pp. 55–56; and Messages of Warning, Admonition, and Instruction, WRHS 75 VIII:B-111, p. 27.

66. This Jane Blanchard of the Church Family at New Lebanon was also called Emma Jane Blanchard.

67. For the Harvard succession from 1791 to 1905, see "Record of Succession in the Ministry at Harvard and Shirley and Journies performed by them," WRHS 32 V:B-59.

68. "Copy of an interesting Narative of some Visionary scenes Witnesed by Eunice Wythe and sent by her to Jane Blanchard, September 22nd 1850," EBK 12,101, pp. 1–3. A second copy of this visionary account is included in another manuscript of Mother's Work, see "Copy of an interesting Narative of some Visionary scenes witness by Eunice Wyeth, and Sent by her to Jane Blanchard. September 22, 1850") in Bathrick, "Visions. Addresses, Extracts," WRHS 75 VIII:B-108, pp. 100–111. The original booklet is owned by EBK, the copy by WRHS, and the painting by HSV. I first noted the connection between the three in my doctoral dissertation, "Spiritual Spectacles: Shaker Gift Images in Religious Context," University of Chicago, 1988.

69. The instrument dated the booklet, at the front, 22 September 1850, and, at the back, 6 June 1851. It is possible that the first date locates the instrument's visionary episode in time while the second specifies the date the record (in word and image) was produced. The painting itself the instrument dated 1851.

70. The Holy City map was attended by a lengthy key or index but this key, the principal function of which was to identify the different sections of the map and to locate them in relationship to the Shaker community, did little more than briefly outline the narrative context of initial visionary event.

71. In a series of allusions to biblical prophets and visionaries Isaiah and Daniel and to Mary the mother of Jesus (here described in a contemplative role), the booklet establishes a similar visionary and contemplative identity for Wyeth and encourages Blanchard in this direction.

72. "Copy of an interesting Narative," EBK 12,101, pp. 2–3.

73. The narrative, which began in 1850, flashed back to a vision experienced in 1815—but soon the visionist, still in 1815, was "seeing" an event that would occur in 1850, then back to 1815, and so on.

74. The communicative mode of an image changes, then, when it is described by words or "translated" into verbal expression.

75. For a rather more extreme statement of this idea ("language unfolds in temporal succession; images reside in a realm of timeless spatiality and simultaneity"), see W. J. T. Mitchell, "Introduction," in W. J. T. Mitchell. ed., *The Language of Images* (Chicago: University of Chicago Press, 1980), p. 3. Mitchell has since modified his position somewhat, see W. J. T. Mitchell, *Iconology: Image, Text, Ideology* (Chicago: University of Chicago Press, 1986).

76. Spiritual gifts of illustrated pocket handkerchiefs were not at all uncommon among Shakers during Mother's Work. See, for example, New Lebanon Ministry to the Elders at Groveland, 24 April 1838, WRHS 20 IV:A-37; "A Beautiful Dress from Holy Mother Wisdom, to the Ministry [at Groveland]," WRHS 63 VIII:A-F7, pp. 13–18; and "Ministry in the City of Peace. Spiritual Dresses for the out families," WRHS 63 VIII:A-F9, n.p., where the handkerchiefs were "tokens of honesty, simplisity, love, peace and purity." One side of "A Little Box of presents," NGA, Index of American Design, 1943.8.13493, the instrument conceived as a handkerchief facsimile; a gift booklet of 1845 (Potter, "Short Notice to Asenith C.," EBK 13,493) included a picture of a pocket handkerchief; and Henry Blinn listed pocket handkerchiefs among spiritual presents received at mid-century (Blinn, *Spiritualism,* p. 84).

77. "Biographical Sketch" of Eunice Wyeth in Eunice Bathrick, Autobiography and Testimony, WRHS 49 VI:A-5, p. 5.

78. "Copy of an interesting Narative," EBK 12,101, p. 5.

79. Harvard Ministry to Hancock Ministry, 21 January 1830, WRHS 19 IV:A-23. This quote is from the first draft of a letter which was itself dated 27 January. The "Square House" mentioned in the letter was noteworthy for its direct connection to the life and ministry of Ann Lee. In 1781, after the death of a non-Shaker "prophet," Shadrach Ireland, Ann Lee occupied his house and converted numbers of his disciples. Later, after purchasing the land from Shadrach's heirs, Shakers gathered the Harvard community on the property. Cf. Garrett, *Spirit Possession,* pp. 178–81.

80. See Harvard Ministry to New Lebanon Ministry, 17 January 1824, WRHS 18 IV:A-22. See also "Domestic Journal of Important Occurrences," entry for 21 May 1846, WRHS 32 V:B-61.

81. "A Communication from Mother Lucy to Jane Blanchard," 1 January 1839, EBK 12,104. Another factor which probably contributed to Blanchard's removal to the Shaker center at New Lebanon involved her fitness for a position of some responsibility in the Mother Church. A "tall" and narrow visually organized calligraphic gift to Jane Blanchard in 1848 simulated, in orientation, shape, and size, a vertical column. The instrument composed the text around an acrostic using the letters of Blanchard's full name. The instrument thus identified Blanchard with "Holy Mother's Silver Column," suggesting that this third generation daughter had herself become a sturdy pillar supporting the Millennial Church. "Holy Mother's Silver Column, or a Notice from Mother Lucy. April 30th 1848," EBK 14,400.

82. In 1830, a friend of Blanchard's from Harvard visited her at New Lebanon and recorded notes about her association with Blanchard. "A Journal kept by Lucy Ann Hammond while on a journey to New Lebanon Hancock and Enfield in 1830," WRHS 30 V:B-39, entries for 17 October–20 November 1830, n.p.

83. See "A Short Communication from Mother Lucy to Jane Blanchard Jan'y 29th 1843," EBK 12,129; and "A Communication from Mother Lucy to Jane Blanchard," 1 January 1839, EBK 12,104. Shaker theodicy assured troubled Believers like Jane Blanchard that the relationship between faith and good fortune was not necessarily reciprocal. If the tribulation born by the faithful seemed great, perhaps they were laboring, as did Mother Ann, for the souls of those less righteous. In fact, only the most spiritually advanced, those closest to perfection, were able to bring other troubled souls and spirits into Ann Lee's gospel in this way. See Bathrick, "Visions. Addresses, Extracts," WRHS 75 VIII:B-108, pp. 212–14.

84. "Copy of an interesting Narative," EBK 12,101, p. 5. For other references to shining stars as gifts and emblems of identification and celestial beauty for true witnesses see "Collection of Sacred Writings at the Second Family New Lebanon," SDL, p. 18; "A few words from Eldress Betsey, to Jane Blanchard March 21st 1869," EBK 12,108; "A Star of Approbation and Seal of the Holy Saviour. Betsy Bates January 1st 1845," WRHS 87 VIII:C-2; and "A Star of Approbation and Seal of the Holy Saviour's Love, Eliza Ann Taylor. January 1st 1845, WRHS 87 VIII:C-2. "A Little Book containing a short word from Holy Mother Wisdom, concerning the Robes and Dresses," WML SA 1072, n.p., has the gift of a star as a "seal of approbation and love."

85. "Copy of an interesting Narative," EBK 12,101, p. 5.

86. Ibid., pp. 8 and 9.

87. Ibid., p. 8. Though the star image and its content appealed directly and specifically to Blanchard, the evidence suggests that others in Blanchard's community knew the image and understood its significance. Implicitly, at least, the picture spoke to Blanchard's third generation companions as well. See "A few words from Eldress Betsey to Jane Blanchard. March 21st 1869," EBK 12,108.

88. Ibid., pp. 10–11.

89. The hymn of testimony, thanksgiving, and praise to the "Holy Savior and Blest Mother Ann," the instrument labeled to indicate that it was "Composed by Eunice

Wyeth Soon after the forementioned vision 1815." The poem was "Composed by the spirit of Eunice Wyeth—1850" and delivered in the "First Order, New Lebanon June 6th 1851." The 1851 date matches the date on the painting.

90. "Copy of an interesting Narative," EBK 12,101, pp. 13–14.

91. Cf. Andrews and Andrews, *Visions,* fig. 7 (*A Present from Mother Ann to Mary H. Nov. 29th 1848*), pp. 42–43, where the central injunction of the image was to use its forms "in remembrance" of Mother Ann. It is useful, in this context, to define sacramental memory as memory which makes present.

Layering metaphor upon metaphor, image was, like other celestial gifts, "heavenly food" intended to nourish and sustain Shakers on earth in times of spiritual famine, a fourth dispensational replacement for the third dispensation sacrament of the Lord's Supper. See, for example, "A true Record," vol. 11, WRHS 76 VIII:B-126, p. 9; Avery, "Historical Sketches," entries for 29 January and 1 February 1843, LC Container 4, Item 53, pp. 176–77, 180–81, and 211–12. See also "A Communication or word of Notice and Comfort from Mother Ann to Amy Reed" (25 September 1848), EBK 12,087. Spiritual food, the food of angels, was as real as natural food. Every crumb had to be saved for a time of need. "Records Concerning the Finding," SDL, pp. 27, 79, and 176–77.

92. Shakers frequently described their instruments as "wholly insensible of the things of time" (New Lebanon Ministry to Sodus Elders, 19 December 1837, "Copies of letters, Begun 1833," WRHS 27 IV:B-8, p. 232). The dead had "closed with the scenes of time" (New Lebanon Ministry to Groveland Ministry, 6 June 1846, WRHS 20 IV:A-39).

93. Eliade, *Myths, Rites, Symbols,* vol. 1, p. 139.

94. See Record of Spiritual Gifts, WRHS 72 VIII:B-52, pp. 39–40.

95. The instrument of a small, liberally illustrated booklet produced in 1845 acknowledged the temporal role of gift images when she specified three purposes for her painted emblems. According to this instrument, the gift booklet, addressed to Shaker minister Rufus Bishop, the Heavenly Parents intended first, "as a memorial of your [Bishop's] holy example when your little ones can see your face no more," second, "to show a mark of this manifestation," and third, "as a representation of what is laid up in the heavens for the truly faithful," Eleanor Potter, "A Short Notice from the Heavenly Father, from Holy Mother Wisdom, and all the Heavenly Parents, with their seals of approbation and blessing. Brought by a Native Spirit called Electa Blanchard; for Br. Rufus Bishop. Holy Mount," 23 March 1845, EBK 13,494, n.p.

96. Cf., for example, *A sheet prepared and written according to Mother Ann's directions,* fig. 11; gift image of a cross placed around Amy Reed's neck by Mother Ann, 1 January 1845, EBK 11,546; and the cross and crown with which Mother Ann adorned Mary Hazard, "A Beautiful Present," 1 January 1843, EBK 11,547. This last gift and one other similar piece by the same hand given a day earlier ("A Precious Present," 31 December 1842, EBK 8116) are the only two certain exceptions to the rule that instruments did not draw or paint gifts for themselves. In these two instances, Mary Hazard was both instrument and recipient.

97. See [Wells], *Testimonies,* 1827, p. 94.

98. See, for example, "A true Record," vol. 2, WRHS 75 VIII:B-117, p. 63; and Eleanor Potter, "A Short Notice, from the Heavenly Father and Holy Mother Wisdom and from all the heavenly Parents with their Seals of Blessing. Brought by a native spirit, and given to Sister Asenith C[lark]," 23 March and 15 April 1845, EBK 13,493, n.p.

99. From the spirit message titled, "A Communication from Elder Sister Spencer to the Elders of the Church," 22 March 1840, New Lebanon, at the back of Journal of trips made by the Harvard Ministry, WRHS 30 V:B-37, n.p.

100. "Mother Hannah's Bequest," WRHS 75 VIII:B-102, pp. 13 and 47; and "Record of the day of Christmas 1845," WRHS 80 VIII:B-179, p. 48.

101. Compilation of Messages to Individuals, WRHS 78 VIII:B- 151, p. 34.

102. "Words of a Shining Roll, Sent from Holy Mother Wisdom to Eldress Ruth Landon," WRHS 67 VIII:A-42, pp. 16–17. Other leaders at New Lebanon (e.g., Asenath Clark, Giles Avery) received similar booklets, again WRHS 67 VIII:A-42, "written" in July and "copied" in August of 1842, given in relationship to the celebration of Holy Wisdom's Passover. Ordinary Shakers, too, the spirits clothed in celestial garments. Cf. "A little Book," WML SA 1072, n.p. The sharp contrast between Shakers as actually clothed in the community and Shakers as decorated by deity bears notice.

103. "A Little Book, Containing a short word from Holy Mother Wisdom, concerning the Robes and Dresses which are prepared for all such as go up to the Feast of the Lord; or attend to Her Holy Passover, Holy Mount July 21st 1842," apparently a copy for the Harvard and Shirley communities, WRHS 67 VIII:A-42, pp. 12–15.

104. Alonzo Giles Hollister, comp., "Some Things of Importance rarely found elsewhere," WRHS 81 VIII:B-201, p. 115; see also p. 114. Cf. Thomas Hammond, Journal of Church Family, Harvard, begun 1816, WRHS 30 V:B-36, pp. 121–22.

105. Leigh Eric Schmidt, "A Church-going People are a Dress-loving People": Clothes, Communication, and Religious Culture in Early America," *Church History* 58, no. 1 (March 1989): 44. The members of the ministry were the most elaborately ornamented. The instruments located other Believers, then, by degree of ornamentation, in relationship to the renewed authority of the ministry.

106. Barber, "Collection of Visionary Scens [*sic*]," EBK 12,316, p. 74.

107. "Collection of Sacred Writings at the Second Family New Lebanon," SDL, p. 57; see also pp. 56 and 58.

108. Bronner's discussion of the human form as a "part of material culture," as an object to "design and manipulate," and the concern of women and men with the "image" they present, with how they "look," is illuminating in this context, Bronner, "Idea of the Folk Artifact," p. 16.

109. A second image largely characterized by a central configuration understood to be "marked" upon a third generation Believer can be found in Sprigg, *Shaker Design,* p. 202 (*A Reward of True Faithfulness From Mother Lucy to Eleanor Potter,* 22 July 1848). The site of choice for such markings (which often included a star or Wisdom's seal crowned by her eye) was generally the Believer's forehead, in close proximity, of course, to the individual's own eyes. Would the star henceforth illuminate the objects of her spiritual vision? Would Wisdom's eyesight sharpen her own?

110. On the divine likeness decorating Believers, especially in relationship to the image of the lamb, cf. quotation from [Bates], *Holy Wisdom's Book,* pp. 7–8, in the discussion of the Shaker concept of likeness, ch. 4. A striking visual similarity exists between the 1844 heart cutout (HSV, verso) addressed to Jane Blanchard (with its prominent lamb motif) and the lamb within the heart on Blanchard's larger gift image of 1851.

111. New Lebanon Ministry to Groveland Ministry, 6 May 1841, WRHS 20 IV:A-38.

112. Ibid. No Shakers were actually marked for destruction during this ritual. See Bennett and Youngs, "Journal of Inspired Meetings," entry for 11 April 1841, WRHS 77 VIII:B-138.

113. New Lebanon Ministry to Groveland Ministry, 6 May 1841, WRHS 20 IV:A-38.

114. "A true Record," vol. 6, WRHS 76 VIII:B-121, pp. 82–85, 158–59; and Bennett and Youngs, "Journal of Inspired Meetings," entry for 11 April 1841, WRHS 77 VIII:B-138. See also [Barber and Reed?] Book of Inspired Visions and Messages, WRHS 87 VIII:C-1, pp. 121–34.

115. Copies of the Roll can be found in Collection of Miscellaneous Inspired Writings, WRHS 80 VIII:B-175, pp. 73–79; and "A Holy Roll written by the finger of Almighty God," WRHS 86 VIII:B-279, pp. 12–26.

116. "A Golden Roll or Holy Gift, from holy Mother Wisdom to the Ministry, copied November 4 1847," EBK 13,492, pp. 10–11.

117. New Lebanon Ministry to [?], 16 November 1847, WRHS 20 IV:A-39. As with other Shaker circular letters, the writer did not specify a single destination. A later letter, from the New Lebanon Ministry to Grove Blanchard of the Harvard Ministry, 15 January 1848, WRHS 20 IV:A-39, noted that the "Christmas gift" at both New Lebanon and Watervliet had been "uncommonly good and interesting, and some [at New Lebanon] had the satisfaction of beholding the Seals when they were given out."

118. "A Record of Sacred Communications from the Spiritual World to Grove Wright," WML 431 SA 1069, p. 41.

119. Rites of purification preceded the reception of the Seal. See New Lebanon Ministry to Groveland Ministry, 6 May 1841, WRHS 20 IV:A-38.

120. In this series of paintings, the instrument surrounded the centrally located heart form with the heavenly treasures and tokens of virtue which ornamented the faithful life. Then she placed the whole within the context of pictorial renderings from the collective historical and sacramental memory.

The cutout hearts of 1844–45 were predecessors of sorts to the central hearts in these layered compositions, the former rendering visible what deity had written and drawn on the individual's own heart, the latter representing an invitation to spiritual union with Holy Mother Wisdom. Multiple references to individuals and groups within Shaker society, as well as to the residences of particular individuals and groups (especially the Church Family at New Lebanon) as "the heart of my temple" confirm the interpretation of hearts as both people and places. See, for example, Barber, "Collection of Visionary Scens [*sic*]," EBK 12,316, pp. 48–51.

121. Hollister, comp., "Some Things of Importance," WRHS 81 VIII:B-201, p. 118. See also Calvin Green, "Biographic Memoir of the Life and Experience of Calvin Green," copied and enlarged by Alonzo Giles Hollister, vol. 2, WRHS 51 VI:B-30, p. 499.

122. Patterson, *Gift Drawing*, p. 23.

123. WRHS 87 VIII:C-6.

124. Ibid.

125. HSV.

126. Goodrich, a longstanding and beloved member of Hancock's ministry, died, at age 79, on 1 June 1848 of consumption, after years of ill health and a "long and distressing" final illness. See "Communications to Cassandana Goodrich," SDL, p. 157. Cassandana (Dana) Brewster succeeded her. The image under consideration Goodrich received on 27 March 1848. Hancock correspondence, beginning in the month of March 1848, expressed anxious concern for Goodrich's life. See, for example, Hancock Ministry to Harvard Ministry, 20 March [1848], WRHS 18 IV:A-19.

127. The reference could mean *Wisdom's* mansion and seal: "From Holy Mother Wisdom. To Eldress Dana or Mother. Copied from the picture of her Mansion and seal." This is a less likely reading, however, and the difference in meaning would be negligible since, even if this is Wisdom's mansion, Wisdom's own mansion has been prepared for Goodrich and will be Goodrich's celestial home.

128. The ship also alludes to the ship *Mariah* on which Ann Lee and her English followers arrived in America in 1774.

129. Vlach, *Plain Painters*, pp. 75–77.

130. The dying Goodrich presumably interpreted this painting in relationship to a collection of pastoral messages gathered in "A Record of Communications from the Spiritual World to Eldress Cassandana Goodrich." Descriptions from one of the book's entries corresponded precisely with the images later pictured by the instrument of the painting. In the manuscript entry as in the painting, Mother Ann promised to send comforting angels and a golden "chariot of beauty" to convey the faithful leader to "the delightful habitations" of Holy Mother Wisdom, "whose protecting eye [pictured in Wisdom's Seal

at the heart of Goodrich's image] is ever upon thee," see "Communications to Cassadana Goodrich," SDL, pp. 115–16.

131. These two images were memorials produced in anticipation of absence and death. The images provided, then, both reassurance to sick and dying leaders and memorials for the people to treasure when the leaders were gone. For another example of an image conceived explicitly as a memorial to a first generation leader produced for the third generation, see "A Short Notice," to Ebenezer Bishop, March 1845, EBK 13,495. Cf. "Mother Hannah's Bequest," WRHS 75 VIII:B-102, p. 55.

132. Bishop's image was probably painted in 1848 or 1849. New Lebanon's Bishop and Hancock's Goodrich were born one year apart. Bishop survived Goodrich by one year. Both were "first born children" of Ann Lee. Lucy Wright appointed Bishop to the parent ministry in 1821. For several years before his death, Bishop lived in almost constant anticipation of his own demise. He wrote his farewell address to members of the United Society in 1842, seven years before he actually died.

133. [Bishop and Wells], *Testimonies,* 1816, pp. 332–33.

134. Taylor became first eldress in 1868 when Betsey Bates died. Taylor was the recipient of many gift images. For useful information on her life, see the obituary notice, "To Our Well Beloved Mother in Israel Eldress Eliza Ann Taylor," 1897, EBK 15,101.

135. Andrews and Andrews, *Visions,* figure 14.

136. Freedberg, *Power of Images,* p. 60.

137. The individual Believer thus became, in a very literal sense, the "true spatial center of worship." (This phrasing originated with Procter-Smith who used it to describe the impact of the New Era phenomenon of experiencing visionary episodes both in and out of communal worship. Procter-Smith, *Women in Shaker Community,* p. 119.)

Epilogue

1. Shakers also referred to their more recent past and the person of the "second Mother" Lucy Wright as a figure of Shaker maternity.

2. Mother Ann herself introduced Holy Mother Wisdom to her mid-century children—and, at least initially, Mother Ann often acted as Wisdom's intermediary. In fact, most official instruments seem initially to have intended Mother Ann and the other heavenly and spiritual parents to depart when Holy Mother Wisdom arrived to take their places on earth. See Youngs, "Concise View," WML SA 760, pp. 130–31, and 143–44; WRHS 75 VIII:B-117, pp. 185–86; and WRHS 76 VIII:B-121, p. 204.

3. Cf. McCracken, *Culture and Consumption,* p. 132.

4. [Youngs], "Preface, or Introduction," WRHS 75 VIII:B-109, pp. 35–36. See also "A true Record," vol. 1, WRHS 75 VIII:B-116, p. 5.

5. See, for example, "A true Record," vol. 2, WRHS 75 VIII:B-117, pp. 121–126.

6. [Youngs], "Preface, or Introduction," WRHS 75 VIII:B-109, pp. 21–22. According to Believers, the "purging of Zion," the departure of the unregenerate, that followed this cleansing work was preparatory to the prophesied ingathering from the world.

7. Cf. Brewer, *Shaker Communities,* pp. 166, 197. Brewer's evidence suggests that changing emphases in the community likely had some marked connection to changing demographics, as Shaker communities in the east came to be characterized by more of the very old and very young and by shifting ratios of women to men.

8. Visionary and prophetic language at Hancock had always been somewhat less harsh in tone than the same mode at New Lebanon.

9. Shakers met twice annually at the feastgrounds until 1852 and sporadically thereafter. They observed the cleansing gift each September through 1850.

10. Cf. McCracken, *Culture and Consumption,* p. 136.

11. Youngs, "Concise View," WML SA 760, pp. 168–69.

12. Ibid., pp. 164–65, and 512.

13. "Sequel to the Holy Orders of God," WRHS 78 VIII:B-150, p. 113.

14. Some of the same qualities which initially made gift drawings and paintings powerful (e.g., that they could be seen, touched, and retained), likely contributed to their eventual cessation. In record and representation, instruments and ministry exercised control over the contours of the spirit world. Ultimately, a spirit world which could be managed may not have been spirit world enough for many Shakers.

15. Visitations and visionary experiences in other forms began in mid–1837. Instruments created the earliest forerunners of religious drawings late in 1839. By the mid-forties the instruments' pictures were relatively common manifestations but the decade of the fifties witnessed the production of the largest, most elaborate, and most colorful compositions.

16. Although instruments continued to produce gift images after the end of Mother's Work proper, the instruments' pictures eventually disappeared more completely and more abruptly than other forms. While Shakers continued to receive the isolated vision, poem, or song until late in the century, only two or three examples of watercolor "gift" images exist from after 1860. And these images might more accurately be called simply "religious pictures" since no evidence indicates that Shakers actually considered any of the three to be a gift from heaven.

17. Cf. Brewer, *Shaker Communities,* pp. 136ff and 158ff.

18. I have qualified my statement of this point because of the problematic character of the evidence. It is somewhat difficult to ascertain, based on surviving gift images, whether the ministry actually received a proportionately large number of images or whether images directed to the ministry were more likely to be preserved. Considering Shaker methods of storing the visionary pictures, it is in fact probable that paintings intended for the ministry received more consistent care than paintings intended for ordinary members. Gifts to the ministry would have been stored in the retiring rooms of the ministry on the second level of the meeting house where fewer people would have had access to them rather than in the larger common dwelling rooms of other Believers. The ministry's images would also have been less likely to come under censure because they already had the approval of their recipients. And members of the ministry exceedingly rarely abandoned their faith, so their gift images remained with them in one place and, at their deaths, passed on to the next generation of ministers to occupy the same habitation. Still, the high proportion of images, and especially of later images, addressed to members of the ministry suggests that this correlation is not entirely accidental.

19. As early as the end of 1843, one inside observer had remarked of other kinds of gift manifestations that "Those gifts have been so abundant and so common that it has diminished the excitement or stimulus; and this has had a tendency to also lessen the respect for those gifts." [Wells and Youngs], "Records Kept by Order of the Church," entry titled "Review of 1843," NYPL 7, p. 219. See also Youngs, "Concise View," WML SA 760, pp. 164–65; and "A true Record," vol. 2, WRHS 75 VIII:B-117, p. 62. What George Kubler calls "aesthetic fatigue" might then account for the cessation of gift images among the Shakers. See George Kubler, *The Shape of Time: Remarks on the History of Things* (New Haven: Yale University Press, 1962), pp. 80–82.

20. This interpretation would see gift images as a psychological safety valve, as a sort of creative disorder which ratified and reinforced traditional communal order. Cf. Albanese, *America: Religions and Religion,* p. 24 for her suggestion that "creative disorder" functions, in some circumstances, to rejuvenate order.

21. Lithography was introduced in America in the early 1820s, photography in 1839. The first American chromolithograph was produced in Boston in 1840. See Marzio, *The Democratic Art.* Shaker instruments made their first heart cutouts in the same years that similar, though secular, sentimental tokens signaled the beginning of the mechanically produced valentine industry in America.

22. This phrasing I have adapted from a comment made by Richard Kathmann, Director of Shaker Village, Inc., Canterbury, New Hampshire, in an informal discussion of 10 October 1986 at National Historic Communal Societies Association meeting. In another context, David Freedberg similarly posits a "need to represent," a "will to image," see *Power of Images,* pp. 55–56. In addition to new sorts of images, in the years between 1830 and 1870 the kinds of images Shakers already understood to be acceptable (maps, charts, architectural drawings, patterns for clothing and manufactured items, marginal sketches in record books, etc.) multiplied rapidly.

23. Marzio, *The Art Crusade,* p. 31.

24. Ibid., pp. 31, 7, 12, 19, 21. See also Vlach, *Plain Painters,* pp. 35, 38, 39.

25. Vlach, *Plain Painters,* p. 54.

26. Marzio, *Art Crusade,* pp. 25–26, 54. See Harris, *The Artist in American Society,* esp. pp. 300–16.

27. Harris, *The Artist in American Society,* p. 304.

28. Ibid., pp. 303–304.

29. Ibid., p. 301; see also pp. 255, 301–16.

30. After the shock of having any religious images at all dissipated, instruments may have found that they could not represent convincingly enough the celestial people, places, and objects that they sought to depict. Cf. comments about visionary splendors that "pen can't paint" in "A true Record," vol. 6, WRHS 76 VIII:B-121, p. 218; Mary Grosvenor to Seth Wells, 2 May 1833, WRHS 19 IV:A-23; and Ministry at Harvard to Ministry at New Lebanon, 3 September 1841, WRHS 19 IV:A-24.

31. By 1871, photography was officially allowed in Shaker communities; it had found an unofficial home there for some years previous, cf. marginal notes on 1871 photo of Frederick Evans in WRHS 122, #60. By the early twentieth century, Shaker amateur artists like Canterbury's Lillian Phelps demonstrated considerable skill in oil painting. Throughout the late 1860s and the 1870s Shaker newsletters and scrapbooks graphically illustrated a changing Shaker aesthetic, cf. examples of newsletters in WRHS 121 and an 1868 "Collection of Sacred Writings," from New Lebanon decorated across the title page with a cut and pasted sprig of roses, possibly from wallpaper, in WRHS 80 VIII:B-192.

32. Shakers realized this quite explicitly, see [Youngs], "Preface, or Introduction," WRHS 75 VIII:B-109, pp. 34–37.

33. See, for example, Giles B. Avery to Hervey Eads, summer 1856, WRHS 21 IV:A-41.

34. See, for example, "Domestic Journal of Important Occurrences," entry for 6 August 1858, WRHS 32 V:B-61; and Youngs, Journal (1839–1858), entry for 6 June 1853, WRHS 35 V:B-134. Frederick Evans and Hervey Eads, in particular, debated the appropriateness of increasing involvements.

35. Youngs, "Concise View," WML SA 760, p. 506.

36. Philemon Stewart, "Poland Book, No. 1," entry for 1 June 1870, WML 139 SA 776, p. 7. See [Barber and Reed?] Book of Inspired Visions and Messages, WRHS 87 VIII:C-1, pp. 152–55, on Stewart's 1854 departure from New Lebanon at the request of the ministry. Stewart saw the decreasing numbers and other difficulties as signs of God's judgment upon Believers for their accommodation to the ways of the world and their diminished adherence to Shaker tradition. Stewart, "Poland Book," entry for 6 September 1873, WML 139 SA 776, pp. 114–15.

37. This reorientation of Shakerism toward the world was reflected, in part, in newly instituted "social gatherings" (see, for example, Antoinette [Doolittle] at New Lebanon to New Lebanon Ministry at Watervliet, 9 August 1860, WRHS 21 IV:A-43; and Polly Reed at Watervliet to New Lebanon, 1 September 1871, WRHS 26 IV:A-83) and in the admission of small "material" pleasures like beards and musical instruments (cf. Brewer, *Shaker Communities,* pp. 168ff).

38. This phrase is taken from one of John Humphrey Noyes' sources, Noyes, *American*

Socialisms, p. 596. From very early in the Era, many expressed considerable concern that manifestations from heaven not be cause for embarrassment among them or between Shakers and the world. According to some, the potential for embarrassment in relationship to gift manifestations motivated the decision to bar outsiders from worship between 1842 and 1845. See "Closing Roll," EBK 12,027, pp. 10 and 24; and Evans, *Autobiography,* pp. 60–61.

39. "Words of Mother Ann to the Ministry," 12 January 1847, PMA 63-160-196-(17).

40. J. P. MacLean, "Spiritualism Among the Shakers of Union Village, Ohio," in *Shakers of Ohio* (Columbus: F. J. Heer Printing Company, 1907; repr., Philadelphia: Porcupine Press, 1975), p. 391.

41. According to Sarah Kinter, archivist at Canterbury Shaker Village, drawings from the Canterbury North Family were destroyed, at least partly in the interests of housecleaning, by Sister Josephine Wilson, Trustee. Personal Interview with Sarah Kinter, 31 August 1984, Canterbury, N.H.

42. Andrews and Andrews, *Visions,* p. 3. Patterson, *Gift Drawing,* p. 7, n. 15, tells a somewhat different story of the "rediscovery" of gift images, with one set found by Alice Smith in an attic in 1925 and another set found by Smith and the Andrewses in the early 1930s, this time in a top cupboard in the ministry sisters' retiring room on the upper level of the closed Hancock meeting house.

43. As told by Wolfe, "Hannah Cohoon": 88. In another source, Faith Andrews tells, with somewhat different details, the story of the first encounter with Shaker visionary paintings. See A. D. Emerich, "A Conversation with Faith Andrews," *Shaker: Furniture and Objects,* pp. 23–40, where Andrews claims that the *Tree of Life* was the first drawing that she and her husband saw. Andrews also notes here (and elsewhere, cf. Edward Deming Andrews and Faith Andrews, *Fruits of the Shaker Tree of Life: Memoirs of Fifty Years of Collecting and Research* [Stockbridge, Mass.: The Berkshire Traveller Press, 1975], pp. 94–96) that Alice Smith and other, earlier, Shakers kept their pictures stored in rolls.

Not only did Shakers intentionally destroy New Era documents, but the fires which raged through many communities in the second half of the nineteenth century doubtless accidentally destroyed drawings and manuscripts that Believers wanted to preserve. Isaac Newton Youngs, Journal (1839–1858), entry for 31 August 1856, WRHS 35 V:B-134 includes notice of fires at Harvard in 1847, at North Enfield in 1849 and 1856, in an Ohio community in 1855, and in the Second Family at New Lebanon in 1855. "A Domestic Journal of Daily Occurances" (1856–1865), entry for 6 February 1875, WRHS 32 V:B-71, includes remarks about a huge fire of 6 February 1875. Furthermore, of the gift images and visually organized manuscripts which do survive, many are unknown to researchers because they are in uncatalogued private collections or because they have been filed in archival collections in such a way as to make their deliberate retrieval unlikely.

44. Youngs, "Concise View," WML SA 760, pp. 176–78.

45. For example, Hervey Elkins, at first "sincerely converted" (p. 54) by the manifestations of Mother's Work, ultimately decided to leave the Society because of the Era's extravagances. He remained convinced, however, that although "much chaff was blended with the precious seed," "the declarations of those inspired beings were true—astoundingly true and superhuman" (p. 35). Hervey Elkins, *Fifteen Years,* pp. 35, 54–75. Frederick W. Evans was encouraged by the experience of having "seen, heard, and felt" for himself the Era's indisputable evidences of divine reality. Evans, *Autobiography,* pp. 39, 60–61.

46. Lamson, *Among the Shakers.* See also Brewer, *Shaker Communities,* pp. 134–35.

47. "Sayings of Mother Lucy," entry for July 1816, WRHS 56 VII:B-60.1. n.p.

48. Eunice Bathrick at Harvard to Adah [Zillah Potter] at New Lebanon, February 1871, "Letters to My Gospel Companions in Zion's Domains," WRHS 26 IV:B-2, pp. 44–49; and Brewer, *Shaker Communities,* pp. 157, 168.

49. White and Taylor, *Shakerism*; and Blinn, *Spiritualism.*

50. See, for example, Polly Lewis, comp., Messages and Visions, WRHS 80 VIII:B-190; and Bathrick, "Visions. Addresses, Extracts," WRHS 75 VIII:B-108, esp. p. 1.

51. See Eunice Bathrick's comments to Adah [Zillah Potter], February 1871, "Letters to Gospel Companions," WRHS 26 IV:B-2, pp. 47–49. See also Lyn Riddle, "Shaker Village Buoyed by New Blood," *New York Times,* Sunday, 28 August 1988, National Section, Y15. In 1985 Sister Frances Carr at Sabbathday Lake, faced with a question about the survival of Shakerism, pointed out that the Shakers in that year numbered no fewer than did the original American band first gathered around Ann Lee.

SELECTED BIBLIOGRAPHY

Manuscript Collections

Collection of the National Gallery of Art. Gift of Edgar William and Bernice Chrysler Garbisch. National Gallery of Art, Washington, D.C.

Collection of the National Gallery of Art. Index of American Design. National Gallery of Art, Washington, D.C.

Shaker Collection. Berkshire Athenaeum, Pittsfield, Mass.

Shaker Collection. Department of Prints, Drawings, and Photographs. Philadelphia Museum of Art, Philadelphia, Pa.

Shaker Collection. Manuscript Division. Library of Congress, Washington, D.C.

Shaker Collection. Manuscript Division. Library of Congress. Microfilm Edition. Washington, D.C.: Library of Congress, 1976.

Shaker Manuscript Collection. Emma B. King Library of the Shaker Museum, Old Chatham, N.Y.

Shaker Manuscript Collection. Hancock Shaker Village, Pittsfield, Mass.

Shaker Manuscript Collection. Henry Francis du Pont Winterthur Museum Library, Winterthur, Del.

Shaker Manuscripts Collection. Rare Books and Manuscripts Division. New York Public Library. Astor, Lenox and Tilden Foundations, New York, N.Y.

Shaker Manuscript Collection. The Shaker Library, United Society of Shakers, Sabbathday Lake, Poland Spring, Maine.

Shaker Manuscript Collection. Western Reserve Historical Society Library, Cleveland, Ohio.

Shaker Manuscript Collection. Western Reserve Historical Society. Microfilm Edition. Sanford, N.C.: Microfilming Corporation of America, 1976.

Printed Materials

Albanese, Catherine L. *America: Religions and Religion.* Belmont, Calif.: Wadsworth Publishing Co., 1981.

Ames, Kenneth L. *Beyond Necessity: Art in the Folk Tradition.* Winterthur, Del.: Henry Francis du Pont Winterthur Museum, 1977.

Andrews, Edward Deming. *The People Called Shakers: A Search for the Perfect Society,* new enl. ed. New York: Dover Publications, 1963.

———. "Shaker Design." *Art in America* 51, no. 4 (1963): 60–63.

Andrews, Edward Deming and Faith. *Fruits of the Shaker Tree of Life: Memoirs of Fifty Years of Collecting and Research.* Stockbridge, Mass.: The Berkshire Traveller Press, 1975.

———. "Sheeler and the Shakers." *Art in America* 53, no. 1 (1965): 90–95.

———. *Visions of the Heavenly Sphere.* Charlottesville: University Press of Virginia, 1969.

Bainbridge, William Sims. "Shaker Demographics 1840–1900: An Example of the Use of U.S. Census Enumeration Schedules." *Journal for the Scientific Study of Religion* 21, no. 4 (1982): 352–65.

Barkun, Michael. *Crucible of the Millennium: The Burned-Over District of New York in the 1840s.* Syracuse: Syracuse University Press, 1986.

[Bates, Paulina]. *The Divine Book of Holy and Eternal Wisdom, Revealing the Word of God;*

Out of Whose Mouth Goeth a Sharp Sword. Canterbury, N.H.: United Society, 1849.

Baxandall, Michael. *Painting and Experience in Fifteenth-Century Italy.* New York: Oxford University Press, 1972.

Benedict, David. *A History of All Religions.* Providence: John Miller, 1824.

[Bishop, Rufus and Wells, Seth Y.], eds. *Testimonies of the Life, Character, Revelations and Doctrines of Our Ever Blessed Mother Ann Lee, and the Elders with Her.* Hancock, Mass.: J. Tallcott and J. Deming, Jrs., 1816.

Bjelajac, David. *Millennial Desire and the Apocalyptic Vision of Washington Allston.* Washington, D.C.: Smithsonian Institution Press, 1988.

Blinn, Henry C. *The Manifestation of Spiritualism Among the Shakers, 1837–1847.* East Canterbury, N.H.: United Society, 1899.

Bode, Carl. *American Life in the 1840s.* Garden City, N.J.: Doubleday and Co., 1967.

Brauer, Jerald C. "Changing Perspectives on Religion in America." In *Reinterpretation in American Church History.* Edited by Jerald C. Brauer. Chicago: University of Chicago Press, 1968.

Brewer, Priscilla J. *Shaker Communities, Shaker Lives.* Hanover, N.H.: University Press of New England, 1986.

Bronner, Simon J., ed. *American Culture and Folklife: A Prologue and a Dialogue.* Ann Arbor: UMI Research Press, 1984.

Butler, Jon. *Awash in a Sea of Faith: Christianizing the American People.* Cambridge, Mass.: Harvard University Press, 1990.

Corn, Wanda. "Coming of Age: Historical Scholarship in American Art," *Art Bulletin* 70 (June 1988): 188–207.

Cott, Nancy F. *The Bonds of Womanhood: "Woman's Sphere" in New England 1780–1835.* New Haven: Yale University Press, 1977.

Dillenberger, John. *The Visual Arts and Christianity in America: The Colonial Period through the Nineteenth Century.* Chico, Calif.: Scholars Press, 1984.

Dixon, John W., Jr. "Art as the Making of the World: Outline of Method in the Criticism of Religion and Art." *Religion and Intellectual Life* 1 (Fall 1983): 78–103.

Dodd, Eugene Merrick. "Functionalism in Shaker Crafts." *Antiques* 98 (October 1970): 588–93.

Douglas, Ann. "Heaven Our Home: Consolation Literature in the Northern United States, 1830–1880." *American Quarterly* 26 (December 1974): 496–515.

________. *The Feminization of American Culture.* New York: Avon Books, 1977.

Dunlavy, John. *The Manifesto, or a Declaration of the Doctrine and Practice of the Church of Christ.* New York: Edward O. Jenkins, 1847.

Eglington, Guy. "Art and Other Things." *International Studio* 80 (Feb. 1925): 418.

Eliade, Mircea. *The Sacred and the Profane: The Nature of Religion.* Translated by Willard R. Trask. New York: Harcourt Brace Jovanovich, 1959.

________. *The Myth of the Eternal Return or, Cosmos and History.* Translated by Willard R. Trask. Princeton: Princeton University Press, 1974.

________. *Myths, Rites, Symbols: A Mircea Eliade Reader.* Edited by Wendell C. Beane and William G. Doty. Vol. 1. New York: Harper and Row, 1976.

Elkins, Hervey. *Fifteen Years in the Senior Order of the Shakers: A Narration of Facts, Concerning that Singular People.* Hanover, N.H.: Dartmouth Press, 1853; repr., New York: AMS Press, 1973.

Emerich, A. D. "A Conversation with Faith Andrews." In *Shaker: Furniture and Objects from the Faith and Edward Deming Andrews Collection.* Washington, D.C.: Smithsonian Institution Press, 1973.

Emlen, Robert P. *Shaker Village Views: Illustrated Maps and Landscape Drawings by Shaker Artists of the Nineteenth Century.* Hanover, N.H.: University Press of New England, 1987.

Evans, Frederick W. *Autobiography of a Shaker and Revelation of the Apocalypse.* New York: American News Company, 1869.

Foster, Lawrence. *Religion and Sexuality: The Shakers, the Mormons, and the Oneida Community.* New York: Oxford University Press, 1981; Urbana: University of Illinois Press, 1984.

Freedberg, David. *The Power of Images: Stiudies in the History and Theory of Response.* Chicago: University of Chicago Press, 1989.

Garrett, Clarke. *Spirit Possession and Popular Religion: From the Camisards to the Shakers.* Baltimore: Johns Hopkins University Press, 1987.

Grabar, Oleg. *The Formation of Islamic Art.* New Haven, Yale University Press, 1973.

[Green, Calvin and Wells, Seth Y.] *A Summary View of the Millennial Church, or United Society of Believers, Commonly Called Shakers,* 2nd ed. rev. Albany: C. Van Benthuysen, 1848; repr., New York: AMS Press, 1973.

Gombrich, E. H. *Art and Illusion: A Study in the Psychology of Pictorial Representation.* Bollingen Paperback Edition. Princeton: Princeton University Press, 1972.

Hall, Peter Dobkin. *The Organization of American Culture 1700–1900: Private Interests, Elites, and the Origins of American Nationality.* New York: New York University Press, 1982.

Halttunen, Karen. *Confidence Men and Painted Women: A Study of Middle Class Culture in America, 1830–1870.* New Haven: Yale University Press, 1982.

Harris, Neil. *The Artist in American Society: The Formative Years, 1790–1860.* New York: G. Braziller, 1966; Chicago: University of Chicago Press, Phoenix Books, 1982.

Hayden, Dolores. *Seven American Utopias.* Cambridge, Mass.: MIT Press, 1976.

Hughes, Richard T., ed. *The American Quest for the Primitive Church.* Urbana: University of Illinois Press, 1988.

Hughes, Richard T. and Allen, C. Leonard. *Illusions of Innocence: Protestant Primitivism in America, 1630–1875.* Chicago: University of Chicago Press, 1988.

Kauffman, Henry. *Pennsylvania Dutch American Folk Art.* New York: Dover Publications, 1964.

Kermode, Frank. *The Sense of an Ending: Studies in the Theory of Fiction.* New York: Oxford University Press, 1967.

Kerr, Howard and Crow, Charles L., eds. *The Occult in America: New Historical Perspectives.* Urbana: University of Illinois Press, 1986.

Kibbey, Ann. *The Interpretation of Material Shapes in Puritanism: A Study of Rhetoric, Prejudice, and Violence.* New York: Cambridge University Press, 1986.

Kleeblatt, Norman L. and Wertkin, Gerard C. *The Jewish Heritage in American Folk Art.* New York: Universe Books, 1984.

Kubler, George. *The Shape of Time: Remarks on the History of Things.* New Haven: Yale University Press, 1962.

Lamson, David R. *Two Years' Experience Among the Shakers.* West Boylston, Mass.: David R. Lamson, 1848; repr., New York: AMS Press, 1971.

Lipman, Jean. *American Primitive Painting.* New York: Dover Publications, 1942.

[Lossing, Benjamin T.] "Visiting the Shakers in 1857." *Harpers Monthly Magazine* no. 86 (July 1857); facsimile repr., n.p.: Shaker Museum Foundation, 1975.

Lowenthal, David. *The Past Is a Foreign Country.* Cambridge: Cambridge University Press, 1985.

Macdonald, Gus. *Camera: Victorian Eyewitness, A History of Photography: 1826–1913.* New York: Viking Press, 1980.

MacLean, J. P. "Spiritualism Among the Shakers of Union Village, Ohio." In *Shakers of Ohio.* Columbus: F. J. Heer Printing Company, 1907; repr., Philadelphia: Porcupine Press, 1975.

Malcolm, Janet. "The Modern Spirit in Shaker Design." In *Shaker: Furniture and Objects from the Faith and Edward Deming Andrews Collection.* Washington, D.C.: Smithsonian Institution Press, 1973.

Marini, Stephen A. *Radical Sects of Revolutionary New England.* Cambridge, Mass.: Harvard University Press, 1982.

Marzio, Peter C. *The Art Crusade: An Analysis of American Drawing Manuals, 1820–1860.* Washington, D.C.: Smithsonian Institution Press, 1976.

________. *The Democratic Art: Pictures of a Nineteenth-Century America, Chromolithography 1840–1900.* Boston: David R. Godine in association with the Amon Carter Museum of Western Art, Fort Worth, 1979.

Maus, Marcel. *The Gift: Forms and Functions of Exchange in Archaic Societies.* Trans. by Ian Cunnison. New York: W. W. Norton and Co., 1967.

Mayo, Edith, ed. *American Material Culture: The Shape of Things Around Us.* Bowling Green, Ohio: Bowling Green State University Popular Press, 1984.

McCracken, Grant. *Culture and Consumption: New Approaches to the Symbolic Character of Consumer Goods and Activities.* Bloomington: Indiana University Press, 1988.

Michaels, Walter Benn and Pease, Donald E., eds. *The American Renaissance Reconsidered.* Baltimore: Johns Hopkins University Press, 1985.

Miles, Margaret. "Formation by Attraction: Vision and Responsibility." *Harvard Divinity Bulletin* (October–November 1983): 3–6.

________. *Image as Insight: Visual Understanding in Western Christianity and Secular Culture.* Boston: Beacon Press, 1985.

Mitchell, W. J. T. *Iconology: Image, Text, Ideology.* Chicago: University of Chicago Press, 1986.

________. "What Is an Image." *New Literary History* 15, no. 3 (1984): 503–37.

________. *The Language of Images.* Chicago: University of Chicago Press, 1980.

Moore, R. Lawrence. *In Search of White Crows: Spiritualism, Parapsychology, and American Culture.* New York: Oxford University Press, 1977.

Noyes, John Humphrey. *History of American Socialisms.* Philadelphia: J. B. Lippincott and Co., 1870; repr., New York: Dover Publications, 1966.

Numbers, Ronald L. and Butler, Jonathan M., eds. *The Disappointed: Millerism and Millenarianism in the Nineteenth Century.* Bloomington: Indiana University Press, 1986.

Orvell, Miles. *The Real Thing: Imitation and Authenticity in American Culture, 1880–1940.* Chapel Hill: University of North Carolina Press, 1989.

Patterson, Daniel W. *The Shaker Spiritual.* Princeton: Princeton University Press, 1979.

________. *Gift Drawing and Gift Song.* Sabbathday Lake, Maine: United Society of Shakers, 1983.

Podmore, Frank. *Modern Spiritualism: A History and Criticism.* 2 vols. New York: Charles Scribner's Sons, 1902.

Procter-Smith, Marjorie. *Women in Shaker Community and Worship: A Feminist Analysis of the Uses of Religious Symbolism.* Lewiston, N.Y.: Edward Mellon Press, 1985.

Quimby, Ian M. G. and Swank, Scott T., eds. *Perspectives on American Folk Art.* New York: W. W. Norton and Co., 1980.

Samarin, William J. *Tongues of Men and Angels: The Religious Language of Pentecostalism.* New York: Macmillan Company, 1972.

Saum, Lewis O. "Death in the Popular Mind of Pre-Civil War America." *American Quarterly* 26 (December 1974): 476–95.

Schaffner, Cynthia V. A. and Klein, Susan. *Folk Hearts: A Celebration of the Heart Motif in American Folk Art.* New York: Alfred A. Knopf, 1984.

Schlereth, Thomas J., ed. *Material Culture: A Research Guide.* Lawrence, Kans.: University of Kansas Press, 1985.

________. *Material Culture Studies in America.* Nashville: American Association for State and Local History, 1982.

Schneider, Gregory. "The Ritual of Happy Dying among Early American Methodists." *Church History* 56 (September 1987): 348–63.

Seidel, Linda. " 'Jan van Eyck's Arnolfini Portrait': Business as Usual?" *Critical Inquiry* 16 (Fall 1989): 55–86.

Sellin, David. "Shaker Inspirational Drawings." *Philadelphia Museum Bulletin* 57 (Spring 1962): 93–114.

Singal, Daniel J. "Towards a Definition of American Modernism." *American Quarterly* 39 (Spring 1987): 7–26.

Sprigg, June. *Shaker Design.* New York: Whitney Museum of American Art in association with W. W. Norton and Co., 1986.

Stannard, David E. *The Puritan Way of Death: A Study in Religion, Culture, and Social Change.* New York: Oxford University Press, 1977.

Stebbins, Theodore E., Jr. and Keyes, Norman, Jr. *Charles Sheeler: The Photographs.* Boston: Little, Brown, 1987.

Stein, Roger B. Exhibition Review. "Winslow Homer in Context." *American Quarterly* 42 (March 1990): 74–92.

Stein, Stephen J. "Shaker Gift and Shaker Order: A Study of Religious Tension in Nineteenth-Century America." *Communal Societies* 10 (1990): 102–13.

[Stewart, Philemon]. *A Holy, Sacred and Divine Roll and Book; from the Lord God of Heaven, to the Inhabitants of Earth; Revealed in the United Society at New Lebanon, County of Columbia, State of New-York, United States of America.* Canterbury, N.H.: United Society, 1843.

Taylor, Michael B. " 'Try the Spirits': Shaker Response to Spiritualism." *Journal of Religious Studies* 7 (Fall 1979): 30–38.

Turner, Victor. *The Ritual Process: Structure and Anti-Structure.* Chicago: Aldine Publishing Co., 1969; Ithaca, N.Y.: Cornell University Press, Cornell Paperbacks Edition, 1977.

———. *Dramas, Fields, and Metaphors.* Ithaca, N.Y.: Cornell University Press, 1974.

Van der Leeuw, Gerardus. *Religion in Essence and Manifestation.* Translated by J. E. Turner. Vol. 2. London: Allen and Unwin, Ltd., 1938; repr., Gloucester, Mass.: Peter Smith, 1967.

———. *Sacred and Profane Beauty: The Holy in Art.* Translated by David E. Green. New York: Holt, Rinehart and Winston, 1963.

Van Gennep, Arnold. *The Rites of Passage.* Translated by Monika B. Vizedom and Gabrielle L. Caffee. Chicago: University of Chicago Press, 1960.

Vlach, John Michael. *Plain Painters: Making Sense of American Folk Art.* Washington, D.C.: Smithsonian Institution Press, 1988.

Watson, Steven. *Strange Bedfellows: The First American Avant-Garde.* New York: Abbeville, 1991.

[Wells, Seth Y. and Green, Calvin], eds. *Testimonies Concerning the Character and Ministry of Mother Ann Lee and the First Witnesses of the Gospel of Christ's Second Appearing.* Albany: Packard and Van Benthuysen, 1827.

White, Anna and Taylor, Leila Sarah. *Shakerism, Its Meaning and Message; Embracing an Historical Account, Statement of Belief and Spiritual Experience of the Church from Its Rise to the Present Day.* Columbus, Ohio: Fred J. Heer, 1905.

Winchester, Alice. "Antiques for the Avant Garde." *Art in America* 51, no. 4 (1963): 53–59.

Wolfe, Ruth. "Hannah Cohoon: Shaker Spirit Painter." *Art and Antiques* 3 (May–June 1980): 88–95.

Youngerman, Suzanne. " 'Shaking Is No Foolish Play': An Anthropological Perspective on the American Shakers—Person, Time, Space, and Dance Ritual." Ph.D. diss., Columbia University, 1983.

[Youngs, Benjamin S.]. *The Testimony of Christ's Second Appearing.* Lebanon, Ohio: Press of John M'Clean, Office of the Western Star, 1808.

[Youngs, Benjamin S.]. *Testimony of Christ's Second Appearing,* 4th edition. Albany: Van Benthuysen, 1856.

"The Youth's Guide in Zion, and Holy Mother's Promises." Mother's Work Series No. 1. Canterbury, N.H.: United Society, 1842; repr., n.p.: United Society, 1974.

INDEX

SALLY M. PROMEY is assistant professor in the Department of Art History and Archaeology at the University of Maryland at College Park.